CITIES AND SUBURBS:
Urban Life in West Africa

CITIES AND SUBURBS:
Urban Life in West Africa

MARGARET PEIL

AFRICANA PUBLISHING COMPANY
NEW YORK • **LONDON**
a division of Holmes & Meier Publishers

First published in the United States of America 1981 by
AFRICANA PUBLISHING COMPANY
A division of
Holmes & Meier Publishers, Inc.
30 Irving Place
New York, N.Y. 10003

Great Britain:
Holmes & Meier Publishers, Ltd.
131 Trafalgar Road
Greenwich, London SE10 9TX

LIBRARY OF CONGRESS CATALOGING IN PUBLICATION DATA

Peil, Margaret.
   Cities and suburbs.

   (New library of African affairs)
   Bibliography: p. 305
   Includes index.
   1. Cities and towns—Africa, West.   2. Urban-
ization—Africa, West.   I. Title.   II. Series.
HT148.W4P44   1981   307.7'6'0966   80-26440
ISBN 0-8419-0685-8

MANUFACTURED IN THE UNITED STATES OF AMERICA

CONTENTS

FIGURES AND TABLES

ACKNOWLEDGMENTS

A research project which includes eight towns in three countries builds up many debts. I am grateful to the Centre of West African Studies of Birmingham University and the Social Science Research Council, which financed the field work, and the Nuffield Foundation, which granted me a Social Science Research Fellowship to spend a year writing up the results. Authorities of the Tema Development Corporation, the Kaduna State government, local authorities in Aba and Abeokuta and the President's Office in The Gambia were both swift and courteous in granting me permission to carry out the research and helpful in providing information about local conditions. Complaints about the inadequacies of bureaucrats are common, but the occasions when they are truly helpful are too often ignored. Many residents of the towns and missionaries of considerable local experience also provided much useful information in casual conversations as well as in more formal interviews; Sacred Heart Hospital provided accommodation in Abeokuta.

I am grateful to Ralph Bailey, Kathy Lang, and John Morris, who gave me inestimable help with the computing, to Sandra Barnes and Clyde Mitchell, whose advice helped to reshape the book in its present form, and to Doreen Taylor for assistance with the typing. Finally, and perhaps most important, I am grateful to my students and colleagues in Legon, Lagos, and Birmingham. Some of them helped with the interviewing; many contributed to discussions of concepts, reformulations of questions, and the analysis of results. Much of what I know about African society is the result of their perceptive comments.

Centre of West African Studies,
Birmingham, England
May 1, 1980

PART 1

SOCIAL STRUCTURE

1 □ INTRODUCTION

In the 29 years following the publication of Busia's study of Sekondi/Takoradi in 1950, there have been at least forty books on individual African cities; these have been supplemented by numerous articles on specific aspects of urban life and books on African urbanization. There is thus a fairly wide body of literature in this area. This book builds on this work by examining many of the assumptions and hypotheses developed on the basis of single studies. Data collected in eight towns in three countries are used to study the interaction of individual and structural variables, to see what characteristics West African towns have in common and which are dependent on a specific environment.

This study compares cities and suburbs, large and small towns, towns where the labor force is largely industrial and others which are mainly commercial and/or administrative, towns in different countries and of varying degrees of ethnic heterogeneity. Since only eight towns have been studied, each must be considered in some sense "typical," but where two or more towns of the same type have been included some of the range of variation within the type will be apparent. Generalizations can be made which are better grounded in empirical data than earlier ones and more specific as to the type of town in which such behavior may be expected.

Historical, cultural, geographical, demographic, economic, and political factors affect the social life in cities. Those founded before the colonial era usually have an economy, a polity, and an ecology which have been modified but not fundamentally changed by the colonial experience. Newer towns grew under different circumstances and should show the effects of this. Location affects density of population (some locations allow little space for expansion) and the ethnic composition of migrants. The social environment in a town with large numbers of young, recent migrants will be different from that of a town with a slower rate of growth, a balanced sex ratio, a high proportion of families with children, and a fair representation of elderly people. The functions a town serves and the size and composition of its labor force are important factors in its attraction for new migrants and therefore in its rate of growth. The characteristics of local elites, the extent of participation in political life, and the level of intergroup interaction and conflict (interethnic, interreligious, interparty, populace/elites, indigenes/migrants, workers/management, and so on) also affect the relationships of residents with one another and their satisfaction with the town as a place to live.

The book is divided into two parts to emphasize the major concerns with the community as a whole and with relations between individual members, but this distinction is somewhat artificial in that structure and interaction are closely related. Part 1 introduces the structural characteristics of West African urbanization and of the eight towns, followed by a brief discussion in chapter 1 of the three aspects of urban structure: the migration process through which the town attracts and keeps new residents, participation in the urban labor force, and the provision of housing.

Chapter 2 examines the migration process and assimilation into an urban milieu. Although natural increase is also important, most towns are growing rapidly as a result of large-scale migration. The migrants' backgrounds, expectations, and intentions of returning home have important effects on the development of the urban community. Satisfaction with life in town varies with the characteristics of the town (its size, demographic and social structure, attitudes toward strangers), with personal characteristics (age, education, marital status, urban experience) and with the place the migrant makes for himself in the political, economic, and social structure of the town; it also varies with personality and expectations, which are more difficult to quantify. The decision to stay in town or go home has as yet been little studied; the data show that house ownership and the retirement process are important factors in this.

The most important reason for migrating to town is to find work. Chapter 3 focuses on the variance in labor force participation in different types of towns, and shows how the opportunities available also vary with age, education, sex, and migration experience. Participation of women in the labor force is high, but most of them are small-scale traders because they lack the education required to take up employment in the formal sector. Occupational mobility, which may or may not involve status mobility, is more common in West Africa than in Europe. Men move in and out of wage and self-employment in order to improve their income, security, or working conditions, to gain independence, or to help out the family, though voluntary turnover has probably declined in recent years because of the intense competition for wage employment. Occupational mobility is also less common than in the early independence period because most good jobs are held by relatively young men and (except in Nigeria) the numbers of jobs in the bureaucracy, school system, and industry are growing very slowly. The situation of craftsmen is examined as the most promising part of the informal sector, since it provides highly valued independence, a satisfactory income to many participants, and reasonably priced goods for the general public.

High housing densities, discussed in chapter 4, are an inevitable result of rapid urban growth and low incomes. The sharing of rooms by transient single men is responsible for much less crowding than large nuclear or extended families living in one or two rooms. In West Africa, neighborhoods are often of mixed housing quality, so that large, well-built houses and poorly constructed shacks may share the same street, especially in newer areas. Even where this is not the case, rooms in most houses are rented out separately and landlords are usually more concerned about ability to pay the rent than about the source of income, ethnicity, or religion, so the average house has a heterogeneous set of tenants. Rich merchants, petty traders, craftsmen, and laborers share the same neighborhoods—if not the same houses—as teachers, clerks, and an occasional lawyer or accountant. This has important implications for interaction between members of different groups. In a particularistic society, categorization mainly applies to groups with which one has had little contact, so frequent interaction as cotenants or neighbors hinders the development of a "we-they" dichotomy based on perceived economic or ethnic inequality.

Part 2 focuses on formal and informal interaction between residents within the framework of kinship, friendship, voluntary associations, and intergroup relations. Chapter 5 examines the role of the nuclear and extended family in urban life. The level of polygyny can be used as an index of the maintenance of customs in spite of changes in other aspects of life. Though education has considerable effect in encouraging women to decline a polygynous marriage, polygyny is still valued by many well-educated men. Urban heterogeneity should increase interethnic marriage, but while ethnicity remains a salient personal characteristic, the barriers to affinal ties tend to remain strong. It is more likely in Muslim societies than in Christianized ones because the tie of Islam is seen as more important than ethnic divisions, whereas Christian sectarianism often reinforces ethnic differences (because missionaries concentrated on certain groups or local areas).

An individual's social life varies with his or her marital status and household composition because these affect the time and other resources available for kin and friends. People tend to think that young, single men have the most active social life, but the difference between single, separated, and married men living with their spouses and children is often more in the use made of free time than in its amount. Married women tend to have less free time than other urban residents because they must combine housework with trading or some other occupation. Some are helped by servants, who are employed in households of modest as well as high income. There are two types of servants: rural adolescents who get a foothold in town by working for kin or people from their village, and long-distance migrants from poorly developed areas who make a career of being stewards or cooks; the latter usually work in more affluent households.

The majority of urban residents value kinship bonds highly and maintain them insofar as their resources and the distances involved permit. They tend to see kin in town often, visit home at least once a year, and send money in emergencies if not regularly. Women's ties to kin are not as strong as men's; their chief sources of support are husband and children, and hometown politics are largely in male hands.

In addition to contacts with kin, most urban dwellers build up a network of friends, coworkers, neighbors and other contacts with whom they spend their free time and to whom they can go for help and advice as needed. Chapter 6 analyzes the nature of these informal social relationships: the level of contacts and the ways in which people prefer to spend their free time. These vary with personal characteristics (especially sex), but also with the structure of the town—its size, rate of growth, and heterogeneity. Most people prefer dense networks (where all one's good friends know one another) and most friendship networks incorporate people of differing origin, education, occupation and/or ethnicity. Friendships between people in quite different societal positions are more common in West Africa than in Britain, partly because of the importance of family and hometown ties and partly because of the social mobility experienced by the elites. The relative accessibility of the affluent members of these societies slows the development of class consciousness.

Formal associations, discussed in chapter 7, are probably less important than in the past because there are now many other sources of mutual aid and recreation. Participation in voluntary associations is only moderately related to other types of sociability. Like contacts with kin or with friends, it provides an alternative means of building networks and spending free time. Associations are, on the whole, more popular with those of moderate resources than with the very rich or very poor, and more popular with members of certain ethnic groups than with others who have less associational tradition. Competition for local or national resources may give rise to association, but many are the result of a more personal need for affiliation.

Most people face emergencies from time to time, and the poor may need help from family or friends fairly often in order to make up for their lack of material resources. Whereas chapter 5 shows what respondents would do with a £100 windfall, chapter 8 examines their response to a series of common problems: the need for money or a job; trouble at work, in the family, or with the police. Both of these questions provide information on societal structure. The first demonstrates patterns of consultation and mutual aid within the extended family as well as the felt needs of various categories of people. The second expands to the use of personal networks and official agencies in a wider variety of situations. Reliance on kinship, friendship, or patronage, or the ability to apply for assistance on a universalistic basis are resources which urban residents can mobilize to get what they need; those with the widest resources are most likely to succeed.

Variations in sources of aid are one measure of inequality in society. This question is further examined through reactions to the size and rationale of income differentials. On the whole, both the rich and poor favor greater equality of income, but there is considerable sympathy for the opinion that those who have "suffered" to achieve a position of eminence or who make a notable contribution to the community should be well rewarded. Few people agree that the salaries of senior civil servants should be lowered; most would argue that equality should be reached by raising the incomes of the poor rather than lowering the incomes of the rich. Farmers should be better rewarded than at present; there is less sympathy for urban laborers. The pattern of responses confirms the findings of Sandbrook and Arn in Ghana (1977) that the majority of urban residents have a populist rather than a class reaction to inequality.

The other aspect of intergroup relations discussed in chapter 8 is the attitudes of hosts and strangers toward each other, which includes but is broader than the issue of ethnicity. Migrants arriving in large numbers can be seen as a threat by the indigenes, and conflict over resources may be exacerbated by cultural differences, especially when the parties only partially understand each other's language. This is a more serious problem in Nigeria than in the other two countries studied, but electioneering and government decisions which affect regional differences in resource allocation can raise the level of conflict in a town which has previously been reasonably harmonious. Thus, it appears that conflict enhances the salience of ethnicity rather than vice versa. The social structure of the town, especially its level of heterogeneity, also affects relations between hosts and strangers and between groups within the latter.

West African Urbanization

Although sub-Saharan Africa has the reputation of being the least urbanized area in the world, certain parts of West Africa have a very long tradition of urban life. In the Sahel, Djenne, Timbuktu, Gao, and Kano were important to the trans-Saharan trade before Europeans appeared on the Guinea Coast. The Yoruba of southwestern Nigeria have a long tradition of urban settlement which had originated in Ife, their spiritual capital, by 800 A.D. Coastal traders found many large towns in this area, though some were new foundations resulting from the breakup of the Oyo empire. The political capitals of Katunga (Old Oyo), Benin City, Abomey, and Kumasi flourished in the eighteenth and nineteenth centuries, often putting considerable obstacles in the way of prospective missionaries and colonial powers (see Hull 1976; Gugler and Flanagan 1978, chapter 1).

Relatively little is known about the social structure of these towns in the past, but the continuity of physical forms suggests that an examination of present-day social life should assume that persistence is as important as change. For example, religious and political buildings often dominate by their size and centrality, markets are an important focus of social life, there are a few wide thoroughfares and many narrow passages, and houses tend to be single-storied and built around a courtyard. Given the manifold influences of the colonial experience, the arrival of the motor car and modern industry, the rapid growth in size and other influences of the twentieth century, why should continuity with the past be so strong, even in towns of relatively recent foundation? The two most important factors appear to be the length and nature of the colonial experience and the indigenes' response to urban life.

The Colonial Experience

Although Europeans exerted influence on West African towns for over four hundred years, the colonial period, during which Europeans could dominate and shape them, seldom lasted more than sixty years and was often much shorter. Before that, local rulers acted to keep Europeans out of their towns and to control those who stayed. European hegemony was greatest in the immediate vicinity of forts such as Elmina, and seldom important away from the coast, especially before protection from malaria was available.

Once established, British and French colonial rule had somewhat different effects on the cities under their control. The British brought in relatively few officials, and these preferred to live on the outskirts of towns, leaving the indigenous centers much as they were. New towns tended to grow from villages, and the indigenes were allowed to keep control over much of the land and supply housing for most of the newcomers. A few housing estates were built, as after the 1939 earthquake in Accra and to relieve conjestion in Sekondi/Takoradi (Busia 1950, pp. 12–14), but on the whole the *laissez faire* policy let the local people build a town that suited them. Where it seemed best to separate long-distance migrants from local people, special areas were designated—the *zongos* of southern Ghana and *sabon gari* of northern Nigeria—but even here the hand of officialdom was light; the residents built a community which largely served their needs (Schildkrout 1978).

French centralization affected the residential location of colonial officials as well as other aspects of urban planning. More French than English came out to the colonies, and these expatriates tended to live in the central part of town rather than in garden estates on the outskirts, as was the British preference. They initially shared the town centers with local people, but soon felt that it would be more convenient if the indigenes and the migrants who came for trade or employment were housed elsewhere. The Madina at Dakar was established as a "native quarter" as a result of the bubonic plague of 1914. Its subsequent growth received little support from the colonial authorities, who concentrated their urban investments in the European sector of the town (Betts 1969). In Abidjan, the local people were expected to live in the "concessions" of Treichville and Adjamé. The dense population and shortage of services in these areas has continued in the postindependence period, though about a fifth of their population now lives in public housing (Cohen 1974, p. 38).

Because the authorities were unable or unwilling to exert a strong influence on the development of these "native quarters," residents tended to build according to their experience and culture rather than to colonial planning specifications. Thus, there are many similarities in the low-income areas of West African towns regardless of who the colonial authority was. The difference appears mainly when one considers the town as a whole. In some towns, the center is modeled on a European pattern, with a cluster of government buildings, hotels, and department stores; high-income residents live in special areas of large, landscaped, and well-serviced houses and the mass of the population must contend with long distances and poor transportation to reach government officials or the hospitals, schools, and jobs to which they should have an equal right. In this situation, there are, in effect, two towns rather than one and meaningful relationships between people at various levels in the social hierarchy may be rare. If, on the other hand, neighborhoods are both economically and ethnically heterogeneous, government offices and facilities are relatively uncentralized and ordinary people have adequate access to them, relationships may be less strained because people feel it is their town rather than a foreign intrusion on their territory. Accra, Banjul, and Lagos appear to be much more African towns than Abidjan or Dakar.

The differences in policy which have been noted were partly a response to the level of urbanization and the opportunities available for urban development. Where a town was founded and shaped by a colonial power, its structure is more likely to show European influence than where colonial administration was merely an additional function for a well-established town. Centralization of function is more evident in Banjul, which the British built, than in Lagos, where they had to compete for space with a very active commercial sector. Nevertheless, Banjul provides a more integrated environment than Ouagadougou, which dates from the fifteenth century but whose transformation by the French began in 1897 (Skinner 1974, p. 23). The number of expatriates in residence is also important. The European ethos of Dakar and Abidjan is a response to the large number of French men and women who have lived there. (The local elites who have taken over have for the most part been socialized into the same expectations.) The foreign presence in Banjul and Ouagadougou has been relatively small; this has resulted in towns more attuned to local than to foreign culture.

In the postindependence period, these differences have gradually narrowed. The major towns in English-speaking countries are acquiring high-income housing estates; these separate the elites from the mass of the population to a much greater extent than in the past. However, attempts to clear residents from town centers in the interests of functional specialization have so far met with strong resistance from residents who value the commercial opportunities of a central location (Aribiah 1974). In both Lagos and Accra, the indigenes have managed to keep their homes and to continue carrying on their businesses within a stone's throw of the offices of modern government and commerce. This does not prevent planners from designing them into obscure, marginal areas, but so far there has not been enough money or political autocracy to enforce such plans.

Freetown and Monrovia are special cases because they were developed by returned slaves who isolated themselves from the indigenes and were a much more pervasive influence than a colonial power could be. They held the power (though, in Freetown, this was as British colonials) and set the standards of status and behavior. Only in recent years have changes in political power and a large influx of migrants lowered the importance of the Creoles and Americo-Liberians as the normative reference group for urban residents. Studies done in the 1950s (Banton 1956; Fraenkel 1964) suggest that these cities were more like those of Ghana and Nigeria than like Dakar, but new studies are needed.

Indigenous Response

The West African form of urban life varies from one town to another, but on the whole it is characterized by a persistence of customary structures. Residents have accommodated, syncretized, and manipulated local customs, European influences, and present-day models to produce urban forms that are suited to their needs (Skinner 1974, p. 447). Therefore, the average migrant finds much that is familiar and most residents are reasonably content. This does not mean that there are no problems or demands for change. There are serious shortages of employment, housing, water supply, and so on in many towns, and social relations between the indigenes and strangers do not always run smoothly. But most people feel that things are moving in the right direction and that the future will be better than the past (Free 1964; Caldwell 1969, p. 179). The towns are seen as offering more of the good things of life than the "bush," and they provide these opportunities within a framework of well-known structures.

The *laissez faire* attitude of colonial overlords allowed urban life to be shaped by traditional forms; continuity is strengthened by the close ties between town and countryside and the intention of most migrants to return home eventually. It is much more difficult to draw a boundary between rural and urban in West than in East or Central Africa because increasing size is only gradually translated into different structures, density is not necessarily related to size, and even large towns may be relatively homogeneous. This does not mean that a new migrant does not notice a difference between his village and Kaduna or Tamale which is more than just size and occupational diversity. But towns shaped by indigenous urbanism (which was structured by customary forms of authority and allowed a high proportion of the population to farm for at least part of the year) provide a familiar milieu for short- if not for long-distance migrants (see Bascom 1959 and Lloyd 1959).

The proportion of farmers in the urban population has dropped considerably in recent years, but there are still a few migrants who go to Lagos, Takoradi, or Tema to farm or fish rather than to participate in modern industry, and significant numbers of indigenes in many towns prefer primary occupations to wage employment. Small-scale market gardening, poultry keeping, and growing food for subsistence needs are common wherever there is land available. This is mainly a part-time occupation to provide supplementary income, but it allows migrants from rural backgrounds to put their spare time and skills to profitable use.

The pace of change in towns is slowed by the interdependence of town and countryside and the frequent interaction between urban residents and their country kin. Few people are committed to one or the other, so the urbanization of the countryside proceeds with the ruralization of the town. Dual occupations and dual residence are important factors in this. The roads into many towns are busy every morning with rural people coming for a day's business, and large numbers of migrants visit home on weekends and on national holidays. Farmers making intensive use of peri-urban land often spend considerable time in town selling produce and firewood, collecting rubbish for compost, and so forth. For example, Hill (1977) shows the mutual dependence of Kano and the villages of the Close Settled Zone. Some men who live in the CSZ have regular work in the city, others are employed there during the dry season, and many participate in urban activities (or, if they live in town, in rural activities) from time to time.

Osborne (1973) reports that many Yoruba families still have both urban and rural homes; members of the family shift from one to the other whenever it is profitable to do so. For instance, they may spend the week in town and the weekend on the farm, or vice versa; others work on the farm for several months and then spend part of the year in town. Thus, some dual households have a constantly shifting membership and it becomes very difficult for census takers (or sociologists) to classify their members as either rural or urban residents.

Close ties are maintained by more permanent residents through visits, messages, and remittances. If a migrant's village is within three or four hours of town, he will go home at least once a year and probably more often for family reunions, community festivals, funerals, other occasions, or just to "see how things are." He will be visited by kin from home when they come to town on business or specifically to check up on his progress (see chapter 5). These contacts can be an occasion for spreading urban values to the countryside; they are also used to exert social control over migrants to ensure that customary values are upheld. It is more difficult to exert this control over long-distance migrants or over the well-educated elite who have less need for the security offered by the extended family, but the former often have kin or people from home living in the same town who can influence their behavior and the latter are sufficiently socialized into societal norms to value their reputation as supporters of their kin. So far, there are few urban residents with no ties to the countryside, though their numbers are growing.

The political and social structures of these towns are important factors in both continuity and change. Democratically elected local government was introduced during the colonial period, but since independence urban politics have often been shaped by the huge expansion of the bureaucracy, fierce struggles for power, widespread corruption and/or a transfer to military rule. Through all these vicissitudes, customary rulers have continued to exercise influence and, in some places, power. The Emir of Kano, Oba of Benin, and Asantehene in Kumasi have less control over their people than in the past, but they are still very much a force to be reckoned with; their advice and aid are sought by government leaders and common people alike. There is considerable competition for customary leadership positions, even in relatively small towns and villages; these offices are more secure than political posts and are a source of considerable prestige even if the potential for material profit is now relatively small.

Lower leadership positions (minor chiefs, headmen, extended family heads) also continue to be important in dispute settlement and, to a lesser extent, in welfare and the support of newcomers. They provide a framework for relatively cohesive subgroups to solve their own problems without recourse to the governmental bureaucracy. Such groups can thus uphold traditional values, adapting them as needed to new situations but maintaining a framework they can understand.

Social structures are also changing very slowly. Urban stratification is a combination of new and old, with success measured in the number of followers and the extent of participation in subgroup affairs, as well as in material resources and high-level occupations. Greeting an elder may no longer involve prostration, but deep bows are often seen. Some young people find kinship obligations onerous and prefer to live on their own, but most people contribute in numerous ways to the furtherance of kin and hometown interests and see kin who live nearby regularly. New associations, centered around church, politics, work, or leisure interests are popular with some urban residents, but more time is spent talking with friends, drinking palm wine or other local brews, or in other pastimes familiar to villagers. Particularism is generally much more acceptable than universalism.

West African towns are, therefore, largely an integral part of the culture. They are also a focus of societal change insofar as they provide the meeting point for heterogeneous populations and the point of entry for new technology and greater specialization. Though not all migrants find the opportunity for social mobility and material success which they are seeking, the majority of residents consider the towns a satisfactory place to spend their working lives.

Types of Towns

Any examination of urban life must take into account the difference between capitals and other central cities, the suburbs which are springing up in increasing numbers, provincial towns (whether precolonial settlements or created for administrative convenience during the colonial period) and industrial towns, including those established since independence. These categories are not mutually exclusive, since provincial towns or suburbs may be largely industrial in function, but certain characteristics of each type can be identified.

Central cities (especially capitals) draw migrants from throughout the country and from neighboring countries, and diplomats, entrepreneurs, and technical advisors from all over the world. They thus have a very heterogeneous and at least partly cosmopolitan population. Most of them have grown very rapidly in the first ten years of independence. Having the most educated population as well as the best amenities and access to government, they attract both local and international industry. These are the towns which attract the most attention, from social scientists among others, and are often seen as typical of African towns. Regional headquarters such as Kumasi, Ibadan, and Kaduna (before the division of Nigeria into states) are central cities on a smaller scale than capitals, somewhat less heterogeneous and cosmopolitan, but having more functions and a much wider hinterland than the average provincial town.

The many provincial towns have received much less attention. They are mostly commercial and administrative headquarters for their agricultural hinterlands. Because they provide opportunities for education and employment close to home, they are also growing, though not as fast as the central cities. Provincial towns range in size from a few thousand people (the country's official boundary to urban status) to several hundred thousand, larger than the capitals of some countries. Urban characteristics likewise vary from the overgrown farm village to the multifunctional city such as Kano. Many house paramount chiefs, emirs, or other ethnic leaders and thus are particularly attractive to members of a particular ethnic group or subgroups. This group contributes a much larger proportion of the population and tends to have considerably more political power in the town than the indigenous people in a central city, though the best jobs in both types of towns may go to better-educated strangers. Self-employment or the "informal sector" is more important in these towns; most of the wage employment is provided by the government. The limited local opportunities may encourage many young people to leave these towns for the central cities; they are replaced by migrants from smaller towns and villages and, on transfer, managers and civil servants from other towns.

Large-scale industry is not usually important in provincial towns, but it is *raison d'être* of a few. Many of these towns were built during the colonial period to develop mineral or timber resources; for example, gold- and diamond-mining towns of Ghana; Enugu, Jos, and Sapele in Nigeria; Harper in Liberia, and Lunsar in Sierra Leone. More recently, Warri has grown rapidly in response to the needs of the oil industry, Liberia has three new iron-mining towns, and the spread of small-scale diamond mining in Sierra Leone has made Koidu a boom town. Transportation is another important source of employment in provincial towns. Ports and railways have brought growth to Douala, Sekondi/Takoradi, and Port Harcourt as well as to many towns along the rights of way; some provincial towns have declined because they were bypassed by the railway or major roads.

The new towns of the independence period, usually established as harbors and/or to promote industry, may be a better indicator of what is to come, since governments are freer in these than in well-established towns to develop the kind of urban environment they want. Unfortunately, new towns are often planned by European or American firms rather than by people who are familiar with local customs and needs. The result may be satisfying to the elite, who are concerned with overseas approval and with their own comfort, but less satisfactory to the majority of the migrants who must live there. Housing built to "acceptable" standards is often too expensive for manual workers. Engaging in petty trade or artisan activities at home is often forbidden, as is rearing poultry. Separation of functions, and the shortage of markets, bars, and other meeting places (including large trees) produce a sterile atmosphere which may take residents a long time to overcome.

The result, in both Tema, Ghana and San Pedro, Ivory Coast, has been the rapid growth of satellite towns where residents can put up housing they can afford, carry on their small businesses without interference, and live within their means (see Haeringer 1973). They aspire to better conditions (paved roads, a regular water supply and electricity, schools, and hospitals), but would rather use their limited income for needs other than rent. These towns tend to be initially insecure, in that the government may consider them slums which detract from the planned town and should be leveled to allow for its expansion. Fortunately for their residents, they soon become too large for the country to bear the cost of replacing them, and they take their place with other suburbs as underserviced signs of the seemingly inevitable urbanization process.

Other suburbs, which provide similar living conditions, are growing on the outskirts of most major towns. They involve squatting less often than is the case in Latin America because landholders have been willing to allot or sell land to migrants, often for remarkably low sums. This, too, is changing, as villagers learn the value of their holdings and speculators move in. In some cases, as in The Gambia and more recently in Nigeria and Ghana, the government has partly or completely nationalized urban land so as to control speculation and suburban growth. It is too soon to see the effect this will have on potential house builders of moderate means. If it severely limits their acquisition of land, squatting may increase. In any case, suburban development seems inevitable, since central cities are already very densely populated and migrants who intend to settle permanently must often find accommodation on the outskirts.

Eight Towns

The Samples

Eight towns have been studied, including all of the types discussed above. A preliminary survey of social activities was carried out in Communities 1 and 4 of Tema, a new port and industrial town in southeastern Ghana, in April 1968. This included a census of randomly selected houses and short interviews with the household heads and their wives. It was followed in July by longer interviews of residents selected from the census sheets and a census/interview survey in Ashaiman, a surburb of Tema (see Table 1.1). In July 1970, interviewers returned to many of the same houses and a few additional ones in Ashaiman to see how much residents had changed in the intervening two years and to carry out interviews on social life which built on the 1968 data.

In 1972, house censuses and interviews based on the Ashaiman 1970 model (with a few changes and additions based on experience or adapted to Nigerian conditions) were carried out in four Nigerian towns: Aba, Abeokuta, Ajegunle, and Kakuri. While lack of house numbers made random selection more difficult than in Ghana, houses were chosen as randomly as conditions permitted, ensuring that all sections of the towns were included. As interviews were done concurrently with census taking, respondents were selected on a quota basis to ensure adequate representation of various categories of age, education, occupation, religion, and

TABLE 1.1
The Samples

	Ghana			Nigeria				Gambia	
	Ashaiman		Tema	Aba	Abeokuta	Ajegunle	Kakuri	Banjul	Serekunda
	1968	1970							
House censuses	143	110	427	95	141	120	95	103[c]	120[c]
Households	799	611	573	472	315	686	617	323	292
Individuals	2082	1494	2724	2383	1244	2587	1778	1603	1599
Interviews	460	98	360	207	202	227	206	204	206
Total houses	1860	2100	9231	NA	NA	5745	1564	2100[c]	3308[c]
Total population ('000)									
At last census[a]	2.6		15	131	187	45	15	39	26
At time of study[b]	28	31	83	300	200	120	30	40	28
Ten-year growth (%)	759		307	143	23	184	111	42	NA
Type of town	industrial suburb		industrial	provincial	provincial	suburb of capital	industrial suburb	capital	suburb of capital

[a]Ghana 1960; Nigeria 1963; Gambia 1973. The 1970 Ghana census found 22,449 in Ashaiman and 60,767 in Tema. Many aliens in Ashaiman hid from government census takers and Section E was probably undercounted.

[b]Estimated.

[c]Compounds, many of which have two or more houses.

marital and migration status; about a quarter of those interviewed were women. Finally, in 1976, the same survey (again with minor changes to suit local conditions and new interests) was carried out in Banjul, capital of The Gambia, and its main suburb, Serekunda.

Why choose these towns? There was a certain amount of chance, because the study was not begun with the whole framework in mind but rather as a much more modest study of social interaction in a new industrial town. This grew out of an earlier study of Ghanaian factory workers, which focused on their life in the factory and raised many questions about what they did outside working hours.

When the opportunity came to expand the work to Nigeria, the most useful course seemed to be to expand the range of size, culture, and labor force, to use different types of towns so that reliable generalizations could be based on patterns found in a wide variety of urban environments. This should help to answer the question, "What is the nature of social life in West African towns?"—at least for towns shaped by the British colonial experience. Each town has, therefore, been selected for characteristics it has in common with many others, though the particular configuration may be in some sense unique because of its location and history.

Four towns were chosen in Nigeria as the maximum which could be handled in the time available. These were selected to include some part of Lagos and one town in each of the former three regions. Lagos is too large to be studied as a whole by an individual researcher. As an area with easily definable boundaries and a heterogeneous population, Ajegunle seemed to offer the best opportunity to study a meaningful community, including many interethnic contacts. Though larger than many, it has the characteristics of suburbs growing rapidly on the outskirts of many African cities.

Another researcher was working in Kano, so Kaduna was chosen as the northern town. Its suburb of Kakuri/Makera is the same size as Ashaiman and is sufficiently similar in its labor force to make a useful comparison in which cultural differences may explain variance in attitudes and behavior. It seemed important to look at provincial towns, on the grounds that they would attract different sorts of migrants and might well have different patterns of social interaction from most of the African towns which have been studied. Much of the Nigerian urban research has been done in Ibadan; Abeokuta was chosen because it is smaller, more "traditional," and more provincial. In the east, Aba had been greatly affected by the upheavals of the 1960s and seemed to be playing an important role in reconstruction. Like Abeokuta, it is mentioned in the history books but has attracted little attention from social researchers.

The Gambia offered a chance to pioneer. This small country had not yet been contaminated by sociological research, but its government was beginning to feel a need for information on the social consequences of development. Gambian migrants are much less likely to have any prior experience of urban life than migrants in Ghana and Nigeria, so their responses might well be different. At the same time, Banjul has a long-established Creole population which can be compared to the indigenes of Abeokuta. The Islamic influence is much stronger in The Gambia than in Kakuri or Abeokuta, which could provide interesting differences in inter-action patterns. Serekunda was included for comparison with Banjul and with the other small towns, though these were much more industrialized; there was no alternative, given The Gambia's level of urbanization.

The resulting towns are by no means ideal for controlled comparisons, as too many variables differ simultaneously. Nevertheless, as the amount of work involved expands rapidly with the addition of more towns, this is as many as can be handled at once. They make it possible to test many hypotheses on a range of data and provide tests of assumptions in the literature which have been accepted on the basis of single reports. As the data show again and again, this is a very risky thing to do. It is hoped that the insights from these studies will be further tested in other towns to assess their validity in varying conditions.

Ghana

Tema was originally one of a series of Ga fishing villages about 27 km. (17 miles) east of Accra. In 1952, the preindependence government of Kwame Nkrumah decided to build a new port and industrial town there to provide improved access for imported goods and to utilize the electricity from the proposed Volta Dam. The government acquired 166 sq. km. (64 sq. mi.) from the traditional owners by compulsory purchase; this came under the authority of the Tema Development Corporation (TDC). Plans were made to move the four thousand residents to a newly built village about 3 km. away (Tema Manhean), freeing the old village site for the new port. There was considerable local opposition, and it was not until 1959 that the move was completed (Amarteifio et al. 1966).

Meanwhile, migrants poured in looking for work on the new town. Many of them settled with the Tema villagers or in an area about 8 km. (5 mi) from the coast; this came to be known as Tema Junction because it was the point on the Accra-Ada road where a turn south was made to reach Tema. By 1957, there were also over one thousand houses built in the new Tema, mainly for low-income workers (Ghana Development Secretariat 1961, p. 31). Some of these were prefabricated units intended for a short life, but it has not yet been possible to replace them.

The town-planning firm of Doxiades was engaged to design a town with modern layout that would fit the climate and social organization of its residents. The plan called for seven communities, each with four neigh-borhoods of three to five thousand people.[1] Each community was to have its own schools, market, and community center. However, the need to spend any available money on more housing has meant that the provision of most community amenities has been delayed. Primary and middle schools have been built[2] and there are some small markets, but the main market, shops, and Community Centre of Kortu-Gon (Community 1) serve as a nucleus for the whole town. The Tema hospital has been built north of the town and is not easy to reach. A patient must first go to the health center and chest clinic in Kortu-Gon unless his case is serious.

By 1975, Tema had about 16,360 houses. They are closely spaced, with four to six "houses" (some are more properly described as flats) in each building; most buildings are of one or two stories. Most of the houses are "Group 4," for low-income workers. The number of rooms allocated is supposed to vary with the tenant's income, so the poor are the most crowded. Group 3 houses, in separate neighborhoods, are larger and situated in more spacious grounds; these provide accommodation for members of middle management, including expatriates from all over the world. A small number of Group 1 houses in one neighborhood in Kortu-Gon have been allocated to the elite. All houses have electricity, running water, and water-borne sanitation, relatively rare amenities in other Ghanaian towns. Since these amenities must be paid for, rents have tended to be higher than for privately owned accommodation, but since they were not raised during the period of rapid inflation they appeared reasonable by the late 1970s.

Because the TDC finds it easier to collect rent from employers, much of Tema housing is block rented to firms who allocate it to their employees. These tenants often sublet rooms to spread the rent bill. Tenants tend to be the more stable and better-paid industrial operatives and clerks or, in Akorley-Djor (Community 5), dock workers. There are relatively few African aliens or northern Ghanaians, because these tend to be laborers or self-employed and thus have very limited access to Tema housing. Small-scale commerce and crafts, so ubiquitous in Ghanaian towns, are hampered by TDC regulations; additions to buildings are forbidden and permission is needed for kiosks. Separation of functions has been surprisingly well enforced considering the pressure of local custom against it, but artisan workshops and private trading in housing areas grew considerably between 1968 and 1978.

Industrial development has been somewhat slower than was hoped, and migration to Tema has continued to outrun the employment available. The country's economic stagnation in recent years has made it a less fertile field for investment than Nigeria, but the thirteen firms with thirty or more workers in 1965 grew to thirty-six firms with 15,178 workers by 1977. Only 5 percent of these employees were women; most were semi-skilled operatives with a middle school education who were committed to a long stay (Tema Development Corporation 1977; Peil 1972a).

As the showplace of the new Ghana, Tema has had more than its share of central government money. It has been administered by the TDC, the Tema City Council, and the Ministry of Local Government (or its equivalent during periods of military rule). There is considerable dissatisfaction with the failure to maintain estate housing and with corruption in the TDC and the Tema City Council, but most residents do not see much they can do about it. A Tema Welfare Association, founded in 1969, draws on the churches and trade unions to support confrontations with authorities over community needs (Peil 1968; Bannerman 1973).

During the early 1960s, Tema Junction became Ashaiman and began to grow rapidly, as the demand for housing in Tema outstripped the supply. The TDC divided the land into four sections, each subdivided into plots for which houseowners pay a small monthly rent depending on size. A road grid was laid out, though the streets remained unpaved and un-ditched. Expansion began in Section B, west of the lorry park and next to the Accra-Ada road (the southern boundary of the residential area until the mid-1970s; the lorry park and several commercial establishments have now been moved south of the road). Early residents were people displaced when Tema village was moved, skilled workmen who came to help build Tema, and men and women from the surrounding rural area who came to farm or trade. Migrants from Upper Volta, Niger, and Mali (usually laborers on the docks) tended to settle in Section D, north of the lorry park and schools, where they built the largest of several mosques. There are several small villages not far from the built-up area.

There is much more variance in housing in Ashaiman than in Tema, as each landlord is free to build what he can afford. Early houses were of swish (mud) with thatched roofs (the site of the original village in the northeastern corner of the town still has such houses) or of packing cases or tin sheets from the docks. More recent houses are of concrete blocks with aluminum roofs, but are well below the Tema standard. Most houses have more rooms than the average Tema house, and many are centered on a courtyard where cotenants can sit and talk, wash clothes, care for children, and so on. Waiting for water at the standpipes also brings people together. Tema residents sometimes come out to Ashaiman in the evenings or on weekends to participate in its lively social life, though others who are not attracted by the numerous small bars and prostitutes look down on it as an eyesore.

The Ashaiman population tends to be more representative of Ghanaian society than Tema's. About a fifth of residents in 1968 were aliens, though about half of these left in the expulsion of 1969–1970 (Peil 1971). There are also more northern Ghanaians than in Tema, more illiterates, low-paid workers and self-employed, though the largest stream of migrants continues to be school leavers from Eastern and Volta Regions, who hope to find work in Tema. There is more space for rearing children in Ashaiman and costs are lower. Skilled workers made redundant as building projects are completed can live there inexpensively and undertake small jobs to support themselves until new contracts are awarded. The only employer of any size in Ashaiman was the Seed Multiplication Unit, under the Ministry of Agriculture, which had twenty workers. The schools and police post also provide employment, but most of the Ashaiman labor force is either self-employed (craftsmen, petty traders, barkeepers, bakers) or works elsewhere. A count taken one morning between 5:45 and 7:45 found 1,026 men and 105 women walking to Tema; in one evening 120 lorries, 12 company and 2 municipal buses and 23 taxis returned workers from Tema and Accra to their rooms in Ashaiman.

Ashaiman is officially under the same jurisdiction as Tema, but gets far less attention because it is conveniently hidden behind the motorway. There has always been a fear that the government will decide to raze Ashaiman and build another Tema community there; for many years investment in amenities was minimal and the town remains a notable slum. In 1968, the TDC built a small estate of 192 houses (in blocks of six with one room and a verandah each); these were assigned to their own workers or employees of large firms or government departments. A group of semi-detached houses, mostly for sale to low-income workers, was built in another area in the mid-1970s. While these areas are well supplied with amenities, these are in very short supply elsewhere. At the time of the study, the private sections of Ashaiman had only about four functioning public latrines and six standpipes for some 25,000 people. A few landlords with their own tap sold water to neighbors; some also had a bucket latrine, but there were many complaints about getting these emptied. Section E, an unauthorized area east of the town, had no services at all until recently and still has no roads.

As the town has grown and finance for rebuilding has not been available, the prospect of demolition has become less likely with every passing year. Ashaiman was in political disfavor with the Busia government because it supported the political opposition and contained many aliens. Nevertheless, residents were becoming increasingly committed to improving their community and through a Town Development Commitee put considerable pressure on the Tema City Council and the Minister of Local Government for improvements. This was rewarded by the investments of the early 1970s: two paved roads, a middle school and clinic, electricity, and more standpipes and public latrines. With the return of military government, the Development Committee had lapsed, and residents had fewer opportunities to make their needs known. Private primary schools and clinics will be needed to supplement government provision for the foreseeable future. Ashaiman remains a town of low-income workers, a dormitory suburb for about a third of the Tema labor force.

Nigeria

Aba and Abeokuta are commercial, administrative, and social service centers. They cover about the same amount of land, but Aba has about 50 percent more people. Aba is the largest town, though not the capital, of Imo State. It is 225 km. south of Enugu (the capital of Anambra State and former capital of Eastern Region) and 77 km. north of Port Harcourt (capital of Rivers state and the major port of eastern Nigeria). It began in precolonial times as a market owned by several nearby villages, at the junction of two trade routes. The colonial authorities soon saw it as a strategic location, and established a military base there in 1901 (Udo 1970, p. 71). Administration and other services (post office, hospital, prison) soon followed, and it became the headquarters for the densely populated Ngwa District. The growth of the oil palm industry, arrival of the railway (in 1915), and its position at a major intersection in the new road network greatly enhanced its commercial functions, though it has been over-shadowed politically by Owerri and Umuahia, smaller towns 64 km. to the northwest and north respectively. Its main claim to a place in history is as the center of the women's riots of 1919 (Gailey 1971).

Aba's large central market is an important focus of activity; it is now being rebuilt after a disastrous fire. The town is also well provided with transportation, educational, and health facilities. The privately owned bus service is supplemented by large numbers of taxis (444 were counted). In 1972 there were six secondary schools with 3733 students, two trade centers with 1267 students, and one training college with 607 students. The nineteen primary schools had 24,089 pupils enrolled. The government runs a large general hospital, a psychiatric and nervous diseases hospital, a dental center, and a community nurses' training school. There are also one Catholic and five private hospitals, plus numerous clinics and maternity homes.

Villages to the south are being encompassed by urban expansion; the town is also growing, through industrial development, along the road to Owerri (the state capital). The administrative boundaries include about 26 sq. km. of built-up area, but there is also considerable suburban sprawl along major roads (Ajaegbu 1976). The dense central part of the city is divided by a grid pattern of streets which were originally paved but are now sometimes impassable because of huge, deep holes. The three sub-sidiary areas within the town boundary (south of Ngwa Street, north of the railway line, and east of the Ngwa River) have a far less organized pattern of streets. These have not been paved, but tend to be somewhat more level than central streets because they get less use. There is a small Government Residential Area (GRA) for senior civil servants. Some of the elite have built houses in the same area and a few others are clustered in several streets near the government offices, in houses shared with ordinary tenants. The rest are scattered throughout the town. In spite of the new bridge, there has been relatively little development in "Waterside" (across the river).

Most of the outsiders in this overwhelmingly Igbo town were soldiers. "Overrail" (across the railway line) had mostly been taken over by the military, and there was another army base in "Waterside." The number of soldiers stationed in the area was declining, but their presence was felt more than that of soldiers in the other Nigerian towns studied.

The two small industrial areas on the outskirts had a textile mill, a brewery, and several soap factories (see Callaway 1970, p. 127). Bakeries and other small-scale industries were located more centrally. The Labor Exchange was crowded with people looking for employment, but many residents were of necessity self-employed. In 1972, migrants were pouring into Aba from their overcrowded and eroded farms, eager for any opportunity to make a living. Many of the craftsmen were underemployed, and there were large numbers of petty traders and small shopkeepers competing for business.

The local authorities were making considerable efforts to repair the streets and collect rubbish regularly, but obviously lacked sufficient equipment and finances. In spite of the heavy rains (which washed out road repairs soon after they were made), there were occasional water shortages because the Ministry of Works lacked equipment to pump water from the river. Water supply is a problem in most Nigerian towns, including Lagos. In 1972, Aba gave the impression of vitality, of a town full of people making plans and actively working to achieve them. By 1978, the enthusiasm had generally declined in the face of government inability to provide roads and other vital amenities, but the values of hard work and self-help still appear to be strong.

Abeokuta, situated on the Ogun River, is 72 km. southwest of Ibadan and 105 km. north of Lagos. It was founded in 1830 as a refuge from the Yoruba wars. The name means "under rock"; some of the first settlers lived in caves in the Olumo Rock. The Egba peoples claim that Omonide, the first wife of the Yoruba progenitor, is buried at Ake, their first capital, and that they are descended from one of the couple's sons. They lived in small villages over a wide area until 1830; these villages are recalled in the city's street and place names. There are five obas, or rulers (the Alake, Osile, Oluwu, Agura, and Onigu), of whom the Alake takes precedence. About 1840, freed slaves returning to Egbaland from Sierra Leone introduced Christianity to the area. The first European missionary arrived in 1843, and Western education (under mission auspices) got an earlier start here than in most other parts of the country. The Abeokuta Grammar School, founded in 1908, replaced an earlier grammar school which was moved to Lagos in 1867. Islam had been introduced to the Egba some years earlier by traders, and continues to be strong in this area; residents are about equally divided between Muslems and Christians (Ajisafe 1948).

The railway line from Lagos opened in 1900, shortening the journey from at least a week to a day and thus facilitating trading contracts. Migration from Abeokuta to Lagos has been heavy for a long time, and many Egba families who have lived in Lagos for two or three generations still claim Abeokuta as their hometown. Development was slowed by the extremely long rule of Alake Ademola II, who reigned from 1920 to 1962. His attitude toward "progress" was very reserved, and in 1972 there was still no cinema or supermarket in the town. A new Alake, formerly a Lagos businessman, was installed soon after the research was completed. Abeokuta was elevated from a district headquarters to a state capital in 1976. This has provided many opportunities for the town's development. By 1978, signs of this were everywhere: new roads, hotels, stores, cinemas, lorry park, public buildings, and large private houses. However, it was evident that most residents were still living as they always had, by trade and crafts.

The city's layout has changed little since the 1930 map was drawn. The main roads around the core and through the center are paved, and most of the houses are set without any particular plan over the hills on which the town has grown. A map based on aerial photographs is available, but the lack of house numbers or even a regular system of footpaths makes it very difficult to census or systematically sample the population. An additional problem for a census is that many families have compounds in town and in nearby villages; household composition may vary from week to week. Some areas are almost empty by urban standards, with space for small-scale farming and roaming goats; land near the main roads is much more crowded. Craftsmen who live "inside" often rent shops facing a street.

Only about 2% of the population is non-Yoruba (mostly Edo from Benin State or Igbo) and two-thirds belong to the Egba/Egbado subgroup; many of the latter are locally born and live in family houses in the central part of town. Higher-income migrants tend to live in newer areas, including the GRA, where amenities are better (Adepoju 1976, p. 19), but many migrants share housing with local people.

Abeokuta mainly provides central place functions for the surrounding countryside. The large daily market and multitudes of small shops serve the ordinary needs of residents. In 1972 the seventy-five primary schools had 25,002 registered pupils, some of whom attended Koranic schools in late afternoon. There are eight secondary schools and three training colleges, which draw pupils from a wide area, In addition, there are many private schools providing commercial or technical training to school leavers, private lessons at primary level, or nursery schooling. The local council runs a large public hospital and two maternity clinics. In addition, the town has a large and widely known government psychiatric hospital, Catholic and private hospitals, several private clinics specializing in maternity care, and a leprosarium. There is no bus service;[3] the large number of taxis (474 were counted in 1972 and this had increased to 2500 by 1978) provide an efficient if noisy and relatively expensive system of transportation.

The government, schools, and brewery are the main sources of wage employment; school leavers usually migrate to Lagos or Ibadan, only returning when transferred by their employers or on retirement. One result of this is that many of the state and district government personnel and teachers in the town are outsiders who have been posted there temporarily. This was said to be as true in 1978 as in 1972; the Egba apparently made no attempt to monopolize state offices.

Politics operates at two levels in Abeokuta, where the traditional hierarchy has maintained considerable importance. Many administrative decisions may be made by outsiders, but local prestige and authority are still affected by one's relationship to the customary rulers. An important sign of success for Yoruba is the bestowal of a chieftaincy title by an oba. Townspeople take these awards very seriously; a car was burned during the survey period by people protesting the award of a title to the wife of a former politician. Where so many residents have grown up in the town, including successful returned migrants, social and political networks tend to be more firmly established than in a new and rapidly expanding town. Abeokuta thus provides a considerable contrast to the other towns studied, a chance to compare "traditional" Yoruba urbanism with colonial and post-colonial towns.

Ajegunle has grown from two villages, Alayabiagba and Onibaba. The latter was founded in 1870 for smallpox patients. Government interest in these settlements was negligible until 1929, when nearby land was acquired for development. Building regulations were introduced in 1940, but people moved beyond the Lagos township boundary to avoid these.[4] The development of Apapa in the 1950s as a port and industrial estate for Lagos led to the rapid expansion of Ajegunle, parts of which are just across the New Canal from Apapa. The newest port development, on Tin Can Island, is reached via a motorway which skirts Ajegunle. Annual growth between 1952 and 1963 averaged 18 percent, and this rate may well have increased in the 1970s (Sada 1970, pp. 41–42).

The built-up area covers about three sq. km. It is divided into fingers of land separated by swamps, which can be crossed on board bridges erected and maintained by groups of residents (who charge a toll) or by short canoe rides. The most southerly finger is known locally as Olodi, the middle as Ajegunle and Aiyetoro, and the more northerly as Amukoko.

Neighboring villages are gradually being absorbed as the town expands westward. Although there are connecting roads and continuous development, Amukoko is considered a separate place because it is under the jurisdiction of the Ikeja District Council, whereas Ajegunle (including Aiyetoro and Olodi) is under the Awori/Ajeromi District Council. It seems likely that the whole will eventually be considered one town. Although mapping and observation were extended to Amukoko, censuses and interviews were confined to Ajegunle because it seemed better to concentrate resources on a smaller area. Differences in background and present social position of the population of the two towns, as well as the nature of their social life, appear to be minimal.

One reason for choosing Ajegunle is that it is the most heterogeneous part of Lagos. Whereas about 80 percent of the Lagos population is Yoruba, less than a third of the Ajegunle population is Yoruba; the rest comes from all over Nigeria, especially the midwest and east. Many Igbo moved there from other parts of Lagos during the troubles of the 1960s. It has also drawn intraurban migrants because land was available at a relatively reasonable price. Most of the land belonged to three families, who had long-established customary ownership. The price has risen with demand, but until recently it was possible for ordinary people to obtain land there.

New streets and houses are constantly being added, though land is now sometimes leasehold rather than freehold. The Land Use Decree of 1978 may have considerable effect here, because there is more open land in Ajegunle than in most other parts of Lagos. A few of the early bamboo, thatch-roofed houses are still in use, but most new buildings are large cement block structures of two or three stories with up to twelve rooms (the legal maximum) per floor. Speculators have moved in, as rental housing is a safe and profitable investment.

While the majority of Ajegunle's residents are low-income workers in either the docks or factories of Apapa or Ijora, clerks in Lagos, or self-employed traders, craftsmen, or fishermen, there are also young middle managers and professionals living in new blocks of flats on Kirikiri Road and moderately successful businessmen throughout the town. Housing is expensive and hard to find in Lagos, and the newer parts of Ajegunle are quieter and more pleasant than many alternatives, especially if one has a car and can arrange for an adequate water supply. These new, higher-income residents may play an important role in the town's development, as they may be more successful than the less secure and less-educated migrants in pressing for more amenities and services. "Tiger Town" may in time become a more respectable place to live. Meanwhile, the self-employed face intense competition. There are four markets (dominated by women) and innumerable hawkers and house traders. The streets are lined with the shops of tailors, carpenters, fitters, repairers of radios and other electrical equipment, and other self-employed workers.

Because Ajegunle is not under the Lagos City Council, urban services are very limited. There is electricity and a small dispensary/maternity unit, but almost no public water supply and no sanitation, rubbish collection, or Labor Exchange. Houseowners dig wells and latrines, often too close together and using the same shallow water table. Considerable money has been invested in 500-gallon water tanks; the owners buy water from tankers and sell it to their neighbors. The sixteen public primary schools, some jointly sponsored with the churches, had 13,242 pupils in 1972. All ran double shifts; by 1974 some were on triple shifts. The only secondary school is beyond the town and accessible only by bus. There are many private schools run on a full- or part-time basis to provide primary education, supplementary studies, or commercial training. Private medical care is also available from clinics, maternity hospitals, and traditional healers.

Ajegunle can be reached via Malu Road from the Lagos-Apapa throughway or (at the west end) from the new Lagos-Badagry highway. The main entrance is only two lanes wide and usually crowded with cars, buses, and lorries moving at a snail's pace toward the lorry park. Cattle awaiting slaughter walk from a penned area just off the throughway to pasturage at the other end of the town, making a considerable contribution to traffic holdups. There were only four paved roads in 1972; one or two more have been paved since. Many roads are impassable because of erosion, accumulating rubbish, and mud; even main roads are partly under water during the wet season. Houses built in swampy areas may be completely surrounded by water if the rains are heavy. In one area where the swamp is being filled by dumping Lagos rubbish, several shops have been built on stilts to make the most of the central location.

Many inhabitants felt that they were being ignored by the authorities, who were seen as more concerned with rural than with urban problems and more interested in building personal careers than in serving the public. It was sometimes possible to organize delegations and use the vote to gain attention when the country was under civilian rule; appointees of the military government were felt to be less responsive because they owed nothing to those under them. In addition, many thought that the military did not look kindly on incipient leadership, so it was better to keep quiet. Community action to clean up and improve the town was much more needed in Ajegunle than in Ashaiman, but there was no sign of it. There was a notable lack of community feeling, a sense of being in Lagos but not accepted by it.

Kaduna is 690 km. north of Lagos and 251 km. southwest of Kano, the largest city in the north. It was founded by Sir Frederick Lugard as the capital for the Protectorate of Northern Nigeria. Housing for the railway construction staff at Kakuri, built in 1911, is thought to be the first permanent part of Kaduna (Bryant n.d., p. 2). As independence approached, it became politically important to invest in northern industrialization, and the logical place appeared to be what was then the capital of Northern Region. The village of Kakuri, about six km. south, was chosen as the site for a new town and industrial estate. Between 1957 and 1964, five large textile mills were built; the estate also has a brewery, asbestos plant, munitions plant, and metal-processing firms. Kakuri/Makera and an adjoining area, Nasarawa, house much of their labor force.[5] This is the largest employment center in the north after Kano; the population doubled between 1963 and 1972. Migrants are largely primary school leavers from Kaduna, Kwara, Benue, and Plateau States.

The northern section of the town (Makera) consists mainly of cement block houses facing streets in a grid pattern. The larger and more populous southern section (Kakuri) has some "modern" houses and streets, but many houses have thatched roofs and are set in irregular fashion along footpaths. Chickens, goats, and pigs wandering about the area indicate that some residents provide their own protein supply; a few men farm full- or part-time and others make their living collecting and selling firewood. Kakuri houses are less likely to have electricity and the rents are lower than in Makera. The town's facilities (chief's office, primary school, main market, government clinic, court, and cinema) are all in Makera. For further education and health care, residents must go to Kaduna. Kakuri and Makera form a single community and are administered together; for convenience, the town will be referred to as Kakuri.

Because migrants are mostly drawn from the ethnically fragmented Middle Belt rather than from the Hausa north, Kakuri is extremely heterogeneous ethnically. The sample census located members of seventy different ethnic groups. Christians are also better represented than in the Muslim north; there are Catholic and Baptist churches in Makera and many separatist sects hold services in Kakuri. Nevertheless, Muslim influence ensures that women are a less important factor in the labor force than in southern Nigeria or Ghana. As many migrants are not yet married, the sex ratio was higher than in the other towns studied; there were two adult men for every woman in 1972. However, by 1978 there was much more evidence of women and children in town (including two shifts for the schools), so it appears that the population is rapidly becoming more balanced.

There was little sign of political activity or interest in Kakuri, partly because Nigeria was under military rule, but also because its government was largely in the hands of distant civil servants with whom the residents could have little contact. As Kaduna was a regional and is now a state capital, local government has been less important than in smaller towns.

There is a chief to symbolize local authority in Kakuri, but most important decisions are taken by state officials in Kaduna. Any improvements in services or amenities would have to get approval in Kaduna, and the general impression was that the trouble taken would probably not be rewarded. Residents are often more concerned with the progress of their hometowns than with Kakuri, which is seen mainly as a place to live while in wage employment. Nevertheless, Kakuri did provide a meaningful community for some of its residents, who felt that it fulfilled their expectations of urban life.

The Gambia

In contrast to Nigeria, The Gambia is one of Africa's smallest countries; its capital is also very small by international standards. Banjul (the traditional name to which it returned in 1973) was founded by the British in 1816. They named it Bathurst and the island on which it is situated St. Mary's Island. The site was not a healthy one; the southern tip of the island is still known as Half-Die in remembrance of the victims of the cholera outbreak of 1869–1870. Nevertheless, its strategic position at the mouth of the Gambia River made it useful for commerce, halting the slave trade, and pacifying warring religious factions in the neighborhood. The streets were laid out in a grid pattern by the Colonial Engineer, Mr. Buckle. Drains were dug in an effort to control malarial mosquitoes. By 1821, it had a hospital and courthouse as well as a fort (Gailey 1964).

With independence in 1965, Banjul progressed from a colonial to a national capital, with Parliament and diplomatic missions. In recent years, a large-scale tourist industry has developed, with package tours mainly from Scandinavia. But it is primarily an administrative and commercial town, exporting the country's groundnuts and importing consumer goods which, if not wanted in The Gambia, are smuggled into Senegal. There are a few small industries (including one of the country's four groundnut decorticating plants about five kilometers outside the town), but a high proportion of wage employment is for the government (civil service, Ministry of Works, docks, and schools).

Banjul is basically a Wollof town and most African residents speak Wollof, but the population is heterogeneous. Over half were born in Banjul, but the rest include migrants from Ghana, Guinea, Liberia, Mali, Nigeria, and Sierra Leone, as well as the more common Mauritanians, Senegalese, and native Gambians. Technical and diplomatic personnel come from Asia and the Middle East as well as from Europe and the United States. Given the small size of the town, the easy tolerance of strangers, and the stable, democratic political situation, there is a cosmopolitan, relaxed atmosphere to which newcomers find it easy to adjust.

The amenities are good. All the streets are paved and in remarkably good condition. The Royal Victoria Hospital attracts patients from Senegal as well as from all over The Gambia. It is supplemented by a maternity clinic, the Ahmaddiyya Clinic, and a mental hospital. The Gambia High School has the country's only sixth form. (There is no university and the only training college is at nearby Yumdum.) There are two other senior secondary schools, run by the Catholic mission, three secondary technical schools (formerly known as junior secondary), a vocational training center and twelve primary schools. In total, there were 5,739 primary pupils and 3,535 in postprimary institutions in 1977; the latter come from all over the country. A private company runs old buses and the Gambian Libyan Arab Public Transport Corporation new ones; in addition, there are large numbers of taxis. There are two cinemas, one large and two smaller markets, a football stadium, and numerous bars and hotels. As a high proportion of the country's few Christians live in Banjul, there are five churches as well as many mosques.

The Banjul Local Council administers an area of 12.7 square kilometers; 8 percent of the country's people live in 0.1 percent of its land area. At 3,099 persons per square kilometer (Gambia 1975, p. 5), Banjul is less crowded than Ashaiman or the Nigerian towns, partly because of the large amount of space given to government buildings and the docks. The government has nationalized all of the land in the Banjul Metropolitan Area, and individuals are allowed only one plot on a twenty-one-year lease; only a few long-established families have permanent tenure. Thus, land ownership is widely spread. Expensive multistoried houses are next to small houses built in traditional style. Most houses are inside walled compounds, which may have two or three buildings in addition to an open space for cooking and recreation. Muslim teachers and self-employed craftsmen also use this area. Thus, much of the social life of the town takes places on private ground rather than in public, as is common in Nigeria and Ghanaian towns.

Serekunda, about 12 kilometers from Banjul, grew from a series of villages (Serekunda, Dippakunda, and Latrikunda), which now form a continuous built-up area and the country's second largest town. It lies in Kombo St. Mary Division and is administered by the Kanifing Urban District Council. With only 25,000 people in a 5-square-kilometer area, it is by far the least dense of the towns studied. Houses are built in walled compounds according to Gambian custom, but as many plots have not yet been built on, there is still plenty of open space. Plots are large; the extra space is often used to grow food, and fruit trees provide shade.

Serekunda houses people of many ethnic groups and all social levels. Over half of the population were born in the Banjul Metropolitan Area. Government ministers, expatriates, civil servants, craftsmen, traders, and laborers find it an attractive place in which to live. Rents tend to be lower than in Banjul and the family can therefore have more space. The main roads are paved and most of the others are passable by car. Electricity and a public water supply are available, though some families dig a well instead of bringing water to the compound or using a public standpipe. Building regulations are not stringent, so a plot holder can build whatever house he can afford, adding to it as his circumstances permit. While there are a few streets where the houses are of uniformly high quality, there is an obvious mixing of people of varying economic levels in many parts of Serekunda.

Given the short distance and ease of travel between Serekunda and Banjul, the former has only a moderate need for central place institutions. There is a market, police post, small private hospital, two secondary technical and three primary schools (with 1,023 and 2,259 pupils respectively in 1976), two cinemas, and a nightclub. The industrial estate to the north of the town is only just getting started, so there is little wage employment available locally. There is a minor traffic jam each morning and afternoon as commuters travel to and from Banjul; this resembles the daily move from Ashaiman to Tema rather than the far more crushing scramble to get from Ajegunle to Lagos and back. During the day, Serekunda gives the impression of a village grown large, and many residents do not find it fundamentally different from their homes except for the higher incidence of services.

Demography

Table 1.2, based on the sample censuses, shows how the towns compare with respect to demographic variables. There are considerable differences both within and between countries, based on locus (city/suburb), history (old/new), predominant culture, labor force, and so on. As over half of the residents of Abeokuta and the Gambian towns were born there and few are recent migrants, it is not surprising to find a balanced sex ratio, but the relative balance in Tema was less expected. However, there are many opportunities for women to earn money in Tema, as in Abeokuta, and the labor force is relatively settled. Kakuri has the least balanced sex ratio and the lowest proportion of women in the labor force. Where it is difficult for women to be self-supporting, husbands often prefer to leave their wives at home and single women are not attracted.

West African migrants generally prefer to have at least some of their children in town with them; at least 30 percent of the population of all the towns was under 15 and children were more likely to be absent because they had become independent than because they were being reared at home. Kakuri has the highest proportion of both men and women in the 15–24 age group. The factory employment available there is most attractive to young primary school leavers, and the married men tend to have young wives. Because of rapid recent growth (except in Abeokuta and the Gambian towns) and because most migrants over 50 have tended to return home, there are as yet few elderly people in most of these towns.

TABLE 1.2
Demographic Background, by Town and Sex (Percentages)

	Ghana				Nigeria								Gambia			
	Ashaiman[a]		Tema[b]		Aba		Abeokuta		Ajegunle		Kakuri		Banjul		Serekunda	
	M	F	M	F	M	F	M	F	M	F	M	F	M	F	M	F
Sex Ratio																
Total	138		112		133		100		135		173		108		102	
Adult	168		134		172		100		153		206		108		101	
Age																
0–5	16	23	17	24	15	20	12	15	15	20	14	19	10	12	18	17
6–14	10	16	20	27	24	33	25	21	17	24	13	20	25	24	24	24
15–24	21	26	19	20	25	22	19	18	23	30	42	37	26	25	18	23
25–34	34	22	24	19	19	15	20	18	30	17	25	19	14	15	16	18
35–49	16	11	9	4	15	9	14	16	12	8	5	4	14	16	15	12
50+	3	2	11	7	2	1	10	12	3	1	1	1	11	8	9	6
Total	100	100	100	100	100	100	100	100	100	100	100	100	100	100	100	100
N[c]	1203	869	1370	1226	1354	1016	623	621	1485	1096	1126	652	833	770	809	790
Education, Adults[d]																
None	39	79	20	50	12	25	20	56	10	32	10	60	13	27	7	26
Primary, Muslim[e]	13	8	7	8	56	45	22	15	38	48	71	32	22	32	43	47
Middle[f]	43	11	49	30	9	8	12	8	23	10	5	2 }	47	30	34	18
More	4	1	19	8	14	12	32	12	23	5	10	3				
Now in school	1	1	5	4	9	10	14	9	6	5	4	3	18	11	16	9
Total	100	100	100	100	100	100	100	100	100	100	100	100	100	100	100	100
N	897	530	868	630	819	478	397	390	995	601	826	400	541	501	467	463

	M	F	M	F	M	F	M	F	M	F	M	F	M	F	M	F
Education, Children 6–14																
None	37	42	8	24	12	31	8	19	11	17	11	26	12	3	1	2
Primary, Mulsim^g	53	54	70	65	84	66	75	71	86	80	86	72	80	84	88	83
Post, primary	9	4	20	11	4	3	17	10	3	3	3	2	8	13	11	15
Total	100	100	100	100	100	100	100	100	100	100	100	100	100	100	100	100
N	118	138	269	318	316	238	152	132	252	263	141	133	177	160	190	199
Conjugal Status^d																
Single	45	15	42	24	56	27	43	18	45	17	60	14	55	33	42	23
Monogamous	53	78	55	67	39	59	38	42	50	67	35	66	34	41	49	54
Polygynous^h	1	4	2	6	4	9	17	33	4	13	4	17	9	16	7	13
Widow, divorced	1	3	1	3	1	5	2	7	1	3	1	3	2	10	2	10
Total	100	100	100	100	100	100	100	100	100	100	100	100	100	100	100	100
N	915	538	859	632	821	481	393	393	975	603	822	410	543	501	471	461
Length of Residence^i																
Under 1 year	14	19	5	6	14	15	4	3	6	7	8	10	5	2	5	5
1–2 years	36	36	17	21	47	47	14	11	29	26	28	29	3	2	6	8
3–5 years	28	28	35	30	3	3	11	9	20	20	38	29	6	5	8	7
6–10 years	15	11	28	31	10	12	10	8	16	16	15	14	8	5	10	8
Over 10 years	6	5	15	12	18	16	11	14	21	20	8	13	15	14	18	10
Birth	1	1	k	k	8	7	50	55	8	11	3	5	63	72	53	62
Total	100	100	100	100	100	100	100	100	100	100	100	100	100	100	100	100
N	887	538	864	626	818	481	396	395	982	592	822	391	542	497	465	453
Occupation^j																
Farmer, unskilled	28	2	11	3	7	8	7	11	13	5	4	4	9	2	13	6
Semiskilled manual	22	3	23	5	6	2	8	1	12	2	53	1	7	2	9	0
Skilled manual	29	2	15	8	14	5	12	8	15	3	11	7	13	3	21	1
Commerce	5	54	8	42	52	42	20	54	24	30	13	23	14	8	10	7
Nonmanual	8	1	29	9	12	10	35	11	27	5	12	3	32	15	26	6
None, Don't know	8	38	14	33	9	33	18	15	9	55	7	62	25	70	21	80
Total	100	100	100	100	100	100	100	100	100	100	100	100	100	100	100	100
N	896	530	865	635	824	481	396	395	986	609	824	399	543	501	471	464

TABLE 1.2 Continued
Demographic Background, by Town and Sex (Percentages)

	Ghana				Nigeria								Gambia			
	Ashaiman[a]		Tema[b]		Aba		Abeokuta		Ajegunle		Kakuri		Banjul		Serekunda	
	M	F	M	F	M	F	M	F	M	F	M	F	M	F	M	F
Employment Sector[d]																
Self-employed	14	60	13	53	42	36	36	61	24	28	10	22	17	10	28	8
Wage-employed	71	2	71	18	43	22	44	15	60	10	78	4	52	20	49	12
Unemployed	14	5	11	5	5	4	2	1	9	4	7	5	7	10	5	10
Not in labor force	1	33	5	24	10	38	18	23	7	58	5	69	24	60	18	70
Total	100	100	100	100	100	100	100	100	100	100	100	100	100	100	100	100
N	907	535	858	630	821	473	392	395	981	608	829	409	543	501	470	461
Religion[d]																
Muslim	20	19	11	7	0	0	43	50	22	28	24	37	90	86	90	84
Catholic	19	15	21	18	43	39	6	5	42	34	28	24				
Protestant	37	33	52	54	33	37	41	35	26	24	27	21	10	14	10	16
Pentecostal, Apostolic	7	11	4	11	21	23	8	8	7	8	20	17				
Other, none	17	22	12	10	3	1	2	2	3	6	1	1	0	0	0	0
Total	100	100	100	100	100	100	100	100	100	100	100	100	100	100	100	100
N	893	521	864	617	809	477	395	397	976	593	823	400	543	501	471	464
Indigenous Ethnic Group	Ga		Ga		Igbo[m]		Yoruba[n]		Yoruba		Gwari		Wollof		Wollof	
Percent of population	23		26		99[m]		98[n]		29		1[p]		47		30	

34

^a1968 data are used as this sample census is larger and more representative than the sample taken in 1970.

^bThirty-nine households with non-African heads have been omitted.

^cThis includes "Don't knows," in no case more than 0.5%.

^dAged 15+.

^eIncludes a few literates who never attended school. There were very few with only Muslim schooling except in Gambia. The proportions for Muslim schooling are 42% male and 28% female in Banjul and 31% and 17% in Serekunda.

^fMiddle school in Ghana; Standard 6 and 7 of primary and less than 4 years of secondary schooling in Nigeria. Gambian respondents did not differentiate between junior secondary (the equivalent of middle school) and senior secondary, so these have been combined.

^gIn school or completed.

^hFor females, refers to wives in a polygynous marriage.

ⁱAdults; based on date of first arrival if the respondent came more than once (chiefly in Aba), and on calendar year regardless of date of interview ("under 1 year" means arrival in the year of the survey).

^jAdults; last occupation has been used for the unemployed and retired. Uniformed services are classed as nonmanual.

^kLess than 0.5%.

^m12% Ngwa, the local subgroup; 36% were Owerri Ibo.

ⁿ69% Egba, the local subgroup.

^p19% were Yoruba, the largest group.

35

However, Tema has only slightly fewer adults over 50 than Abeokuta and Banjul; this is because well-established migrants in good jobs have greater access to Tema housing than newcomers. Elderly people in Ashaiman tend to be landlords and their wives who have settled there rather than go home. This will be further discussed in chapter 2.

As low rents attract the poor to the suburbs, it was expected that suburban residents would have a lower level of education and occupation than people living in the central city. Provincial towns were expected to attract less-educated migrants than the more industrialized towns. These hypotheses were partly confirmed, but local factors must be taken into consideration. Ashaiman, with the lowest level of education of the towns studied, is well below Tema in the education of both men and women. Serekunda adults are not less likely than those in Banjul to have attended school or to be still in school when surveyed, but fewer of them got beyond the primary level. Thus, in these two cases, there is evidence that the less educated settle in the suburbs. However, adults in Ajegunle and the provincial towns are better educated than adults in Lagos (Morgan and Kanisto 1973, p. 20). In this case, relatively well-educated migrants are moving to the suburb, whereas many local people have not been much concerned about education because they specialize in trade.

The split in attitudes toward education in Abeokuta is evident in the relatively high proportion of illiterates and the large number who have gone beyond three years of secondary schooling. Many of the latter are migrant civil servants. Women's education lags behind that of men in all towns, but Islam appears to be less of a hindrance to the educational progress of women in The Gambia than in northern Nigeria (Kakuri) or Abeokuta.

Local factors affect the use parents make of urban educational opportunities. Although according to government statistics the proportion of the child population attending school was higher in southern Ghana than in southern Nigeria and lower than either of these in northern Nigeria and The Gambia, the proportion of sampled children in school was highest in The Gambia and lowest in Ashaiman. Whereas many unschooled children were merely late starters, many Ashaiman parents appeared to be uninterested; quite a few children had been dropped from the school register because of truancy. This may have been the result of the drop in confidence in the benefits of education which was sweeping Ghana at the time, but it also reflects the low level of literacy among Ashaiman adults. The Gambia provides an exception to the international norm that boys get more education than girls. Boys in Banjul were less likely than girls to be sent to school, and in both Gambian towns somewhat more girls than boys had gone beyond primary school. Islam seems to be an important factor here in limiting the educational progress of the boys; nearly twice as many boys as girls attend Koranic schools.

All of the towns have a fairly high proportion of young single men (and Banjul, of young single women). There are few widowed or divorced people (except for women in The Gambia) because most remarry or, having reached old age, return home. The higher proportion of women in this category is due to the preference of older women for staying in town with their children or grandchildren rather than going home, and to the migration of some widowed or divorced women to town to find new husbands or live with their sons. As more educated young men settle with their families in stable urban jobs, the migration of grandmothers will probably increase. Polygyny is more common in Nigeria and The Gambia than in Ghana, partly because of the limited spread of Islam in the latter and partly because it has not been common among the matrilineal Akan who form such a large proportion of the Ghanaian population. The Abeokuta sample was, on average, older than the others, and hence more likely to be polygynous, but polygyny is also fostered by both Yoruba and Muslim values and for the freedom it allows women for participation in trade, for which Yoruba women are particularly noted.

The towns can be divided by average length of residence into stable towns, with a high proportion of locally born and many long-term migrants (Abeokuta and the Gambian towns), new towns (Kakuri, Ashaiman, and Tema), and a relatively balanced middle type (Aba and Ajegunle). The stable type is often ignored in descriptions of Third World urbanization, and provides an important contrast to the more frequently studied capitals. Norms are well established in these stable towns; migrants face a different sort of adaptation process than is the case when most other residents are also new arrivals. The war produced a sharp discontinuity in migration to Aba; over three-fifths of its population had arrived since the end of hostilities in 1970, but a quarter of the population were long-term residents who could provide a normative base on which to build. Ajegunle is also growing rapidly, but has been doing so for many years and hence has a social structure geared to the steady influx of newcomers.

Farming and unskilled work tend to be more common among suburban men than among those in the central cities, partly because of the tendency of low-income people to move out to the suburbs and partly because the open land available there permits farming. The difference is more notable in Ashaiman than in Serekunda. Small-scale farming is also carried out in open spaces in most towns, usually as a part-time supplement to other economic activities. Semiskilled work, mainly in factories, was the chief occupation in Kakuri, where half the men were semiskilled and over three-fourths were in wage employment. Most of the men in Ashaiman and Tema were also working for wages, but less than a quarter were in semiskilled jobs in spite of the predominance of factories as employers. Many of the skilled workers in Ashaiman were employed on construction jobs in Tema and carried on private businesses in the evenings, weekends, and whenever they were temporarily without wage employment. Skilled workers (especially fitters and carpenters) often prefer a suburban site because there is more space for a workshop. Skilled workers are more common in Ashaiman than in Tema and in Serekunda than in Banjul, but there appears to be no difference between Ajegunle and Lagos and there are relatively few skilled men in Kakuri.

The few women are employed in manual work (mainly as farmers, laborers, or seamstresses). Commerce, on the other hand, is very attractive to West African women, especially those in the towns of southern Ghana and Nigeria and preeminently to the Yoruba (Peil 1975a). Half of the women in Ashaiman and Abeokuta were engaged in trade, as were two-fifths of those in Tema and a third of those in Ajegunle. Most operate on a small scale, which is nevertheless an important addition to household income. Ghanaians tend to consider petty trading a job for women or aliens; few Ghanaian men engage in it, though they do run shops and larger businesses. Yoruba and Hausa men, on the other hand, often look to trading as preferable to wage employment (Peace 1974). Igbo men are somewhat less enthusiastic, though many do trade; the high proportion of men in Aba who were trading (either on their own or as apprentices to kin) was partly due to the lack of other opportunities. The few factories had only a small labor force and trading required less training or capital than most crafts.

The incidence of nonmanual workers in the suburbs depends on the amount and cost of housing in the central city. There were relatively fewer residents in nonmanual occupations in Ashaiman and Kakuri than in the other two suburbs, though none of these towns have much local non-manual work. Teachers and clerks often find it easier than semiskilled or unskilled workers to get accommodation near their jobs, but as rooms are hard to find and expensive in Lagos and Banjul, nonmanual workers in these towns must often move to the suburbs. In Tema and Kaduna, they can find rooms in town.

Self-employment is far more important for women than for men be-cause of the former's relative lack of education and the regular hours demanded by employers. A higher proportion of men are self-employed in the provincial towns and, to a lesser extent, in Ajegunle and Serekunda, than elsewhere. In the industrial towns of Tema and Kakuri, men with a modicum of education can find factory jobs and need not risk self-employment unless they are strongly attracted to it. Where these oppor-tunities are less available, it may require more education (or contacts) to find wage employment, and a higher proportion of men are self-employed.

The census takers in these studies left it to the respondent (or the household head) to say whether he or she was unemployed, and relatively few identified themselves as such. Given the large volume of literature on urban unemployment in Africa, the consistently low proportion of unem-ployed in these towns must be noted. While some of the unemployed may be "sleeping rough" in markets or other public places and thus not reached by house censuses, evidence of these and other studies of unemployment suggests that their numbers are probably not large; most young men have kinsmen or friends who will provide a roof during periods of unemployment. Rather, the number of unemployed is kept down by the prevalence of opportunities for self-employment or casual work in West African towns (Hart 1973). Income from such work is often small and irregular, but the young man who is totally without work for more than six months is probably a secondary school leaver who is determined to wait until a desirable job comes up (Peil 1972b, 1977).

A somewhat different criterion was used for women than for men. Few women are dependent on wage employment; they can enter and leave trading more easily than men and thus it is difficult to establish an objective definition of unemployment. Therefore, the figure given includes the few who said they were unemployed but also any woman who was not in charge of a household (housewife), a mother of resident children, or retired, and was not participating in any economic activity— that is, all those who were available for employment regardless of whether they were looking for it. This produces a realistic figure for most towns, because girls expect to trade or carry on some activity until they marry and during at least some part of their marital career (see chapter 3). However, it is too high in the Gambian towns, where the participation of women in the labor force is much less common than in southern Nigeria or Ghana. Gambian girls who have been to school often say they are looking for work, but many do not take this search very seriously and their families do not press them. True female unemployment in these towns is probably 2 to 3 percent.

Most of these towns are as hetereogeneous in religious affiliation as they are in other variables. This is least true of the Gambian towns, where nearly 90% of the population are Muslim and the Islamic ethos is pervasive. Islam is also strong in Abeokuta, claiming nearly half the population, compared to between a fifth and a quarter of the population of Ashaiman, Ajegunle, and Kakuri, and no one in the Aba sample. There are so few Christians in The Gambia that church affiliation is seldom reported, but Catholics are in the majority. They also outnumber Protestants in Aba, Ajegunle, and Kakuri, whereas most of the Christians in Abeokuta are either Anglicans or Baptists; in Ghana the Presbyterians and Methodists are well represented among southerners whereas a majority of northern Christians are Catholic.

The proliferation of separatist churches in southern Ghana and Nigeria is most evident in Aba and Kakuri, where about a fifth of the adults are affiliated to one of a large number of pentecostal and apostolic groups. About fifty-two such churches were found in Aba, some with several branches. Although the proportion of participants is much smaller elsewhere, there are numerous signs of separatist activities in all of the Nigerian towns studied. The "other" category includes Jehovah's Witnesses (especially active in Kakuri), Salvation Army (in Abeokuta and Aba), and those following traditional religions. It was far more common to claim adherence to traditional religion (or none, which may have meant the same thing) in Ghana than in Nigeria.

The Ga are numerically a small group compared to the Akan and Ewe, so it is not surprising that they are grossly outnumbered in a migration center such as Tema. In addition, they have taken less advantage than they might have of Western education and as a result, have seen most of the wage employment in their towns go to outsiders while they continue to follow their traditional activities of trading, farming, and fishing. Much the same thing has happened to the indigenous Yoruba in Lagos, but a majority of the migrants there are of the same ethnic stock. Ajegunle is the only part of Lagos where the Yoruba are are not an overwhelming majority, and even there they have a strong position in house ownership and trade. The Gwari have a reputation of being uninterested in towns, which is confirmed by their small contribution to Kakuri. The two Nigerian provincial towns are ethnically homogeneous, though Abeokuta has a strong majority of members of the local subgroup, whereas in Aba the local Ngwa are outnumbered by the neighboring Owerri. As traditional land-owners, the Wollof are in a stronger position than migrants in Banjul and have had less need to move out to Serekunda. They are the largest group in both towns, but there are almost as many Mandinka as Wollof in Serekunda.

These demographic data show the towns to have many differences which affect the nature of social life. The implications of these will be explored in succeeding chapters.

2□MIGRATION

Olantunji Sogbesan was a Yoruba of 61 living in Kakuri.[1]
He grew up in Lagos and claimed to have attended Kings'
College, a prestigious secondary school. At 16, he started
work as a "boy" and later became an engineering assistant
on a ship. He spent most of the 1930s as a crane driver or
winch operator in Lagos. With the outbreak of World War
II, he joined the army and spent time in Burma, East
Africa, and South Africa. He came out a trained driver, and
worked in Lagos until transferred to Kaduna in 1956.
With the exception of one year on a course in Lagos, he
stayed in Kaduna until 1966, working for several employers because of his independent disposition. He belonged to the drivers' union, but "got nothing from it."
With the outbreak of "Ojukwu's war," he rejoined the
army at 55, but left after a year because his third wife died
and he had to look after the child. He returned to Kakuri,
where he owned a small house. He worked for a month as
a driver, but then went into semiretirement. He sold part
of his plot and earned money from rents and as a part-time
fitter/blacksmith (for which he had no specific training).
He considered Abeokuta his hometown, though he had
never lived there and had not visited since 1966. He said
he would go there when he retired or gets a "good wife"
(he divorced two and two have died), but it seems unlikely, since he has already retired in Kakuri and the
family house in Abeokuta has been sold. His eldest son was
in secondary school in Lagos and his other two children
were with him in Kakuri. Although a Jehovah's Witness,
he participated in no religious activities. He had no
contact with kin and claimed to have no friends, but was
obviously well known in the neighborhood; his chief
recreation was drinking with cronies.

With the exception of Abeokuta, the Ghanaian and Nigerian towns
studied were growing rapidly through migration; the social environment
was being shaped by newcomers who were attracted by the possibility of
improving their standard of living and who were seldom committed to
permanent residence. This chapter will examine the migration careers of
residents, their adaptation to urban life, and their retirement plans, showing how these factors affect participation in urban society and how they
differ in various types of towns.

Career Migration

Both censuses and surveys tend to measure migration only by comparing the respondent's birthplace and current residence. But many Africans move more than once and a large number eventually return home, so that a migrant's birthplace and present residence may be the same even though he moved many times in his life. This problem has been handled by asking where every individual in the sample censuses was born, grew up, and lived before moving to his or her present residence and, in the Nigerian and Gambian interviews, by recording every place where the respondent lived since the age of 15 or the time he left school. Various aspects of migration have been examined with these data: direct and indirect or multiple migration, the nature of multiple moves and what sort of people make them, long- and short-distance migration, the age at which migration takes place, and changes in these types of migration over time. The difference between male and female migration patterns is also examined.

Studies of Ghanaian factory workers (Peil 1972a, p. 139) led to the expectation that a high proportion of migrants would have gone directly to the city in which they were interviewed and that step migration (movement up the size hierarchy to a small town near home and then to a larger town or city) would be relatively unimportant. This type of migration has been reported as useful in helping migrants in Zaire and Sierra Leone adjust to urban life (Pons 1969; Riddell and Harvey 1972), but so many southern Ghanaians and Nigerians can visit towns to see what they are like before actually migrating that such a gradual approach is unnecessary. If step migration varies with the level of urbanization, it should be more common in The Gambia and central Nigeria than in southern Nigeria or Ghana. Long-distance migrants might experience more indirect migration than those who have moved only a short distance because they would have more alternatives, have greater difficulty learning about distant towns, and have a greater adjustment to make when crossing cultural boundaries. However, even long-distance migrants often come directly because the opportunities available in a capital or large industrial town are known throughout the country and even to potential migrants in nearby countries.

After an extensive study of migration in Thailand, Goldstein (1976) suggested that direct migration is more common to central cities than to provincial towns. This may also be true in West Africa, where migrants to provincial towns tend to be of two types. The main stream brings people to trade or engage in other small-scale self-employment which will be more fruitful in town than in a village. They may have limited aspirations, not want to chance a big city, or just prefer being near home and kin; most are short-distance direct migrants, as there is seldom much point in going a long distance for this type of work. The other migrant stream to provincial towns involves relatively well-educated administrators and professionals for whom job transfers are a frequent occurrence. Soldiers, policemen, and railway workers must also accept frequent moves from one small or middle-sized town to another. Grillo (1973) and Jacobson (1973) have described this pattern, and its implications for the people involved, as it occurs in Uganda. Both of these migrant types were evident in Aba and Abeokuta.

Age is important because of the time it gives for additional moves, but also because opportunities change over time. Young migrants should be more flexible and find it easier to settle down than those who do not leave home until they are over 35. However, migrants who arrive at the peak ages of 20–24 probably face stronger competition from others who have an equal amount of preparation for employment and equally high aspirations, whereas men who arrive when they are older may have more experience to help them find employment and adjust to their new environment, especially if they have moved before. Today's migrants should have more information about where to go and what their qualifications are worth than their predecessors, and probably have more contacts, in more places, who can help them. Therefore, we would expect direct migration to be more common among recent migrants than among those whose last move was ten or twenty years ago.

Single and Multiple Moves

There is little difference between men and women in most categories, indicating that they have similar origins and migration experiences. Women are slightly more likely to be of rural origin and men to have experienced both urban and rural life before moving to where they presently reside. Many men still send back to the rural areas for wives rather than marrying local women, and many migrants prefer to settle down in town before marrying or sending for their wives, so wives make somewhat fewer moves than their husbands. Only in Aba had as many men as women been direct migrants. In most towns, men were somewhat more likely to have come from a distance; the difference was greatest in Banjul, where about a fifth of the long-distance migrant men must either marry local or short-distance migrant women or leave their wives at home. But in the provincial towns and Kakuri somewhat more women than men had come from a distance. Some of these were wives of men who formerly moved farther away and have now returned to their own area, such as the Abeokuta man who had spent thirty years working for the railways and brought his wife with him when he returned home upon retiring.

At least half of the migrants to all of the towns had made only one move. The hypothesis that step migration, as an early response to the problem of adjustment to urban life, declines over time, is not supported. It seems likely that it was never very important in these countries. Instead, multiple

TABLE 2.1

Type of Migration by Town, Sex, and Place of Origin (in Percentages)[a]

Origin and Type of Migration	Ghana				Nigeria								Gambia			
	Ashaiman[b]		Tema		Aba		Abeokuta		Ajegunle		Kakuri		Banjul		Serekunda	
	M	F	M	F	M	F	M	F	M	F	M	F	M	F	M	F
Direct, near																
From rural	34	43	30	35	46	42	10	11	17	22	34	33	32	50	36	43
From urban	11	14	21	26	25	26	24	24	22	29	26	26	21	2	6	5
Direct, far																
From rural	7	4	8	5	b	1	0	0	15	16	6	5	33	29	36	31
From urban	5	3	6	4	3	2	17	20	23	17	9	14	19	9	10	13
Indirect, near																
All rural	10	9	1	3	4	4	1	2	2	2	2	2	1	3	1	1
All urban	3	2	8	7	5	5	31	29	3	2	7	7	0	1	0	0
Mixed	17	14	19	15	13	11	9	6	8	5	11	6	1	2	4	1
Indirect, far																
All rural	3	1	c	1	c	0	1	1	c	c	c	0	2	1	3	1
All urban	5	4	3	2	1	5	6	6	5	4	2	4	3	2	1	1
Mixed	5	6	4	2	3	4	1	1	5	3	3	3	8	2	3	4
Total	100	100	100	100	100	100	100	100	100	100	100	100	100	100	100	100
N	827	516	859	650	716	411	221	181	811	450	741	326	161	107	190	168

[a]Nonmigrants and migrants who arrived before age 15 have been omitted. Near is south and central Ghana for Tema and Ashaiman; the same state for Aba and Abeokuta; Lagos, Bendel, and Western States for Ajegunle; states included in the former Northern Region for Kakuri; Kombo, Western, and North Bank Divisions for Banjul and Serekunda. The rural/urban line is at 10,000 for Ghana and Nigeria and 2,500 for Gambia.

[b]Ashaiman data are for 1968 unless otherwise labeled.

[c]Less than 0.5 percent.

44

migration appears to be neither more nor less common now than in the past. While an increasing breadth of contacts in towns may now make it possible for migrants to try more than one place and a wider range of opportunities makes it easier to move on if one is not satisfied, the majority continue to prefer to minimize the number of moves by choosing what looks like the most promising destination and settling there.

Neither of the provincial towns clearly exemplifies both characteristics described above, but Aba has the most migrants from nearby and Abeokuta the most indirect migrants (usually transfers). The Gambian metropolitan area is shown to have the wide attraction of a primate city, however small; Banjul and Serekunda show similar proportions in all categories and few indirect migrants, even from a distance. Migrants come in considerable numbers from neighboring countries as well as from all parts of The Gambia. With the exception of Bekau, which is near several of the tourist hotels, there is little in other Gambian towns to attract migrants; the major alternative migration opportunity is for groundnut farming.

Differences between towns are often greater than differences between people of varying age or origin within the same town. Towns vary in the labor force they attract, and also in the nature of their hinterland (a much higher level of urbanization in some areas than in others) and because of circumstances which have affected their development (the establishment of migrant streams and pressures on certain groups to migrate to a particular place). Neither provincial nor industrial towns consistently attract more rural or more multiple migrants. The proportion of migrants who have lived exclusively in rural places is relatively high in Aba (49 percent) and low in Abeokuta (13 percent) because of the level of urbanization in their respective hinterlands. In addition, most of the wage employment available in Abeokuta requires education or training which has been available mainly in urban areas. Ashaiman and Tema share the same hinterland, but more migrants to Tema came from towns in the early days; many of the jobs giving access to Tema housing required more education than the factory or construction jobs which were prominent among the Ashaiman labor force. The Gambian towns have a more rural hinterland and a larger proportion of migrants of rural origin than the Nigerian or Ghanaian towns.

Aba demonstrates the importance of special circumstances. Disturbances in eastern Nigeria between 1967 and 1970 made the population of Aba more mobile than they would otherwise have been. This does not show up fully in the data because many returned to their home villages before moving to Aba. Nevertheless, both men and women who first moved to Aba shortly before the war were most likely—and those who moved there since the war least likely—to have made more than one move. The former flooded into Aba and other eastern towns as a result of civil unrest in the north in 1966 and the latter left home because it was so difficult to make a living there in the aftermath of the war. Two-fifths of the men and a quarter of the women interviewed in Aba reported spending at least six months at home since they had first migrated and a quarter had lived in four or more places since reaching adulthood; this was over twice as many as in other towns. Large numbers of migrants were arriving in Aba in spite of its relative lack of opportunities because conditions at home were worse and because many did not feel safe outside East Central State or could not return to their former residences (they were no longer welcome in Rivers State).

While it appears from the table that indirect migrants are likely to have originated fairly close to their eventual destination, this is due to the high proportion of short-distance migrants. A comparison of short- and long-distance migrants shows that the latter are more likely to have made more than one move in The Gambia (often to a town in Senegal or Guinea) and the Nigerian provincial towns, but that there is no difference in Ghana and the Nigerian suburbs. The important factor seems to be the nature of the local labor market and the town's consequent attraction for migrants. Industrial towns appear to exert an equal attraction to migrants over a very wide area, so that those from a long distance come directly at about the same rate as those from the immediate hinterland.

Occupation

The overwhelming importance of economics (migration as a means to employment) is confirmed in the differing migration experiences of men in various types of occupations. Traders and manual workers are more likely to be direct migrants than men in nonmanual occupations, especially soldiers and policemen. Multiple moves of the latter tend to be due to official transfers rather than free movement. For example, a primary teacher had taught in four towns and a policeman had served in Lagos, Calabar, Maiduguri, Ilorin, and Ibadan before being sent to Abeokuta. He seldom stayed longer than two years in a town and some tours lasted only six months. Quite a few older men in both Ghana and Nigeria had traveled while in the army during World War II. Experience of other countries or even distant parts of their own country had often broadened their outlook and, at the same time, gave them opportunity to acquire new skills and thus a better chance of urban employment after discharge.

While some traders and businessmen move from place to place, most try to build up businesses in the towns selected as offering them the best opportunity, the towns in which they have the best contacts, or those closest to their homes. Similarly, semiskilled operatives are likely to continue working in the factory which has employed them or, if this job is lost, to seek work in another factory in the same town. The main exception to this was semiskilled workers in Aba, and in this case migration preferences were affected by the civil disturbances of the late 1960s.

Unskilled and skilled workers show a more variant pattern, sometimes higher and sometimes lower than average mobility for their towns. This is due to the diversity of positions they hold within the labor force. There are large numbers of craftsmen in both wage and self-employment, and while some watchmen and laborers have settled down in town and have histories of stable employment, others come for short periods and pick up jobs by the day. Self-employed men were more often direct migrants than the wage employed except in Kakuri, where wage employees were mainly semiskilled and the skilled had mostly come from a long distance.

The opportunities attracting migrants and competition from other towns affect the number of moves. Skilled and unskilled workers are freer to move on if they choose, taking their skills or strength with them, than are qualified nonmanual workers, who must usually go through elaborate employment procedures, or factory workers, who are limited to industrial towns. The high rate of indirect migration to Ashaiman is largely due to the mobility of skilled workers seeking construction projects (many came down to the Tema area after the Volta Dam was completed) and to self-employed international migrants who worked in other Ghanaian towns and villages before moving to Ashaiman when new opportunities developed there.

The migration patterns of women are less clearly related to their participation in the labor force than those of men, because women are less likely to make migration decisions for themselves. Successful women traders have more freedom of movement than most women. They travel about the country collecting produce for sale, leaving their husbands in town or on the farm, or remain in town when their husbands go elsewhere on business or return home. A palm oil trader in Abeokuta received supplies weekly from her husband. Either he came to town to spend the weekend with her or she went to their village, where he stayed with another wife and all of their children. Several Ga women had come to Ashaiman for two or three months of trading. Men who do not intend to settle in town for more than a few years tend to leave their wives (if any) at home to continue the farming. If the stay in town is longer, the wife will probably try to persuade her husband to let her join him. But this is not always the case. One woman who was asked how long she intended to stay in town said that she considered it a great waste of time. She wanted to return to her trading at home as soon as she got pregnant.

Age

The only notable relationship between age at arrival and distance or size of place of origin is that direct male migrants to the four more industrialized towns who arrived before the age of 15 were more likely to be from nearby towns than males arriving later. The migrant himself does not make the decision when he moves at this age, so this suggests that

TABLE 2.2
Age at Arrival and Number of Moves, by Country and Place of Origin, Males (Percentages)[a]

	Ghana				Nigeria								Gambia			
	Near		Far		Industrial				Provincial				Near		Far	
					Near		Far		Near		Far					
Age at Arrival and Number of Moves	R	U	R	U	R	U	R	U	R	U	R	U	R	U	R	U
0–14: 1	20	22	14	8	9	12	5	6	11	7	18	18	26	21	19	17
2+	14	9	8	4	2	1	1	1	2	1	9	9	0	0	0	0
15–24: 1	21	23	22	22	54	52	46	36	38	31	27	28	20	33	34	30
2+	22	14	20	28	19	14	15	13	7	9	9	20	4	0	9	3
25–34: 1	8	16	10	13	8	11	19	26	18	27	0	15	31	33	18	21
2+	12	9	16	15	6	5	6	10	10	11	18	5	3	0	6	9
35+: 1	2	5	3	6	1	3	6	7	9	8	5	3	14	13	12	16
2+	1	2	7	4	1	2	2	1	5	6	14	2	2	0	2	2
Total	100	100	100	100	100	100	100	100	100	100	100	100	100	100	100	100
N	956	361	228	187	742	390	304	233	560	275	22	65	159	24	162	57

[a]The locally born have been omitted. See table 2.1 for definitions of near and far, rural and urban. Age at first arrival is used for returnees.

industrialized towns are less of an attraction for men who grow up in other towns in the same area than they are for the rural-born or, taking the friction of distance into account, the urban-born of other areas. This may be due to the greater ability of the locally born to take advantage of certain opportunities in less industrialized towns, a topic which will be discussed in the next chapter.

The rush of school leavers to town and the consequent pressure on jobs by recent migrants aged 15 to 24 is evident in Table 2.2, but it is considerably more important in the Nigerian suburbs (both offering industrial employment) than elsewhere. The provincial and Gambian towns, on the other hand, show relatively high levels of migration after age 35. Goldstein (1976, p. 141) argues that in Thailand migration to provincial towns is more rational than migration to Bangkok because individuals have lower aspirations and a better understanding of the opportunities available and what they will do in town. Therefore, there is less of a rush to migrate immediately on reaching adulthood and migrants tend to be older. This hypothesis can be expanded to include towns like Banjul and Serekunda, which are not provincial in the Gambian context but offer much the same sort of opportunities as provincial towns elsewhere. Lower levels of education in The Gambia than in Ghana or Nigeria also probably help to make migration less age-selective, as pressure to leave home soon after finishing school certainly increases the numbers of men who migrate in their late teens.

Child migration (usually with parents, but occasionally alone, for schooling) has apparently been more common in the Gambian and Ghanaian towns than in Nigeria, though Ghanaian parents in the interview samples were least likely to have all of their children with them. The relatively high levels of multiple migration among Ghanaians who arrived before age 15 reflects the secondary nature of such migration to the Tema area during the town's early years as well as the custom of fostering children with kin, so that many Ghanaian children whose parents remain at home grow up in villages or towns other than those where they were born (see chapter 5).

Table 2.3 shows that indirect migration usually increases with age, but that differences between towns are greater than age differences in the same town. Multiple migration is more common at all ages in the Ghanaian towns than at any age in the Gambian towns, due to the former's recent and rapid development. There is no difference between the suburban and provincial towns in Nigeria up to age 35, but after that indirect migration increases in the provincial towns and decreases in the suburbs. This is also probably related to differences in pull factors; the industrial suburbs place a premium on young school leavers and are relatively unattractive to older, experienced migrants, whereas quite a few older men see provincial towns as good places to run small businesses in their declining years.

Men are more likely than women to move more than twice and to move

TABLE 2.3

Proportion of Indirect Male Migrants, by Country and Age at Arrival[a]

Place	0–14	15–24	25–34	35+
Ghana	34(110)	39(745)	54(612)	55(266)
Nigeria				
Suburban	15(171)	25(1077)	31(316)	23(95)
Provincial	18(123)	20(403)	33(273)	40(123)
Gambia	6(64)	11(175)	14(114)	24(49)

[a]Number in parenthesis is base for percentage.

after the age of 34. However, there is a small stream of elderly women moving for the first time to join their children in town after their husbands' deaths. This seems to be a relatively new phenomenon, but is likely to grow. Ten percent of the Nigerian men and 8 percent of the women over 50 had arrived within the past three years, which suggests that many younger individuals in these samples have further migration ahead of them.

It might be expected that most people returning to their places of birth would be ready for retirement, but return to an urban place of birth appears to be based more on opportunity than age. Caldwell (1969, p. 196) found that the proportion of Ghanaian migrants who had returned to their rural homes doubled after age 25 and nearly doubled again after 45, whereas in these towns differences in the proportion of returnees in different age groups were usually very small. Locally born men between 25 and 34 were more likely than those who were older or younger to have returned to Aba, and three-fifths of returnees to other towns were under 35. Therefore, it appears that there is at least no impediment to an early return to the town of one's birth. Some of these young men returned after further education or training; there is no university in any of these towns and no postsecondary institution in Banjul. Others came back on transfer. Many people prefer to live near home if they can find a job there, even though they have been educated abroad, and men who are born in a town have a better chance of returning home without changing jobs than the rural-born.

Education

Because of the access it provides to formal employment, education is an important cause of migration. Caldwell (1968) reports that the more education rural Ghanaian children receive, the more likely they are to leave home. Byerlee (1976, pp. 36, 48) found that a quarter of rural-urban migrants in Sierra Leone were students. The average "educated" migrant left home at age 12 and spent six years in school in a town. Educated migrants were more mobile than the uneducated; only a quarter were working in the town where they finished school.

Because of the wider provision of postprimary schooling in Ghana and Nigeria than in Sierra Leone, migration for education is less common there. Nevertheless, these studies show that the more education people receive, the more often and farther they are likely to move. Illiterates were overrepresented among nonmigrant men and women in Abeokuta and Kakuri; children who go to school leave for better opportunities elsewhere even when they grow up in town. Both men and women who had gone beyond secondary modern school in Nigeria or middle school in Ghana were more likely than those with less education to be multiple migrants; in Nigeria, they were also more likely to have lived in more than one part of the country. These differences are not statistically significant in all six towns, but they are all in the same direction. Primary education does not seem to have any notable effect on the number of moves, perhaps because it is no longer of much consequence for the type of employment obtained. At this level, access to training becomes particularly important (see chapter 3).

It is generally assumed that, because they have the best access to schools, people who grow up in a large town will be better educated than those who migrate to it. However, this depends on the level of educational provision. It is true in The Gambia, where secondary education is largely concentrated in the capital, but nonmigrants in Abeokuta (and the few in Ghana) had less education than migrants, and in the other towns the differences were not significant. Returned migrants born in the Banjul area were also significantly better educated than nonmigrants. This is partly because university education must be obtained abroad, but there are also a large number of senior civil servants from Banjul serving in small towns throughout the country. The principle seems to be that because the best educated leave the countryside and the urban indigenes who get little or no education usually remain at home, migrants to West African towns tend to be at least as educated as the average nonmigrant. This has important implications for labor force participation, which will be discussed in the next chapter.

Contacts

Both Hill (1977, pp. 150–51) and Byerlee (1976, p. 48) point out that the cohesiveness of kin groups is an important factor in migration. Regardless of the relative economic advantages of migration, one potential migrant may not leave home until his father dies, while another may go because his parents urge him to. Migrants tend to choose one town rather than another because they have kin there who can help them, and they often return home in middle age because the time has come to take up lineage land or assume lineage responsibilities.

A few questions were asked in Tema and Ashaiman of all respondents who had arrived within the previous six months, in the expectation that they would have the clearest memory of the migration process. A third of the men and nearly half of the women said they had come to the Tema area because they knew someone there; the proportions were even higher for migrants under 25, men who were not yet employed, and women over 50. These results suggest that young men in particular take the availability of kin as well as opportunities for work into consideration in deciding where to go. An older woman often comes for a few months after the birth of a grandchild or to join her son's household on a more permanent basis. Men over 35 and in clerical, professional, or skilled occupations were least likely to choose Tema because they knew someone. They were usually experienced migrants, able to settle in a new town without help from kin and qualified to find work by themselves; they were also most likely to come on transfer.

Rather surprisingly, there was no difference among the men of varying levels of education or distance from places of origin in the proportion choosing Tema because they knew someone there. Illiterates and long-distance migrants might be expected to want more security on arrival in a strange place than well-educated migrants or those from nearby who can visit the town and make arrangements before actually moving. However, the northerners and alien men who come to Tema tend to be less educated but more experienced and older on arrival than southern migrants. Men who came directly from a rural place (mostly young southern Ghanaian school leavers) were more likely than either indirect migrants or those who came directly from towns or cities to choose Tema because they knew someone there. The characteristics of this type of migrant have been fictionalized in *The Gab Boys* (Duodu 1967).

Women very seldom move to a place where they lack contacts. Only 4 percent of the wives in the Ashaiman census had arrived before their husbands; these had usually migrated with their parents. Three-fifths came at the same time or within the same year as their husbands and another 10 percent came the following year.[2] Four-fifths of the women migrants in the Gambian towns said their husbands or families sponsored their moves; a few of these joined sisters in Banjul in hopes of finding husbands there. Nearly half of the Nigerian women interviewed (differing little from one town to another) said they had had no choice about migration; they went where they were expected to go.

The relative who supports the migrant in town is most often a sibling, spouse, or parent (44 percent of the men and 80 percent of the women in

Tema or Ashaiman who said they knew anyone in the town). Only 9 percent of the women but 37 percent of the men mentioned nonkin (friend, family friend, or someone from the same hometown) drawing them to Tema. This demonstrates again how much more controlled female migration is; women may be quite independent economically, but they are expected to live under the protection of either husband or kin, at least until they are middle-aged. This and the lower pressure to find employment probably make it easier for women than for young men to settle down in town, and this probably affects their perception of urban life and their intention to remain indefinitely.

Urban Adaptation

An examination of the adaptation process is useful in assessing the amount and nature of change which living in town requires and the ease with which various types of migrants make these changes. As discussed in the last chapter, West African migrants probably have less difficulty adapting than migrants in other parts of the continent because of the cultural continuity provided by the maintenance of traditional norms in both the long-established towns and the newer ones. Tema may be an exception to this because of its European design and industrial base, but the spread of urban values and norms in southern Ghana, from which most of the Tema population comes, makes this less of a problem than it would be if Tema had been established in a less urbanized area.

A Model

Goldlust and Richmond (1974) suggest that adjustment to urban life is a complex process which varies with the premigration characteristics of the migrants, the condition of their migration, the nature of the society into which they move, and the length of their stay. The attitudes and behavior of migrants are likely to be changed in the process of settling down in a new town, but they may also bring about modifications in this society, especially if they arrive in large numbers and/or are able to assume positions of political or economic power. Where the host population is better educated and has better access than migrants to economic, political, and social resources, the migrants may suffer discrimination and feel the need to group together for mutual protection and support. In West African towns, however, it may be the indigenes who feel discriminated against (Baker 1974; Peil 1976b, p. 142).

The Goldlust and Richmond model (see Figure 2.1) was developed from a study of immigrants to Toronto; it will be tested here to see how well it survives in quite different cultural and urban conditions. Because of the relatively small number of women in the interview samples, the

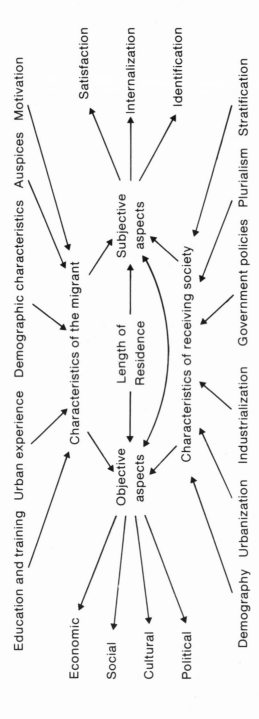

Figure 2.1 A Model of the Migrant Adaptation Process (Adapted from Goldlust and Richmond 1974, p.198.)

discussion will focus on male adaptation, though female reactions will be included for comparative purposes.

Premigration characteristics may be cumulative, giving some migrants a far better chance of easy adaptation than others. The migrant who has completed secondary school (and, preferably, some further training), who has some prior experience of urban life, who is young, who has close kin to help him get settled, and who plans to spend his working life in town should find it easier to adapt than the illiterate who has never been more than a few miles from his village, the older first-time migrant who is set in his ways, or the man who knows no one in the town and/or plans only a short stay.

Education and training provide a framework for success in town both occupationally and socially. Those who find employment quickly and earn an above-average income should see the town in a more positive light than those who are long disappointed in their search for work and then earn just enough to survive. However, those with little or no education may have lower aspirations than the well-educated and hence often find satisfying self-employment more quickly than the secondary school leavers who feel they must wait for clerical jobs. Education is also a help because it provides at least one additional language, English. Other indigenous languages may also be learned, either from fellow students or formally. For example, Akan is part of the Ghanaian primary curriculum. This provides an initial advantage when migrating to a new area, though many unedu-cated West Africans also pick up local languages when they find it useful to do so.

The importance of prior urbanization depends on how much difference there is between rural and urban life. There is probably less difference in West Africa than in Canada because of the high proportion of recent migrants and the low standard of living of most urban residents. However, migrants who have grown up on relatively isolated farms or in distant villages are likely to find urban social life much more of a change than those who have grown up in large villages or small towns; the change seems greater for Middle Belt migrants to Kakuri than for those moving from southwestern towns to Ajegunle or from most parts of southern Ghana to Ashaiman.

Sex, age, and marital status affect the position one can establish in urban social life. A high proportion of migrants to most towns are young and single. They have considerable free time to associate with their peers, though this is less true for young women whose kin take their responsi-bility seriously. Migrating soon after leaving school under the auspices of a brother or uncle is easier than going completely on one's own. The kinsman will provide a place to stay, advice on what to do and not to do and, if one is lucky, help in finding work. Marriage often results in a more circumscribed social life, with fewer opportunities to meet strangers and thus to discover different ways of doing things. Older people are often beginning to think about going home for good, and hence pay less attention to urban roles and have less interest in adapting to new ways. Elderly women may seldom go out.

The receiving society may present formidable barriers to adaptation or may make it easy for migrants to feel at home. The demographic situation in the towns studied has already been discussed. Migrants seem to find the stable towns most congenial, probably because they are most like home. Competition for jobs and housing is greatest in the new towns and the most rapidly growing old ones; these may provide the best opportunity for success but also the least security. Imbalanced sex ratios and the consequent distortions of social life are less common in West African towns than elsewhere on the continent, because migration there was not controlled by colonial government regulations and because towns have long been a normal feature of life in many areas.

Industrialization and urbanization vary within towns as well as between them; this is partly a question of where the migrant lives—in the center with the indigenes, in elite "quarters," or on the periphery. Those who find work in large factories, or move from villages to Accra, Lagos, or Abidjan, have more adapting to do than those who grew up in towns or who settle into self-employment in Aba, Abeokuta, or Serekunda. Though conditions may seem bad to middle-class Europeans, the quality of life in towns is generally higher than in the countryside; there are more amenities available and most urban residents have more material goods than most villagers. Social life is somewhat more varied than in a village and one has more choice of friends, but spare time tends to be spent in the same sort of activities, especially in small, low-income suburbs such as Ashaiman or Kakuri and in sparsely settled Serekunda (see chapter 5). Large numbers of men and women in these towns are self-employed, and many of these work at home instead of having separate places of work and residence. Housing must be shared with nonkin, and it is necessary to adjust to people of differing ethnicity and religion; nevertheless, women sometimes share cooking and child care as they would in a compound at home.

Government policies do not hinder migration and provide a *laissez faire* atmosphere which allows small-scale entrepreneurs to carry on their businesses without undue government interference. The lack of welfare provision and the lower attention given to rural than to urban amenities encourage migrants to maintain contact with kin for mutual security and to contribute to the needs of their villages in the expectation of returning there eventually. Though the government does relatively little about rural problems, it eulogizes rural values, making it more difficult for the sophisticated urban resident to look down on new arrivals and helping the latter to feel that they are important carriers of local culture. Government propaganda also fosters nationalism ("We are all Ghanaians"), though this tends to be lost in election campaigns and competition for national resources.

Cultural and religious pluralism are widely acknowledged; though ethnic prejudice and economic stratification cause difficulties for some migrants, it is generally held that opportunities for advancement are still open. Government policies encourage this view and promote multicultural nationalism whereby only aliens are at an official disadvantage. Even this has received little attention (insofar as African aliens are concerned) in Nigeria or The Gambia. The Ghanaian government, on the other hand, has been much stricter in excluding non-Ghanaians from the country and, should they enter, from various occupations; this has made nationality (which in this case means membership in a Ghanaian ethnic group) far more relevant than it was in the past. Though most migrants find it fairly easy to pick up another language if they need to, they continue to prefer their first language for home use. Cultural change is slow, but this does not appear to hinder adapatation in other respects.

Finally, the stratification system remains open, though perhaps more so at the subjective than at the objective level. Its influence on adapation to urban life is that migrants feel that the town offers many opportunities; they can usually point to kin or neighbors who have done well, and this strengthens their belief in their own future (see Peace 1979: chapter 3). There is considerable competition for industrial and clerical jobs, but those who feel themselves unsuited for such work find other more or less attractive opportunities open to them. Though the highest-paying employment goes to those with the most education, self-employment can still bring the able but illiterate entrepreneur both financial success and prestige. The proportion who reach the top may be declining (there are no figures), but the proportion who are sufficiently successful to satisfy themselves, their kin, and acquaintances appears to be fairly large. The mixing within houses of people at different economic and prestige levels will be demonstrated in chapter 4; its effect is to minimize the separation of the less advantaged from the rest of the society.

Length of residence takes the central position between the characteristics of the migrant and of the receiving society which affect adaptation and the objective and subjective results which this adaptation may have. It serves as an important intervening variable. It is hypothesized that the longer a migrant remains in town the more he adapts to the life around him. Those whose background presents many difficulties or who face barriers from the receiving society on arrival tend to either overcome these problems in time or leave. This is not to say that all long-term residents have accommodated perfectly to local values and behavior, but only that time should moderate the differences in background between migrants and help them to become more like the indigenes, to take on the prevailing cultural characteristics if they wish to.

Political, social, cultural, and economic adjustment can, to a certain extent, be measured objectively. Do migrants take part in local politics and pressure groups or are they indifferent or aloof from local concerns? Are their social networks primarily composed of kin and people from home or have they also good friends among the local population? When they come from a different cultural area, to what extent have they learned the local language and adopted local foods or broadened their value system beyond the norms learned at home? Have they found regular employment in the formal or informal sector or do they have considerable economic insecurity? Is their participation in the economic system limited to their point of entrance or have they been occupationally and socially mobile? To what extent has their use of income adapted to new values (buying consumer goods or building houses in town rather than sending any spare cash home)?

The three subjective aspects of adjustment are more difficult to measure, but they may be more important indices of how well the migrant has adapted himself to urban life. Identification, a transference of loyalty to a new "home," is rare in West Africa. It is closely tied to ethnic or subethnic identification, which gives people their place within the national society; it also seems to involve a denial of kinship with one's ancestors, a potentially dangerous thing to do.

Internalization is a change of attitudes and values that goes deeper than the outward conformity that can be measured objectively. Fear of sanctions may bring about changed behavior, but the migrant will only be a full member of the new society if he internalizes its values. Lastly, the migrant will not adapt to the new society if he is not satisfied with it. This satisfaction will be based on comparisons of his present situation with his position at home before migration, at the present time (if he had stayed at home) and in the future (should he return) as well as comparisons of his success in town with that of other migrants and the indigenes. His comparative reference groups may change over time; the new migrant will more often estimate how he stands relative to his peers at home, whereas the long-established migrant will look at his position in relation to successful urbanites.

Application

As the surveys were carried out before the article by Goldlust and Richmond appeared, the data do not correspond precisely with their categories. Nevertheless, except for cultural aspects and auspices, sufficient data are available to test the strength of relationships predicted by the model. The following measures have been used:

1. Premigration characteristics: education, prior experience of urban life and other cultures, and age at arrival. Training has been omitted because almost the only specific occupational training which cannot be included under education is the apprenticeship of skilled workers or short, on-the-job training of the semiskilled. This is often obtained after arrival in town and appears to have no effect which is independent of education and occupation.

2. Social aspects: frequency of seeing kin in town and visiting home, membership in voluntary associations, and a variety of measures of social interaction which will be discussed in chapter 6.

3. Economic aspects: occupation, unemployment, length of time on the job, and income.

4. Political aspects: belief that ordinary people can make their needs known to government, whether the respondent has ever tried to do so, and the use of bureaucratic agencies to handle problems.

5. Length of stay, counting from first arrival in town or metropolitan area.

6. Subjective aspects: intention to go home, the ease with which the respondent makes acquaintances and satisfaction with the neighborhood.[3]

The correlation coefficients of scale scores, shown in Table 2.4, vary considerably from one town to another; those for males are seldom above .30. Premigration characteristics are most consistently related to economic success and, to a lesser extent, political participation, whereas length of residence appears to be more important to social activity and subjective satisfaction with life in town. Insofar as the model is designed to predict adaptation to urban life, it is unfortunately no more useful than a set of background characteristics; the scales taken together predict only about 4 percent of the variance in subjective satisfaction among Nigerian and Ghanaian respondents, varying considerably between towns. The R^2 is higher for The Gambia, but is not statistically significant given the small number of migrants in the Gambian samples.[4]

In order to test the impact of specific background characteristics, they were transformed into dummy variables and all the samples were combined. Table 2.5 shows that many of them are useful in explaining subjective satisfaction, but most explain little of the variance in the other scales. By far the most important factor in satisfaction is location; the urban environment appears to have more to do with this than any personal characteristic. Thus, the respondents in the two Gambian towns are most satisfied and those in the two Ghanaian towns least satisfied. Although subjective and economic scores are seldom closely correlated, in the economic score location is also important (after education) because the

TABLE 2.4
Correlation Coefficients of Adaptation Measures, by Town, Migrants[a]

	Ghana						Gambia				Nigeria							
	Tema		Ashaiman 1968		Ashaiman 1970		Banjul		Serekunda		Aba		Abeokuta		Ajegunle		Kakuri	
	M	F	M	F	M	F	M	F	M	F	M	F	M	F	M	F	M	F
Premigration																		
Social	.37	.21	.10				.53	.55	.48	.52					-.16			
Economic[b]	.42	.23	.24		.19		.25	.63	.31	.66	.32	.47	.51	.46			.18	
Political[c]							.35	.59	.41	.47	.16	.40	.23	.73	.24			
Arrival[d]					.15	-.25	.22	.38		.42					-.22			
Subjective																		.41
Social																		
Economic	.19	.32	.14				.26			.39	.32	.27			.29	.45		
Political[c]							.25						-.18					.23
Arrival[d]	.27	.18	.25	-.22			.27		.21		.25	.39	.56	.42				.25
Subjective	-.28	-.10											.46	.40		.24		.24
Economic																		
Political[c]							.25	.51	.39	.65		.58	-.18		.49	.42	.18	.42
Arrival				.14			.24					.24	.19			.34	.18	.34
Subjective	-.15										.14							
Political[c]																		
Arrival[d]							.27	.42	.18	.33								
Subjective								.47	.21	.36			.46				.25	
Arrival[d]																		
Subjective	-.14	.12					.33		.29	.47	.16		.33		.40	.26		
N	203	147	313	141	72	25	96	23	90	26	151	55	97	43	163	50	154	45

[a]Only significant correlations (.05 or better) are listed.
[b]Occupation only for Tema and Ashaiman 1968.
[c]Not enough data for Ghana.
[d]Length of residence in this town.

TABLE 2.5

Percent of Variance Explained by Background Characteristics, by Scale and Sex[a]

Variable	Subjective M	F	Social M	F	Economic M	F	Political M	F
Country	.56	.55	.05		.13	.06	.02	
Town	.57	.54	.08		.19	.10	.04	
Income	.44	.29	.05		c	c	.08	.18
Length of residence	.28	.32	.01	.06	.02		.04	
Age at arrival	.21	.23					.03	
Religion	.16	.17	.02		.02			
Origin[b]	.14	.17	.06	.07				
Marital status	.04	.17	.01		.05		.01	
Occupation	.09	.09	.03		c	c	.07	.15
Employment sector	.10				.06	.64	.04	.17
Education	.04	.06	.02		.14	.22	.06	.18
Age	.03				.07		.01	

[a]Only R^2s significant beyond the .05 level are shown.

[b]Rural or urban background and distance of home from town.

[c]Included in the scale.

nature of local economic activities affects the use which can be made of education and the income which can be earned.

The next most important factor is income. A high income increases satisfaction with urban life and also participation in politics. In this case, education is more important than income; the R^2 for income drops considerably when education is added to the equation, though high income still makes a significant contribution.

Length of residence is important mainly in increasing satisfaction, though it has a small effect on the other three scales for men and on women's social activities. Age at arrival, religion, and the size and distance of place of origin mainly affect the subjective scale, though coming from a long distance significantly lowers the social participation of both men and women. Marital status is more important for women's than for men's satisfaction, but it has more effect on the other scales for men. Occupation, employment sector, and education have very little effect on social position and less effect on the other scales than anticipated. They matter more to women than to men; the uneducated housewife is in a poor economic position and unlikely to be politically active, whereas the well-educated woman holding a professional job is in a better position to exercise influence. Last, age is a poor predictor of any of these aspects of urban life. These relationships will be analyzed in future chapters.

Overall, this exercise confirms the impression that these societies are still remarkably open to people of a wide variety of backgrounds. Personality, initiative, and luck have been important to success in the past, especially in business, and the increasing centralization and bureaucratization since independence have not yet cut off avenues for advancement, though they may have decreased the number of men and women who are able to use them. Political, social, and economic achievement are not closely related. Political pressure from below is often strong and insistent and the wealthy are given social prestige only if they share with less fortunate kin and clients.

In what sort of social structure does the model fit best and least well? The mean correlations are highest for Abeokuta and Ashaiman (1968) and lowest for Ashaiman (1970) and Ajegunle. Abeokuta has the highest mean scores on all but the political scales, the highest correlation nine times and the lowest four times. There are many aspects of this town which set it and its migrants apart from the general trend of West African urbanization, though these characteristics may be common in many provincial towns of southwestern Nigeria. Age is more important there than elsewhere and premigration characteristics are more closely related to economic and political (but not social) factors. This reflects the separation between the migrants, many of whom are administrators on government transfer, and the social life of the town, which is centered on the locally born with their traditional ties. A similar dichotomy is probably found in many long-established provincial towns.

Ashaiman in 1968, on the other hand, was a typical new town, full of young migrants struggling to make a place for themselves. Its high correlations of subjective identification with social and political factors reflect the development of home ownership and community attachment among the long-established aliens and migrants from the immediate neighborhood. Although interest in community improvement was considerably greater in 1970 (when, unfortunately, political factors were not measured), any local identification developed by aliens was lost when the government ordered mass expulsions. The poor economic situation meant that fewer migrants were drawn to the Tema area and many who lived there either lost their jobs or felt insecure. Average age and length of residence of migrants were higher in 1970 than in 1968, but older men with promising backgrounds apparently moved out; the correlation between age and premigration characteristics is reversed. The older men of long residence who stayed were often long-distance direct migrants who had little or no education but maintained a wide circle of contacts and a relatively comfortable economic position.[5]

Ajegunle might be considered typical of what is worst in Third World urbanization, and here the model provides little help. Subjective attachment does increase with age, and objective factors are also somewhat more favorable for older men, but the most interesting findings are the negative correlations between social factors and political and economic factors. The less social also tend to be more politically active in Abeokuta and, to a lesser extent, in Aba. It is the less-educated migrant of rural origin who is more socially active, whereas the economically successful (especially in Abeokuta) often seek official sources of assistance instead of relying on kin—the basis of scoring on the political scale.

Insofar as Ajegunle and Ashaiman in 1970 provided the most difficulties for migrants in terms of adverse government policies (Ajegunle was suffering from benign neglect, to say the least), conflicts over ethnicity, and (in Ajegunle) a more divisive system of stratification than other towns, the model predicts that migrants will have more difficulty in adjusting. The correlations suggest that it is the relationships between variables which are affected: given unfavorable conditions, prior advantages such as education or urban residence and objective factors such as social or economic success may not pay off in increased attachment to the town or satisfaction with what it provides. On the other hand, the low level of urbanization, tolerant pluralism, and helpful government which are found in Serekunda do not appear to raise the correlations, though they do improve the migrants' general satisfaction.

Tema, with a maximum of industrialization and government intervention, comes out about average. Those with advantageous premigration characteristics are more satisfied in Tema than in other towns, but age, length of residence, and objective success are relatively less important there. Tema provides opportunities for young, educated migrants, but it is difficult to become attached to a town when one has only a limited chance for promotion and little prospect of owning a house.

In conclusion, the model is mainly useful in providing a framework for analysis, though much more careful measuring of its variables is necessary than has been possible in this study. Its utility as a predictor of behavior is limited. While some of the variance between towns can be explained in terms of situational determinants, other aspects cannot. Towns which appear to have fairly similar social structure show widely differing results on some variables, and similar correlations appear in towns which seem to be quite different in structure and/or opportunity. The underlying relationships are obviously very complex.

Going Home

While a great deal of attention has been given to studies of migration to the towns, there has been much less concern with the return home. Plotnicov's suggestion (on the basis of his work in Jos [1965]), that few migrants return relies too heavily on conversations with the few who stayed rather than the many who left. It is far easier to contact the former than the latter. The proportion who remain in town after retirement may be increasing, but the shortage of migrants over 50 in most towns suggests that many former residents have gone home. Given the rate of influx into many towns over the past thirty years, the total population would be far larger if most had stayed.

Though circulating migration was probably more common in southern and East Africa than in West Africa, today's rural-urban migrants in all areas are probably more likely to plan a long stay than in the past. This is partly because they tend to have some education and to be interested in the sorts of jobs that are found mainly in towns, but also because land shortages in many source areas make it difficult for them to take up farming (except in subservience to their fathers) and because the urban standard of living is sufficiently higher than the rural standard to make it worthwhile to live in town until retirement. Nevertheless, some migrants only stay for a short time. If they cannot find work in six months to a year, young migrants may try another town, but many go home. Some try again later when conditions look more promising, but many give up their plans for an urban career and either become farmers or find local wage employment.[6]

Attempts to trace the unemployed are often frustrated because they have left town; the "hard core" unemployed are likely to be over 25 and either locally born or long-term migrants who find it more difficult to leave than do newcomers. For example, long-term unemployment in Banjul affected mainly local school leavers still living with their parents. A study of unemployment in Lagos found that a third of the men who had been unemployed for up to six months but half of those without work for over two years were over 25 years of age (Peil 1972b). Given the large numbers of young men who come to Lagos each year looking for work, it is evident that many who are unsuccessful do not stay.

Caldwell (1969, p. 186) asked rural respondents in Ghana whether many migrants fail to return home; 70% said no. Two-thirds of these indicated that migrants usually return on retirement, in old age, or when they become too sick to continue working. However, Caldwell reports (ibid., p. 190) that substantial numbers of southern Ghanaians return home in mid-career to take up cash-crop farming. A man often inherits a farm at this time, and may have some savings invested in a house as well as skills which he can use to advantage at home. Northern Ghanaians, on the other hand, have had little alternative to subsistence farming at home, but have tended to stay only a few years because the unskilled work available to them was physically hard and not very remunerative. Their situation is now changing with the spread of cash crops at home and with education, which puts them on a more equal footing with the southern school leaver. Insofar as young men from northern Ghana and the Middle Belt of Nigeria have greater access to land for farming at home than migrants from areas with a dense rural population nearer the coast, they will be more likely to return home before retirement, especially if faced with prolonged urban unemployment.

House Ownership

The best measure of intention to stay is the acquisition of a house in town, though it is probably more accurate for migrants over 40. Rent from urban property provides a means for continued residence in town; the landlord's children, who inherit the house jointly,[7] are more likely than first-generation migrants or the children of tenants to change their allegiance from the ancestral hometown to the new place of residence. A few owners of urban houses live at home and come to town periodically to collect the monthly rent or they may allow a kinsman to supervise the property and collect the rent, but, in general, there is a high correlation between urban house ownership and the intention to remain permanently in town. People at all income levels acquire urban houses, but long-term planning is needed and the decision must usually be made by the time the prospective owner is middle-aged. Thus, attitude toward remaining in town permanently is a relevant factor in property ownership (Barnes 1974).

Likewise, while the elites often build at home because of the strong social pressure to do so and all those who own a house at home do not return to live in it permanently, the completion of a rural house tends to signify a commitment to rural retirement which is usually fulfilled if the owner lives until retirement. Those who cannot afford to put up a house at home, or even add a room of their own to the family house, may feel that they would not be welcome. If the urban cost of living should make it impossible to accumulate savings which can be sent home for family support and investment in housing, this could raise the proportion who feel they are too poor to go home; so far, there is little hard evidence that this is happening. All but 4 percent of Caldwell's urban respondents (1969, p. 147) had hopes of rural house or room ownership and 31 percent already owned or were building rural accommodation. About half of the respondents in Tema and Ashaiman who were over 50 and intended to stay indefinitely owned a house in town or said that it was now home (often because they had a child settled there with whom they could live).

Gambian respondents were asked whether they owned houses in the Banjul area or at home or hoped to do so. The difference in orientation reflected in house ownership comes out clearly in Table 2.6. Those who already owned a house in town were more likely than tenants to be born in the area; those who planned to buy or build houses there were most likely to say that they did not intend to return home; those who owned a house at home were most likely to plan to return there in old age; and those who

TABLE 2.6

Male Home Ownership and Intention to Remain in Town,
Gambian Samples (Percentages)

	Local Origin	Will Return Home		
		Never	When Old	Soon
Owns here	32	17	8	2
Plans: Here	42	54	13	10
Home	0	0	8	18
Owns at home	0	1	38	25
None of these	26	28	33	45
Total	100	100	100	100
N	140	93	24	40

neither owned a house nor planned to do so showed the greatest inclination to return home in the near future. The patterns are identical in Banjul and Serekunda.

Only male responses are shown in the table because a woman is less likely than a man to have enough capital to buy or build a house of her own (especially in The Gambia). In addition, women frequently have access to urban housing that does not entail ownership. Nevertheless, 15 percent of the women interviewed in The Gambia owned a house and 17 percent hoped to do so eventually; some of these had inherited the family compound. Only a quarter of the women owners were migrants; Barnes (1974) found that it usually took women in Lagos at least two generations to become house owners. The means used to acquire houses and the potential of individuals of varying characteristics to be house owners will be discussed in chapter 4. Suffice it to say here that motivation appears to be at least as important as income, which is why ownership is such a useful index of intention to stay.

The Decision to Leave Town

Given that the majority of migrants are still young and have not accumulated enough savings to build a house, their own estimate of their intentions is often the best measure available. Less than a tenth of respondents in Tema and Ashaiman thought that older people should stay in town with their children rather than go home when they retire. Three percent mentioned the possibility of staying in town if one owned a house there, but over half felt that old age should be spent in the company of family and kin; separation may be necessary for employment, but there is no need to prolong this into retirement and, if at all possible, one should die and be buried at home.

TABLE 2.7
Migrants' Estimates of their Eventual Return Home, by Town and Sex
(Percentages)

	Nigeria								Gambia			
	Aba		Abeokuta		Ajegunle		Kakuri		Banjul		Serekunda	
	M	F	M	F	M	F	M	F	M	F	M	F
Never	4	2	2	25	2	4	12	23	47	45	70	50
Eventually	91	90	72	31	63	40	60	52	14	15	15	18
Soon	4	6	16	36	35	54	24	14	38	35	14	38
Don't know	1	2	10	8	0	2	4	11	1	5	1	4
Total	100	100	100	100	100	100	100	100	100	100	100	100
N	147	54	61	36	170	52	156	44	79	20	87	24

Table 2.7 shows that only a small proportion of the Nigerians and Ghanaians questioned expected to stay permanently, compared to about half of the Gambian migrants.[8] Women in Abeokuta and both men and women in Kakuri were more committed to a permanent stay than other Nigerians. The Gambians appear to be staying because they can get access to land to build houses and because they find that the Banjul area provides a higher standard of living and better amenities than their village without demanding much cultural change. The peri-urban atmosphere and low standard of housing are probably similar assets, and financing a house there is not difficult.

In addition, several of the migrants intending to stay were older women who had come to town after their husbands' deaths and settled into sons' households. A mother's presence may encourage the son to acquire a house, since the need for visiting and supporting parents (which focuses attention on the hometown) is removed. This is one reason why villages so strongly support the return of all their members on retirement and the building of a house at home; it puts pressure on the next generation to maintain their ties with the village (Kaufert 1976). The stability of the migrant women in Abeokuta is largely due to their marriages to local men and to their continuing role in trade and/or looking after their grandchildren while their daughters trade.

Women's stated intentions may be less reliable than men's because they often allow men to make their migration decisions for them; they go home when their husbands decide to go and they may be sent home if the husband dies or it is decided that the children should get some of their schooling in the village rather than in town. With large-scale inflation in Ghanaian towns in the 1970s, many men have sent their wives and children back to the villages to raise their own food.

Two carer histories might by hypothesized. First, a new migrant might feel ill at ease and think he would stay only a short time, but gradually he settles down and, as he feels more at home, decides that he may as well stay indefinitely. The longer he stays, the harder it is to leave his friends and his local position and return to a village with which he feels increasingly out of touch. Alternatively, the new migrant might feel that the town is the best place to be, that he is much more a part of things there than in the village (where he can have only an insignificant position until he is much older and a family head). As he ages, he begins to take a more active part in hometown affairs, either through the improvement association in the town where he is living or on visits home for holidays and funerals. By the time he reaches retirement age, he sees the village as a proper and prestigious place to live and is glad to return. While one or the other of these types undoubtedly occurs in some cases, neither is sufficiently typical to be clearly evident in the data. Most people represent a composite of these types.

It seems logical that the proportion of migrants who remain in town permanently should increase over time. Present-day migrants are, on average, better prepared for urban life than previous newcomers. In addition, urban conditions are tending to improve faster than rural conditions even though all residents do not participate in these improvements. However, Ejiogu's data on Lagos (n.d., p. 127, collected 1964) and Gugler's on eastern Nigeria of 1961–1962 (1970, p. 27) suggest that intended stability might have been greater shortly after independence than it was in the aftermath of the civil war. Ejiogu reports that 8 percent of the migrants under 30 and 56 percent of those over 50 planned a permanent stay in Lagos. His sample included some elite housing and several areas with a more settled population than Ajegunle, so his respondents may have felt more secure and many were certainly more financially successful than people in the Ajegunle sample. Gugler found that 96 percent of "ordinary" people but only 65 percent of professionals and successful businessmen intended to retire to their hometown. This difference was not evident in my 1972 samples.

Length of stay in towns appears to have the most effect on stability; age, economic success, and distance from home are less important than was assumed. The relationship between length of residence and intention to stay is fairly strong in The Gambia (r = .38 for men and .37 for women), but weak in the Nigerian samples (r = .10 for men and .13 for women). Migrants who had lived in Nigerian towns more than ten years were most likely to plan a permanent stay, but this was only 8 percent of the men with long-term residence. For those who had spent less than ten years in town, the pattern is less clear; age and opportunity are probably more important. For example, almost no one in Aba planned to return home in the near future, compared to about a quarter of migrants in Kakuri; in both, the newest arrivals had a slight lead in the proportion who expected only a short stay. On the other hand, men who had lived in Ajegunle between two and ten years were significantly more likely than those with either less or more experience to plan to leave soon. It appears that the scale of Lagos, the high cost of living and level of unemployment (with associated job insecurity) put extra strain on residents of Ajegunle, especially middle-aged men with family responsibilities.

Though young men and recent migrants tended to be somewhat more interested than men of middle age in going home soon, this was most notable among the unemployed. Evidently, initial feelings of insecurity and possibly transitory residence were overcome fairly easily once work was obtained. The proportion who planned to stay indefinitely increased with age among men in Kakuri, Abeokuta, and Aba (over 50 only) and among women in Abeokuta, but the differences were seldom statistically significant. The proportion of migrants over 50 who intended to go home was still very high (from 43 percent in Serekunda to 93 percent in Ajegunle), so a major increase in the numbers of elderly people in towns seemed unlikely in the near future, except in The Gambia.

Some older men will continue to put off their return, but many are likely to go, and some of those who intend to stay may also change their minds because it becomes more advantageous to return, or because of pressure from kin or an inability to support themselves in town. With the exception of women in Ajegunle, most Nigerian respondents expected to go home only after many years, usually on retirement. This does not mean that they are not open to sudden opportunities, but rather that they expect it to be advantageous to remain in urban employment over a long period. Inheritance of farm land or improved chances of success in trade or craftsmanship at home may encourage them to change their minds.

Length of residence and age proved to be less important factors in the stability among Ghanaian factory workers than among Nigerians. The stabilized included about a quarter of workers interviewed in Accra, Takoradi, and Tema, and 37 percent of those in Kumasi (the Akan capital, which many migrants considered their true hometown). Recent migrants were least likely to say that they planned to stay indefinitely, but there was no difference between younger and older men in Tema, Kumasi, or Takoradi. In Accra, workers over 30 years of age were more likely than younger men to say they intended to go home when they stopped working, but some of the younger men may have interpreted "when you stop working" as referring to leaving their present jobs rather than retiring from the labor force (Peil 1972a, pp. 181–85).

A good education, leading to a high-level occupation and income, should make it easier to settle down in town permanently. However, successful migrants normally retire to a satisfying and relatively comfortable life as local leaders and patrons in their hometowns rather than remaining in the city; this arrangement allows them considerable prestige and minimal duties in their declining years. It has been suggested that new "elder statesmen" roles will develop in the towns, but these will be open to few. The elites are usually under strong pressure to build at home; since they may vacate job-related housing in town when they retire it simplifies things if a house in their own hometown is ready and waiting. Even if the house serves only as a monument to success and residence for kin, it is important for prestige. Some migrants (from all occupational categories) take a middle course by settling in the nearest town to their home; they can be culturally at home while still enjoying urban amenities.

Professionals and administrators who originated in towns like Abeokuta are especially fortunate in being able to combine retirement at home with urban life. It is probably more satisfying to settle permanently in a provincial town, where one can participate in local and state politics and be seen as a "big man" than in a metropolis where younger men are competing strongly for prestige and power or in a suburb which is governed by decisions made elsewhere and which has few roles for local "big men" other than the landlords' association or the church or mosque. A landlord's association may be an important factor in local politics (formal or informal) and thus give landlords both a reason for remaining and a role when they decide to do so (Barnes 1977). However, there is less evidence of landlord interest in Ajegunle than Barnes found in Mushin, perhaps because only half the Ajegunle landlords lived there. The scope for leadership in religious affairs varies with the importance the religious group gives to formal training and hierarchy, but for most migrants there is probably at least as much scope at home as in town.

Though education is an important factor in the decision to migrate, it appears to play little direct role in the decision to remain in town. The only significant relationship was in The Gambia, where men with primary schooling were more likely than those with more or less education to say they would go home on retirement. A high income from a professional or commercial occupation should make it easier to stay in town, but the effect of income on motivation is mixed. While men earning over £750 per year were more likely than those with lower incomes to intend to stay permanently in the Nigerian provincial towns, all of those earning over £500 in Kakuri and Ajegunle intended to go home, usually in the distant future. All but two men in the £300–499 income group in all four towns intended to go home.

At the other extreme, men earning nothing were more likely than those earning something to plan a return in the near future. Some of these were already retired and some had not yet started working, but the distribution of those intending to stay gives no support to the "too poor to go" hypothesis. This does not mean that a few of the poverty-stricken do not get stuck in town, since they are least able to do as they choose, but many families send indigent kin home because it is easier and cheaper to care for them there and it is normative that they should go. However, unemployed men in Aba were committed to staying there, probably because they saw no alternative.

The self-employed, especially those in trade, have more control over where they live than those who depend on wage employment; whether they choose to stay in town or return home varies from place to place. Nigerian men in commercial occupations were more likely than either manual or nonmanual workers to be stabilized in town—except in Ajegunle, where all but one planned to leave eventually. This may reflect the intense competition among traders in Lagos, making business there more attractive to younger men. Income from self-employment tends to be less secure and regular than wages, but a successful venture may provide enough capital to invest in a house, more than the wage earner is likely to accumulate at one time. Self-employment is the goal of a high proportion of Nigerian wage earners, and those who can make the change successfully are also more likely to be able to plan ahead, build a house, and settle down as local figures of influence.

Distance from home is a similarly poor predictor. Migrants from a short distance might be more willing to remain in town because they can visit their homes regularly, or long-distance migrants might become more committed to urban life because visits home are so expensive and difficult that they take place only at long intervals. However, there is considerable variance between towns in whether short- or long-distance migrants are the most stabilized and the differences are not statistically significant. Though distance from home and contacts with kin probably play a part in migrants' intentions, other factors are more important.

Abeokuta is a useful place to study migration because, though larger and offering more wage employment than a village, it has a long history of out-migration and a strong sense of identity which pulls migrants back in their old age. A comparison of nonmigrants with returnees shows that the latter's children are more likely to be migrants in their turn, though most nonmigrants with children over 20 had seen some of them try their luck away from home. Lagos and Ibadan were almost as popular with their children as with the children of migrants, and both had children living in England. Thus, the rate of migration seems likely to increase. It will be affected in two ways by the creation of new states in 1976: the new position of Abeokuta as capital of Ogun State has made more jobs available locally, in construction and the civil service, and thus decreased the need to migrate. For those who go, discrimination in favor of local people in neighboring states will probably make Lagos an even more likely destination than it has been in the past.

The Abeokuta sample census located thirty-seven men and thirty-six women who had been born in Abeokuta and returned there after a period away. Eight of the men and five of the women had grown up elsewhere, and there were several other Egba in the sample "returning" to a hometown in which they were neither born nor grew up. There is much more work to be done on patterns of allegiance to a hometown, but these data confirm that it is by no means lost by the children of migrants. Three-fifths of the women returned with their husbands and a seventh were widows; one joined her husband and another her son, and two had husbands who were away. There were three housewives and two teachers; all the rest traded.

Three-fourths of the men had returned before reaching 35 years of age. Most of these younger men were in wage employment and might be transferred away again. Two of the three who came home while in their forties were also employees. Just as the desire for a wage may be the primary reason for migration, so migration may be necessary in order to qualify for a wage job at home.

It appears that migrants who want to go home to set up their own businesses are seldom able to do so before late middle age. The exceptions may have been unsuccessful in finding steady wage employment in larger towns or unusual in some other way; as they were not interviewed, it is impossible to say. For most migrants, the large town appears to offer the most opportunities for wage or self-employment until they reach their fifties or sixties. Then, as death seems closer, they feel it is time to go home.

Retirement

The age of retirement varies between countries and jobs, but 55 or 60 is probably the most common official norm. For farmers and the urban self-employed, retirement involves a gradual lowering of effort rather than the sharp break which the wage employed experience. The attitudes and economic position of three categories of people over 60 will be examined here: migrants who have not returned home, people born in the survey city who have returned there after working elsewhere, and nonmigrants. Few people in their sixties were interviewed, but they provide examples of factors which affect older people's decisions, the extent to which they continue to participate in the labor force, and their sources of support.

Figure 2.2 (p. 74–75) shows that participation in the labor force declines considerably for both men and women who remain in town after the age of 60, except for men in Tema. The decline is least for men and women in the Ghanaian towns and for men in Kakuri; it is greatest for men and women in Aba and Banjul and women in Abeokuta. Thus, the industrial towns maintain a high level of labor force participation (and those who stop work go home), whereas provincial towns and the Gambian capital (whose environment has many provincial aspects) are seen by many as convenient places to retire. Women's retirement appears to be more normative than men's. Most women stop trading at some time in their fifties, when their children urge them to or their husbands die; in both cases, the grandmother role provides an attractive substitute.

Mandatory retirement of men from wage employment at 60 or 65 may be a waste of manpower, at least in Nigeria. Those who retire in their early fifties are more likely to move into entrepreneurial occupations than those who keep their jobs until a later age, because the former still have energy for new ventures. Of the elderly men interviewed in Abeokuta, one had changed from cloth trading to the less demanding but less remunerative sale of cigarettes and sweets at about 60, and another had let his business run down to about one contract per year. However, two others had not retired until they were 67 and 70. Of the three migrants still active, one had retired at 55 to become a trader after a six-months rest, the second had returned home at 53 to become a *mallam* (Muslim teacher) and the third had also returned at 53 to continue his cattle trading at home. The Gambia allows voluntary retirement from the civil service, with pension, at any time after 45, an arrangement which encourages men at the top to move on and make room for younger men.

The fifty-seven men and thirty-seven women interviewed in Tema and Ashaiman who were over 50 were asked how much longer they intended to stay, where they would go when they left, and why. All those who intended to leave said they would go to their hometown. Half thought they would leave within the next five years, an indication that the fifties and early sixties are seen as the proper time to retire to one's hometown. A third of the men but only 11 percent of the women said they would stay for more than ten more years, but a quarter of the women said that the decision was not theirs to make. An eighth of the men were not sure what they would do.

Half of the men and three-quarters of the women felt that an old person's proper place was at home. A driver from Ada summed up the prevailing feeling of the men that they owed it to their hometown to return: "You are made what you are by your native town, and must go to help somehow." It is felt that migrants have a duty to rejoin the kin group (or whatever part of it still maintains a place in the village) and, especially, to die at home. Men are occasionally called on to return home to take charge of lineage affairs. Very few people are buried in urban cemeteries; it is important to be buried with the ancestors, and much more convenient for the family if one dies at home (Aronson 1971; Kaufert 1976).

Three of the five men who planned to stay owned their houses; the other two were aliens from the north who said they felt at home in Tema/Ashaiman, though both had arrived within the last ten years. Most of the rest stayed in town because of their work. Only two were retired, a fisherman who had come recently for medical treatment and would leave as soon as this was completed, and a civil servant who spent most of his

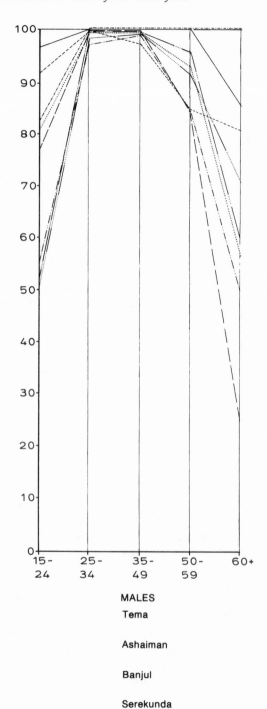

MALES

Tema

Ashaiman

Banjul

Serekunda

Figure 2.2 Labour Force Participation, by Sex and Age

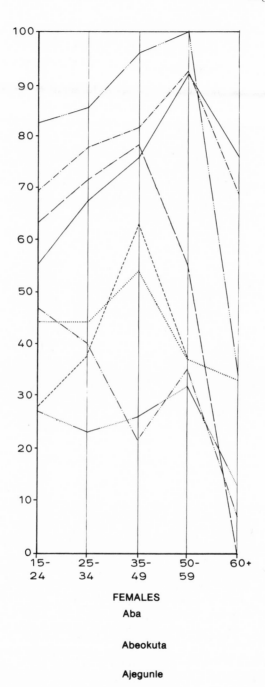

Aba

Abeokuta

Ajegunle

Kakuri

Figure 2.2 (continued)

time at home but came to town for a week each month to collect rent from his tenants and visit his wife and children, who still lived in Ashaiman. Several men said they were only waiting until they were pensioned to go home, and a Hausa planned to return to Nigeria as soon as the war ended. Another Hausa planned to go soon to build his house at home; he preferred to supervise this himself. A Yoruba who had built in Ashaiman still planned to return to his hometown to live with his children. An Ewe storekeeper felt that it was best to go home, but was unsure about returning because he had not managed to build there. Thus, men identify living in town with participation in the labor force and see retirement as a time to pay off debts to one's hometown.

Women, on the other hand, feel their indebtedness to the family rather than the village. Women exchange the role of trader for grandmother as they "retire," and tend to choose town or home (if they have a choice) according to the location of grandchildren. The only woman who wanted to stay had three grandchildren with her and said there was nothing for her to do at home. Thus, as children and grandchildren of migrants grow up in town, the proportion of women who return home seems certain to decline.

Only fourteen elderly migrants who had not yet returned home were interviewed in Nigeria, three or four in each town. In addition, there were eight who had returned to Abeokuta after working elsewhere and nineteen who had remained at home in Abeokuta.[9] Of the fourteen, five were definite that they would never leave and it seemed likely that six more would stay, two because they had already spent many years in retirement, two because they owned land in town, one because she was a widow living with her son, and the last because he had all of his children with him in Ajegunle. One of the pensioners seemed to be unsure that his pension would be maintained if he left Lagos. Of those who were sure they would stay, two had become chiefs, one had been farming near Kakuri for twenty years, one had been in Abeokuta since 1912 and married there, and the last was a moderately successful trader who said, "I have no investment at home, so I have no cause to go home finally; most of my investments are here in Lagos."

Two of the three probable returnees were recent arrivals: a herbalist who moved to Ajegunle at 61 hoping to increase his income, having left most of his children at home, and a supervisor of a mission school transferred to Kaduna from the south at 57. The last, a lawyer in Aba, had left his wife and younger children at home after the war. Only his unemployed eldest son was in Aba. Only two of the twelve migrants over 60 interviewed in The Gambia planned to go home. One said he would leave when his sons set up separate compounds in Serekunda and the other was a recently arrived *mallam* who planned to spend the rainy season at home. The two women both chose to stay in town with their children.

Nonmigrants in Abeokuta were more likely than returnees to be economically active after age 60; the formal act of retiring from wage employment and returning home was the signal for all but three of the latter to stop working. Only three of the nonmigrants had ever had wage employment and only one still had part-time salaried employment. As traders, contractors, farmers, and craftsmen, the nonmigrants were able to moderate their work load as they grew older and thus seldom faced the symbolic end of a working life which characterized the returnees. In The Gambia, five of the twelve nonmigrant men over 60 were fully retired and only two were self-employed, compared to no retirees and six self-employed among the ten migrant men. In this case, the greater ability of local men to get wage employment allows them to retire (usually in their fifties), while most migrants remain in the labor force until at least their mid-sixties. Perhaps because they were still economically active, migrants seldom reported receiving money from children, whereas over half of the nonmigrants did—often considerable sums.

Conclusion

The majority of men and women, in all types of towns, have migrated only once. Whether they grow up in villages or towns or migrate to nearby towns or ones which are in another area or even another country, most prefer (and are able) to settle down at their chosen destinations until the time comes to return home. This is not to deny that some West Africans are very mobile, but most of these fall into three occupational categories: members of the uniformed services, upwardly mobile government administrators, and skilled construction workers.

Sex, age, education, and contacts also affect the migration process. Contacts in town are especially important for women, who are somewhat less mobile than men. They are less likely to make their own migration decisions and also to obtain an education and participate in the labor force, two factors which are important in male migration. However, once in town they may be less likely than the men to return home; the role of elderly women in urban family life and as landladies deserves further study.

Age and education are important factors because of their interrelationship with occupation. Migration to industrial towns appears to be more age-selective than migration to administrative or commercial centers with little industrial employment. This is because so many recent school leavers hope for wage employment in factories and flock to the towns which might provide it. People with a high level of education or none at all seem better able to plan their migration strategy, and the migration which accompanies it, than primary- and especially secondary-school leavers. This problem will be discussed more fully in chapter 3.

The Richmond and Goldlust model of migrant adaptation provides a useful framework for the analysis of the interrelationships of premigration characteristics, urban demographic and social structure, and the objective satisfaction of the migrant. However, it explains only a small proportion of the variance in these West African towns. The effect of background characteristics and objective factors in adaptation and satisfaction varies considerably from one town to another in ways not necessarily related to urban social structure. Further model development will require more information than is now available.

It is still normative for West Africans to go home on retirement, to die and be buried there. A few people defy convention and their kin by remaining in town; this decision is often symbolized by the acquisition of an urban house and (seldom in Ghana and southern Nigeria but relatively frequently in The Gambia) identifying the present place of residence as one's new hometown. Although intention to remain in town does increase with age and length of residence, the very high proportion of migrants who plan to leave means that these are not very strong relationships and that most of today's residents will in fact go. This should have the advantage of slowing urban growth somewhat. Education and economic success appear to be relatively unimportant in changing this strong value orientation, which supports the hypothesis to be developed in chapter 5 that for most people at all levels of the society links to the extended family continue to be important.

Concern for the young, who are such a large proportion of the African population, has meant that little attention has been given to retirement or the elderly. Yet, modern medicine has increased the life span; far more families than in the past must now make provision for grandparents who are no longer self-supporting. Villages which could provide prestige and responsibility for half a dozen elderly men may find it more difficult to give satisfying roles to two or three dozen. Thus, early retirement from wage employment, which not only makes room for the next generation but encourages retirees to take up small-scale entrepreneurship, is likely to be more advantageous to the community than maintaining a retirement age which has become conventional in more industrialized countries. Women tend to retire from the labor force earlier than men, but an alternative role helping to care for grandchildren awaits most of them. This is increasingly likely to be performed in town rather than at home.

3 □ WORK

Alieu Sise was a Serere executive living in a rented house in Serekunda with his wife, three children, and two relatives who were staying with him while they attended school. He was born in Banjul, completed his secondary schooling at 18 and started work as an accounts clerk. After five years, he moved to another clerical job, but after seven more years he decided the "inconvenience" was too great and took a job as a factory hand. This job lasted four years. Meanwhile, he had been studying and saving as well as starting his family. At 34, he went to London and obtained a university degree. On his return to The Gambia, he obtained his present post and moved out to Serekunda. He now considers Serekunda home, but sees his numerous kin in Banjul once or twice a week. He also participates regularly in a work association and a sporting club.

Kweku Mensah was a 30-year-old mallam living alone in a rented room in Ashaiman. He had moved from the Ashanti Region village where he grew up and attended Koranic school to another village to learn photography, but after two years changed to a carpentry apprenticeship. On finishing this, he married a girl from the village and moved with his wife to Ivory Coast to establish a business in Abidjan. However, after about five years he went bankrupt, so when his father invited him to come to Ashaiman he sent his wife and four children back to their village while he established himself as a mallam. After six months in Ashaiman, he preferred it to Accra, which he thought was too artificial and raised too many expectations: "Here I can live as I like." Neither of his two close friends was either a Muslim or an Asante.

Most migrants come to town for work. This chapter will examine participation in the labor force, the occupational careers of men and women, and the position of craftsmen, who form a relatively large component of both the self- and the wage-employed. Although there are difficulties with certain categories, such as farmers and businessmen, because they have varying levels of income and prestige, occupation is the best single indicator of status in West African towns, as in more industrialized parts of the world. First, wage employment tends to be on government-set pay scales and relatively few of the self-employed do better than those with

79

comparable wage employment. Second, education and occupation are at least as highly correlated as in advanced countries. Third, wealth and literacy are strongly related to life-style. Occupation is a much less useful measure of women's status than of men's for three reasons: cultural factors affect women's participation in the labor force, a high proportion of women who are economically active are traders and thus difficult to place, and a woman's position may be dependent on her husband's (especially if he is a member of the elite) or be partly or fully independent of his.

Occupational Categories

Many problems arise in the classification of occupations in Africa. Some authors, such as Hinderink and Sterkenburg (1975) follow the International Standard Classification of Occupations (ISCO), which is used by several national censuses and divides the working population into professionals, administrators and executives, clerical workers, sales workers, farmers and fishermen, transport and communication workers, craftsmen and production process workers, and service workers. However, these are much more industrial than occupational categories; two people doing exactly the same work could be in different categories. More important, most of these categories are socially and economically very heterogeneous and therefore tell us little or nothing about the relative position of the present holder of the position in the society. One category, craftsmen and production process workers, includes most manual workers from highly paid printers and electricians to the lowest-paid laborers, a majority of the wage-employed population in many African towns.

Treiman's detailed classification (1977), which is an extension of Duncan's prestige scale (1961) intended for use in developing as well as developed countries, is better than the ISCO, but as Treiman had few African sources he inevitably omitted some occupations common in African cities. Other occupations are rated higher than they deserve in these societies, where they are carried out by people with much less education or training and receiving much less income than is common elsewhere.

Given the ease with which people can move from one type of self-employment to another in West African towns, many occupations classed as service by the ISCO and Treiman are best grouped with commercial occupations; others can be classified according to the nature of the work performed and its relative prestige. For example, many West African prostitutes also trade and report themselves as traders. If prostitution is classed as a commercial rather than a service occupation, there is no problem of which source of income is preeminent.

Given the relatively small sample sizes in these studies, it has seemed most useful to code occupations in a small number of categories which correspond to the socioeconomic position of most of the people doing this work. Farming and fishing have been combined with unskilled manual work because there were few people in these urban samples devoting themselves exclusively to these primary occupations and, except for being mainly nonmigrants, they share the laborer's position in society. Above these, the hierarchy rises through semiskilled and skilled manual, commercial, clerical, and supervisory to administrative and professional (see Peil and Lucas 1972 for the codes used).

Commercial (and personal service) occupations have been placed between manual and nonmanual work for three reasons. (1) Far more manual than nonmanual workers aspire to go into commerce; traders and businessmen seldom aspire to any other type of work. (2) Some nonmanual workers do go into business, especially on retirement, but the level of income of the average trader and the insecurity involved mean that manual workers are more likely than clerical workers to see a move into trading as a step up. (3) Trading has been particularly attractive to international migrants (and, in Nigeria, interregional migrants) for whom farm labor tends to be the chief alternative. Extensive contacts across boundaries give the long-distance migrant an advantage over the local trader in certain goods such as cattle and cola nuts (Meillassoux 1965; Cohen 1969). In these days of nationalist discrimination against aliens, international migrants may be expelled or their trading activities limited precisely because of this success (Peil 1971), but those who remain still find that self-employment offers them better opportunities than the wage market.

The distinction in prestige between skilled manual/technical and clerical occupations is also problematic. Prestige-ranking studies in Ghana (Peil 1972a, p. 118) and The Gambia put typists at about the same level as skilled craftsmen, with senior clerks considerably higher. As the trades with the largest numbers of practitioners (tailoring, carpentry, weaving, blacksmithing) are usually ranked below typist, it seems fair to say that the average clerical worker has greater prestige than the average craftsman. This is more due to the respect shown to education and white-collar jobs than to differences in income or job satisfaction. Some men leave lower-level clerical jobs for semiskilled factory work.

Technicians have been classified with skilled manual workers rather than with professionals because the distinction is vague for most West Africans. Technician sounds higher, but the level of work performed and its remuneration may be equal. The few technicians in the samples tend to have the same amount of technical education as the better-educated craftsmen and are otherwise indistinguishable from them. Therefore, it would misrepresent the position of technicians to class them as the ISCO does. This will probably change as technical education becomes more widespread.

Members of the uniformed services have been included with clerical workers. Less than 2 percent of the men in the Gambian and Ghanaian samples and 5 percent of Nigerian men were in the army or police, so although their migration experience and job opportunities cannot be considered typical of clerical workers, it is not worthwhile keeping them separate. Soldiers and policemen tend to be rated with clerks (as of middle-level status), though many people feel ambivalent about their role in the society because these jobs are seen as providing both well-paying opportunities for people of limited education and a source of oppression and corruption (Mitchell 1966, p. 267; Peil 1976b).

With the exception of primary teachers (who rank at about the same level as policemen and typists) and traditional healers (who have about the same prestige as typists in Ghana but considerably more in The Gambia), most occupations in the administrative and professional category are held by members of the elite or subelite of the society. The samples include government ministers, doctors and lawyers, priests and mallams, accountants and secondary teachers, officers in the uniformed services, and executives in government departments. Some live in government housing or in the better sections of towns like Ajegunle or Tema; others share family houses in Abeokuta or Banjul, or have their own houses or rented rooms. They are only a small part of the population, but the similarities and differences between them and the less successful members of the urban community, and the social roles they fill, should be neither ignored nor overemphasized.

It is more difficult to order self- and wage employment as measures of success than to order occupations, because much depends on the income gained and the status of the person doing the ranking. Wage employment is the initial goal of most migrants, but self-employment, either in town or at home, is the eventual goal for many, especially in Nigeria. Wage employment is often seen as more secure than self-employment, especially by the young, but many older men with little education would rate successful independent entrepreneurship higher. Those in well-paying jobs are unlikely to look to self-employment until they are ready to retire, but educated men who are willing to take the risk of business and succeed at it have at least as much prestige as local managers of transnational firms and senior civil servants. As sources of support for political parties, they may have considerably more political influence than administrative employees during periods of civilian rule.

The factors of importance here are income and how it is spent. On the basis of average income, wage employment can be counted as better than self-employment for most but by no means all. It also fosters greater stability of migrants; voluntary movement is more difficult for employees than for the self-employed, though the former are occasionally subject to transfer. However, successful businessmen can usually spend more lavishly on consumer goods than men in salaried employment (especially for the

government) and win the approbation of the general public for such behavior. Civil servants can be attacked for corruption if their style of life
appears to be higher than their salary warrants.

Those who were currently unemployed or retired were classed according to their previous occupation, if any, since this gave them an
identity within the urban hierarchy. Women move in and out of the labor
force more easily than men, so they were classed according to their
current self-identification as housewife or trader, but according to last
occupation if they considered themselves unemployed.

Labor Force Participation

Movement in and out of the labor force and between occupations varies
with education, age, sex, and migration status, as well as with the opportunities available in different types of towns. These interrelated variables
produce a complex picture, which is further complicated by the ability of
some individuals to substitute personal contacts, diligence, or luck for
more obvious advantages, and the inability of others to make the most of
an initially favorable position. Labor force participation is high for both
men and women in most towns, and openness to opportunity is probably
the most characteristic feature. The widespread belief in the possibility of
upward mobility may bring disappointment to many, but others achieve at
least a moderate success in spite of their disadvantages.

Education

Education is the most basic factor in a man's labor force participation,
affecting his chances of employment, the occupation he undertakes,
whether he is working for wages or self-employed, and (through its effect
on migration decisions) where he lives. The most important distinctions in
level of education which affect job opportunities are (1) between those
who have never attended school and those who have and (2) between
those who have at least some form of secondary certificate and those who
have not. The lower boundary is less important than the upper one
because many who got three years or less of schooling are not functionally
literate. A few who became literate through evening classes and, in Ghana
and Nigeria, the few who reported attending only Koranic school, were
included with those who attended primary school because this was very
seldom carried to a high level and was of little help when entering the
urban labor force. There was a much higher incidence of Koranic schooling in The Gambia and several respondents were highly trained; therefore, this type of schooling was kept separate in order to examine its
effects.

A middle level of education, roughly comparable to Ghanaian middle schooling, was designated for analytical purposes in the Nigerian samples. This included all those who had more than six years of primary school and less than four years of secondary school. Until the late 1950s (the date varies in different parts of the country), Standard I followed two years of infant school, so those reaching Standard VI had completed at least eight years in school. Secondary modern schools, which began in 1955, and are most popular in southwestern Nigeria, offer three years of schooling after Primary 6. Many students starting secondary modern school do not complete the three years, and many who enter secondary grammar school do not obtain the Secondary 4 certificate or the school certificate after completing Secondary 5. Although the proportion in the "middle" category is much smaller than in Ghana, it is possible to compare their occupational placement with that of men with one to six years of education.

Gambian postprimary education is in junior and senior secondary schools, which are often reported as "secondary" by respondents. Junior secondaries were at one time called secondary modern, and have recently been redesignated secondary technical. They provide four years of education, leading to an internally examined certificate. There is little movement from them to the far more prestigious senior secondaries, which cater to small numbers of students selected directly from primary schools. As in Ghana and Nigeria, the goal is passes in several "O"-level examinations, followed by two years in sixth form or (occasionally in Ghana and increasingly in Nigeria) direct entry into a university.

The expansion of junior secondary schools in The Gambia is recent and therefore the distinction is most relevant for men under 25. Men over 35 reporting secondary schooling should have been rare enough in their cohort to merit good jobs. As there are few with postsecondary schooling in The Gambia, all those with postprimary education have been put in a single category. However, it should be kept in mind that the secondary education reported by young men usually has considerably less value in the marketplace than that reported by older men, because for most it is a new and less rigorous form. Secondary education has been devalued in Ghana and Nigeria as well, but more by expansion of the academic system than by creating a new form.

Many of the patterns shown in Table 3.1 are as expected; the proportion of men in unskilled work declines, and in nonmanual work increases, with education. Nevertheless, it is worth pointing out that in every town there are men with no state education in professional roles (mallams and traditional healers) and only in Tema is no one with secondary education doing unskilled work; semiskilled work by secondary school leavers is fairly common, especially in Kakuri. Education provides opportunities, but there are no rigid barriers or guarantees. Commerce and skilled work, which may provide equal or greater income than many nonmanual jobs, illustrate even further that while education may be a help to status or class mobility it is neither necessary nor sufficient in the present West African situation. Only in Banjul and Tema are less than a fifth of the unschooled doing skilled work. Though many of these earn relatively little, others build up sizeable businesses.

Commerce provides even greater opportunities for a few and a satisfactory income for many who might be considered disadvantaged because they lack education. While the complexity of modern business, especially manufacturing, favors men with at least secondary education (Kennedy 1974), the educational system turns most students away from commerce and toward bureaucratic roles. Fortunately, there are still many types of businesses in West Africa which can be successfully carried out by men and women with little or no education. Where it becomes evident that literacy is an advantage, some traders acquire these skills as adults, but large-scale operations can be carried out, even over long distances, by men using trust and memory rather than written records of transactions (Cohen 1969).

Certain ethnic groups, such as the Fula, Hausa, Kwahu, Sarahuli, and Yoruba, are noted for their commercial activities. Personal contacts and patron/client relations are important in building up a business, and the aspiring entrepreneur sometimes gets considerable assistance from more experienced members of his group (Hill 1966; Aronson 1971; Garlick 1971; Yusuf 1975; Eades 1979). For example, Eades shows how Yoruba traders in Tamale brought in kin from Nigeria as their businesses grew and how these became independent after a period of training; Yusuf provides a diagram of the economic, social, political, religious, and kinship links maintained by a successful Kano trader which help him to carry out his business and uphold his position in the community.

As used here, wage employment includes any work done under direction; apprentices, family workers, and others in an ambiguous income position have been classed as working for wages, though some of them earn no more than subsistence. They are at least not responsible for their own support, as they would be in self-employment. Such arrangements were most common in Aba; many new migrants there lacked capital even for small-scale trading and therefore apprenticed themselves to kin who were established traders or craftsmen. Some of these young men earn money on their own as well as for their masters, and the proportions of men with little or no education who are self-employed would be even higher if they were included.

Nevertheless, the pattern is clear. Self-employment is much less important for those who have gone beyond primary school than for the relatively uneducated, though self-employment in all educational categories varies with the level of alternative opportunities. In Aba and Abeokuta, where there is relatively little wage employment, there are more self-employed secondary leavers than in the Ghanaian towns, where

TABLE 3.1

Male Occupational Placement, by Education and Town (Percentages)

Town and Education	Farmers, Unskilled	Semi-skilled	Skilled	Commerce	Non-manual	Unem-ployed	Total[a]	N	Self-Employed
Ashaiman 1968									
None	50.0	9.4	25.0	9.9	2.6	9.9	106.8	352	20.2
Primary, Muslim	33.9	15.2	35.7	6.2	4.5	13.4	108.9	112	25.0
Middle	7.5	37.3	30.3	2.3	11.3	18.8	107.5	389	8.5
Post-middle	0.0	11.4	34.3	2.9	34.3	20.0	102.9	35	0.0
Tema									
None	42.5	15.6	16.9	14.4	6.9	8.8	105.1	160	27.5
Primary, Muslim	13.8	29.3	20.7	20.7	10.3	6.6	101.4	58	31.0
Middle	4.8	37.0	19.3	4.6	27.6	11.4	104.7	435	10.1
Post-middle	0.6	7.4	9.9	2.5	75.2	8.1	103.7	161	5.0
Aba									
None	15.3	4.1	25.5	51.0	3.1	3.1	102.1	98	72.4
Primary	11.6	8.8	18.5	55.2	4.0	3.1	101.2	455	47.2
Middle[b]	2.7	10.0	19.2	50.7	11.0	12.3	105.9	73	49.3
Secondary 4+	0.9	1.9	10.3	15.9	59.8	11.2	100.0	107	17.8
Abeokuta									
None	22.7	16.0	21.3	34.7	4.0	1.3	100.0	75	84.0
Primary, Muslim	7.3	17.1	20.7	41.5	12.2	1.2	100.0	82	63.4
Middle[b]	4.9	14.6	14.6	19.5	46.4	0.0	100.0	41	36.6
Secondary 4+	1.6	0.8	5.8	5.8	84.3	2.4	100.7	121	9.7
Ajegunle									
None	18.0	15.7	30.3	24.7	9.0	3.4	101.1	89	48.3
Primary, Muslim	24.1	15.8	19.0	20.0	11.8	11.8	102.5	374	37.4
Middle[b]	9.4	17.0	19.3	13.9	36.8	5.8	102.2	223	19.3
Secondary 4+	0.4	4.0	13.3	8.0	64.0	13.3	103.0	225	4.4

TABLE 3.1 Continued

Male Occupational Placement, by Education and Town (Percentages)

Town and Education	Farmers, Unskilled	Semi-skilled	Skilled	Commerce	Non-manual	Unem-ployed	Total[a]	N	Self-Employed
Kakuri									
None	15.4	38.4	23.1	10.3	7.7	6.4	101.3	78	21.8
Primary, Muslim	3.6	67.4	9.5	5.4	7.3	7.8	101.0	577	7.8
Middle[b]	0.0	47.6	9.5	16.7	26.2	2.4	102.4	42	16.7
Secondary 4+	1.2	20.2	26.2	1.2	42.9	8.3	100.0	84	7.1
Banjul									
None	37.1	18.6	11.4	37.1	2.9	6.0	103.1	67	49.2
Muslim	13.9	21.1	15.3	29.2	11.1	9.4	100.0	64	43.8
Primary	31.0	16.9	44.9	6.9	6.9	3.4	100.0	29	31.0
Post-primary	1.7	3.8	14.3	9.3	61.2	11.4	101.7	237	7.2
Serekunda									
None	23.1	19.2	42.3	3.8	3.8	7.7	100.0	26	30.8
Muslim	25.3	13.3	30.1	24.0	7.3	1.4	101.3	147	57.8
Primary	9.4	15.1	41.6	7.5	22.6	3.8	100.0	53	30.2
Post-primary	3.9	5.8	15.6	3.9	63.0	11.0	103.2	154	11.0

[a]Totals are over 100 percent if some of the unemployed reported their prior occupation.

[b]Standard VI and VII, Secondary Modern and Secondary Grammar 1 to 3.

wage employment is much more important. There are more self-employed men with secondary or technical education in Kakuri than would be predicted; they are all in skilled trades, and may be self-employed because there are so few openings for skilled men in the Kakuri factories. All but one were from the south, so their presence in Kakuri was probably due to the opportunities it offers for independent craftsmen rather than to accidents of propinquity.

There are two factors involved in the relationship between education and self-employment, both working in the same direction. Schooling fosters a knowledge of the working of bureaucratic organizations and an appreciation of the rewards available to those who participate in them; it also makes it easier to get wage employment. However, a majority of adults in these countries are still independent farmers and many societies promote the values of individual achievement and independence and denigrate the subservience implied in working for someone else. Thus, young people who do not go to school are likely to favor self-employment, and their lack of education gives them few alternatives to it. Trading and self-employed craftsmanship are also popular among older men who have not been to school, whose main alternatives are laboring and security work. Boys with secondary education who become skilled craftsmen tend to go into printing, electrical work, or photography, though there were some in every craft singled out for study. Of these three, only photography is practiced mainly by the self-employed.

It was thought that just as state education fosters an attraction to bureaucratic roles, so Muslim education might foster an attraction to trade. Islam was spread by traders, and Muslims continue to be among the leading traders in many towns. Alternatively, since trade is greatly helped by contacts, Muslim education (as a symbol of greater attachment to Islam) might serve as a useful base for a career in trade. However, insofar as entry to commercial occupations is concerned, the relationship is ambiguous at best. Muslims in The Gambia who had Koranic education were more than twice as likely to be in commerce as those who reported state education or none at all, but the relationship was reversed in Ghana and Nigeria; men reporting Koranic education there were less likely to be traders than other Muslims.

Thus, in a country with a large majority of Muslims (where the differentiating value of religious ties would be less important) the relationship between Muslim schooling and trading appears strong, but where the proportion of Muslims is lower (and the religious distinction might therefore be important), Koranic education is apparently less relevant. It might be that a distinction should be made between commercial leaders such as the Sabo landlords described by Cohen (1969) and more ordinary traders, which is not possible with these data; but it appears that the attraction of trading is probably more directly related to a lack of extensive state education than to socialization in Koranic schools or the contacts made there.

Age

Figure 3.1 shows the pattern of economic activity for different age groups. Only about half of the men in the 15 to 24 age group are in the labor force in Abeokuta and the Gambian towns, compared to about four-fifths in Aba, Ajegunle, and Tema, and over 90 percent in the industrial suburbs of Ashaiman and Kakuri. There were large numbers still in school in Abeokuta and the Gambian towns, children of local families and a few young men who had moved to town to continue their education. The completion of schooling and drop in unemployment after age 25 means that almost all males between 25 and 49 are not only in the labor force but employed. Between 4 and 15 percent of the men in their fifties have already retired, with the Ghanaian towns the only ones maintaining full employment until age 60. Retirement, as described in chapter 2, then takes place, though the number of men who remain in town after retirement is so small in some towns that the margin for error in the data increases considerably.

The age variance in women's participation in the labor force is much greater than men's. It is highest in Abeokuta until age 60, then drops dramatically as most women traders retire. Tema and Ashaiman show the same rising participation with age until 60, but a much less precipitous drop, probably because women who retire are more likely to leave these towns. The other three Nigerian towns show rising economic activity until the 35 to 40 age group, but in Aba and Ajegunle participation by women in their fifties is lower than for women aged 15 to 24. This suggests earlier retirement, with women staying in town to care for grandchildren.

The Gambian patterns are quite different. Participation is low, as this Islamic society prefers that women remain at home; Christian women are more likely to be economically active than Muslims. More young women are employed in Banjul than in Serekunda, but the difference is relatively small after age 35. The proportion drops in both towns for the 25–34 age group, showing that some women leave the labor force for marriage and child rearing. It rises again for the 35 to 49 age group in Serekunda, but continues dropping in Banjul; it rises for both towns for women in their fifties. Half of the women over 50 were widowed or divorced and another 15 percent were not living in the same households as their husbands; a woman probably enters the labor force at this period because she no longer has a man to support her but still has children to care for.[1] After 60, they again drop out of the labor force because at least some of their children are old enough to care for them.

Female Participation

The high participation rates for men follow from their main reason for coming to town; those for women require further explanation. Women in the coastal and forest belt towns of West Africa between southern Ghana and southern Cameroon have higher rates of economic activity than women in most cities of Western Europe or America, and have maintained these rates over a long period of time. Women's participation in farming and trading has given them economic autonomy and sometimes political power in these societies, most notably in the case of the Yoruba of Nigeria. They are able to support themselves and their children and are often expected to do so (Peil 1975a).

Though age and education are also relevant, marital status is the most important factor in women's participation in the labor force. Table 3.2 shows that, with age and education held constant, married women living with their husbands are only about half as likely as other women to be participating in the labor force. The drop is less in the provincial towns than elsewhere, but even here women tend to take a few years off when they marry, either because their husbands expect it (they may object to their working for wages and promise to furnish trading capital in a year or two), or in order to care for the first child. Women with several children often take only a few months leave for a new addition, but the initial introduction to motherhood usually justifies a longer break.

The distinction between the separated and the widowed or divorced is somewhat artificial, since some of the older women were probably widows and there are other women in the separated category who are no longer involved in a meaningful marriage; formal divorce proceedings are not necessary to end a marriage unless it was under the marriage ordinance. However, the somewhat lower labor force participation rates of the separated than of the widowed or divorced up to age 50 suggest that some of the former are being supported by their husbands (and under their influence remain housewives) whereas the latter are on their own. The older widows can often rely on their children for support, whereas younger women must provide for themselves and their children. However, insofar as the younger women are more often divorcees than widows, they may be more independent than other women and prefer economic autonomy to remarriage.

Another group of economically independent women was the prostitutes, of whom there were considerable numbers in Kakuri, Ajegunle, and Ashaiman. About half were under 25 and most were illiterate, though one was over 50 and a few had gone beyond primary school. Better-educated girls who engage in casual or regular prostitution usually have other jobs in which to categorize themselves.[2] Illiterate prostitutes often do some trading, but they are easy for interviewers to spot. Most of the prostitutes

Proportion of Women Who Are Economically Active, by Location, Education, Marital Status, and Age[a]

Marital Status and Age		Islamic			Industrial			Provincial		
		None	Primary, Koranic	More	None	Primary, Koranic	More	None	Primary, Koranic	More
Single:	15–24	42(43)	29(28)	65(77)	72(109)	66(41)	61(97)	100(20)	74(50)	76(25)
	25+	93(15)	38(8)	83(23)	91(55)	100(7)	93(15)	d	d	60(10)
Married:	15–24	11(128)	16(129)	33(33)	37(266)	31(207)	46(126)	71(31)	40(94)	62(21)
	25–34	14(130)	13(121)	41(27)	62(365)	46(121)	64(101)	75(71)	67(95)	85(52)
	35–49	14(85)	11(76)	43(28)	61(165)	55(40)	59(22)	87(107)	70(27)	94(18)
	50+	25(8)	19(21)	71(7)	88(24)	d	d	96(27)	d	d
Separated:[c]	15–24	50(6)	16(19)	56(18)	76(37)	80(10)	75(24) ⎱	100(7)	86(7)	88(8)
	25–34	64(11)	13(15)	40(10)	83(48)	71(7)	80(20) ⎰			
	35–49	64(14)	36(11)		93(56)	d	92(13)	94(16)	d	100(6)
	50+	29(7)	43(7)	67(6)	88(17)			50(14)	d	d
Widowed,	15–34	89(9)	50(12)	67(9)	92(13)	86(7)	d	d	d	d
Divorced:	35–49	75(8)	67(15)	28(7)	93(27)	100(12)	d	100(11) ⎱ 14(7)		d
	50+	19(21)	8(40)		65(20)	60(5)	d	41(27) ⎰		d
Total		25(485)	18(502)	54(250)	63(1202)	47(465)	63(422)	80(332)	61(293)	81(144)

[a] The numbers in parentheses are bases for percentages.

[b] Islamic towns: Banjul and Serekunda. Industrial: Ajegunle, Ashaiman, Kakuri, and Tema. Provincial: Aba and Abeokuta.

[c] Married but not living in the same household as her spouse.

[d] Less than 5 cases.

91

said they were single, and most of the rest said they were divorced, but two were living with their husbands. Only a few of the divorced women appeared to be prostitutes, and some of these had recently come to town in hopes of finding new husbands. The houses in Ashaiman which had several prostitutes in 1968 still had them in 1970, but none of the same women were living there.

The division of the towns into Islamic, industrial, and provincial demonstrates another influence on women's labor force participation. Although only a minority of residents in Kakuri are Muslim, the influence of Islamic values keeps many women at home and the large market makes it difficult for home traders (Hill 1969) to compete. Thus, Kakuri women are only slightly more likely than those in the Gambian towns to be economically active. At the other extreme, the norm of female participation is strong in many provincial towns, though more so in Yoruba and Ga towns than in those dominated by the Igbo. In addition, the woman in Aba faced severe competition from male traders, which probably kept some of them out of business. Nevertheless, women in nearly every age and education category were more likely to be economically active if they lived in a provincial town than if they lived in a town where Islamic influence was strong.[3] Women in the industrial towns tended to be in between, with higher participation in Ashaiman and Tema than in Ajegunle.

The effect of education is curvilinear. Women who have primary or Koranic schooling are less likely to be economically active than women who have never been to school, whereas those who have gone further have the same participation rate as illiterates in industrial and provincial towns and double it in Islamic towns. Thus, it seems that increased education for girls will initially result in some decline in their economic activity but that in the long term they will continue to have much higher levels of participation than European women; competition with male school leavers for clerical and teaching posts is certain to increase. The development of postprimary education for girls in Islamic areas may lead to demands for more equal opportunities for employment; they want to use what they have learned. Less than a quarter of the women in The Gambia with less than secondary education are in the labor force, compared to half of those who attended secondary school and 77 percent of those who continued their education beyond this. Kakuri women who had at least completed Secondary 4 were twice as likely as other women to be in the labor force.

The decline in participation of women with primary schooling appears to be due to changing expectations of employment. Women with no education take it for granted that they should become traders. Girls who do not reach School Certificate level are less interested in trading than illiterates (though many take it up), but are not well enough qualified for clerical jobs given the present level of competition. Some become seamstresses, but others remain outside the labor force; their education has to this extent been counterproductive. Well-educated girls have a far wider range of job opportunities than their sisters, and most of them continue to work, except perhaps for their first few years of marriage, because it is expected and rewarding and because it gives them a measure of autonomy within their (often elite) marriages (see Oppong 1970, 1974). The high proportion of educated women who remain in the labor force or return to it suggests that female education should be an important consideration for manpower planners.

Migration Experience

Education not only affects the decision to migrate (because rural parents who have paid school fees implicitly or explicitly expect some return on their investment), but also affects the direction of migration (a rural area for farming, the nearest provincial town, the capital). Illiterates and primary school leavers in Ghana are likely either to stay home or become farm laborers, leaving urban jobs for middle- and secondary-school leavers (Caldwell 1968). Many primary-school leavers in Kwara State migrate north to Kaduna rather than south to Lagos or Ibadan because they realize that with such limited education they will have better opportunities in Kaduna, where the educational level is low. But those seeking self-employment may be attracted to a town where the educational level is relatively high because people in good jobs will have more money to buy their wares or use their services. This is what draws Senegalese and Mauritanians to Banjul.

Once the migrant has arrived in town, his place of origin as well as his education may affect his ability to get certain types of work. His impression of opportunities in the labor force will be shaped by what he has heard from earlier migrants before leaving home, by what he is told, and by the help he is given by the people he stays with on arrival. Granovetter's finding (1973) that a wide range of ties, especially weak ties, is important in the process of locating work, can be applied here.

The hypothesis is that the locally born will have the best-established networks for finding employment, that migrants from a short distance will normally have many people (in a variety of occupational roles) to whom they can turn for help, and that the contacts of long-distance migrants will, on average, be fewer and less influential. Thus, with a given level of education, the locals should be able to get the best jobs, the short-distance migrants the next best, and the long-distance migrants should be most limited in the occupations to which they have access. These differences are probably most important in large cities such as Lagos and Accra/Tema, which draw from a national or international hinterland and where long-distance migrants are from areas which are different culturally and tend to have lower levels of education and development than areas nearer the city. In provincial towns such as Aba and Abeokuta, the hinterland is smaller, migrants are more homogeneous, and long-distance migrants are likely to be sponsored by their employers (such as the army or police).

Tables 3.3 and 3.4 show the patterns of employment for men and women of differing migration background. It appears that culturally influenced preferences and access to education have more effect than the distance traveled on placement in the labor force. For both men and women, self-employment is most prominent among the locally born in Abeokuta, but it is highest among migrants from the north in Ajegunle and among alien migrants to the Ghanaian and Gambian towns. Over half of the long-distance male migrants to every town but Serekunda are in wage employment, which suggests that discrimination against them, where present, is not strong. However, the advantage of the locals is shown in their higher levels of wage employment in Ajegunle and the Gambian towns.[4]

Locals are at least as likely to be suffering from unemployment as migrants, though new arrivals tend to have the highest rates. Many of the unemployed school leavers are locally born; these have the best access to support while seeking the work they want. Men from outside the state living in Abeokuta and easterners in Ajegunle had relatively high levels of unemployment; the easterners tended to be recent school leavers and/or new arrivals who were hoping (like the local young men) for wage employment.

Women's employment is more closely tied to cultural expectations than men's. Because so few have enough education to qualify for clerical or professional jobs and because many husbands consider trading the most acceptable occupation for a married woman, a large proportion of employed women in Ghana and Nigeria are traders. Because of the influence of Islam discussed in the last section, women from northern Ghana and Nigeria and from western Gambia are less active in the labor force than other women, though in Ajegunle it is the eastern (and Christian) women who stay at home. Igbo women have traditionally been much less economically active than the Yoruba, who show no sign of being limited by adherence to Islam. Where one might expect local women to profit by their contacts to expand their opportunities for trading, at the participation level they seem to have no advantage, except in Abeokuta. In The Gambia, it is educational opportunities in town which allow local women greater participation than those from the surrounding countryside.

Comparison of the income of locals with near and distant migrants also fails to support the hypothesis that local people have an advantage. Differences are seldom statistically significant, regardless of whether

Type of Economic Activity, by Town, Sex, and Distance of Migration (Percentages)[a]

Town and Birthplace	Males					Females				
	Self	Wage	None	Total	N	Self	Wage	None	Total	N
Ashaiman: Near[b]	13	70	17	100	620	57	4	39	100	430
North	3	90	7	100	74	26	0	74	100	27
Alien	26	64	10	100	194	63	3	34	100	74
Tema: Near[b]	11	77	12	100	460	55	18	27	100	531
North	19	76	5	100	58	61	4	35	100	26
Alien	30	58	12	100	116	63	12	25	100	60
Aba: Here	43	48	9	100	44	36	20	44	100	25
Near[c]	47	48	5	100	644	42	23	35	100	383
Far	41	55	4	100	49	18	35	47	100	17
Abeokuta: Here	61	38	1	100	146	77	9	14	100	199
Near[d]	30	69	1	100	149	54	28	18	100	110
Far	38	54	8	100	24	61	18	21	100	51
Ajegunle: Here	9	76	15	100	55	37	20	43	100	51
Near[e]	25	67	8	100	449	32	9	59	100	330
Far: East[f]	25	62	13	100	288	9	17	74	100	107
North[g]	41	54	5	100	117	42	4	54	100	83
Kakuri: Here	29	71	0	100	17	7	0	93	100	15
Near[g]	7	85	8	100	627	18	3	75	100	287
Far	24	71	5	100	139	45	6	49	100	63
Banjul: Here	9	79	12	100	243	9	26	60	100	342
Near[h]	30	62	8	100	74	13	7	80	100	71
Far	65	58	7	100	97	21	17	62	100	48
Serekunda: Here	24	68	8	100	200	8	17	75	100	241
Near[h]	38	57	5	100	104	8	5	87	100	101
Far	52	46	2	100	81	11	12	77	100	73

[a] Males not participating in the labor force and female students have been omitted.
[b] Southern and central Ghana, including Ashanti and Brong/Ahafo Regions.
[c] The former East Central State.
[d] The former Western State.
[e] Bendel, Lagos, Ogun, Ondo, and Oyo States.
[f] Anambra, Cross River, Imo, and River States.
[g] All states of the former Northern Region.
[h] Kombo St. Mary, North Bank, and Western Divisions.

occupation is held constant, and usually favor long-distance migrants. This supports Stouffer's (1940) "intervening opportunities" hypothesis that people only migrate a long distance if there is a measurable gain for so doing, but the modest relationship suggests either inadequate information or the greater importance of other factors.

Even among women traders, for whom one would suppose contacts and experience to be most important, women from a long distance appear to earn more than local women except in Ajegunle. The hypothesis that this is due to age differences (locals make less because more of them are young and inexperienced) proved to be incorrect; local women are overrepresented among the young and distant migrants are overrepresented among the older traders only in Ghana, where income was not recorded. Another explanation might be that long-distance women migrants have fewer alternative demands on their time than local women and feel a stronger need to work hard in order to overcome their initial disadvantages; further study would be useful.

The hypothesis of local advantage accepts the assumption of both functionalist and conflict theorists of migration that migrants come in at the bottom of the occupational structure, allowing those who have lived longer in town to move up. Richmond and Verma (1978) point out that this is no longer true in Canada; these data show that it cannot be accepted for West African towns either, except where urban educational advantages are substantial. The tendency of the better-educated to migrate means that they enter the labor force at all levels. In many towns, the poorest jobs are held by illiterate local people with low opportunity costs while most of the best jobs are in the hands of migrants. This situation may increase the locals' feelings that their town is being taken over by strangers (see chapter 8).

Locally born Gambians and southern Ghanaian migrants to the Tema area have a clear advantage in nonmanual jobs because they are usually better educated than other job seekers. In Nigeria, on the other hand, long-distance migrants appear to select a town because it provides either good jobs for which they are qualified or particularly favorable trading opportunities. Migrants do better than locals in finding nonmanual work in Abeokuta, Kakuri, and Aba. Three-fifths of the nonmigrants in Abeokuta are self-employed, and few of these have gone beyond primary school. The young men with more education have tended to look for better jobs in other towns, and Ogun State administrators are mostly migrants. Young men born in Kakuri or Kaduna have so far been unable or unwilling to capitalize on their position as the town has grown around them; their situation may improve as state education becomes more popular in the north. The same lack of concern for education and wage employment has characterized the few original families in Ashaiman and many Ga

TABLE 3.4

Male Occupational Placement, by Town and Distance of Migration (Percentages)

Town and Place of Origin		Farmers, Unskilled	Semi-skilled	Skilled	Commerce	Clerical, Uniformed	Administrative, Professional	Total	N
Ashaiman:	Near[a]	18	29	39	4	8	2	100	566
	North	73	9	10	3	4	1	100	71
	Alien	34	18	26	15	3	4	100	113
Tema:	Near[a]	6	32	20	4	26	12	100	598
	North	56	18	0	12	12	2	100	57
	Alien	25	12	16	27	12	8	100	113
Aba:	Here	17	7	25	42	7	2	100	41
	Near[b]	10	8	19	51	7	5	100	621
	Far	10	6	19	42	15	8	100	48
Abeokuta:	Here	14	12	18	28	13	15	100	152
	Near[c]	3	9	11	19	31	27	100	150
	Far	4	4	8	33	33	17	100	24
Ajegunle:	Here	4	8	27	10	48	2	100	48
	Near[d]	11	19	25	12	29	4	100	418
Far:	East[e]	22	8	16	19	32	3	100	263
	North[f]	19	15	11	35	18	2	100	111
Kakuri:	Here	28	33	0	33	6	0	100	18
	Near[f]	4	68	11	4	11	2	100	578
	Far	4	39	27	12	16	2	100	134
Banjul:	Here	6	6	24	9	43	14	100	243
	Near[g]	28	17	7	19	22	7	100	69
	Far	21	10	9	43	9	8	100	97
Serekunda:	Here	11	7	30	6	32	14	100	189
	Near[g]	22	15	25	15	16	7	100	100
	Far	21	18	21	24	6	10	100	84

[a] Southern and central Ghana, including Ashanti and Brong/Ahafo Regions.
[b] Western State.
[c] The former East Central State.

[d] Bendel, Lagos, Ogun, Ondo, and Oyo States.
[e] Anambra, Cross River, Imo, and Rivers States.
[f] All states of the former Northern Region.
[g] Kombo St. Mary, North Bank, and Western Divisions.

families in Accra. Access to land and the convenience of familiar ties and customs may make them less inclined to accept change.

Migrants from nearby are often relatively highly involved in semi-skilled work as operatives in factories or as drivers, seamen, butchers, cooks, and so on, whereas the locally born (except in Kakuri) have profited from greater access to apprenticeships to take a slight lead in skilled occupations. Commerce (again, except in Kakuri) is most attractive to long-distance migrants, who tend to have less education or access to training than those from nearby. Contrary to the expectation that employees in central cities will have higher qualifications than provincial workers, it appears to take more education to get a nonmanual job in a provincial town than in a place where industry is more developed. Competition may be increased because many people prefer to work near home and/or because there are only a small range and number of alternative wage jobs available. Abeokuta had the best-educated nonmanual workers, and Aba was second; 77 and 75 percent respectively had at least four years of secondary school, compared to 52 percent in Tema and 51 percent in Ajegunle.

It is often assumed that women applicants have an unfair advantage in applying for clerical jobs, that their educational qualifications count for less than personality and pulchritude. However, the census data indicate that women clerical workers are educationally as well qualified as their male counterparts. Their underrepresentation probably involves some discrimination in a field which has historically been considered the best source of jobs for men. It is only in recent years that enough women have had the education to move into clerical work in significant numbers, and they now face demands for relatively high qualifications and the intense competition of males who leave school, who are equally able to use personal contacts and may make the case that their need for work is greater.

Given the difficulty women have in entering administrative and professional occupations, it was a considerable surprise to find that in six of the eight towns women in nonmanual occupations were more likely than men to be in administrative or professional jobs. This is further evidence of discrimination against women applicants for clerical posts, but the social background of educated women is probably also a factor. Women who complete secondary school, and especially those who go on to university, are usually of higher status than comparable male students, often daughters of professionals or higher-level civil servants. Thus, they are probably more likely than their male colleagues to see education as leading to professional jobs and to have the resources to obtain employment in these categories. (They may well aim at nursing or teaching whereas the men aim at law or medicine, but both sets of occupations are classed here as professional.)

Another factor is the economic independence of West African women; their sex limits their aspirations much less than in Europe, and as more of them achieve a high level of education they will take it for granted that they can compete with men on equal ground. It must be emphasized that only a small proportion of women have reached this level, but the numbers will no doubt grow considerably in the future.

It was expected that urban experience would also be of help in finding satisfactory employment. Those who are born in a town or grow up there should be better prepared to enter the urban labor force than those who know only village life, both because they have greater access to education and because they will know about a wider variety of occupations. They should therefore be better able than adult rural-urban migrants to make the most of the opportunities available. Migrants from other towns should have some advantage. They will know less than the locals about the norms of a particular town, but they will only migrate if opportunities seem better than at home. The data indicate, however, that origin in a rural or urban place and length of stay in town have a relatively small role in occupational placement, which depends largely on the factors already discussed.

Experience and the growth of contacts seem to be somewhat more important for women than for men. The few women doing unskilled work tend to be newcomers and participation in commerce increases with length of residence in Tema and the Nigerian towns. There is usually strong competition for market stalls in these towns, and prospective traders on all but the lowest level need time to acquire capital and arrange for regular supplies. Locally born women have probably been trading since they were children, whereas women who migrate from areas where their role has been farming rather than trading need time to acquire the new skill.

Of the factors discussed, education is by far the most important (for women, after marital status). The limits it sets on occupational achievement are greater today than at independence and seem likely to grow, but there is still scope for the talented individual who lacks education to succeed as an entrepreneur and for someone who enters an occupation with minimum qualifications to rise through ability or contacts. The next two sections will demonstrate two other areas of flexibility, occupational mobility and craftsmanship. The level of occupational mobility is still considerable, so that one's first job is only a moderate predictor of position ten or fifteen years later. The easy access to apprenticeship training makes upward mobility possible for many young men of limited education, and movement within artisanship illustrates the willingness of many West Africans to take up opportunities for wage or self-employment as they seem most promising.

Occupational Mobility

Many West Africans have their first work experiences helping their parents on the farm and take up a variety of occupations simultaneously or sequentially. Farmers become artisans or traders during the dry season, and young men often accept a series of short-term jobs while they wait for their "big chance" (Aronson 1970, p. 169). Many urbanites at all school levels engage in entrepreneurial activity on the side: university lecturers run egg businesses behind their houses, women teachers sell cloth from the boots of their cars, soldiers become self-employed tailors or carpenters on weekends, and anyone with the necessary contacts may engage in more or less legitimate "income transfer" activities such as commodity specu-lation and smuggling (see Hart 1973).

In addition to this, there is fairly considerable occupational mobility in full-time jobs over time in response to business cycles and new oppor-tunities (such as opened at independence). West Africans tend to be relatively flexible, willing to leave one occupation for another which pays better, avoids the disadvantages of the present job, or merely provides a change. Many teachers moved into jobs in the civil service or politics at independence. This caused considerable difficulty at a time when the educational system was expanding rapidly. School dropouts who find low-level clerical jobs may leave them for factory work, and craftsmen who become dissatisfied with their trades may move to others or become semi-skilled workers or watchmen. Many manual workers, especially in Nigeria, aspire to become traders, and teachers study privately for many years in hopes of moving into administration or law. During the civil war, clerks and traders in the east became farmers, craftsmen took up trade, and men from all types of occupations joined the army or civil defense forces.

There has been considerable concern in recent years that opport-unities for upward mobility are declining, that the disadvantaged seldom have an opportunity to overcome a poor background. Typically, interest is limited to the elites, with the more common short-distance mobility from unskilled to skilled worker or lower to higher clerical worker being ignored. If there is increasing rigidity within the stratification system, the development of class consciousness seems inevitable, but much more evidence is needed before these (often ethnocentric or ideological) hy-potheses can be confirmed. Since many people migrate in order to be occupationally mobile, towns are good places to measure the type and amount of mobility experienced by people in various types of work. Be-cause occupation is only one factor in social status, the implications of mobility are not always clear, but at least some aspects of the subject can be examined.

Respondents in Nigeria and The Gambia were asked about all the jobs they had had since leaving school or reaching age 15. Some comparisons can be made with similar career data on Ghanaian factory workers (Peil 1972a, pp. 49–59). About half of the men in the Gambian and Nigerian towns had held only one type of job (farm, unskilled, semiskilled, skilled, commercial, clerical, uniformed, or administrative/professional). A fifth (39 percent) had held two types and 13 percent had worked at three or more types; a quarter had done both manual and nonmanual work. (The proportions for the Ghanaian workers were 22, 47, 31, and 31 percent respectively.) Differences between the Nigerian provincial, Nigerian suburban, and Gambian towns were often remarkably small, though Nigerians were more likely than Gambians to have done both manual and nonmanual work.

As expected, administrative/professional, clerical, and skilled workers were more likely both to have worked at only one level and to have stayed on one side of the manual/nonmanual line. However, the three-fifths of men in these categories who stayed at the same level did not necessarily keep to the same work. One teacher became an electrical engineer and another a prophet, laborers became watchmen and drivers factory operatives. Mobility within nonmanual work tends to be through promotion or by clerical workers becoming administrators, though a few dispensers and teachers became clerks. Movement into clerical, administrative, or professional occupations from manual work is limited because of educational requirements, but 14 percent of men in nonmanual work had managed it. Sometimes it is the result of delayed studies (a man works until school fees can be paid), but a farmer or laborer may decide to become a traditional healer or mallam, or a man who starts as a semiskilled worker may find a clerical post.

The relatively small amount of mobility into and out of the skilled trades is due to the emphasis on early apprenticeships (88 percent of apprentices located in a series of studies were under 25 years of age) and, more important, the general satisfaction of craftsmen with their work. Most of the skilled workers who had done other work had farmed before starting an apprenticeship or worked for a period at another job to pay for their equipment. Only in Tema, where there were relatively few skilled jobs and where semiskilled factory employment paid more than many craftsmen could earn on their own, were more than a fifth of the men trained in a skill not practicing it; the proportion was only 10 percent in the Nigerian towns. A few men never manage to save enough for their tools and others are too inadequate as businessmen to continue if other work is available; these may drift into farming or laboring.

Men in commercial occupations (including contracting and running a restaurant or other business as well as trading) were the most mobile of all; two-thirds had held other types of jobs. The placement of commercial occupations between manual and clerical work in the hierarchy is supported by the fact that commerce attracts mainly manual workers; half of the men currently in these jobs had done manual work in the past and of the sixty men who had formerly been traders, two-thirds were doing manual work when they were interviewed. There is considerable interchange between unskilled work and trading because petty trading is relatively easy to enter and is seen as a useful supplement to a low income or a stopgap in times of unemployment. But trading at this level is also insecure, so many men change to wage employment if they get the chance. Others place a high value on independence and leave wage employment for trading in mid-career, or take up trading after retiring from "a job."

There was considerable movement into the Nigerian army in the late 1960s, and many Igbo in the sample had served with the civil defense forces during the war. Thus, while members of the uniformed services in The Gambia (which has no army) were more stable than any other group (71 percent had held only one type of job), Nigerians in uniform had been unduly mobile (67 percent had held other jobs, half manual and half nonmanual). As the army has remained much larger than necessary, recruitment is at a low level. It seems likely that the army will attract mainly young, career-oriented school leavers in the future. This will probably lower the understanding soldiers have of civilian life, especially as most will be housed in barracks rather than among the civilian population as has been common during the past ten years.

Most mobility, especially across the manual/nonmanual line, takes place during the first few years in the labor force. The proportion who had worked at both types of jobs increased from 15 percent of men under 25 to about 30 percent in each of the older age groups. Stability was highest among 15 to 24-year-olds in The Gambia (83 percent), but dropped to half of the men aged 25 to 34 and less than two-fifths of the older men. At the other extreme were men in the Nigerian provincial towns; a third had held more than one type of job by the time they were 25, but nearly half of the older men had remained at the same level throughout their careers—an indication of the lack of alternatives for employment in these towns.

Stability declines more regularly with age in Ajegunle and Kakuri, where the range and newness of opportunities have given men who want to move their chance to do so. Young men have gone into semiskilled work, but older men have been more mobile at the status extremes—some retiring into farming, the unsuccessful moving down into unskilled work, and others carving out new careers in the professions. While the relatively high level of stability among young men may indicate declining opportunities, the fact that half of the men between 25 and 34 have changed suggests that mobility is still normal.

Occupational mobility is involved in at least half of job changes, a far higher proportion than in Europe. This is yet another indication of the flexibility of the West African labor force. Although there is only a small number of major employers, workers are able to shift between self- and wage employment and are willing to try new types of work. This helps to shorten periods of unemployment and insures that there will always be plenty of candidates for any job with moderate training requirements and adequate pay. The main reasons for leaving jobs in Nigeria were the war (29 percent), the desire for improvement or change (20 percent), and low income or lack of capital (18 percent). About 8 percent, mainly clerks and semiskilled or unskilled workers, had been laid off, and another 8 percent (largely traders and craftsmen) chose to migrate. While many men were able to return to the same or similar jobs after the war, some (especially Igbo who had been clerical workers or traders in other parts of the country) had to find new occupations or at least new locations because others were working in their places.

After about 1960, there was a decline in the proportion of men changing jobs in order to improve themselves. It is probably harder to find a job now than in the period before independence, and the proportion who farm as a first job may also have declined as a higher proportion of entrants to the labor force are school leavers. The continued importance of the level of income in job satisfaction indicates that job mobility is often due to a search for a higher standard of living. This does not just apply to wages; aspirant traders must also give serious consideration to their ability to overcome strong competition and bring in at least a subsistence income. It may seem that trading is often the last resort of men who can find nothing else, but the number of ex-traders in other work is evidence that not all unsuccessful traders are condemned to stay in this occupation.

Most of those who reported their reasons for leaving farming were looking for improved income and conditions in a "job" as a relief from the hard, dirty work in the fields. Government plans to cut down rural-urban migration must take this into account. The unskilled work that often falls to the ex-farmer in town may not be much of an improvement, but many feel that the change is worthwhile, at least for a few years. At the other extreme, about an eighth of nonmanual jobs had been left for further study, which confirms the impression that this route to advancement has been frequently used over the years. Some entrants to the labor force who are not satisfied with the level of education they have reached still continue to study privately, apply for scholarships, and move up to higher-status occupations. While a high proportion of the successful ones are teachers, many others make the attempt. The popularity of correspondence schools in West Africa deserves serious study.

Craftsmen

Craftsmanship has a long history in West Africa. Blacksmiths, weavers, potters, silver- and goldsmiths, and leather workers were active long before the colonial period; carpentry and tailoring were introduced by early missionaries and soon spread widely. Printers worked in several towns in the nineteenth century. New trades (such as TV repair) are eagerly adopted, since they provide additional opportunities for wage employment or independent entrepreneurship. Craft skills have been particularly popular in Ghana, where few men are traders. A quarter of the Ghanaian urban male labor force in 1960 was skilled (Ghana 1964), and Ghanaian craftsmen also find work in Ivory Coast, Liberia, Sierra Leone, and Togo. Nigerians and Togolese craftsmen also find work in Ghana, though most of these left when the aliens were expelled in 1969/1970 or when economic conditions became much better in Nigeria.

Craftsmen make an important economic, educational, and social contribution. Although many earn relatively low incomes, others do as well as some professionals and their collective annual income, even in a town as small as Banjul, would be well over £100,000. They provide clothing, furniture, and other consumer goods and repair motor vehicles, shoes, watches, and radios at considerably lower prices than large-scale organizations. This is of considerable assistance to the low-income population, but they are also patronized by the more affluent who can thus get their houses built and cars repaired at reasonable cost. Their service in training apprentices makes a much greater contribution to manpower development than technical schools, which are few, expensive, and seldom geared to the conditions under which most skilled workers practice their trades. The apprentice not only learns the techniques of his craft, but also how to run a business, for a fee that has remained remarkably low. Finally, because of their location and frequent underemployment, self-employed craftsmen sometimes serve as a focus for social life.

Distribution

As part of the observation of the social and economic activity of the towns, the location of all self-employed craftsmen who could be seen from the street was recorded on sketch maps. The four Nigerian towns were remapped fully or for selected streets in 1978. The maps include some men who had wage employment but worked for themselves in the evenings or on weekends, a practice which appears to be more common in Ghana and Nigeria than in The Gambia. This exercise was omitted in Tema because private entrepreneurial activity was not permitted in its public housing. (By 1978, it maintained a lively, though only semilegal existence.) In the other towns, there was a high density of craftsmen near the town centers and along major roads, but it was a rare street that had none at all. Craftsmen tend to work at or near the house where they live, though fitters must find a vacant lot with access to a road and others who can afford it may rent a room or set up a shelter on a main street if their living room is too isolated. Tinsmiths and tailors are often located in markets; there were eighty tailors in the main market in Banjul.

The number of craftsmen is roughly proportional to the size of the town (212 were located in Serekunda and 1896 in Aba), but small towns tend to have a somewhat higher density than large ones. The range is wider in large towns, but overconcentration in some trades is evident everywhere. Ashaiman's 137 carpenters and Banjul's 272 tailors are often grossly underemployed, and the same is probably true of many of Aba's 66 printers. Tailors top the list in every town studied in The Gambia and Nigeria, though the proportion of tailors varies considerably. Where women are most independent and many become seamstresses, fewer tailors are needed than in towns where tailors make female as well as male clothing.

The increasing output of local clothing factories and consequent spread of retail outlets for ready-made clothing is likely to lower the income of self-employed tailors; many will have to take up factory work because independent operations no longer pay. This change was already evident in the decreasing number of tailors in three of the four Nigerian towns between 1972 and 1978. However, those working in factories often run small businesses on the side, and may stay home for a day or two if private jobs pay more than they lose in wages.

Carpenters also find it easy to combine wage and self-employment. The elite of the trade have jobs with public works departments or large construction firms; the majority, on the margin of subsistence between construction jobs, attract what private business they can (Peil 1969). So far, only a few have found work in furniture factories. Skill levels vary more widely in carpentry than in the other trades observed, from the production of crude furniture from scrap wood with the simplest tools to superbly finished work at least equal to the best being manufactured. A worker making chairs to tide himself over a layoff in his Kakuri textile factory is an example of the former and several carpenters in Aba are in the latter category. Apprenticeships in The Gambia tended to be shorter than elsewhere, and the work was generally below the standard of Ashaiman and the southern Nigerian towns.

Shoemakers probably face more severe competition from manufactured goods than any other craftsmen, and shoe factories seem to have little need for them. Many of the shoemakers interviewed in a study of Lagos craftsmen would have preferred wage to self-employment if they could have found any, and the numbers appear to be dropping in several towns. Leather workers in Banjul produce amulets for local consumption and handbags, pouffes, and other leather items for tourists. This type of work may provide new outlets for shoemakers who are able to adjust to it, but cooperatives would probably be more profitable than individual production. Cooperatives of leather workers and calabash carvers in Oyo sell their products to large stores in Ibadan and Lagos as well as to local tourists (Oyeneye 1979).

Metal workers include blacksmiths, steel benders, welders, and tinsmiths. Steel benders tend to be employed by construction firms, but a few work on their own account. Some welders work with fitters and auto electricians in repair yards; others are rather difficult for an outsider to differentiate from blacksmiths. This field is open to the entrepreneur and likely to grow in importance as development raises the demand for small-scale engineering. Tinsmiths often recycle oil drums and other metal scrap into household objects such as stoves, pails, oil lamps, and kitchen utensils. They will be affected by the increasing availability of electricity and plastic kitchenware, but local stoves are still so much cheaper than European means of cooking that this item appears to have a long future use.

Photographers are part of the conspicuous consumption which custom requires at weddings and graduation ceremonies. In spite of the expense of equipment, this field is recruiting far more than can be supported. Accessibility to the local elites and to tourists improves the business of goldsmiths and silversmiths; they do much better (and are found in larger numbers) in Banjul than in more isolated Serekunda. Goldsmiths in poorer areas, such as Ajegunle and Ashaiman, may spend much of their time cleaning and repairing jewelry rather than making new objects; their numbers are declining.

Printers need more capital investment than other craftsmen to become independent, and most of them are in wage employment. Printing is the only trade in which apprentices are regularly paid a wage while they learn, but this attracts some apprentices who see it only as a job and leave before they are qualified. The demands of a newly literate and increasingly affluent public should provide many opportunities for Nigerian printers, especially those who can get contracts to supply the school system or install equipment to produce inexpensive books. (Onitsha printers established a reputation for cheap books in the 1960s.) Printed business and memorial cards, calendars, invitations, and greeting cards are becoming so popular that many small printers with minimal equipment can also be supported.

Repair work flourishes in a society where goods must be made to last as long as possible. Repairing lorries, cars, and motorcycles is important business in Aba and Abeokuta, which are transportation centers for a densely settled hinterland and which also support large numbers of taxis. Much of the motor repairing for the Tema area is done is Ashaiman, because space is available there. Radio and TV repairing is most common in Ajegunle, but this field is expanding everywhere as more people are able to afford such equipment. However, both radio and watch repairing suffer because luxury goods may not be collected if their owners are short of funds.

Electricians often sell electrical goods as well as install wiring and repair appliances; it is not always possible to tell whether a shop is merely a retail outlet or also a workshop. There appears to have been an increase in electricians in Nigerian towns in the late 1970s as more people can afford fans and refrigerators. This expansion has been partly at the expense of radio repairmen, as some electricians also repair radio and TV sets.

Other craftsmen, seen in smaller numbers, include masons and painters (expecially in Ashaiman), who tended to be missed because they do not have shops, and crafts requiring less skill than most of those which have been discussed and often lacking apprenticeship programs: mat and mattress makers; tire vulcanizers and fabricators of rubber products from old tires; upholsterers in Banjul; organ builders in Aba; basket weavers and plumbers, a net maker, and a clothing reweaver in Ashaiman; potters in Abeokuta; and cloth dyers in Abeokuta, Banjul, and Serekunda.

Economic and Social Position

Data on craftsmen's careers and income from the interviews seldom provide enough information on members of specific trades for comparative purposes. However, this can be supplemented by data from studies of self-employed craftsmen in Accra and Lagos. Each interviewer located twenty masters in a specified trade in the section of town assigned to him, Six trades were included in Accra and thirteen in Lagos (Peil 1979).

Most craftsmen spend three to five years learning their trades and, if they plan to work on their own account, a year or two earning enough capital to get started. This employment may bear no relation to their training; it may be farming or any wage job from laboring to teaching. A few move immediately into another apprenticeship. Between 10 and 20 percent (depending on trade) leave before completing their training and about 10 percent never actually practice the skill they have learned. Most of those who find wage employment in their trade and stay longer than two years settle down in formal sector employment until retirement, but many of these also build up private businesses on their own time and redundancy pushes others, especially those into he building trades, into temporary or permanent self-employment. A new industry may draw in men in mid-career who do not see themselves as giving up their businesses but as adding other and more stable sources of income.

Even under conditions of extreme competition, large numbers of apprentices are being trained (350 were counted in Ashaiman in 1970). Craftsmen are under pressure from kin and school leavers seeking training, and some find it hard to get along without any apprentices, but there appears to be no feeling that numbers should be kept down. A man still gets prestige from the number of his followers, and master craftsmen tend to have a paternalistic rather than exploitative relationship with their apprentices.

Craftsmen have an advantage over other workers in that it is relatively easy for them to move from one town to another if conditions for business look more promising, and their ability to take their work with them also makes it easier for them than for men in other occupations to return home when they decide to do so. About half move after completing their apprenticeship; those specializing in construction are among the most mobile men in the samples. Akinnusi (1971, p. 12) found that the proportion of migrant small-scale entrepreneurs (mainly craftsmen) in ten divisional headquarters towns in southwestern Nigeria varied from 9 to 54 percent, with the more isolated towns where earnings were likely to be higher having the highest rate. Abeokuta, with Ibadan and Lagos nearby, was among the lowest in gross annual earnings and in the proportion of migrants.

Discussions of the informal or nonenumerated sector have tended to assume that the self-employed barely earn enough for subsistence, but little hard data are available. Hinchliffe (1974, p. 64) shows that informal sector workers in Kaduna "appear to earn less per hour than farmers, once relevant adjustments have been made," whereas workers in a large textile factory earn 5 to 40 percent more. However, the necessity of focusing on illiterate craftsmen in order to make the comparison with farmers means that his figures do not represent the average artisan, and even these may be earning less in the north than they would in the south, partly because of a lower level of training. Bryant (1976, p. 21) found that self-employed craftsmen in a Ghanaian mining town in the early 1970s were earning more than they would in wage employment.

Some authors (i.e., Sandbrook and Arn 1977, p. 25) argue that lucrative markets developed by craftsmen are quickly taken over by large, foreign-controlled firms. However, King (1977) shows that small-scale producers in Kenya are capable of competing with better-equipped manufacturers, and Kennedy (1977, p. 192) points out, on the basis of studies in Ghana, that multinationals and small producers may have no interest in assimilation or collaboration because neither find this advantageous. Both of these authors stress the flexibility of the small producer and his ability to perceive and fill gaps much more quickly than more bureaucratic firms. However, Jules-Rosette (1979) points out that the artist/craftsman catering for an elite/tourist market is likely to be more concerned with innovation in technology and style than the carpenter, tinsmith, or basketweaver caught in a highly competitive, low-income market.

Johnson (1978, pp. 264–69) suggests that the effect of factory products on local craft production varies with the craft and from one area to another. Local production of handwoven textiles and clay pots may well be as large as in the past, though this forms a diminishing proportion of the total textiles and pots used. Bead making has nearly ceased, but blacksmithing is flourishing. Fapohunda (1978, p. 129) found that only 22 percent of 2025 informal sector entrepreneurs interviewed in Lagos thought that competition from large firms significantly decreased their income; 54 percent thought they had no effect. On the other hand, 49 percent felt there was too much competition from small-scale enterprises in their field. Thus, the multinational corporation and the locally owned factory are less important sources of competition than fellow craftsmen. With the exception of clothing and shoes, where factories are making significant inroads into the artisan market (at least in large towns), small-scale enterprises continue to thrive; mass production caters to different markets.

The main difference in income between the self- and wage-employed skilled workers located in these studies was the greater range of the former's income. Men working for wages tend to have a somewhat higher average wage than the self-employed, but some craftsmen do much better on their own. Even though it is sometimes ignored by small firms, the government minimum wage raises employees above the level of the least successful of the self-employed. However, wages have a relatively low upper limit unless one is promoted to a supervisory position; craftsmen on their own, especially in printing and building contracting, can do better than this. Differences in favor of wage employment are signficant in The Gambia and the Nigerian provincial towns but not in the suburbs; the opportunity to build a private business is greatest in towns like Ajegunle, where rapid growth means that many households need furniture and equipment. A large population earning relatively good wages keeps craftsmen busy. For example, the Udoji wage increases meant that many Ajegunle households could afford locally made water tanks.

Some trades pay better than others, regardless of the source of income. Printers and electricians are usually among the best paid, whereas carpenters and blacksmiths do relatively poorly; this is reflected in the prestige of these trades. Fitters and carpenters appear to earn more in wage employment, but tailors have a good chance of doing better working for themselves. This is probably related to the incidence of small, sweatshop clothing firms which provide wage employment for tailors and seamstresses. Printers had the highest average income, but a self-employed electrician who claimed to have earned £5000 in the past year was the best-paid craftsman in the samples. At the other extreme, no shoemaker or painter in the Lagos study earned over £200 per year. Signs advertising "Doctor of Shoes" and "Engineer of Watches" are an attempt to improve the status of these poorly paid trades.

Most craftsmen work alone, with one or more apprentices, or with a single colleague; few have paid employees. Their status inhibits informal socializing with apprentices, but there is often time for gossiping with friends, and friendliness is good for business. Pons (1969, pp. 186–88) provides a case study of a carpenter who had settled in Kisangani and had many friends and visitors while he worked. In the absence of community centers or other formal, institutionalized recreation, craftsmen may be nuclei of social groups. Young men gathered at a photographer's shop or around a working carpenter or tailor are a fairly frequent sight in the late afternoons or on weekends in many West African towns.

However, the data suggest that these groupings are as related to the personality of a particular craftsman as they are characteristic of his occupation or his freedom for informal conversation while he works. Self-employed craftsmen in some towns know more of their neighbors than wage-employed skilled workers, but on the whole self-employment makes little difference to the sociability of craftsmen and skilled workers are not more sociable than men in other occupations. This will be discussed more fully in chapter 6.

Conclusion

Although almost all men between 25 and 49 are in the labor force, the participation rates for younger and older men differ considerably between towns. The more the labor force is concentrated in manufacturing, the higher the proportion of men under 25 who are employed; in less industrial towns, over 40 percent of the young men may still be in school. Older men have been less likely to stay in industrial towns once they leave the labor force, whereas older and more balanced towns have a larger component of retired, elderly men.

Education has much more effect on the level of labor force participation than other variables, but there is still considerable variability in the education of people doing various types of work and flexibility in shifting to other jobs by acquiring more education or training. Those who lack education may achieve higher income than those who have it if they can build successful businesses, since education produces a taste for bureaucratically structured wage employment which relatively few who go beyond primary school manage to overcome. Muslim education, on the other hand, appears to have no effect on labor force participation *per se*; work opportunities for men who do not become mallams depend on study in state schools.

Religion, custom, and need for support are the most important factors in women's participation in the labor force. Islam decreases it, except among the Yoruba; customary economic autonomy increases it for certain ethnic groups; and support from husbands living in the same household make it less necessary for women to be economically active. However, many married women prefer to be financially independent and others are forced to support themselves and their children because their partners are unable or unwilling to do so. The spread of secondary education for girls seems likely to increase their demands for a share of middle- and high-level jobs; education is especially important in increasing labor force participation among Muslim women. The sharp drop in participation over age 50 shows that a majority of women leave the labor force when their children are old enough to support them.

If their educational levels are similar, local people and migrants from nearby have little advantage over long-distance migrants. If the locals do not take the educational opportunities open to them they lose the good jobs to better-educated migrants. This has happened in several towns. Likewise, long residence in town apparently does not result in a widening of contacts which improves job opportunities, though it may be helpful to women traders who face severe competition for market stalls.

Within educational constraints, there is considerable short-distance occupational mobility, especially in middle-level jobs (semiskilled and clerical work, teaching). Since this is largely the first generation out of farming, there is little attachment to specific urban jobs and considerable willingness to try something new if it looks more promising. This makes for a flexible labor force, which should help to overcome gaps in middle-level manpower occasioned by development.

Craftsmen have been among the most satisfied sectors of the labor force and have provided inexpensive training for large numbers of apprentices. Many face severe competition because of oversupply in their trade and, to a lesser extent, from cheap manufactured goods (both local and imported). The shortage of jobs in the formal sector ensures a continuing demand for training, and so far craftsmen have made no attempt to limit access to their trades. While the opportunity to build their own businesses is highly valued by many craftsmen, the proportion who are self-employed varies with the craft and the presence of alternative opportunities. Given the choice, many craftsmen maximize their income by participating in both sectors—holding wage employment and carrying on businesses outside normal working hours.

4□HOUSING

Comfort Ameh was a 55-year-old Adangbe landlady in
Ashaiman. She had grown up in Ningo, a coastal village,
and learned kenkey trading while attending primary
school. At about 25, she married, moved to Accra and took
up cloth trading. This prospered, and in 1965 she was able
to acquire a plot in Ashaiman and put up her own house.
She had a stall for petty trading in Ashaiman, and liked it
better than Accra: "You won't make any living in Accra,
but here you gain a lot from petty trading." Her husband
and children had died, but she had an 11-year-old grand-
daughter living with her in 1968; the girl had not been
sent to school. Her house has eleven rooms, some of which
were empty in 1970 because five tenants had been ejected
for misbehavior. The tenants included an Akwapim mason,
his wife, and a young sister; another mason and his half-
sister; a Buem clerk and his wife, two children and wife's
brother's daughter; and an Adangbe carpenter. The three
skilled men all worked for the same firm in Tema. She has
two rooms; each tenant has one.

She has a bed in the stall, and sleeps and sells all day.
Her tenants buy for her in the market, and friends come
and chat. She listed nine friends, all neighbors whom she
saw several times a week. About half were from her
hometown and the rest from a 50 km. radius; the women
were traders or seamstresses and the men in semiskilled or
skilled work or storekeeping. She saw her sister's daughter
(a neighbor) every day and visited a half-sister in Accra
bimonthly.

After employment, the major problem faced by migrants to the towns is
finding a place to live. Given the rapid growth of most towns, housing is
hard to find and crowded. Various aspects of the housing situation will be
examined in this chapter; the ethnic and occupational heterogeneity
which characterized these houses, the reasons why people move from one
house to another, the level of amenities and crowding they experience,
the relationship between household composition and housing density and
the role and characteristics of landowners, especially those living with
their tenants. This chapter thus provides a description of the conditions in
which urban residents live, as the basis for the analysis of their social life in
the chapters which follow.

Heterogeneity

Ethnic and status mixing within houses and neighborhoods can been seen as a continuum from the ethnic or income ghetto (enforced, administratively promoted, or completely voluntary) to the highly mixed area where people of widely differing background and level of success live in close proximity, On the whole, housing in West Africa is at the integrated end of this continuum, which is potentially very important for the nature of urban society.

Heterogeneity may be an indicator of tolerance and social mix, or merely of a very tight housing market in which people must accept whatever accommodation they can find. Propinquity can encourage understanding and friendship, or merely raise tensions which would be absent if people of differing norms and values had no need to interact so closely. Although the data from these studies are insufficient to measure these effects, some tentative conclusions can be drawn. At least, data on the extent and nature of heterogeneity contradict widely held views on ethnic and income segregation.

Colonial authorities often encouraged segregation in housing. They built cantonments known as Government Residential Areas (GRAs) for themselves, provided special housing for certain categories of employees such as railway workers and policemen, and set aside areas (*zongos* and *sabon gari*) for long-distance migrants. These last had been somewhat segregated by local custom, but their numbers vastly increased during the colonial period and they substituted an alliance with the colonial rulers for dependence on traditional rulers. These changes often resulted in a decline in harmonious relations between strangers and the local population.[1]

Segregation of strangers went furthest in northern Nigeria. Plotnicov (1967, pp. 41–50) describes the separation of Jos into a Native Town and a separate Township for Europeans, Asians, and southern Nigerian clerks and traders. Amenities were much better developed in the township and its residents were under a separate administrative and judicial system. Separation in Kano was even more complex. Paden (1971, pp. 117–18) divides Kano into six residential sectors "distinctive in terms of ethnicity, standard of living, and recency and rate of immigration." Three have people of all income levels; two areas of recent growth house mainly low-income northerners; and the Township, originally set aside for non-Africans, houses upper-income Nigerians as well as expatriates. The largest areas are Kano City, the old central core inhabited by Hausa/Fulani families, and Sabon Gari, established for southerners early in the colonial period. The density per room in these areas shows the effect of discrimination in access to housing; in the early 1960s it was 1.4 in Kano City and 7.0 in Sabon Gari.

Strangers' quarters tend to be more ethnically heterogeneous than other parts of the town, though they may have a prevailing culture if one group is longer resident and better represented than others. Between 60 and 80 percent of the Kano Sabon Gari population in the early 1960s were Igbo. In Ghana, it has tended to be the Hausa who set the cultural pattern for the *zongos*. Though they are no longer in the majority there, Hausa tends to be the *lingua franca* of *zongo* residents and Islam tends to be the dominant religion. With increasing numbers of southerners moving into *zongo* areas, the spread of literacy in English and the fostering of a national culture, this ascendency is declining (Dinan 1975; Schildkrout 1970, 1978).

Residential segregation may be useful in fostering an economic monopoly. The Hausa maintain their control in the Sabo area of Ibadan, and prefer isolation because it promotes the continued dominance of Sabo leaders over the cattle and kolanut trades. Networks of clientage would be weaker and local competition would be harder to overcome if the traders were residentially dispersed (Cohen 1969).

Segregation by income appears to be much less prevalent in West Africa than in Europe. Extended family ties often bring together people of widely different income and education, and public housing (with its inherent segregation by ability to pay rent) is poorly developed. Spatially separate housing is generally not highly valued by the wealthy; many who could afford to isolate themselves are content to live in areas crowded with people who can afford much less. Fraenkel (1964, p. 51) reports that Monrovian landlords allow huts to be built behind their own houses as a profitable way to use unneeded land. Marris (1961, p. 69) points out that

> [T]he shabbiness of the houses in central Lagos disguises how widely the residents vary in prosperity. Only the chrome-tipped fin of a Pontiac, edged into the angle of a lane, may distinguish the home of a business man with a profit of several thousand pounds a year from that of his neighbour, who earns perhaps £200 as a carpenter for the railways.

The limitations of space, which make it impossible for all members of the second or third generation to find rooms in a family house, and the desire for a higher level of amenities on the part of those who have obtained higher education are gradually modifying this pattern to increase the spatial segregation between rich and poor. Where they are not provided with government housing, the elites are increasingly building houses in new subdivisions, accessible only by car and accommodating families like themselves. This is often encouraged by the government, which allocates land for high-income housing estates. For example, it is Gambian government policy that wealthy applicants build at Fajara, leaving plots in Serekunda for lower-income people. This division was not yet very successful; several expensive houses were being built in Serekunda.

Source of income (commerce versus government or profession) and education appear to be more divisive factors in housing preference than income *per se*. Businessmen often find the maintenance of a wide network of ties to clients and potential customers profitable and have a life-style which differs little from the majority of the population, whereas some of the highly educated elites have other values and prefer a more European life-style, including isolating their children from "unsuitable" companions (B. Lloyd 1966, p. 166).

There was a high level of mixing of people of different ethnicity, religion, occupation, and income in the sample houses. A large majority of houses with more than one household, and many of those with only one household, accommodate members of more than one ethnic group (or subgroup in monoethnic towns). Although ethnicity appears to be a more salient factor in social relations in Nigeria than in Ghana or, especially, The Gambia, ethnic mixing in housing is more common in Nigeria. The variance appears to be due to structural factors rather than differences in preference. While half of the people in multifamily houses have at least one cotenant of the same ethnic background as themselves, this increases to three-fifths in the Gambian towns because they have a relatively small number of ethnic groups. Nevertheless, even though most houses in Banjul and Serekunda are relatively small, nearly nine out of ten multifamily houses have residents of more than one ethnic group. The high proportion of Muslims in the Gambian towns, on the other hand, means that relatively few houses have adherents of more than one religion.

Tema has only a few Muslims, but even with a majority of single-family houses half have members of more than one branch of Christianity. Occupational mixing, in turn, is low in Tema and Abeokuta because there is only one man working in most houses. It is very high in Ajegunle, where houses are larger and there is a wide variety of opportunities open to residents; men doing manual and nonmanual work share most large houses. Tenants in one Aba house included a hotel manager, a barrister, a clerk, and a driver. Insofar as cotenancy and neighboring lead to meaningful contacts, the development of class consciousness could be inhibited because many nonwork relationships are with people of differing perspectives.

Even with considerable heterogeneity, it is possible that some ethnic groups which are closer to each other on cultural or political grounds might tend to cluster and that other groups might find themselves, or prefer to be, isolated in housing. Therefore, two techniques were used to measure ethnic clustering: hierarchical linkage (Mitchell 1974, pp. 4–13) and smallest space analysis (Guttman 1968). Both are based on the number of household heads who share accommodation with members of other groups. This matrix is scaled by the root of the diagonals (to take account of the varying numbers in each ethnic group in the sample) to produce the similarity index used in both procedures. Hierarchical linkage

TABLE 4.1
Heterogeneity in Housing by Town (Percentages)[a]

	Ashaiman	Tema	Aba	Abeokuta	Ajegunle	Kakuri	Banjul	Serekunda
Ethnicity:								
More than 1 group[b]	86(128)	83(171)	94(82)	97(67)	98(114)	84(86)	89(87)	85(75)
Household head with no cotenant of same group[b]	32(797)	56(300)	48(468)	66(252)	51(677)	63(612)	38(383)	39(319)
Religion:								
More than 1	83	52	87	42	86	91	18	19
Christians and Muslims	38(136)	8(359)	0[d](94)	34(141)	49(120)	67(95)	15(102)	13(120)
Occupation of males:[c]								
More than 2 types	55	10	54	15	73	63	44	35
Manual and nonmanual	59(137)	23(350)	73(94)	28(127)	85(118)	70(92)	66(102)	48(116)

[a]Numbers in parentheses are bases for percentages. Houses with only one adult were omitted.

[b]Houses with only one household were omitted unless they were multiethnic. The Akan in Ghana were divided into Fante and Twi. Subgroups were counted for Igbo in Aba and Yoruba in Abeokuta. Extended family houses in Abeokuta were omitted even if they were shared by several households unless they were ethnically heterogeneous.

[c]Houses with no employed adult males were omitted.

[d]No Muslims in Aba sample.

117

is simpler and nondimensional; the result is a diagram with links at various levels indicating smaller or greater distance between groups. Smallest space analysis produces plots in two or more dimensions of Euclidian space.

On the whole, the results largely confirm the hypothesis that there is little ethnic clustering in West African urban housing. There was a division in Ashaiman in 1968 between southerners and northerners and between Ghanaians and aliens (see Figure 4.1), but Tema was more mixed, as was Ashaiman in 1970 (when many of the aliens had left). Igbo and Yoruba appear to have been further apart in Ashaiman in 1970 than in 1968, perhaps as a result of the war in Nigeria. The greater separation of Ewe from Ga and Akan in 1970 may be related to their political isolation at that time. In 1968, it was the Ga (the local group in Tema and Ashaiman) who were separated from the Akan and Ewe. In all three plots, the majority of southern Ghanaian groups can be seen as central; the isolation of all three Nigerian groups in 1970 is evident. (The expulsion of aliens was mainly aimed at Nigerians.)

The picture for Nigeria and The Gambia is much less clear; there is no consistency in results using different methods and the plots show little evidence that members of certain groups seek each other out. In the few cases of meaningful grouping, there are usually other groups in the cluster whose presence cannot be accounted for. For example, the Igbo, Ijaw, and Edo (all southerners) might be seen as a cluster in one series of Kakuri plots, but the Hausa nearby cannot be explained and hierarchical linkage puts considerable distance between the Igbo and Edo. Separating small and large houses often produces different results, which may mean different bases of choice but could easily mean that any clustering found is spurious.

Hierarchical linkage of the Gambian data suggests that the Mande are isolated in Serekunda and the Jola in Banjul, whereas smallest space analysis isolated the Aku in Serekunda and the Sarahuli in Banjul. Again, there is no sign of real clustering; note how most groups join singly in Figure 4.2. This suggests that there is no underlying structure in housing choice, that ethnicity is not an important factor when seeking accommodation. Insofar as clustering occurs, it involves members of a single group, often joined at a lower level of affiliation than ethnicity—by ties of kinship or common hometown—and is probably greatest among the indigenes of the town.[2]

Chapter 6 demonstrates a relatively high level of interethnic and inter-status friendship and chapter 8 discusses the varying levels of preference for ethnic distance in housing. While it is difficult to assess the effect of mixing in housing, neighborhood, or work on behavior or attitudes, those who have had opportunities for interaction with members of other groups find it more difficult to categorize than those who lack such contacts and

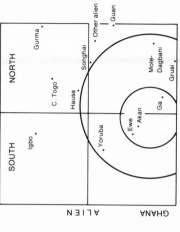

Tema 1968. Two Dimensional solution,
Guttman-Lingoes Coefficient of Alienation .135.

Ashaiman 1968. Four dimensional solution, vector 2 plotted
against vector 1. Guttman-Lingoes Coefficient of Alienation .082.

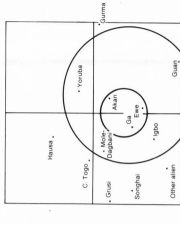

Ashaiman 1970. Two dimensional solution,
Guttman-Lingoes Coefficient of Alienation .137.

Figure 4.1 Smallest Space Analysis of Interethnic Housing in Ghana,
Euclidean Metric

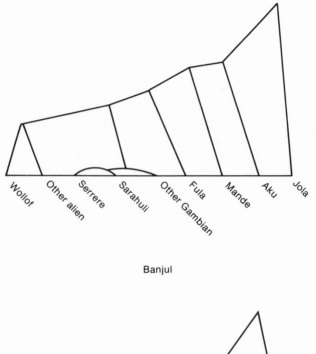

Banjul

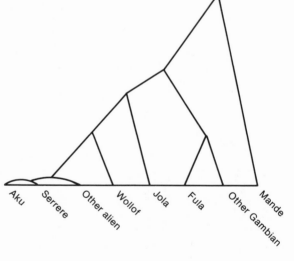

Serekunda

Figure 4.2 Hierarchical Linkage of Interethnic Housing
in The Gambia

quite a few friendships grow from accidental meetings. Thus, the high level of heterogeneity in urban housing probably makes a substantial contribution to community integration. Insofar as public housing lowers this heterogeneity, it may lay the seeds of future conflict. The separation of southerners in the Kano Sabon Gari was one of the causes of the interethnic riots there (Paden 1971, p. 131).

Conditions

Research on the quality of life usually includes measures of housing conditions and satisfaction. For most people in these towns, housing is poorly provided with amenities and crowded. It is least expensive for those with good salaries who live in government-subsidized housing, but it is relatively inexpensive for many of the poor because the *laissez faire* attitude of government toward private housing has permitted a larger supply of rooms for rent than in countries where the housing market is more under government control (see Peil 1976a). On the whole, rents have risen much more slowly than other prices. Housing density is as much a result of the larger size of households as of inability to pay for more space; a version of Parkinson's Law operates here in that households tend to grow to fill the space available—kin visitors stay longer if there is room for them.

Expectations

Except for Tema, where almost all housing is owned by the Tema Development Corporation, government housing in these towns is largely limited to the elites and the military. Professionals and senior administrators live in the Government Residential Areas (GRAs) of Aba and Abeokuta, which are relics of colonial times; there is also some middle-level government housing in Aba. The TDC has built 192 one-room houses in Ashaiman, which are available to government employees or sublet to their workers by large firms; it recently built a few larger houses for sale. The other major supplier of official housing is the army, though the shortage of barracks means that some members of the armed services live in private housing (some officially and some privately rented). Policemen are housed under similar conditions. The majority of the population is dependent on the private housing market, which has several disadvantages in comparison with subsidized housing but at least allows a choice of where to live.

The lack of amenities in most West African housing makes living there seem grim to anyone used to a European level of accommodation. Gambian houses were, on average, the best provided with amenities. Two-thirds of the sampled compounds in Banjul and three-fourths of those in Serekunda had piped water, electricity, and a latrine; most of the other Banjul houses lacked piped water, which is available from the many standpipes in these towns. At the other extreme, Ashaiman had no electricity (though it has been installed since) and few houses had either piped water or latrines. The number of standpipes and latrines has increased since the study, but the water supply cannot be depended on and servicing of latrines remains a problem. Most of Ajegunle lacks a public water supply; households depend on shallow wells or buy water brought in from Apapa by tank truck or bicycle. Some tenants complained vociferously about the state of the latrines provided by the owners; even if otherwise satisfactory, these latrines were used by far too many people. In addition, rubbish collection is a severe problem in most Nigerian towns.

As land becomes more expensive, the standard of building (and the rents) tend to go up because only better-off people are able to get access to building land. "Swish" (earth) walls are giving way to cement block walls and cement floors in newer houses, though sandcrete blocks are used to save money. There are still a few houses with bamboo walls in Ajegunle and far more in Ashaiman with walls made of tin sheets or packing cases. Nevertheless, the norm of using cement or sandcrete is now so well established that new owners wait until they can afford to use these materials. Unfortunately, this often means a long delay before the house can be lived in, and intensifies the shortage of rooms for rent.

There is considerable movement from one house to another within towns; the reasons given for these moves provide information on the importance of physical, social, and economic factors in housing choice. Morgan and Kannisto (1973, p. 13) estimate that about 45 percent of Lagos residents moved in 1967–1968, but this is probably abnormally high due to the wartime situation. A third of the households surveyed in Ajegunle had moved at least twice, but many of the rest had spent many years in the same house. Moving was somewhat less common in the other towns, where relatively few household heads reported moving more than once. Nevertheless, two-thirds of those in the Gambian and Nigerian suburban towns had moved at least once. Except in Ghana, women were as likely to report moving as men.

The most common reason for the move was the physical condition of the house; people left because the house lacked water, electricity, or toilets, which were available in the new house, or because the roof leaked, or the house was old and in bad condition, crowded, too hot, or badly located. Location is particularly important in a town like Ajegunle, where transportation is poor and work may be far away. The greater space of Serekunda and Ashaiman draw people even though fewer amenities are available than in Banjul or Tema. Destruction by fire or rain sometimes makes it necessary for all residents of a house to move.

Next come social reasons. Women usually move when they marry and accompany their husbands on their moves. Young people move out when they can afford to be independent. (This was a reason for leaving family compounds in Abeokuta and crowded rooms shared with kin elsewhere.) Individuals who feel that cotenants are hostile, or have nothing in common with them, or who are annoyed by quarrels or children, move in search of more congenial company. A teacher left "to live with literates" and another "to move away from the traditional people in my family." A single man left a house "inhabited mainly by family men" whose "children always disturbed me with their noises." The anonymity of the town can make a move a useful means of escape. One young man felt it necessary to "move away from a girl friend who was too frequent in my place." Thieves in the neighborhood may also make it advisable to move. The landlord sometimes asks tenants to leave because of disagreement (with himself or other tenants) or because he "wants the house," which may mean using the room for kin, rebuilding, or merely raising the rent.

Economic reasons are less important than physical and social ones, perhaps because there is relatively little variance in the price of the type of rented room most of the respondents can afford and therefore little to be gained economically by a change. Rents tended to be £2 per month or less in Ashaiman and Aba, £2 to £3 in Kakuri and £4 to £5 in Ajegunle and Tema. Serekunda rents, from £5 up, were reported to be about half of those in Banjul. This represents the equivalent of 10 to 25 percent of average male income in these towns, highest in Ajegunle and lowest in Abeokuta.

A major problem for many who want to move, especially young people, is the landowner's demand for "key money," usually equivalent to at least two months' rent, and/or the requirement that three to six months' rent be paid in advance. This is not just avarice; landowners are often remarkably tolerant about rent once the tenant is known (allowing several months' leeway in times of unemployment), but they consider their best interests in requiring that prospective tenants prove their financial solvency. In high-rent housing, advances involve large sums, which can be put to work immediately in the construction of more houses.

There were several respondents in most towns who had moved into houses of their own, either inherited or newly built. This house may initially have fewer amenities or be less conveniently located than the house which is left behind, but new houses are probably in better physical condition and the savings on rent plus the possibility of income from tenants make this an attractive proposition to those who intend to stay in town permanently. House owners may consider the economic factor more important than the physical one; Abloh (1967, p. 75) reports that a man who builds a new house in Agona Swedru often remains in the old house in spite of its bad condition in order to rent out all of the new one.

Density

The expectations that residents have of housing and their limited ability to pay for it affect their satisfaction with physical and social constraints. Aside from lack of amenities, the most obvious problem with urban housing in West Africa is the level of crowding. It has often been assumed that overcrowding is detrimental to family life and aggravates conflict in neighborhoods, but recent studies in Europe and North America have produced ambivalent results. In any case, they have seldom involved densities as high as those which are common in West Africa, and so may not be relevant.[3]

The applicability of their findings is also limited because the need for privacy and feeling of being crowded are at least partly culturally based. People who grow up in large family compounds are socialized not to seek privacy (B. Lloyd 1966, p. 167), and take sharing of sleeping rooms by several people for granted. The climate helps, as even in the rainy season daytime hours can often be spent in the courtyard and the rooms are used mainly for sleeping and storage. (This is less true for Aba, which gets much more rain than the other towns studied.)

Table 4.2 shows the highest densities in Tema Group 4, Ajegunle, and Aba; the lowest are in Abeokuta, the Gambian towns, and Ashaiman. Pressure from new migrants is probably the most important source of crowding, which tends to be greatest in rapidly growing towns and especially their central areas. A central location is important to traders and craftsmen because it brings business past the door (see Marris 1961), but also to wage employees because the poor state of urban transportation makes it necessary for many to walk to work. An extreme case of central crowding is the estimated average occupancy of Lagos Island in the mid-1970s as over four per room. At this level, compounds are full of household goods which can no longer be stored in the sleeping rooms and people must sleep on verandahs and even in the open because there is just not enough floor space inside. Many rooms have only 7.4 sq. meters and few are larger than 13.4 sq. meters.

Although there are a few detached houses classed as Group 1 and several areas of Group 3 housing (semidetached houses with gardens and servants' quarters or large flats, for senior staff, many of them rented to expatriates), 80 percent of Tema accommodation is Group 4 (four to six "houses" per building, for ordinary people). With high rents and very high demand, it was usual for official tenants of a Group 4 "house" to sublet all but one room to other families, so that two or three households often shared a single house. The most crowded house in the Tema sample had thirty-two people in four rooms and, on average, households were over twice as crowded as in Ashaiman. However, at some point density does force people to move out. The precipitating factor was usually finding

TABLE 4.2

Housing Density

| Town | Mean Number | | | | | % of Households | | | Number of | |
| | Per House[a] | | | People per | | Per Room Over | | In 1 Room | | |
	Rooms	Households	People	Room	Household	2.5	3.5		Houses	Households
Abeokuta	6.3	2.2	8.8	1.4	3.9	12	4	37	141	315
Tema, Group 3[c]	3.1	1.0	5.6	1.8	5.6	13	2	0	44	45
Serekunda	7.3	2.4	13.3	1.8	5.5	16	5	21	120	292
Banjul	8.8	3.1	15.6	1.9	5.0	27	11	27	103	323
Ashaiman 1970	6.5	5.6	14.0	2.1	2.5	23	8	82	110	611
1968	6.3	5.6	14.5	2.3	2.6	28	11	89	143	799
Kakuri	8.1	6.5	18.7	2.3	2.9	30	18	83	95	617
Aba	8.3	5.0	25.4	2.9	5.0	54	30	58	95	472
Ajegunle	7.2	5.7	20.9	3.0	3.8	47	26	81	120	686
Tema, Group 4	2.1	1.4	6.9	3.0	4.5	48	30	62	383	528

[a]Compound in Banjul and Serekunda.

[b]Children under 5 counted as half.

[c]Upper-income housing; non-African households have been omitted.

stable employment (enabling dependent kinsmen to be independent), marriage, or the expected arrival of yet more migrants. A quarter of household heads in the Ashaiman 1968 sample had come from Tema.

Crowding in Tema rather than moving out to Ashaiman suggests a preference for amenities and a good location over space and cost. Rents in Ashaiman were about half those in Tema, but most houses lacked the water supply, toilets, and electricity available in Tema houses. Ashaiman also had a reputation as a "rough" town, with many thieves, and so had little appeal to the better-paid, more stable workers who could qualify for housing in Tema. Turner (1972, p. 165–66) shows that housing priorities vary according to one's position in society; access to jobs and security of tenure are most important for low-income people who need to know what work is available and to have somewhere to stay through periods of unemployment. Security of tenure is relatively unimportant in West Africa because most migrants plan to return home and can do so if necessary; hence, they put more emphasis on low rent than on house ownership. Most Tema families have relative job security and are not worried about being put out by the TDC, which, like private landlords, has been slow to take action against defaulters. Hake (1977, p. 144) points out that space is a relatively unimportant consideration for Africans. If given the choice, they prefer to "eat well and sleep crowded," to economize on space. Thus, while Tema residents often complain about the lack of space (Peil 1968, p. 13; Potakey 1975, p. 3), they prefer to stay where they are.

Space was as short in Aba as in Tema; several houses had signs warning prospective tenants that they were fully occupied. Aba had filled up rapidly in the eighteen months since the war ended; there had not been time to rebuild many houses destroyed during the hostilities, much less expand the housing stock, and many houses in the Overrail area had been taken over by the army. In Ajegunle, on the other hand, crowding was based on economics rather than on an absolute shortage of rooms. There were signs directing prospective tenants to absentee owners and 11 percent of the houses studied had at least one empty room.

The other two towns with over 80 percent of the population living in single rooms, Ashaiman and Kakuri, have a higher proportion of people living alone than Ajegunle, so they are not as crowded. In Ajegunle, 15 percent of the households in single rooms have five or more people. Ten people appears to be the absolute limit of a single room; households with more than ten people (in Ajegunle and other towns) had at least two rooms. There is an economic as well as a space factor in this. A household with seven or eight people may include only the head, his wife, and dependent children. Beyond ten, there are usually also adult kin, who are bringing in money which can be used for rent.

Abeokuta and the Gambian towns are relatively uncrowded on all of the measures used. The average is less than two people per room and less than a third of households have more than 2.5 people per room.[4] A large majority of households in these three towns have more than one room (unlike Ashaiman, the other relatively low density town), so the presence of large households is a lesser problem. The mean number of people per house was lower in Abeokuta than anywhere except the Group 3 houses in Tema. Many family compounds had only a few elderly residents, with empty rooms available for migrants to use on visits home.

Households in a single room are more likely to be severely over-crowded (more than 3.5 per room) than those with more space, but this difference is not found in Kakuri or Abeokuta and in all the towns house-holds with more than one room are as likely as those with only one to be moderately crowded. Density increases with the length of time spent in town and with the addition of kin to the nuclear family. There is strong normative pressure on urban residents to accept new arrivals and help them get on their feet, even though this results in a deterioration of housing conditions for themselves. So far, it appears that the majority accept this responsibility even though it is heaviest on the middle-aged, who are already crowded by the size of their nuclear families.

The nature of the local housing market is a better guide to density than size of house; large and small houses have almost equal proportions of crowded households. Neither are houses near the centers of towns neces-sarily more crowded than those farther out.[5] A density gradient was present in Aba (partly because upper-income people tended to live in relatively peripheral housing), but not in Ajegunle; central, middle-range, and peripheral houses had about the same average density. If the avail-ability of rooms decreases and the higher cost of new houses leads to higher rents, the peripheral houses may eventually show a higher density than those at the center. The absence of a gradient in Ajegunle may be because the whole town is peripheral to Lagos; the expected dif-ferential does occur to a limited extent between central Lagos and Ajegunle and Mushin. Similarly, density declines between Tema and Ashaiman; differentials within Ashaiman are not notable.

Household Composition

The growth of households by the addition of children, kin, servants, apprentices, and friends inevitably increases the crowding in urban houses; an extra room cannot be built or rented just because the family has increased in size. Household composition is examined here for its effect on housing density. Its relationship to family life will be discussed in chapter 5.

There are many difficulties in the accurate assessment of household composition in West Africa. There may be considerable variance over time, and people living in one place may be only part of a wider domestic network. Therefore, household composition reported here is *de facto*: the people sharing a recognized household at the time the census was taken. Residents of houses were allowed by interviewers to divide themselves into households according to their sleeping, eating, and financial arrangements. People who jointly rent a room or rooms in which they share domestic activities usually count themselves as a single household.

Separate households signify a degree of independence between people who may see a good deal of each other: a wife who prepares meals for and sleeps with her husband in rota with other wives, a son who is still financially dependent on his father and prepares meals for him but has a separate room, two friends whose settlement in town is being aided by a cotenant, but who have a room of their own and take care of their own cooking. On the other hand, servants may have separate quarters but still be considered part of the household and a child of the household may sleep with a neighbor because there is no space for him or her in the family's room.

A wife may have a separate household from her husband even in a monogamous marriage if he is working elsewhere or if custom decrees separate female quarters or continued residence with her kin. In Ghana, Ga, and to a lesser extent, Akan, wives customarily have separate households. A Yoruba trader may live alone in town, being joined periodically by her normally village-resident husband. Osborne (1973) found that many Egbado Yoruba have two households, one in the village and one in Abeokuta; they move between the two seasonally or whenever it is opportune to do so. In this case, household composition at any given time is at best a sample of a geographically extended household.

The type of household varies with the life cycle, migration customs, availability of housing, and, to a certain extent, income. The variance shown in Table 4.3 demonstrates all of these factors. One-person households were most common in Ashaiman; Serekunda and Abeokuta had the highest proportion of nuclear families, and extended family members or nonkin were most often present in Tema and Aba. Young residents of Ashaiman and Kakuri were living alone because they had not yet married. Ashaiman also had many long-distance migrants who had left their wives and children at home in accordance with custom; many of these lived alone. The low proportion of extended families (either by the addition of adults or children) in Ashaiman is a result of the availability of housing and its relatively low cost, and is also reflected in the comparatively low level of crowding there. Kakuri's higher density is probably caused by more unmarried young men sharing with kin.

Group 3 housing in Tema is seldom crowded because several rooms are available to a household, but two-thirds of these relatively affluent families share their rooms with people who are outside their nuclear family. Servants increase the number of nonkin in the household, though some

TABLE 4.3
Household Composition, by Town (Percentages)

	Single Person	Nuclear only[a]	Nuclear, plus			Head, plus			Total	N	Households with Extra	
			Kin	Nonkin	Both	Kin	Nonkin	Both			Adults[b]	School-age Children[c]
Ashaiman 1968	35	41	7	1	0	12	3	1	100	799	22	9
Ashaiman 1970	37	36	9	1	1	12	4	0	100	612	21	4
Tema, Group 3[d]	11	24	40	9	16	0	0	0	100	45	46	27
Tema, Group 4	12	37	29	3	3	13	2	1	100	528	58	16
Aba	13	27	22	15	12	10	2	4	100	472	48	39
Abeokuta	23	51	10	5	1	6	2	2	100	325	27	13
Ajegunle	16	43	18	3	1	17	1	1	100	686	35	15
Kakuri	27	38	8	1	1	20	3	2	100	617	31	9
Banjul	10	45	29	2	2	6	4	2	100	323	50	20
Serekunda	14	54	25	1	2	1	2	1	100	292	43	12

[a]Spouses or parent(s) and children.

[b]Anyone over 14 and not in school, excluding head and spouse.

[c]Anyone aged 6–14 or still in school who is not a child of head or spouse. (14-year-olds who have left school after Primary 6 are not counted.)

[d]More spacious, higher-rent houses than Group 4.

relatives also act as servants. The difficulty in getting accommodation in Tema means that many Group 4 households must also make room for kin, though more of these are sharing with a single household head than in Group 3 houses.[6]

There were some young migrants living alone in Abeokuta, but there were also elderly widows and widowers who had rooms of their own in the family house. For them, a single-person household signaled the retention of some independence without social isolation. In this type of community, there is little need for kin to share rooms and relatively few do. As in all the towns, extra adults in the household are more common than extra school-age children. In Abeokuta, these adults are usually sons or daughters of the head of the household who have not yet married or fellow migrants (where young men share a household). Most of the government workers transferred to Abeokuta have their families with them, even though they expect to stay only a few years.

The distribution of household types in Ajegunle is similar to that of the Gambian towns, though heads of households are less often living with their spouses in Ajegunle. Banjul and Serekunda shown a norm of settled family life, often extended to include grown-up sons and daughters, the children of rural kin who have come to town for schooling, or other relatives from the country. There is some evidence that young migrants initially share rooms in Banjul and then move to Serekunda when they marry. Gambian households are as large as those in Aba, but are twice as likely to contain only a nuclear family; the supply of housing is much more adequate in The Gambia.

Landowners

The ownership of housing has important political, economic, and social implications in an urban community. Because owners are usually more committed to urban residence than their tenants and have property to defend, they tend to develop political networks which, in turn, enhance their power in the neighborhood and their ability to exercise patronage. They serve as dispute settlers and advisors and help to socialize new migrants to urban life (Schildkrout 1973, p. 54, 1978, pp. 110–19; Barnes 1974, 1977).

The ownership of land also has important implications for the subethnic identity of the local people. These are still largely agricultural societies, where communities are identified with the land in which their ancestors are buried; the threat of strangers taking over the land from the traditional owners has been a source of conflict in many towns (see Lloyd 1974). In addition, should a few wealthy owners (often referred to in the press as "speculators") gain an increasing monopoly over housing for the

poor, this would exacerbate feelings of exploitation and class consciousness. To the extent that owners share their houses with tenants, so that
they interact frequently on a personal level, they are likely to be seen as
elders and businessmen or women with an interest in the neighborhood
community, much more socially acceptable roles.

The availability of land and distribution of ownership varies considerably between towns. All of the land in the Banjul metropolitan area has
been taken over by the government. With the exception of a few long-
established family plots in Banjul, it is allocated to applicants on renewable
twenty-one-year leases, officially limited to one per family, and sales must
have government approval.

Acquiring urban land in Ghana and Nigeria is more complex and less
secure. Few titles are registered and the agreement of all owners must be
obtained for a legitimate sale. As houses are jointly inherited by all
children of the previous owner, after two or three generations there are
often so many owners that a purchaser risks a series of lawsuits and having
to buy off claimants who appear several years after his purchase. The two
main results of this are (1) a relatively small market for older houses
(which tend to remain in the family of the builder) coupled with a strong
demand for new building land on which to establish new family houses
and (2) the development of associations and other forms of social support
by owners to help defend their titles should they be challenged (Aronson
1978a; Barnes 1974, 1977).[7]

It was assumed that many tenants would know little about a non-
resident owner, so the only information collected was their place of
residence and ethnicity. This is available for almost all houses. In addition,
the standard census data are available for all resident owners, and some of
these were included in the interview samples. Both the poor and the rich
build for residence and income, but given the relative affluence necessary
to own more than one house, resident landlords were expected to be more
representative of poor than of rich owners, especially in the suburbs.
Nevertheless, the data give some indication of the possibility of house
ownership by the less advantaged and provide information on the type of
people who are prominent in neighborhood affairs.

Economists complain that in Africa, surplus funds are too readily invested in housing rather than in projects which contribute more to
national development. However, the relative security of housing investment and the high rate of return make it a popular use of capital. Since
land is cheaper and much easier to get in the suburbs than in the city
centers, a high proportion of suburban housing is owned by residents of
nearby towns. The proportion of resident owners varies from just over a
quarter in Ashaiman (1970) and Kakuri to about four-fifths in the Gambian
towns.

Most absentee owners in Aba were reported to be living nearby, but half of the owners in Ashaiman, Ajegunle, and Kakuri lived outside the suburb. Nevertheless, in both Ashaiman and Kakuri it was rare to have an outsider collecting the rent; either the owner came himself (70 percent in Ashaiman and 39 percent in Kakuri) or he appointed a tenant (usually a kinsman) to take his place. This arrangement effectively puts in the house someone in authority with whom the tenants can develop a personal relationship. The relationship of tenants with their landlords tends to be more commercial in Ajegunle, where rent-collecting agencies cater to owners who prefer to have nothing to do with their tenants.

House ownership is usually seen as a male prerogative, just as heading a household is. However, except in Abeokuta and Kakuri, women are slightly more likely to be resident owners than to be tenant household heads. A third of the resident owners in Ashaiman and a quarter of those in Banjul were female, compared to only 3 percent in Kakuri. Both female ownership and tenancy appear to be more common in the older parts of central cities than in the new and largely migrant suburbs. The most common way for a woman to become a house owner is through inheritance, which means that women who are first-generation migrants are even less likely than male migrants to own houses. As the more successful young people move out to the suburbs to establish homes of their own, widows and other women who have inherited a family house remain behind. Robertson (1976, p. 126) reports that 27 percent of the Ga women over 50 whom she interviewed in central Accra owned a house.

Ashaiman, on the other hand, is a new town where there is little scope as yet for inheritance, but where the majority of houses have involved only moderate cost. The women owners there are mainly short-distance migrants who have come to Ashaiman for trade and invested their profits in housing. This route is used by successful women traders in many towns, though they often prefer to build houses to rent to expatriates or local elites rather than as accommodation for themselves. This is sufficiently common in some towns for government officials to complain that "most of the decent buildings" are "owned and controlled by women and the so-called petty traders" (Anon. 1971).[8]

It usually takes many years of planning and saving to build or buy a house, so most owners have spent at least ten years in town and few are under 35. The locally born have a considerable advantage in towns where they are a long-standing majority; 87 percent of resident owners in Abeokuta and 79 percent in Banjul were locally born, compared to 11 percent in Ashaiman and the other three Nigerian towns. Migrant owners are more likely to be under 50 than the locally born, which suggests that the latter often wait to inherit a family house. Acquisition of a house is a more active process for migrants, based on a decision taken relatively early in their careers. Age adds to the owners' status in the community and makes it easier for them to exercise leadership.

The local ethnic group is about equally represented among resident and absentee owners; the indigenes appear to have no greater preference for building for accommodation or for income than migrants. Only in Abeokuta does the local group have a near monopoly on housing; at the other extreme, 78 percent of the owners in Aba and 97 percent of those in Kakuri were strangers. At this level, the indigenes may justly complain of losing their land. This is only a minor problem in Kakuri, as Kaduna has never been considered "owned" by any group, but in Aba it is obvious that the neighboring Owerri have made better use of the opportunities of urban growth than the local Ngwa. The increasing ownership of housing in Ashaiman by aliens was a source of discontent in 1968. By 1970, many of these aliens had been forced to leave as a result of the Aliens' Compliance Order, and a few Ghanaians had earned substantial sums selling their houses for them. Some of the swish houses were left to disintegrate, an indication of their low economic value.

Using the two best measures of social status, education and occupation, considerable breadth of ownership can be demonstrated. Administrators and professionals are less likely to be resident than other owners, but it appears that they own only a small minority of houses in most towns. They are under considerable pressure to build at home, and are less oriented toward the investment aspects of urban housing than businessmen. The uneducated tend to be better represented than those who are relatively well educated; two-thirds of resident owners in Ashaiman, at least a quarter in each of the Nigerian towns, and about a tenth in Banjul and Serekunda had no education at all. On the whole, it is the people with only primary or middle-level education who seem to do less well in the competition for housing. However, this discrimination may be more apparent than real, because so many migrants with moderate education are young. Most of these have not yet had time to save for a house, whereas older illiterates have.

The proportion of resident owners who were manual workers varied from 55 percent in Kakuri in 14 percent in Aba, suggesting that many people in this sector of the labor force are able to acquire houses if they decide to settle down in town. But traders and businessmen are the most interested in housing; they are overrepresented among resident owners in all towns and especially in the provincial towns (71 percent of resident owners in Aba and 42 percent in Abeokuta, compared to between a sixth and a quarter in the other towns). This may be due to the conservatism of provincial businessmen and women, but is probably related to the limited alternatives for investing capital in this type of town.

Finally, an additional index of economic position is income, on which data are available for the 126 resident male owners who were interviewed at length. This also indicates remarkable access to housing; 15 percent had annual incomes of less than £100, 40 percent earned between £100 and £500, and only 35 percent earned more than £500 in the previous year. Owners are, on average, wealthier in relatively stable areas where family houses predominate (Abeokuta and the Gambian towns); very few in Aba, Ajegunle, or Kakuri had incomes over £500. It might be argued that absentee owners are likely to be wealthier than residents, especially in Ajegunle and Kakuri, where they tend to live outside the suburb. They are manifestly able to build a house for rent while accommodating themselves elsewhere. However, the available information casts some doubt on this. There was no difference between resident and absentee owners in the mean number of rooms in their houses, except in Ajegunle and Aba, where the resident owners had, on average, larger houses than the absentees.

This also supports the contention that housing style is less closely tied to wealth or status in West Africa than in Europe or America. A large house in an unprestigious neighborhood which will accommodate the owner's family and paying tenants as well is considered a good business proposition. The fact that owners living outside the neighborhood tend to have smaller houses than either residents or absentees living in the neighborhood belies the image of the distant owner as a Rachmanite speculator. The farmer's attitude toward land ownership remains an important value for most urban residents, so owners do not usually treat their houses as just another business.

Owners are more likely than tenants to have the use of two or more rooms, but nearly a third of those in Ashaiman and the Nigerian suburbs had only one. As a result, though owners are usually less crowded than their tenants, in Ashaiman and Kakuri the owners were somewhat more often overcrowded. Owners seldom live alone, but only in The Gambia are they more likely than tenants to have people outside the nuclear family staying with them. There appears to be little pressure for ethnic, occupational, or religious homogeneity on the part of residential owners. Heterogeneity can be useful in that it is easier to collect rent and get rid of undesirable tenants if there are no connecting ties. On the whole, tenants of resident owners seem to be better satisfied than those living in the house of absentee owners; turnover is lower where the owner lives in the house.

Conclusion

Housing is the most basic component of the urban environment. The concern of prospective migrants to have a place to stay is often as important factor in their decision on where to go. Urban housing is usually overcrowded and lacking in amenities by European standards, but most of it is of a higher standard than is available to villagers. On the whole, it appears to correspond fairly well with the expectations if not the aspirations of urban residents, partly because most can find a room at a price they can afford to pay.

Because so many houses are large, with the majority of tenants renting only one room, there is considerable scope for mixing among cotenants. Ethnic, occupational, and religious heterogeneity is the norm in these houses, and neighborhoods usually have representatives of most social categories even though certain groups predominate. This is potentially a source of friction, but it may also provide an impetus to overcome ethnic or religious particularism and an opportunity to know personally people whose economic and social position is quite different from one's own— which may, in turn, raise aspirations and slow the development of class consciousness. These possibilities will be further examined in chapters 6 and 8.

Though some members of the elites might not agree, a case can be made that housing is a less important factor in the standard of living and self-image of a West African than of an Englishman or American. Individuals and families are often content to live in less space than they can afford, and this is not necessarily because alternative accommodation is impossible to find. More prestige is gained from building a large, ostentatious house at home than in town, even though it is seldom occupied. Many wealthy people prefer to live less conspicuously in town, using their money for productive investments, their children's education, cars, and clothing rather than for spacious accommodation. Furniture also tends to be limited to functional necessities (with the exception of a television set and a radio-phonograph if these can be financed) rather than conspicuous display, perhaps because the norm was set by government provision for colonial officers. Dahlberg (1974, p. 178) found a similar attitude in East Africa.

The educated elites have sometimes been socialized into new housing values, but for ordinary residents housing is not very important other than as a place to sleep, store belongings, and receive shelter from rain; life can more easily and pleasantly be lived out-of-doors. Social life is not centered on a set of rooms but on the space outside them. It might be argued that rooms are not used because they are too crowded; on the other hand, their crowding is less an inconvenience because they are not wanted for daytime activities. That this is the direction of causation can be seen by comparing Banjul and Ajegunle. Banjul houses are seldom overcrowded by the standard used here, yet the compounds are in active use all day. Rooms in Ajegunle are much more crowded, yet they are often used for talking with friends because outdoor space is so limited. Thus, the preference is for relaxing and entertaining out-of-doors. Insofar as new urban housing is built without provision for the residents to cook and sit with friends outside, dissatisfaction with housing density is likely to increase.

Landlords are, on average, older, better established and more interested in municipal and neighborhood politics than their tenants. Nevertheless, many of those who share their houses with tenants are doing the same sort of work (or did before they retired) and have the same, moderate incomes. Absentee ownership, with its potential for class-type divisions, is more common in suburbs because the opportunities for investment are there and most of the tenants who seek housing there are too new to the town to be able to build their own houses. If these communities stabilize, the proportion of resident owners seems likely to increase, though increased speculation in land could make it much more difficult than in the past for manual workers and small-scale traders to become house owners.

Our West African migrants have now settled down in town, with a job and a place to live. Part II will examine the social life available to them: the family life which spreads outward from the household to kin in the neighborhood and elsewhere in town and to the extended family at home; friendships which develop with other urban residents; and the use made of formal associations. The final chapter will assess the ways in which these relationships can be manipulated when problems arise and the effect on community relations of attitudes toward ethnic and economic differentials.

Map 1   THE SURVEY TOWNS

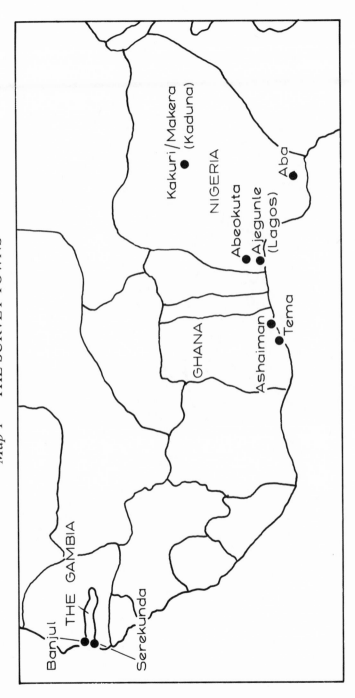

Map 2   TEMA

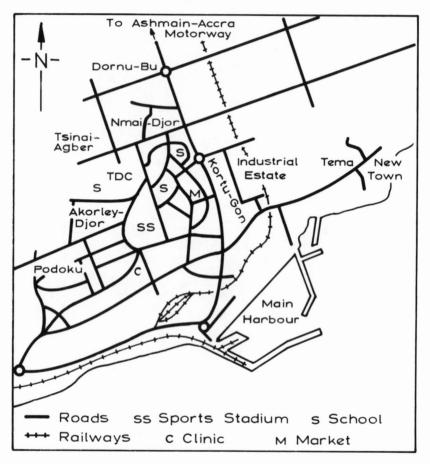

Map 3 ASHAIMAN

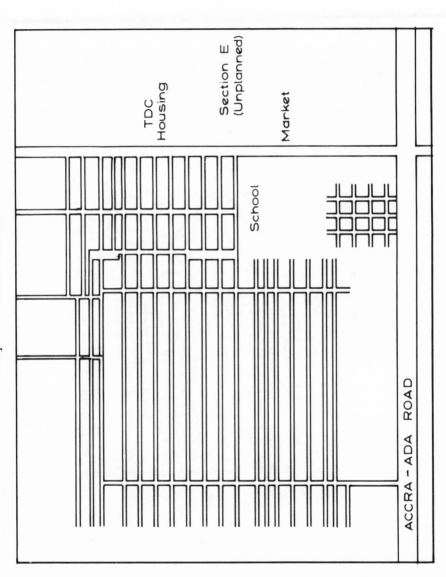

TDC
Housing

Section E
(Unplanned)

Market

School

ACCRA - ADA ROAD

Map 4   ABA

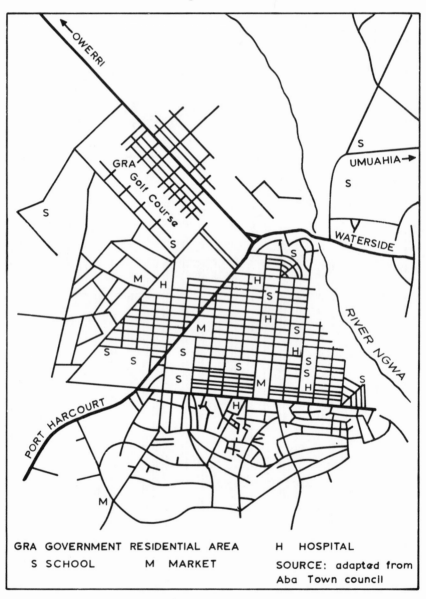

OWERRI

GRA
Golf Course
S
S
S

S
UMUAHIA→
S
WATERSIDE

M H
H
S
H
M
S
S
S
H
S
S
S
M
H
S
H
PORT HARCOURT
RIVER NGWA
H

M

GRA GOVERNMENT RESIDENTIAL AREA   H HOSPITAL
     S SCHOOL   M MARKET   SOURCE: adapted from
                                       Aba Town council

Map 5 ABEOKUTA

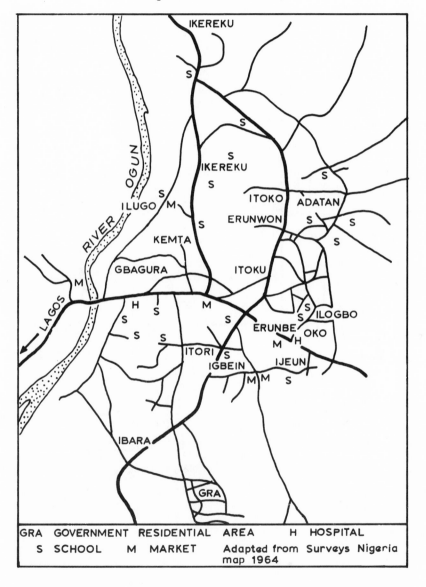

GRA GOVERNMENT RESIDENTIAL AREA   H HOSPITAL
  S SCHOOL   M MARKET   Adapted from Surveys Nigeria
                                map 1964

Map 6   AJEGUNLE

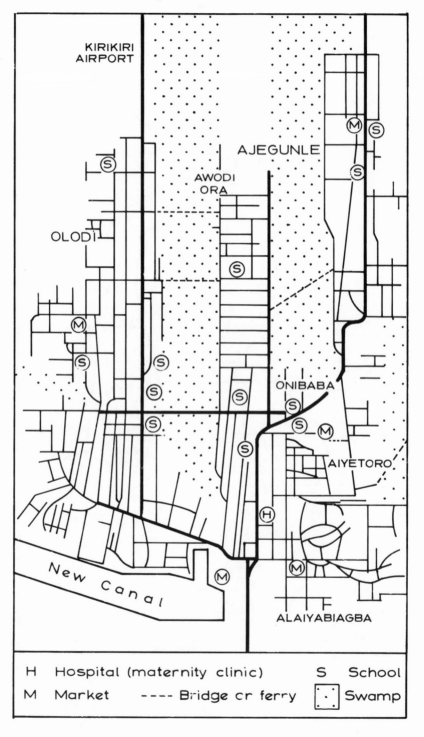

KIRIKIRI AIRPORT

AJEGUNLE

AWODI ORA

OLODI

ONIBABA

AIYETORO

New Canal

ALAIYABIAGBA

H   Hospital (maternity clinic)   S   School

M   Market   - - - - Bridge or ferry   Swamp

Map 7   KAKURI/MAKERA

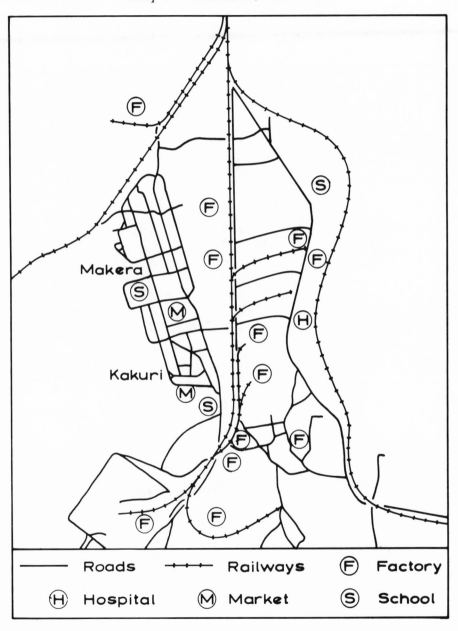

Map 8   BANJUL

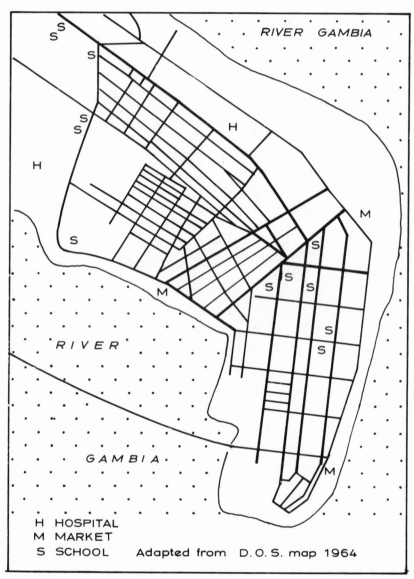

RIVER GAMBIA

H

M

S

S

S

S

S

S

S

H

S

M

RIVER

GAMBIA

M

H HOSPITAL
M MARKET
S SCHOOL   Adapted from   D.O.S. map 1964

Map 9   SEREKUNDA

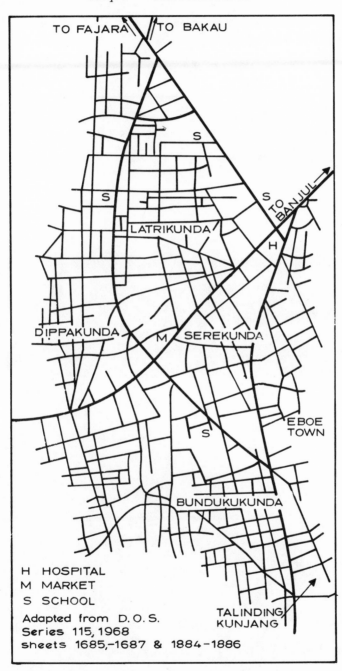

TO FAJARA   TO BAKAU

S

S

S
TO BANJUL

LATRIKUNDA

H

DIPPAKUNDA

M   SEREKUNDA

E BOE
TOWN

S

BUNDUKUKUNDA

H HOSPITAL
M MARKET
S SCHOOL

Adapted from D.O.S.
Series 115, 1968
sheets 1685,-1687 & 1884-1886

TALINDING
KUNJANG

1. Grave of a founder next to the family house. **2.** Shops line the street; water is sold by the bucket. **3.** Storeyed house with a beer parlor.

4. Bridge across the swamp.　**5.** Industrial refuse dump and market.　**6.** Private commercial school.

7

8

7. A young apprentice mechanic.   **8.** A carpenter and friends.

9. Restaurant.　**10.** Independent church.　**11.** A popular sport.

PART 2

SOCIAL INTERACTION

5□FAMILIES

Johnson Wagu was a 54-year-old unemployed ex-policeman living in Aba. He had grown up in a village in Owerri Division, completed two years of secondary school and joined the police at age 20. Over the next eighteen years, he had twelve transfers. He retired at 38, moved from Port Harcourt to Aba, and took up produce buying. He farmed at home during the war and had not yet found employment on his return to Aba, though he had some income from rent on his house. He did not marry until he was 34, but at the time of interview he had three wives (one home "on leave") and six children under nine years of age. Two of his wives were Efik rather than Igbo; as market traders, they were probably supporting the household. The first wife was married while Johnson was living in her hometown.

Johnson had three cousins living in Aba. He saw the two who lived nearby every day and the more distant one about three times a week. Given his financial circumstances, it is not surprising that he was unable to send money home, but he tried to visit at least twice a year, staying as long as two weeks and taking £5 and foodstuffs with him. His second wife had probably taken gifts when she went to their hometown. He belonged to a "family meeting" in Aba and the police pensioner's association, and was active on the committee of the Cherubim and Seraphim church. His hope for money to restart produce trading was based on an in-law in Lagos who was "in a position to help me."

The social life of West African towns is strongly influenced by the fact that the majority of adults are or have been married and that migrants seldom cut themselves off from their families or kin. Rather, they prefer to establish family life in town and, at the same time, maintain contacts with kin at home. Men and women may have different friends and spend their free time separately, but much time each day is spent on family affairs. This chapter will explore the types of marriage, its effects on social life, and the contacts residents maintain with their extended families in town and at home. The main theme is that considerable continuity with the past in both attitudes and behavior coexists with a variety of adaptations to present circumstances. The result seems to produce far less strain than an outsider might expect, because strong family relationships are still very highly valued in these societies.

Marriage

The early literature on African towns, especially reports on southern and eastern Africa, gave the impression of largely male populations and little family life; wives and children were left on the farm while the husbands came to town for short periods of wage employment. This was perhaps inevitable, as many of the towns studied were newly established for administration or to service European-run industries such as mining, and the housing was often designed for single men. The indigenous towns of West Africa and the Swahili coast of East Africa provided more scope for family life, though those which grew rapidly during the colonial period or since independence have had an increase in the proportion of young, unmarried men and, probably, a decline in the incidence of extended families living together. However, since most migrants now settle in town for some years, married men usually want to have their wives with them, and wives exert pressure on their husbands to come.

As a result, the sex ratios in many towns are tending toward balance. For example, between 1960 and 1970, the sex ratio of Tema dropped from 147 to 121, that of Accra from 115 to 103 and that of Kumasi from 113 to 102 (Ghana 1962, 1972). However, the sex ratio of Ashaiman has remained almost the same (141, 140); this town continues to attract large numbers of young, unmarried men and long-distance migrants who prefer to leave their wives at home. Table 1.2 shows that in the towns studied, the sex ratio generally increases with the proportion of recent migrants. The exception is Kakuri, which has the highest sex ratio but only as many migrants who arrived within the last two years as Ajegunle. This difference appears to be due to the lower average age of arrival in Kakuri than in Ajegunle; newcomers to the former are, therefore, less likely to be married.

As shown in Table 5.1, the rates of marriage and polygyny both increase with age, but there are notable differences in the marital patterns of men and women. The early marriages of many women, to husbands who are at least five and often more than ten years their senior, is partly due to the competition engendered by polygyny, but marriage of males is also delayed in order to complete schooling. While most men over 50 are still married, many women in the Gambian and Nigerian towns have not remarried after being widowed or divorced. Second marriages are more likely to be polygynous than first marriages. Some older women "retire from marriage" by returning to the family home or living with their grown-up children rather than with their husbands, though these usually report themselves as married.

Rates of Marriage and Joint Residence, by Sex and Town[a]

		% Married				% of Polygynous Marriages			% of Households with		
		15–24	25–34	35–49	50+	Early	Middle	Late[b]	Both Spouses[c]	All R's Children[d]	Children[e]
Ghana											
Ashaiman:	M	21(256)	59(409)	84(187)	91(43)	5(239)	19(94)	12(21)	70(467)	40(53)	38(795)
	F	77(222)	89(194)	94(96)	94(17)	8(147)	19(105)	23(63)	79(425)	47(19)	
Tema:	M	9(264)	67(330)	94(207)	98(57)	1(245)	5(192)	12((56)	78(489)	...	63(572)
	F	50(262)	94(246)	95(110)	94(34)	3(126)	8(234)	11(124)	84(481)	...	
Nigeria											
Aba:	M	2(326)	49(259)	93(202)	100(26)	2(133)	11(188)	42(26)	81(360)	68(94)	74(472)
	F	50(218)	86(151)	83(95)	46(11)	10(108)	6(130)	30(74)	92(338)	84(45)	
Abeokuta:	M	3(117)	57(127)	94(85)	92(65)	5(75)	35(80)	58(60)	88(219)	57(94)	65(314)
	F	39(110)	97(112)	96(99)	71(72)	16(43)	39(109)	55(176)	91(293)	68(44)	
Ajegunle:	M	13(319)	63(429)	96(183)	94(47)	4(312)	8(175)	30(44)	78(518)	64(90)	58(686)
	F	73(318)	88(184)	82(83)	64(11)	12(233)	14(162)	23(75)	93(469)	73(41)	
Kakuri:	M	16(471)	65(283)	87(55)	100(13)	6(261)	27(48)	38(13)	85(281)	77(70)	42(617)
	F	82(239)	85(126)	81(26)	75(8)	15(195)	27(107)	33(27)	93(299)	78(32)	
Gambia											
Banjul:	M	4(216)	34(117)	89(120)	84(89)	10(50)	28(107)	24(75)	86(226)	53(107)	62(323)
	F	30(197)	74(114)	87(127)	48(64)	19(59)	39(84)	25(142)	81(275)	74(39)	
Serekunda:	M	5(150)	61(129)	88(122)	93(69)	1(85)	16(108)	19(64)	88(237)	73(109)	70(294)
	F	44(174)	85(143)	88(92)	49(47)	19(77)	17(122)	18(104)	84(283)	71(40)	

[a] Numbers in parentheses are bases for percentages.
[b] Early = 15–34 for males and 15–24 for females.
Late = 50+ for males and 35+ for females. 1970 data used for Ashaiman.

[c] Married individuals only.
[d] Interview data, respondents with children only.
[d] Dependents under 15 or still in school.

Men in Serekunda between 25 and 34 years of age are almost twice as likely to be married as those in Banjul; this is because so many young married men move out to Serekunda for housing. The low marriage rate of men in Aba in this age category is probably due to wartime delays and insecurity. Very few men under 25 had married in either the provincial or the Gambian towns. These young men were more likely to be still in school than suburban residents and were probably more dependent on parental support to enable them to marry.

Polygyny

Of the three countries studied, polygyny rates are lowest in Ghana and highest in Nigeria, especially in the provincial towns. The matrilineal Akan of southern Ghana (who contribute the majority of the population of Tema and Ashaiman) have historically been less polygynous than the patrilineal peoples of northern Ghana. Gambians appear to get an earlier start in polygyny than Nigerians, but while the former's rates remain fairly stable after the middle of the marital career or even decline, elderly Nigerians are more likely to be polygynous than the middle-aged.

Polygyny is both more prevalent and more intense in Abeokuta than in the other towns; over half of the men over 50 and the women over 35 are involved in polygynous marriages, and this is the only town with substantial numbers of men having more than two wives. An interesting corollary of this is the freedom it gives to both men and women to establish liaisons outside of marriage. An older man with several wives had a female friend with whom he spent considerable time, and a woman in a polygynous marriage had a male friend whom she had known well for several years and visited nearly every day. The interviewers explained that polygynous husbands are less likely to be watchful or jealous than monogamous ones, and presumably a woman who remains in a polygynous marriage cannot complain if her husband makes other alliances.

Studies of the relationship between polygyny and social change have shown that education, religion, ethnicity, economic position, and urbanization affect the level of polygyny. Education appears to be more important for women than for men. Educated women can use their scarcity value to require formal monogamy of their husbands, though they may be less successful in preventing the establishment of "outside wives" (see Harrell-Bond 1975). Clignet and Sween (1969, p. 143) suggest that some educated women in Abidjan find the power attached to the position of senior wife attractive or that a moderate education gives little bargaining power when a husband wants another wife. However, Ohadike (1968, p. 381) found that each increased level of schooling resulted in a substantial drop in the proportion of Lagos women in polygynous marriages. Education made much less difference in the proportion of Lagos men who were polygynous, except for those with university or professional training, who find it relatively easy to support outside wives.

Although it sometimes results in percentages based on only a few cases, polygyny rates are given by age group in Table 5.2 because overall figures are often misleading. As younger people are likely to have more education but to be less polygynous than those who are older, the effect of education on polygyny must be tested for people of relatively the same age. There is also considerable interaction between education and other variables, but the size of the samples makes it necessary to take these one at a time. A clear relationship between level of education and incidence of polygyny among men is found only for Nigerians over 35 and Ghanaians with at least secondary education. Gambian men with secondary schooling were as likely to be polygynous as those who never attended school.

The effect of education is also stronger among Nigerian than among other women; in all age categories, more education means less acceptance of polygyny. In Ghana and The Gambia, however, primary education has little effect. None of the Ghanaian women who had gone beyond middle school had a polygynous marriage, but Gambian women with secondary schooling were only somewhat less likely than their less-educated sisters to have polygynous husbands. Contrary to Clignet and Sween's findings, there is almost no evidence in these samples of educated women settling for the position of senior cowife. The wives in most polygynous households all had the same amount of education or, where this was not the case, the junior wife was more likely than the senior to have attended school. This is probably because she was younger and had benefited from the increased access of her cohort to education. Men who want additional wives these days are likely to find that a majority of the eligible women have at least had some primary education.

The major differences in the religion sections of Table 5.2 are between Muslims and Christians. (There were few people who identified themselves as followers of traditional religions in the Nigerian samples and none in the Gambian samples.) Religion tends to reinforce education in that Christians have usually had more Western education than Muslims. Christianity may cut down polygyny somewhat, but it has had far less influence than most of its leaders would like, because the societal value system has remained relatively unaffected. Islamic acceptance of up to four wives is one of its important attractions.

The Muslims in the Ghanaian samples, who were predominantly aliens, had higher rates than other Ghanaian respondents, and these rates were increased slightly by Muslim education. This suggests a greater allegiance to Islamic values on the part of those who get such training. As this effect is also present in Nigeria but not in The Gambia, it may be related to the minority position of Muslims in Ghana and southern Nigeria, both as religious adherents and as members of ethnic groups centered in areas

TABLE 5.2

Proportion in Polygynous Marriages, by Country, Age, Sex, and Socioeconomic Background[a]

MALES	Ghana			Gambia			Nigeria		
	15–34	35–49	50+	15–34	35–49	50+	15–34	35–49	50+
Education									
None	2(168)	9(169)	8(47)	0(13)	26(27)	6(18)	9(91)	20(103)	53(55)
Muslim	6(16)	4(26)	29(17)	10(41)	21(72)	25(54)	5(19)	42(19)	70(10)
Primary	5(75)	5(37)	11(9)	0(16)	25(24)	26(19)	5(336)	15(198)	43(35)
Middle	2(437)	9(144)	12(32)	3(61)	20(89)	15(48)	1(144)	13(84)	38(24)
More	0(92)	5(63)	0(9)				3(189)	7(85)	21(19)
Religion[b]									
Muslim	2(96)	6(77)	24(37)	5(119)	24(196)	21(125)	11(166)	30(103)	65(36)
Traditional	4(88)	8(83)	7(15)	…	…	…	25(4)	36(11)	50(4)
Sect	4(54)	13(45)	9(11)				3(106)	13(64)	54(13)
Protestant	1(378)	7(167)	6(36)	0(16)	0(18)	0(14)	2(231)	13(151)	36(42)
Catholic	4(167)	6(64)	8(13)				2(262)	7(138)	23(35)
Occupation									
Farm, unskilled	2(123)	10(83)	16(37)	0(12)	27(33)	5(19)	3(60)	8(53)	53(19)
Semiskilled	2(236)	8(77)	16(19)	5(19)	25(24)	0(8)	1(190)	16(68)	27(15)
Skilled	5(260)	9(137)	9(11)	4(25)	17(42)	18(33)	7(122)	18(92)	47(19)
Commerce	0(32)	3(38)	17(12)	10(21)	31(42)	31(26)	8(136)	20(163)	57(44)
Clerical[c]	0(108)	8(64)	4(22)	6(36)	16(49)	17(29)	3(212)	9(72)	33(15)

MALES

	Ghana			Gambia			Nigeria		
	15–34	35–49	50+	15–34	35–49	50+	15–34	35–49	50+
Administration, Professional	0 (18)	6 (34)	8 (12)	0 (16)	16 (25)	28 (18)	7 (42)	12 (41)	26 (26)
Urbanization[d]									
Rural	3 (379)	12 (171)	14 (49)	4 (50)	30 (69)	23 (31)	2 (245)	11 (151)	40 (30)
Mixed	4 (199)	6 (132)	14 (22)	0 (7)	18 (11)	33 (3)	4 (125)	17 (99)	32 (22)
Urban	1 (210)	5 (135)	9 (43)	13 (8)	14 (22)	0 (10)	4 (321)	14 (188)	40 (55)
Here	NA	NA	NA	3 (67)	18 (108)	18 (93)	6 (90)	32 (53)	64 (36)

FEMALES

	Ghana			Gambia			Nigeria		
	15–24	25–34	35+	15–24	25–34	35+	15–24	25–34	35+
Education									
None	6 (270)	9 (346)	14 (213)	18 (22)	39 (69)	20 (92)	17 (180)	28 (220)	45 (229)
Muslim	9 (11)	43 (14)	20 (10)	28 (54)	19 (84)	27 (97)	62 (13)	53 (15)	44 (9)
Primary	2 (41)	13 (39)	0 (10)	21 (14)	32 (19)	26 (19)	11 (295)	15 (176)	32 (53)
Middle	4 (115)	3 (87)	0 (26)	9 (43)	15 (34)	16 (36)	7 (59)	9 (47)	10 (10)
More	0 (8)	0 (22)	0 (13)				5 (21)	4 (48)	4 (27)
Religion[c]									
Muslim	7 (55)	22 (69)	18 (54)	25 (320)	26 (168)	29 (42)	28 (120)	39 (168)	56 (118)
Traditional	4 (67)	6 (87)	8 (56)	…	…	…	50 (4)	60 (5)	67 (12)
Sect	4 (48)	4 (66)	14 (37)				12 (85)	9 (76)	38 (39)
Protestant	2 (177)	6 (212)	5 (92)	0 (22)	0 (24)	0 (12)	9 (165)	12 (139)	27 (99)
Catholic	10 (94)	6 (69)	10 (31)				7 (195)	8 (111)	21 (56)

145

TABLE 5.2 (continued)
Proportion in Polygynous Marriages, by Country, Age, Sex, and Socioeconomic Background[a]

FEMALES	Ghana			Gambia			Nigeria		
	15–34	35–49	35+	15–34	35–49	35+	15–34	35–49	35+
Occupation									
Housewife	4(228)	8(157)	14(59)	21(108)	29(174)	26(196)	12(407)	17(245)	28(81)
Commerce	6(174)	11(267)	12(174)	0(6)	15(13)	16(25)	19(113)	31(181)	46(215)
Manual	9(36)	5(59)	7(29)	25(4)	20(5)	8(12)	0(34)	0(31)	33(15)
Nonmanual	0(7)	0(26)	0(10)	11(18)	0(14)	0(13)	9(23)	6(48)	5(20)
Urbanization[d]									
Rural	7(256)	10(274)	14(133)	29(34)	36(78)	25(57)	10(212)	14(154)	27(67)
Mixed	4(85)	4(94)	19(32)	0(2)	20(5)	0(1)	8(51)	13(55)	26(35)
Urban	3(102)	10(138)	8(82)	18(6)	25(20)	21(14)	12(299)	20(208)	32(122)
Here	NA	NA	NA	16(94)	18(101)	22(172)	21(117)	36(91)	58(108)

[a]Numbers in parentheses are bases for percentages.

[b]Traditional includes a substantial number of "none" in Ghana. Most non-Muslims in The Gambia are Catholic.

[c]Includes supervisors and members of the uniformed services.

[d]Size of places where R grew up and came from. Urban = 2500 in The Gambia, 10,000 in Ghana, and 20,000 in Nigeria. Those who grew up in Tema or Ashaiman are counted as rural, as they were villages until recently.

146

which are less developed than the coastal belt. Almost half of the Yoruba are Muslim, but other southern groups have relatively low proportions of Muslims.

Given their relative animosity to polygyny, it was expected that, among Christians, Catholics would have the lowest incidence of polygyny and members of some of the indigenous sects the highest. However, while this was evident to a certain extent in Nigeria, it was not apparent in Ghana. No polygyny at all was found among the Gambian Christians interviewed. They are such a small minority that it is probably easier there than else- where to enforce monogamy as a distinctive characteristic. In Ghana, finer distinctions based on individual churches (see Aryee 1967, p. 104) show that certain sects have higher rates than Muslims, but differences between Catholics and most of the Christian Council churches are small.

Therefore, the assumption that the spread of education and Chris- tianity will rapidly cut down the incidence of polygyny in African societies must be questioned. It may do so among peoples with relatively low levels of polygyny in the past and, to a lesser extent, in communities which convert as a group to Christianity, but the high level of education needed for a large-scale shift in male attitudes, especially among Muslims, suggests that the decline in polygyny rates will of necessity be very slow. It should be noted that a fifth of the Nigerian men over 50 who had at least four years of secondary school (a high level of education for their generation) had more than one wife.

The effects of socioeconomic position and urbanization are similarly difficult to separate from education, since people who hold good jobs are likely to be better educated than those in unskilled occupations. Never- theless, the possibility that there are additional effects from these in- fluences needs to be examined.

On the basis of studies in Abidjan, Clignet and Sween (1969) argue that urbanization is much less effective in lowering polygyny rates in some groups than in others. Peoples who have traditionally had low rates of polygyny show more decline with urbanization than other groups for whom polygyny is culturally more important. Whereas education and the high-status occupations to which it gives access are expected to lower rates of polygyny, the most successful members of highly polygynous groups may use their increased resources in traditional ways, by taking additional wives and seeking local leadership roles. Members of the urban population who are the least touched by "modern" forces (illiterates who continue to practice primary occupations such as farming or fishing or who rely on jobs as unskilled laborers) could also be expected to maintain an attraction to polygyny as a symbol of success and to take a second wife if they can manage it. It was found that the men in the middle (with moder- ate incomes and education) are most likely to be monogamous, as eco- nomic stringency reinforces pressures for value change.

These data do not support these hypotheses, though perhaps further controls are needed for an adequate test. There is some evidence that men in commercial occupations (who tend to have relatively little education but, by the time they are 50, enough money for a second wife) are most attracted to polygyny, but this is certainly influenced by the relatively high proportion of Muslims in commerce. Differences between men in other occupations are generally small and not consistent from one age group to another. Professional and administrative occupations are certainly not a bar to polygyny, but the rates of men in these occupations are neither consistently high nor low. The same is true of men in primary and unskilled occupations; only Nigerians over 50 have notably high rates.

Insofar as polygyny may appeal to women traders because it frees them from exclusive responsibility for housekeeping and child care, it was expected that they would be overrepresented among women in polygynous marriages. This is the case in Nigeria, but in Ghana traders and housewives are about equally likely to have polygynous husbands. Pressure on Muslims who can afford it to keep their wives in seclusion means that Gambian women in polygynous marriages are housewives more often than traders; this is much less true in southern Nigeria because of the general acceptance of trading as a female occupation. The low proportion of women doing nonmanual work who have polygynous marriages is a direct result of the education needed for such jobs, but their ability to hold nonmanual jobs probably makes it easier for them than for women of equal education who are not participating in the labor force to enforce monogamy on their husbands.[1] If an educated woman wants a monogamous marriage but only a small family, she may encourage her husband to take an outside wife. This accommodation to male values is fairly common in Lagos (S. Barnes, personal communication).

Where urban experience affects polygyny rates, it appears to increase them. Growing up in a town or city seems to make little difference; the relatively high rates for Nigerian nonmigrants are due to Abeokuta polygynists, who are often Muslims with low levels of education. Men and women in all age categories who have lived in the Gambian or Nigerian towns more than ten years are slightly more likely than newer arrivals to be polygynous. While most of these differences are small, their consistency suggests that, if anything, urban residence tends to increase rather than decrease the incidence of polygyny. This supports Clignet and Sween's finding (1969, p. 130) that several Ivorian cities have higher rates than their hinterlands. Urban life provides a better economic position than farming, and some residents use this to support polygyny.

In summary, these data indicate that polygyny will continue to be an important aspect of marriage in African cities, though more so in Nigeria and The Gambia than in Ghana. Education and Christianity have made a mark, but the traditional value remains remarkably strong. As long as economic conditions permit it and women do not strongly object, older men will continue to demonstrate their success in life by taking second wives, and will attract prestige by so doing.

Interethnic Marriage

Marriage between peoples of differing ethnic background may be an index of interethnic tolerance or merely of opportunity. Neighboring people may intermarry because cultural barriers between them are minimal or because there is a good deal of social mixing, but they may intermarry on a small scale in spite of substantial cultural and social barriers against it. Some peoples place much more emphasis on endogamous marriage than others, but even for those who accept it exogamy is likely to be greater among migrants, especially if they are in a minority and far from home, than among people who stay within their own area.

Parents often favor marriage within the local community for pragmatic as well as ethnocentric reasons. They think that marriage will be more likely to last if both parties have similar backgrounds and expectations and if the arrangements are made between families as well as between the two individuals. In addition, they fear that children who marry out will lose interest and fail to provide for them, that they will be expected to make long and expensive journeys to attend the funerals of affines, or that because of different inheritance patterns the children will not belong to any lineage or people. Therefore, they put considerable pressure on migrant children to choose spouses known to them, and interethnic marriage remains relatively rare. It tends to be more common among Muslims than among Christians, as for many Muslims Islam is seen as superceding ethnicity (Salamone 1975).

Table 5.3 shows that interethnic marriage is, as expected, most common in The Gambia and least common in Nigeria. Subgroup intermarriage was measured for the Ga and Akan in Ghana and the Igbo, Katab, Hausa/ Fulani,[2] Urhobo, and Yoruba in Nigeria. As for intermarriage of more inclusive groups, subgroup intermarriage is slightly more common in Tema and Ashaiman than in Kakuri or Ajegunle, but it appears to be most common among residents of provincial towns. This is partly due to the more accurate reporting, but it also seems likely that spouses in interethnic marriages are seldom taken to provincial towns because they feel too isolated in them and that barriers to subgroup intermarriage are lower in such towns than in more heterogeneous places. In the latter, social pressure is for endogamy, and those who are willing to cross subgroup boundaries feel that they can choose their spouses freely.

The effect of distance and majority/minority position on propensity to marry out can be measured by comparing various ethnic groups in the same town and the same group in different towns. Long-distance migrants

TABLE 5.3
Interethnic Marriages, by Town (Percentages)

Town	Ethnic Groups	Including Subgroups	Number of Marriages[a]
Banjul	27	...	249
Serekunda	21	...	222
Tema	14	23	394
Ashaiman 1968	15	20	337
Ashaiman 1970	13	20	238
Kakuri	9	11	326
Ajegunle	4	8	451
Abeokuta	0	15	262
Aba	1	10	299

[a]Only those where the spouses were coresident have been included.

were expected to marry out more than migrants from nearby, as the latter could more easily find wives at home or among the more numerous women of their own group in town. For the same reasons of propinquity and choice, members of minority groups could be expected to have more exogamous marriages than people belonging to the local majority. These hypotheses are generally upheld, though there are some exceptions. In The Gambia, the Wollof, Mandinka, and Creole or Aku people are more endogamous than people who contribute smaller proportions of the population. (The Creole are distinguished by Christianity in a largely Muslim society, which should inhibit exogamy even though they are a minority.) With the exception of southern Nigerians and Hausa (who have about average levels of exogamy), aliens in the Ghanaian towns are more likely to marry out than Ghanaians. However, the Ga and Akan make up much of the difference through subgroup intermarriage.

During the early period of migration to towns, migrants probably married local women more frequently then they do today. Ga women in Tema and Ashaiman have only slightly higher out-marriage than other southern Ghanaians, and only two Yoruba women in the Ajegunle sample had married non-Yoruba. The highest rates in Kakuri are for the Ketab and Igbo; they contribute only 8 percent of marriages, but one-third of inter-ethnic marriages. The latter are less represented and from a longer distance than the former, but both are small minorities in Kakuri. The highest rates in Ajegunle are for the Edo and Efik, each three times the average for the town. Both are minorities from ethnically plural states, but other peoples from the same states show considerably lower rates, so their prominence may be an accident of sampling.

Levels of exogamy can be compared for members of the three largest Nigerian ethnic groups in several towns. Both the Yoruba and the Hausa/

Fulani have higher rates of interethnic marriage in Ghana than in Nigeria and higher in Kakuri than in Ajegunle, though subgroup exogamy in Ajegunle brings the Yoruba rate there up to the Kakuri level. Thus, these two peoples appear most likely to marry out when they are far from home and in a minority position; the ethnic competitiveness of Ajegunle seems to inhibit intermarriage among both strangers and locals. The numbers of Igbo in Ghana and Kakuri are small, decreasing the reliability of the figures. However, the finding that about one Igbo marriage in twelve in Ghana and Ajegunle compared to a quarter of those in Kakuri was interethnic suggests that insecure situations promote exogamy. Those who stayed in the north in spite of the troubles or went there soon after the war may have been more likely than other Igbo to marry exogamously, either because they lacked common prejudices or as a form of security.

There are no observable cultural preferences among those who marry out; except for differential opportunity due to numbers in town or growing up in town, choice appears to be random. A few polygynous men have one wife belonging to another group; others have no wife of their own group.

An examination of the education and occupation of spouses in interethnic marriages suggests that in most towns they are a fair cross section of married individuals. The exception is Ajegunle, where nearly two-fifths of the husbands in such marriages were in the uniformed services and a third had at least four years of secondary school. There appear to be stronger barriers to interethnic marriage in Ajegunle than elsewhere, probably related to the position of Lagos as the center of ethnic competition for national resources. In such a situation, the people who can withstand social pressure best are probably those who are often transferred (making for looser ties to kin and friends) and the well-educated (who have secure employment and can pay their own marriage expenses). In other towns, especially in The Gambia, where interethnic marriage is more acceptable, people at all social levels feel free to choose spouses on other grounds. In several Gambian ethnic groups, over half of the marriages were exogamous.

Effect on Social Life

Marital status affects social life through community expectations about the behavior of single and married men and women and because of the demands a family makes on one's time. Young people tend to have more time (and sometimes money) to spend on recreation than older, married people, though unmarried women are often watched by their families to ensure that they avoid trouble and make satisfactory matches (if, indeed, they are allowed to come to town before marriage). Married men and women usually spend more time than the unmarried with other members of their household; the women have cooking and washing to do, and many men spend some of their spare time watching and playing with their young children, especially on weekends. While this means they have less time for frends, they may have a wider circle of friends than young newcomers if they have spent several years in town. Therefore, it was expected that the married would have more friends, but see them less often, than the unmarried.

The position of men and women not living with their spouses (hereafter referred to as "the separated" to distinguish them from cohabiting married people) may be somewhat ambiguous. Insofar as they are known by the community to be married, certain behavior might be expected. This effect may be minimal, given urban anonymity, but age (in a society where marriage and adulthood are considered synonymous) and, especially for women, the presence of children (though these might have been conceived outside marriage) would lead neighbors to expect individuals to behave as if they were married. A man living without his wife and children may choose to spend his time enjoying himself with friends or working to speed his return home; he may make few friends in town because he goes home every weekend. Long-distance migrants to southern Ghana often leave their wives behind and have little money for recreation because they are mostly unskilled laborers. Many migrants to Aba, on the other hand, are close enough to maintain regular contact with home and thus have little need to make new friends, though they usually have friends from home living nearby.

The situation of a married woman whose husband lives elsewhere is difficult to assess without knowing where her husband is, the reason he is there, and the frequency of his visits. If he lives nearby (as in a polygynous marriage or in the customary Ga arrangement of separate sex households), the separation is more apparent than real, the result of using data collection methods designed for another culture. However, the spouses are more autonomous, especially in their use of time, than they would be if they shared the same household.

A second pattern involves one or more wives left behind while the husband carries on a business elsewhere, sometimes with another wife and children in another town. If this type of household is large, the wife who takes charge may have considerable authority and, from the social point of view, may be one of the neighborhood's more important married women, whose advice is sought by younger women. A man who is transferred by his employer may also leave his wife behind, but this appears to be less common, perhaps because a businessman can spend part of the year in each town whereas an employee on transfer usually assumes that he will spend several years in the new place. Unless the wife does not want to leave her own work, she will probably expect to move when her husband is transferred.

A third pattern, less less common than the others, is the wife who comes to town to trade, leaving her husband and children behind in the village. She is probably a short-distance migrant who goes home frequently for supplies as well as to visit her family, and she may plan only a short stay in town. Establishing an active social life in town may be unimportant, but she will probably make friends with other traders.

The questions on social contacts provide data with which to compare the size and range of social networks of the single (including, for this discussion, the widowed and divorced) and separated respondents with those who are married and living with their spouses. Although there is considerable variance, on the whole the separated reported knowing somewhat fewer people, had a somewhat narrower set of regular contacts, and were more likely than either the single or the married to report having no friends or only one. The married tend to have a social life that differs more in quality than in quantity from that of the unmarried.

An early question asked the respondents, "Which do you think gets to know more people, a man (woman) who lives alone or one who is living with his wife (her husband)?" It was expected that people would tend to say that their own state gave more opportunities but, beyond this, there would be some agreement that single people have the advantage. Both of these tendencies are present; there were more married people who said the single know more people than single respondents who gave the advantage to the married. The separated in Ghana and the Nigerian suburbs felt that you could know more people if you lived alone, but both sides were equally favored in The Gambia and those in the provincial towns gave the advantage to the married. In each case, the pattern was the same for both men and women, which indicates that there are real differences in the environment these towns provide.

Where there are large numbers of unattached adults, social life is probably centered around them; there are dances, football matches, and similar activities at which they can seek entertainment and make new acquaintances. Provincial towns, on the other hand, tend to have a much larger core of long-established, married residents whose lives are centered around their families (both nuclear and extended). In such a situation, separated individuals could feel more "married" and cut off from contacts common to this state.

Single people tend to emphasize the lack of outside control over their movements; they are free to come and go as they like. Some married men agree with this picture, suggesting that their wives keep closer track of them than they would prefer. For example, a married contractor pointed out, "A single person will have more friends because he can leave his house at any time and he can come back whenever he likes; in addition, he moves with a different type of people." A married clerk reported, "When one is single both male and female will be free to enter his house, but if married the wife might think and be suspicious." Although these societies are male-dominated, many married women appear to achieve a measure of ascendency in their households, at least in the popular stereotype.

However, there are advantages accruing to the married as well. Married people reported that they have a chance to know their spouse's kin and friends as well as their own, thus extending their networks. Ceremonies such as weddings and outdoorings (taking a newborn child out of the house for the first time), provide additional opportunities to meet people; the married are more likely than the unmarried to have formal parties.

Switching from generalizations about the community to personal experiences, we can examine the respondents' reports on the numbers of their friends, where they met them, how often they see them, and also on their less close contacts: the number of neighbors they know and the people with whom they frequently sit and talk. Some friendships continue after marriage, but about two-thirds of the respondents mentioned only friends of the same marital status as themselves. This is partly a question of age, but social expectations concerning the single and married states are sufficiently different that it is easier to have friends of the same marital status as oneself.

Single men in Ghana and The Gambia and single women in Nigeria and The Gambia are more likely to report three or more friends than the separated or married. For Nigerian men and Ghanaian women, the differences are small and/or favor the married over the single and the separated. At the other extreme, the separated in Nigeria and The Gambia are most likely to report that they have no friends or only one, which suggests that they have more tenuous contacts with the people around them than the single or married. For some, this is because they only plan a short stay; a long period spent in town would increase the pressure to bring their wives and children to town. However, the separated are as likely as the single or married to report meeting friends at work and elsewhere in town, so the majority are not rejecting urban contacts. True to expectation, the separated are as likely as the single (and in some towns more likely) to see their friends daily; it is often the married men and women who see their friends least often.

The evidence on the numbers of neighbors the respondents know well is also mixed, but overall suggests that the separated are the most isolated group. Similarly, when asked about frequent conversations with cotenants, neighbors, coworkers, and kin, the separated are most likely to show a narrow range of contacts, talking with people in only one of these categories. It is important to emphasize that the results on all these questions vary considerably from one town and country to another. While it appears that the single have the widest and most varied social life and the separated the least, on no measure is this unequivocally true for all the samples.

Marriage seems to result in a gradual shift in relationships with one's friends and neighbors, but age, socioeconomic position, and other factors to be discussed in the next chapter are also important. The absence of a spouse can mean that one cannot fully participate in the roles of the married even though one is no longer oriented toward single roles. This may result in a narrower social life, though in some situations and for many individuals it does not do so.

Children

Marriage in Africa is not considered complete without children; fertility rates remain high and there is often considerable pressure for the dissolution of childless marriages. Children are desired to continue the lineage, to provide support in old age, and to signify the sexual competence of the partners; all of these goals are as important today as in the past. The value of children to the kin group as a whole is demonstrated in the prevalence of fostering and the provision of school fees and other support for the children of close kin.

The incidence of children in the household (see Table 5.1) varies with the age of the household head and the importance of local provision of education. Young, unmarried migrants' households usually contain only adults, though occasionally a young sibling is sent to continue his education in town. Married couples generally prefer to have their children with them in town, though the children (with or without their mother) may spend months or even years at home if opportunities for schooling seem better there, if inflation makes food very expensive (as in Ghana in the 1970s), or to increase family solidarity and ensure that they are socialized into their hometown culture. Later in the life cycle, some children go off for secondary school or further education and most establish their own households after marriage; few are lucky enough to have a room in an urban family house available to them and not all of these want to continue to live with their parents.

Other children come into the household through fostering or as maids, nursegirls, and houseboys. Fostering is common in some parts of West Africa, though probably more among villagers than city dwellers. The latter are more likely to be foster parents than to give their own children to foster parents. In addition to solving the problem of what should be done with children if their parents die of if they are being neglected after a divorce and remarriage, fostering is also useful in reinforcing real and fictive kinship ties and in providing training in certain skills which cannot be given at home. Foster parents are expected to treat the child as their own, and often support him or her until marriage (Goody 1966, 1970; Schildkrout 1973). Children are usually sent to towns with the expectation that they will be educated or trained in specific skills such as trading crafts; the amount of formal education they receive probably varies with the closeness of their relationship to their guardians. In any case, they will be expected to help with household tasks.

Fostering should not be overemphasized; most of the children in urban households were living with one or both parents, and a majority of the respondents' children who were not living in the household were either with their other parent or married. At least 85 percent of the children in all the towns except Aba and Banjul and at least 70 percent in these towns were sons or daughters of the household head and/or his wife, and quite a few of the other children were living with a parent who was not the household head. (The most common cases are sisters and their children and grandchildren of the head.) Most of the children are closely related to the head, suggesting that pressure for urban fostering is mainly from a narrowly defined extended family. Children are more likely to be living with grandparents, uncles, or aunts in Ghana and The Gambia than in Nigeria, whereas children who are siblings of the head or his wife are more common in Nigeria and Ghana than in The Gambia; more distant relationships are rare in all towns.

It appears that Nigerian children are more often sent to their siblings in town to complete their schooling, whereas schooling is a less important reason for child migration to Tema or Ashaiman. Less than a seventh of the Nigerian "extra children" were under school age, compared to about two-fifths of those in Ghana and The Gambia; in the latter, half of the "extra children" were with their grandparents, usually as part of three- or four-generation households. However, Gambians are as likely as Nigerians to be continuing the education of extra children who are over 15 years old; the superior provision of postprimary education in the Banjul area (and in Lagos and Kaduna) continues to draw considerable numbers of adolescents to these towns. Migration for education is mainly a male phenomenon; girls must usually be satisfied with whatever education is available at home, though about 6 percent of the extra girls in Nigeria and The Gambia were over 15 and still at school.

Servants

Because servants have been almost unmentioned in the literature, it is useful to examine the background of those in the samples for information on patterns of recruitment. These data do not give a full picture of servants because members of the extended family are seldom identified as servants even though they have come to town for this purpose (girls) or are making themselves useful as a way of paying for their support while they attend school or search for employment (boys). Given their usefulness around the house, girls are more often sent to town as maids and baby nurses than as scholars, and are therefore less likely than boys to be living with kin.

Duodu's *The Gab Boys* (1967) describes a boy's reaction to finding himself a servant in town.

Three patterns of recruitment can be seen. Young people are taken on as servants on compassionate grounds, to provide training, and on a business basis, in which case being a servant is a career or job like any other.[3] There were far more servants in Aba than elsewhere (189, compared to 68 in the other Nigerian towns, 48 in Ghana, and 9 in The Gambia). Many families in Aba were repaying wartime debts by taking in the children of friends who faced economic difficulties in the postwar period, but they also were supporting young strangers to a rather surprising extent given the difficulty of the times. About two-thirds of the Aba servants were from the same town or village as the head or his wife, but a quarter were from elsewhere and had a different ethnic or subethnic identification. Two-thirds were between 10 and 19 years of age; most of the other girls were younger (one was only six), while most of the other houseboys were in their twenties.

Generally, the younger servants are most likely to come from the head's or his wife's hometown, but there are notable exceptions (in several towns) of children who appear to have been sent to work for strangers at a very early age. However, given the mobility of many families, there may be an extended family tie in these cases which was not recorded. The unusual circumstances in Aba are also evident in that 80 percent of the young men acting as servants had been to school, compared to less than half of the girls in Aba and both boys and girls in other Nigerian towns. The severe competition for employment in Aba made such jobs more acceptable than they would otherwise have been.

While Aba had about equal numbers of male and female servants, a large majority in the other towns were female. The age distribution was the same in all Nigerian towns; a quarter of the males but only 5 percent of the females were over age 20. The youngest was a "nursegirl" aged four in Kakuri. She was born in Kaduna and apparently had two infants in her charge. There were considerable differences in the origins of male and female servants in these towns. Three-quarters of the girls but only two-fifths of the boys shared the hometown and ethnic background of the head or his wife, while 44 percent of the boys but only 12 percent of the girls came from different places and ethnic stock.

The sex differentiation demonstrates the other two forms of servant status. Females are mainly recruited from home, and the contract tends to be based on some personal relationship between the employers and the parents (to whom the wages, if any, are often paid). Males in service are, on average, older. For them, service is but one type of unskilled employment in which they may make a career, whereas for girls such work stops when they marry. There was some evidence in Aba of girls following the male "job" pattern. This may become more common elsewhere if alternative opportunities for women to earn money (such as trading) become too crowded.

The distinction is even clearer in Ghana then in Nigeria. The male servants were mainly northerners or eastern Nigerians and two-thirds were over 15. Certain groups have a reputation for specializing in cook/ steward employment, whereas members of other groups (especially educated southern Ghanaians) look down on such jobs as beneath them. Female servants, like the males, have seldom been to school, but they are more likely than the males to come from southern villages. Some elite families have rural dependent families from which they have drawn servants over several generations (Oppong, personal communication); girls are sent to town between the ages of 10 and 14 to learn housekeeping and trading skills as a preparation for marriage and to earn money for marriage expenses. Two-thirds of the female servants in Tema were in this age category and none were over 19.

By the late 1970s, male career servants had almost disappeared in Ghana. Nigerians could make more money at home and northern Ghanaians found they could do better farming than in urban service jobs. Female school leavers tended to demand higher wages than most families could afford. Except in the highest-income households, therefore, a large proportion of servants were in the compassionate category, and most households had to do without them.

There were only nine servants in the Gambian samples, though many households could have afforded a servant. It is not clear whether some Banjul servants live out or whether these tasks are done by kin in extended families. However, many migrants who take employment as servants during the dry season had gone home to farm at the time the study was being done; it was reported that it is very difficult to keep servants during the farming season. All those identified as servants were illiterate females, mainly from Cassamance; all but one were Jola. This appears to be an extreme case of an ethnic monopoly, but a dry season sample is needed to confirm this.

About four-fifths of the male servants and half of the females in Tema were working for families in which the head of the household was in professional or administrative employment; the rest were about equally divided between heads in other white-collar, commercial, and manual work. This concentration in well-off families was much less evident in other towns, where less than a fifth of servants had employers in the professional/administrative category. This suggests that servants are often self-financing (their assistance with trading pays for their keep) and/or that many families of average or even below average income have servants because of pressures from home to take in young people who want to migrate to town. One steward, himself a household head, had a houseboy of his own.

Uses of a Windfall

An important component in the mythology of success in African towns is the windfall—the sudden acquisition of a lump sum which can be used for pressing needs or as capital for entrepreneurial ventures. It can provide the "take-off" for a migrant otherwise without opportunities, or a chance to pay off debts or to send home a significant sum and thus enhance one's prestige. The windfall may result from a tip (leading to successful speculation), a contact with someone in a position to exercise patronage, a large order for a small businessman, or a win at the pools. There is no evidence on how many or what sort of people actually get a windfall during their careers, but many can point to friends, neighbors, and"big men" who have been lucky in this way. The possibility of a windfall is thus taken seriously. It was used in the interviews as a measure of economic need and aspirations. The answers also provide an indication of the extent of money transfers on these occasions, especially between spouses and close kin. In this sense, the results can support or question other data on the strength of kinship and hometown ties.

Nigerian and Gambian respondents were asked, "If someone gave you £100 (local equivalent), how would you use it?" This was a relatively unimportant sum to some respondents, but for most was the equivalent of at least several months' income. The proposition was taken seriously, and the answers show something of the division of economic responsibility within the household and the economic ties with kin as well as the respondents' long-term aspirations and the use they make of ready cash. Table 5.4 allows comparison of Nigerians and Gambians of varying economic status. Nigerians are more interested in business ventures and paying school fees, whereas Gambians need money for food and clothing and put more emphasis on making gifts to kin, building houses, and accumulating savings than Nigerians.

Nearly half the Nigerians, compared to about a fifth of the Gambians, would use a windfall to increase their capital or equipment if they were already in business, to invest in a business of their own, or to help their wife or kin (usually their mother) with trading funds. While men who were already in business were most likely to give this response, the enthusiasm for sideline ventures was evident in the considerable number of Nigerian men and women in other occupations (from laborers to professionals) who would use a windfall as capital to increase their income. Not all would invest in trade or in the town. Craftsmen wanted to buy tools, sewing machines, and printing presses, an agricultural officer said he would spend it on his poultry farm, and several others would pay for farm equipment and labor.

Nigerian housewives were six times as likely as Gambian ones to aspire to trading if they could get capital to start. In addition, both male and

TABLE 5.4
Use of £L100 Windfall, by Country, Sex, and Income (Percentages)

	Nigeria						Gambia					
	Males			Females			Males			Females		
	£0-199	200-499	500+	None	£1-199	200+	£0-199	200-499	500+	None	£1-199	200+
Business, investment												
Self	61	38	21	60	58	25	29	24	16	10	41	19
Spouse	3	8	5	4	0	2	0	0	1	0	0	0
Kin	1	1	0	4	1	2	0	0	1	0	0	0
Household												
Food, clothing	7	4	2	17	18	12	18	19	17	45	22	25
Consumer goods	3	6	7	8	3	2	6	6	11	15	4	6
Other	2	4	5	0	2	0	10	4	6	10	0	8
Spouse, n.e.c.	0	0	0	9	6	16	0	0	3	10	4	6
Give to Kin												
Send home[a]	7	10	4	13	12	11	22	13	11	40	22	22
Schooling												
Children	7	8	16	4	6	5	0	2	4	0	4	0
Self	2	5	0	2	2	2	0	0	2	0	0	0
Siblings	2	1	3	0	0	4	0	0	0	0	0	0
Save	10	16	16	9	8	18	18	33	25	5	15	28
Housing, land	11	11	11	0	8	4	22	24	18	10	0	6
Other	6	5	2	2	4	4	4	2	6	0	4	3
N[b]	322	213	94	53	107	56	49	84	105	20	27	36

[a]School fees are listed separately below.
[b]As multiple answers were common, no total percentage is given.

female Nigerians were willing to provide trading capital for their spouses, mother, or brothers (in order to make the latter independent of further assistance). The independence provided by £100 would allow several respondents to return home. An Igbo watchman in Ajegunle said he would "rush home and start trading" and an unemployed school certificate holder had the same idea. A Senegalese woman in Banjul was saving to trade at home and thought the windfall would make it possible. Some, who thought £100 would allow them to "open a very big store and sell something" or "buy a lorry to give out for hire" appeared to have only a vague idea of the amount of capital needed for such ventures, but many others (especially Gambians) would add the money to long-term savings for the object of their aspirations: a lorry, a house, and so on.

Working women often take a major responsibility for providing food and clothing for themselves and their children as their contribution to domestic finances. Hence, a sixth of Nigerian women would spend a windfall on daily needs of the household. The importance of the food category for Gambian men at all economic levels is due to the high price of rice at the time of the survey; many men said they would buy several bags of rice for their wives and/or kin.

Consumer goods, on the other hand, tend to be seen as the duty of the husband to provide, though several women saw the windfall as a chance to get something they wanted. An interesting division can be seen in this. Though the differences are small, in both countries housewives (with no income) were slightly more likely than working women or the poorest men to mention consumer goods, men earning more than £200 per year were next, and women with their own income were least likely to do so. This suggests that women who can afford to buy consumer goods for the home tend to let their husbands assume this duty if possible, while women on more constrained budgets would use an unexpected windfall to satisfy a long-felt want. The consumer goods desired vary with country and level of income. Nigerians, especially at lower income levels, would buy furniture, whereas several Gambians aspired to mobylettes or cars and furniture was seldom mentioned.

The "other" category under "household" often means an ambiguous response. The money would be spent to take care of family affairs or to pay off debts. It was not always clear whether family affairs referred to the nuclear or extended family, so this probably includes some sending money home. Quite a few women would just give the money to their husbands and let them decide what to do with it; this was most common in Aba. As one women trader there put it, "I would hand it to my husband, and it will be a big relief." This type of response was more characteristic of well-educated women (such as teachers) than of illiterates in Nigeria, but in The Gambia illiterate women were less likely than educated ones to have the confidence to make their own decision. This difference is probably due to the active trading careers of so many illiterate Nigerian women, which encourage them to see money as their own; Gambian women are less likely to have such experience.

Although actual gifts to kin will be discussed more fully below, this question provides an opportunity to see how often relatives are remembered in times of good fortune. When anyone specific was mentioned, it was usually the respondents' parents, as support for parents is seen as a very important duty. Children contribute to improvements to the family farm as well as to family wedding and funeral expenses and their siblings' school fees. Women are more generous in intention than men, with the smallest differences between the sexes for those in moderate circumstances; the wealthiest remembered their kin slightly less often, but the differences are very small. Gambians with the lowest income were more willing to share than those who were better-off, perhaps because under normal circumstances they seldom have money to give.

The expenses of schooling include school fees, the provision of books and uniforms and, among personal aspirations for a few, the expense of a trip overseas. All this is of more concern to Nigerians than to Gambians, especially to the relatively affluent Nigerian men who expect to provide private nursery and primary schooling for their children as well as pay secondary school fees. There is little private schooling in The Gambia and fees for state schools are low. Although school fees are usually seen as the father's responsibility, mothers are often willing to help to ensure that their children get as far as possible.

Respondents concerned about further schooling for themselves tended to be recent school leavers and either unemployed or in routine clerical work, though an illiterate trader aspired to an adult education course and a policeman with a school certificate hoped to go overseas. A young Urhobo man in Ajegunle, who obviously felt that he had left school too early, said he would "go immediately to any school, pay fees, and start." Relatively few men specifically allocated money for their siblings' schooling, but some of those who said they would send money home may have known it would be used for this purpose.

Many of the people who said they would save the windfall also said what they were saving for: a house, further studies, a vehicle, a business. The relatively large number of people at all income levels who think in terms of savings suggests less desperation than some commentators on urban life in developing countries assume and also an optimism and interest in planning for the future even though present life is a struggle. It is important to note that the poor are as likely to save as the better-off. The nest egg may be used for daily needs over a long period (especially by the unemployed) or for emergencies, but at least their immediate needs (or debts) are not so great that any money coming in is spent immediately. Men are more likely to save than women, which owes more to differences in family responsibilities and long-term aspirations than to differences in relative access to cash; women may find it easier than men to satisfy their wants for £100.

As with savings, there is no income differential in the proportion who would put the money toward housing. Saving for a house is usually a long-term process; rather than saving in a bank, some men buy bricks, cement, or aluminum sheets for the roof and store them until they have accumulated enough to call in a builder. Many houses are built a room at a time, or a wall at a time, which makes it possible for the poor to finance a house over a considerable period. Several elderly men would use the money to repair their houses. Younger men in The Gambia often thought in terms of buying plots of land in Serekunda or Kombo St. Mary as the first step to homes of their own. Women were less concerned with housing, which is usually the husband's responsibility, but some women hoped to acquire houses to rent out.

The "other" category includes fifteen men who would use the money to marry, five young people who felt that bribes would help them find employment, four women who would seek medical help for infertility, and several people who would tithe or give some of the money to charity. Fourteen men, at various economic levels, would spend at least part of the money on recreation; a Methodist factory worker said he would enjoy half of it, "because man can join the dust at any time."

Kinship

The general assumption of many studies of modernization has been that with increasing urbanization and industrialization kinship will become less important as a source of social and economic support or, at least, that extended kinship networks will be contracted and the nuclear family emphasized (see Goode 1963). Social and geographical mobility tends to separate members of extended families and give them conflicting interests because of their differing financial resources. Kin are often not immediately available when help is needed, so that the support they do give is more often for long-term commitments than for short-term crises (Litwak and Szelenyi 1969).

Reports from Rhodesia (Lukhero in Lloyd 1966; Weinrich 1976) have shown a decline in kinship networks, at least among the more successful Africans, but in other parts of Africa kinship continues to be a strong bond for people at all social levels (see Pfeffermann 1968, p. 223 for Dakar; Parkin 1969 for Kampala; Oppong 1974 for Accra; Ross 1975, p. 48 for Nairobi; and Aronson 1978, for Ibadan). On the whole, there has been much more research on the links between migrants in town and their kin at home than on the relationships between kin living in the same town.

Since the latter are available in crises, these contacts are a more important test of the theory.

Contacts with kin may be somewhat less frequent and involve fewer people in town than in a village, but nevertheless they are a regular feature of life for the majority of urban residents.[4] Those who have no kin living in the same town (which is most likely in new towns) may have some in a nearby town and will probably be visited from time to time by kin from home. Because a large majority of Ghanaians and Nigerians intend to retire eventually to their hometowns, their kin and people from home remain a salient reference group; visits and messages are exchanged and many who have little money to spare help to support parents, siblings, and even more distant elderly kin at home, either regularly or in emergencies.

The various measures of kinship contact have different implications for the individuals concerned and for the society. Frequent visiting in town suggests a high level of social as well as economic support and a continuance of customary patterns in an urban environment.[5] The prevalence of illiteracy and the uncertainty of letters sent through the mail increase the importance of visits for the maintenance of kinship ties. Visits to kin in town can be an important means of socialization for intending migrants; visits home imply a continuing commitment to the village and its welfare as well as to the kin who live there. Village leaders often stress the importance of the regular return of migrants and put considerable effort into insuring that major public holidays are spent at home (Kaufert 1976).

Income transfers are the least personal source of kinship contacts, but they symbolize a continuing concern on both sides. The amounts remitted to individual families may be small, but they represent an improved standard of living for large numbers of Africans who never leave home and greater equality of income between urban and rural areas than is evident in official figures on earnings. Although interest has mainly centered on the money migrants send home, students and the unemployed often receive money from home which makes their continued stay in town possible. Their later commitment to sending money home is often a repayment of help received as well as a recognition of customary responsibility.

Finally, the continued importance of kinship ties is an important factor inhibiting the development of social classes in the Marxian sense in West Africa. As Jahoda put it (in Lloyd 1966, p. 202), "The sense of loyalty to both tribe and kin, as well as feelings of dependence on these, remain sufficiently strong to ensure the persistence of frequent personal contacts ... among people of widely disparate status levels." Blood ties, through which various forms of aid are exchanged for status and prestige in the community, are the basis of meaningful social relationships between rich and poor, successful and unsuccessful.

Women tend to have less contact with relatives outside the household than men. First, they are less likely to have any. A man migrates to the place where he has kin to help him; his wife may have none in that town. Second, they have less time available for visiting. Many are full-time traders, yet are responsible for housekeeping, meals, and child care. Finally, their mobility is somewhat limited. This is partly a question of time, but also of custom.

It was expected that women would have less spatial mobility in town but visit home more often than their husbands because few are tied to wage employment. However, only in Ghana are women more frequent visitors at home than men, and this is because they more often come from nearby. Women find it more difficult to send money home, as few have sizeable incomes, and most rely on their husbands to make the decision to return home. Thus, men's contacts with their kin have more important behavioral and attitudinal implications than those of their wives; women's contacts are more purely social.

Urban Visiting Patterns

Three sets of questions were used to measure contacts with kin in the urban environment. Respondents were first asked if they had any relatives living in the town and, if so, where they lived, how often they saw them, and what they did on these occasions (talk, share meals, and so on). They were then asked if anyone from their family had come to visit them during a specified period and, if so, where they had come from and whether any gifts had been exchanged. Gambian respondents were also asked if there was anyone living with them six months earlier who was not there now. This was designed as a measure of the level and nature of dry season migration to the Banjul area. In order to get a more precise view of the amount of visiting, respondents were then asked about anyone who had spent a night with them in the last two weeks (Nigeria and The Gambia only).

Differences between towns are related to the size of the town, the distance migrants have come, and their relative security (see Table 5.5). Contrasts between towns illustrate the effects of these factors. The proportion of Abeokuta residents recorded as having no kin in town is deceptive, as many live in family compounds; they have no kin living elsewhere in town because of the high level of out-migration. Most in-migrants are from nearby towns and villages, and many Abeokuta families have kin in these villages (Osborne 1973). In contrast, most migrants to Ajegunle come from more than 180 miles away. Only a fifth of the Ajegunle residents who were interviewed had no kin in the Lagos metropolitan area, but they see less of them, and have fewer contacts with kin left at home, than Abeokuta residents.

Distance of migration is probably the most important cause of these differences, but the size of Lagos, the state of its transportation system,

TABLE 5.5
Visits with Kin, by Town and Sex (Percentages)

	Ghana				Gambia				Nigeria							
	Ashaiman		Tema		Banjul		Serekunda		Aba		Abeokuta		Ajegunle		Kakuri	
	M	F	M	F	M	F	M	F	M	F	M	F	M	F	M	F
Visits kin in town																
Daily	17	14	21	13	31	35	38	42	22	13	22	14	10	11	27	20
1–6 times per week	13	13	23	24	42	47	46	28	49	42	40	33	56	43	35	33
Less often	6	6	3	6	9	8	5	15	12	9	7	11	15	24	10	16
No kin in town	64	67	53	57	18	10	11	15	17	36	32	42	19	22	28	31
Total	100	100	100	100	100	100	100	100	100	100	100	100	100	100	100	100
N	314	140	204	150	152	51	152	53	152	55	138	64	172	55	161	45
Visits by kin from elsewhere																
Within two weeks	...	...	...	...	18	16	22	26	24	27	27	34	10	18	22	13
Longer period[a]	37	37	34	38	31	29	23	23	78	75	64	61	40	44	58	53
N	316	144	209	151	152	51	152	53	152	55	138	64	172	55	161	45
Visits home[b]																
Less than 1 year	35	33	45	36	60	65	54	68	12	24	15	33	49	67	45	64
1–3 per year	50	42	27	25	28	30	38	32	44	58	46	56	47	31	52	36
More often	15	25	28	39	12	5	8	0	44	18	39	11	4	2	3	0
Total	100	100	100	100	100	100	100	100	100	100	100	100	100	100	100	100
N	283	109	194	139	75	20	82	19	146	51	59	36	165	51	147	39

[a] Ghana: the past year; Gambia: any kin living in the household six months before who was not there at the time of the interview; Nigeria: the last six months.

[b] Indigenes and migrants who arrived in the year of the study and have not yet gone home have been omitted.

and the cost of living are also relevant. The ecological structure of Abeokuta and the prevalence of cheap taxis mean that kin anywhere in town can be reached in about fifteen minutes; in Lagos, it could take more than two hours and so is best left to an occasional weekend. The average income of respondents in Abeokuta and Ajegunle was similar, but the cost of living is considerably higher in Lagos; this leaves less for traveling or sending to kin at home.

Far fewer respondents in Tema and Ashaiman than in the other towns had kin nearby whom they could visit, though quite a few had relatives in Accra, only twelve miles away. There seemed to be a higher level of conscious rejection of kinship ties among Tema residents than elsewhere. Although most were southern Ghanaians who could get home easily, only three-fifths went home at least once a year; they were also less likely than residents of other towns to send money home, though most had relatively well-paid employment. This may be partly self-selection of middle-school leavers seeking "modern" industrial employment without the pressures of coresident elder kin.

Because most of the Tema housing goes to the more established workers, whose jobs are relatively safe, they are less dependent on kin for help in emergencies. They can thus afford to pay less attention to kinship networks, at least until they reach middle age, than migrants who are less confident of a regular income. Ashaiman residents tend to be somewhat older, less secure (more often in self-employment or in lower wage categories), and more often from a long distance; although only a third have kin in town, they see them as often as Tema residents, and the men in Ashaiman are more likely to visit home at least once a year and to send money home. Thus, kinship contacts are a more important part of social life in Ashaiman than in Tema.

The small-scale, relaxed nature of urban life and lack of salience of ethnic boundaries make it possible for even first-generation migrants to the Gambian towns to transfer their allegiance and begin to think of Banjul or Serekunda as home. The result is lowered contacts with kin at home, though contacts in town are maintained at the high level expected of a small town. Only a fifth of the respondents who did not intend to return eventually visited home more than once a year, though the majority sent money at least occasionally.

With the exception of a few provincial migrants (especially in Aba) whose villages are so near that they can visit home or be visited weekly, most of the relatives seen by urban residents are also urban dwellers. The majority of people living in the Nigerian and Gambian towns have kin living in the same town, and most see these relatives at least occasionally. There is no evidence that certain categories of migrants are either avoiding their kin or centering their social life around a kinship network. For instance, clerical workers and professionals appear to see as much of their kin as the unskilled.[6]

Contrary to expectation, housewives do not see their kin more often than women who are either trading or in wage employment. Although the latter have less time, they probably have more freedom of movement than housewives. Male newcomers to Gambian and Nigerian suburban towns tend to see their kin more often than migrants who have spent more than ten years in town, which may indicate a greater dependence on relatives during the early years. This should be less important in provincial towns because home is closer and the change between life at home and in town is relatively minor.

Given the considerable variance between towns in visiting patterns, it seems reasonable to assume that residents are about equally motivated to associate with their kin (regardless of age, education, place of origin, or occupation) and that variance in the frequency of visits is largely due to differences in opportunity and the nature of the kinship tie: the number of kin living in town, their distance, the closeness of the relationship, and how well individuals get on with one another. A person with several relatives in town is more likely to see at least one of them often than a person who has only one uncle living at a distance.

Distance affects the frequency of visits more than either the sex or the respondent or the closeness of the kinship tie. In every town kin living at a distance are seldom seen daily and at least a quarter of them are seen less than once a week. Distance makes somewhat more difference to women than to men, because the latter sometimes work in other parts of town and can see kin as part of the daily round. Women tend to work fairly near where they live and seldom get to other parts of the town or, in the case of suburbs, into the city. Table 5.6 shows that women see both nearby and distant kin slightly less often than men; the differences are small but consistent.

The size of the town is also a factor, partly because of the way distance has been defined (town/suburb). In small towns such as Kakuri, Ashaiman, and those in The Gambia, over two-fifths of the men and a third of the women who have kin anywhere in town see at least one of them every day. This declines to about a fifth of men and women in the Nigerian provincial towns and a seventh in Ajegunle.

The relatively large size of Ajegunle and Aba may be partly responsible for the low proportion of nearby kin who are seen daily, but conditions of employment are also important. Many Ajegunle workers spent more than two hours each day getting to and from work, and thus had time for visiting even nearby kin only on weekends. Aba males were more likely than men in other towns to be self-employed, and many were trying to establish businesses in the face of severe competition. Long hours of waiting for customers apparently left many of them with little visiting time; when they

Frequency of Visits with Urban Kin, by Sex, Location, Distance from Kin, and Nature of Tie (Percentages)

	Males					Females				
	Daily	1–6/ Week	Less Often	Total	N	Daily	1–6/ Week	Less Often	Total	N
Ghana										
Near: Nuclear[a]	56	40	4	100	137	64	33	3	100	58
Extended	35	50	15	100	144	49	46	5	100	41
Far: Nuclear	11	62	27	100	56	6	60	34	100	71
Extended	3	60	37	100	67	6	49	45	100	47
Gambia										
Near: Nuclear	52	43	5	100	194	31	58	11	100	78
Extended	41	49	10	100	177	29	61	10	100	59
Far: Nuclear	4	67	29	100	207	3	63	34	100	32
Extended	3	66	31	100	181	4	27	69	100	26
Nigeria										
Provincial Towns										
Nuclear	20	67	13	100	281	14	54	32	100	117
Extended	21	59	20	100	294	24	48	28	100	58
Kakuri										
Near: Nuclear	61	33	6	100	83	44	44	12	100	16
Extended	45	50	5	100	20	33	33	33	99	6
Far: Nuclear	9	64	27	100	158	3	55	42	100	31
Extended	13	67	20	100	39	18	55	27	100	11
Ajegunle										
Near: Nuclear	12	78	10	100	178	23	52	25	100	44
Extended	20	66	14	100	51	6	75	19	100	16
Far: Nuclear	2	48	50	100	117	2	28	70	100	43
Extended	2	27	71	100	66	0	50	50	100	12

[a]Near = residence in the same town as respondent; far = residence in a nearby town or suburb. Since few provincial kin were clearly living far away, all were classed as near. Nuclear = parents, siblings, spouses, and children.

could get away they went home. In Kakuri, on the other hand, most workers were free for the day at 2:00 P.M., which left considerable time for visiting within their small town or in Kaduna. They were twice as likely as men in Ajegunle to visit distant kin at least once a week.

It was expected that women would show closer ties to their nuclear families than men and that both men and women would visit parents and siblings more often than more distantly related kin. However, the difference in average frequency of visits between nuclear and extended family members varies from one town to another. Personal preference may be as important as the degree of kinship. An uncle or cousin with whom one gets on well may be visited more often, regardless of where he lives, than a brother with whom one has little sympathy or who is continually asking for money. Kinship roles are much less specific than in the past, and any member of the extended family may be chosen.

Except in Kakuri, most parents are visited at least once a week regardless of where in the urban area they are living. Siblings are more often visited daily than parents, even when both live nearby, but parents, spouses, and children are more likely than siblings to be visited at least once a week. Children living independently feel responsibility to visit parents regularly, but they may want to see more of a sibling if the bond is close; weaker sibling ties result in less frequent visits. There appears to be little sex selectivity in sibling visits, though men see somewhat more of their brothers than of their sisters. The reverse is less evident for women, as brothers may be an important source of support if a woman has trouble with her husband.

While relative ages cannot be ascertained from the data available, there appears to be a tendency to see relatives of one's own generation more often than members of other generations (siblings and cousins more than parents or aunts). This is least evident for the uncle-nephew relationship; many uncles are seen daily or several times a week. In some societies (such as the matrilineal Akan), nephews inherit from their uncles, but the common occurrence of these visits suggests that uncles are an important source of advice and aid to large numbers of young men in many towns— they serve as father substitutes. Aunts are much less important for women.

Women were somewhat more likely than men to have parents living in the town, or to mention the presence of a spouse or children in answering this question. This may be because they come to town with their parents more often than male migrants. Spouses and children were often omitted because the question asked for family and kin; spouses and children are not always considered as being in these categories. More nuclear than extended family members were mentioned by both men and women, presumably because they are more salient. The presence of other kin is sometimes evident from answers to other questions, but their omission appears to be accidental.

Perhaps because of the difficulty of finding a room, kin do not tend to cluster together in towns. Parents, siblings, and more distant kin are equally likely to be living near or far from the respondents; just over half of both lived nearby. When respondents listed several kin, they usually lived on different streets. Thus, a man with several relatives in town may have one living in the neighborhood, who helped him find his room and whom he sees every day, but he will probably also have others in various parts of town whom he visits at most once or twice a week. Ten percent of Ashaiman respondents and only one in Tema had kin in adjacent houses. This dispersion means that social life is not confined to the neighborhood as an "urban village"; many people get to other parts of their towns at fairly frequent intervals, which gives them opportunities to meet people living in these areas.

Visits are usually for conversation. A distant uncle, seen rarely, is "greeted"; those who are better known pass on news of home and discuss family affairs (of all segments of the family). Some are seen mainly when money is needed, but other kinds of help are also sought and given. One man reported that his sister saw him often to complain about her husband, and a woman cooked meals about twice a week for a nephew in boarding school. Weekend meals are often extended family affairs. Young people keep track of the health and well-being of parents and elderly kin; they also share their recreation with brothers and cousins: going to the cinema, dancing, and similar activities. Most visits are informal, but Yoruba family meetings on Sunday afternoons in Ajegunle sometimes involve rented chairs and formal procedures.

Visits from Home

Kin from home may come for the day or stay for several days or even several months. Sometimes a visit is in reality a trial migration. If the visitor finds a job, he will stay in town; if not, he will return home for the next farming season. Dry-season migration to town was probably more common in Ghana and Nigeria in the past, because jobs are now hard to find and wage employment tends to require more education than the temporary migrant has. However, this circulating pattern is still common in The Gambia, so that respondents were asked about anyone who was living in the household in January as well as about visitors during the previous two weeks.

About a quarter of respondents said that someone in the household in January was no longer there, though relatively few of these appear to have been labor migrants. About half of the visitors were unemployed at the time of their visit, but reports that they were seeking work (or had left to farm at home) came from only 28 percent of Serekunda respondents who had visitors and 13 percent of those in Banjul. Some were merely making social visits and some were schoolchildren who had (in July) gone home for the school holiday. A few had died; 15 percent of those reporting visitors (in January or recently) said they had come for medical attention. The official death rate in Banjul is probably increased by its inexpensive medical facilities, which attract sick people from Senegal as well as from all of The Gambia.

The most common reason for a visit from home is social, to maintain solidarity in a geographically extended family. Kin visitors are usually closely related to their hosts; they are mostly parents, siblings, or children. They come to see how their brothers or children are getting on, to discuss family problems, and pass on hometown news. They may be looking for money for school fees or farm equipment, but they also bring foodstuffs which are a welcome contribution to the urban household. While in town, they shop, sell produce, and take care of business with the government (while housed at their kin's expense), but social ties tend to be pre-eminent. Less than 5 percent of visitors are not kin, and these tend to be either long-term family friends or fiancés. Only in Ashaiman was there evidence of households having to accommodate migrants from home with whom they did not already have strong ties, and this is probably due to the nature of Ashaiman as a new town.

With improvements in roads, visits to town will certainly increase. They can be useful for national as well as family solidarity in that people who live far from the metropolis will feel less cut off from "progress" if they can visit occasionally and get a taste of urban life. A large increase in the number of visitors to West African towns may lead to the development of more inexpensive hotels and hostels for them, such as are found in many South American cities. This has begun in some Nigerian cities, though most hotels still aim at the elite and expatriate market. However, most visitors prefer to stay with relatives, and as long as kin are willing to accommodate them the demand for alternative accommodation will probably remain low.

Nigerian respondents were asked about visitors over a longer period, the last six months. Women were somewhat less likely than men to be visited by members of their families of orientation (parents and siblings) and somewhat more likely to be visited by spouses and children. It appears that husbands more often travel to visit wives than vice versa, but husbands are more likely than wives to go off on business, so it is up to them to come back from time to time. There was no significant difference between towns in the proportion of respondents who had been visited by parents or siblings. However, respondents in the provincial towns were not only more likely than those in the suburbs to have visitors, they had more visitors who were less closely related to them. Nearly a third of the men and a sixth of the women interviewed in Abeokuta reported visits of members of their extended families (uncles, cousins) compared to about an eleventh of both men and women in Ajegunle.

Abeokuta respondents were also most likely to have been visited by their spouses and children. This is due to their higher average age (they had more grown-up children living independently who might visit) and the somewhat greater frequency of residential separation of spouses in Abeokuta than in the other Nigerian towns. Some of the Ajegunle men had left their wives at home, but these appear to visit less often than absent wives or husbands of Abeokuta residents, probably because the latter live much nearer. The crowded housing in Aba made it easier for urban spouses to go home for a visit than to be visited in town, and this may have been true in Ajegunle as well.

Nevertheless, Aba respondents were more likely than those in other towns to have had visitors from home. Ties to kin are strongly maintained in this area and because distances are often short the visit need not last more than a few hours. Some migrants were visited more than once a week by kin living in nearby villages. It is very difficult to draw a line between town and country here, and some kin are so close that the distinction in residence is administrative rather than social.

Migrants also occasionally visit friends in nearby towns on weekends. About a quarter of the women and nearly a fifth of the men in the Nigerian towns reported visitors who were not living in their hometowns, compared to about a seventh of the Gambian respondents. The proportion was about a third of both men and women in Abeokuta, where the extended family may be settled in nearby villages or towns and see the urban members when they travel on business or just make social visits occasionally.

Visits Home[7]

Most migrants in Ghana and Nigeria go home at least once a year, though this is less common in The Gambia. These visits are important in maintaining family solidarity and in bringing new ideas and economic support to the villages; they symbolize the migrants' continued interest in local affairs. While long-distance migrants may maintain their interest over many years without a visit, migrants who have not been home for many years are often, rightly, considered lost to the village; they are less likely to return eventually than the migrants who visit every year or two. While much visiting is casual, at times convenient to the migrants, there are also formal occasions when their presence is expected. The most notable of these are funerals (for those who are not too far away) and village festivals.

Many villages in Ghana and Nigeria have an annual celebration which leaders hope will bring the migrants home. The harvest festival has lost ground in recent years to Christmas and Easter because employees usually have at least four days free at these times. There are dances and social events as well as lineage and community meetings, where plans are made for local development and contributions are solicited. Igbo villages have probably gone furthest in developing this form of communal expression of solidarity, but the Yoruba and Ewe, among others, also give it considerable importance.[7] It is a way of exerting pressure on migrants to maintain contacts with their communities of origin and remind them of their eventual return home (and the present obligations this entails). The migrant who lives far away, where there is no one else from home, is less easy to influence and will probably not return every year, but if several years pass without his attendance efforts will be made (insofar as his whereabouts are known) to bring him back to the fold.

A woman may sometimes accompany her husband to his hometown, but visits by people at all social levels are often as individuals rather than as families; an elite man and wife often take separate holidays, each to his or her hometown. Children may be taken on visits to both places, but it is considered particularly important that they get to know their lineage hometown if they are to maintain contact with it as adults. They may be sent home for schooling or holidays to ensure that they become proficient in the local language and get to know their extended family. Elite children are least likely to have this experience, and thus most likely to "forget their home."

It may be quite hard for an urban child to fit into rural life. Even the poor miss urban conveniences; they feel awkward when they cannot do things their country cousins take for granted and when they cannot distinguish large numbers of kin who have known each other from infancy. Thus, the adaptation process faced by the migrant on arrival in town must be handled by his children on their visits, long or short, to his place of origin.

The continuing importance of the family home to the second generation is shown in the finding that Nigerian men who had lived in their hometown but not been born there were more likely to visit home at least monthly than those who were born and grew up in the place claimed as hometown. Size of place of origin appears to make little difference in the frequency of visits, though a town would probably be easier to get to than many villages. It is the importance of the place as the home of one's lineage rather than the number of people who live there which counts; a house in a back street in Lagos is as much a family home as a large, isolated compound in Ghana's Upper Region.

Visits usually require more giving on the part of the visitor than can be returned by those at home (either in food to take back, in status within the local society, or in promised security in old age). Therefore, those who want to conserve their resources for the upward climb might be expected to visit as rarely as possible, and those who do not intend to settle at home in their old age could find it convenient to let their contacts with home lapse. In practice, the second happens more often than the first. Lux (1971) reported that some Yombe migrants in Zaire send money home in order to avoid sanctions from their kin, but rarely visit because of the loss of independence which often results from such visits. Few Gambians who have decided to stay in town go home as often as once a year. However, the pressure on migrants to visit regularly is still very strong in Ghana and Nigeria, and is reinforced by the intention of most of them to retire to their homes eventually.

As with visiting in town, the most important factor in the frequency of visits home is the distance which must be traveled. If a journey costs very little in money or time, the migrant can go every week or two; if it takes several days and costs a week's wages, he may not go every year. In all three countries, there is no difference between men and women from nearby in the frequency of visits, but men who come from a middle or long distance are more likely than women to go home at least once a year. In Nigeria and The Gambia, only a minority of women coming from a distance go home as often as once a year, whereas about half the men go at least that often.

With distance controlled, the frequency of visits varies more clearly with income and occupation than with age. Men with higher incomes generally make more visits than those earning less. This might be expected in the light of the costs of such visits in fares, gifts, and promises of further assistance which must be made, but it is contrary to the assumption of those arguing that upper-class members of these societies are increasingly cutting themselves off from their less successful kin. The data show fairly clearly that visits increase with income. Clerical workers and professionals are especially likely to be frequent visitors if home is only a few hours away, whereas unskilled workers who are short-distance migrants seldom visit home more than once a year. The strongest indication of their disadvantage is in Aba, where only 12 percent of all migrants but 35 percent of unskilled migrants visited home less than once a year.

As migrants are likely to seek more important positions in the home community the closer they are to retiring to it (Amachree 1968, pp. 234–35) and older people are expected to participate in more funerals, it might be expected that the frequency of visits would be directly related to age, but insofar as the differences are significant the relationship appears to be curvilinear for men and indirect for women. Young men tend to go home rarely (unless they are courting) because they have little status at home. Middle-aged men (35–49) in Aba and the Gambian towns go more often than those who are either older or younger. These are beginning to play roles in hometown politics, and their parents are often still alive. Older men in Ashaiman and older women in all but the Nigerian provincial towns very seldom go home as much as once a year. Some of these have "retired" to the town; most of the women will have their main ties in town and thus have little need to travel home.

Reports from East and Central Africa suggest that housewives there often spend the growing season at home, joining their husbands in town only for the dry season (Parkin 1969, p. 60; Weinrich 1976, p. 135). This pattern appears to be rare in West Africa, where urban women are often traders or otherwise employed. Housewives may visit home once a year if it is not too far away, but on the whole they go home less often than women in the labor force. This suggests that women usually pay their own way instead of relying on their husbands for expenses. Few women traders go home often enough to use a home area as a source of supplies.

Gift Exchange

Few visitors come empty-handed if they can avoid it, unless they come very frequently. Gifts are often useful in themselves, but they also maintain a continuing social exchange which symbolizes the mutual dependence and support of the parties concerned and the importance of kinship ties (Mauss 1925). As might be expected because they usually come from farming areas, visitors to urban kin tend to bring food with them. This does not come frequently enough to be a substantial or reliable contribution to urban subsistence, but it is welcome nevertheless. Table 5.7 shows that, except in Serekunda, at least half of the vsitors brought food with them. Other gifts, mainly money or cloth, were most common in The Gambia and Abeokuta. Women are more likely than men to receive some gift from their visitors, and women and the unemployed are most likely to be recipients of money. The amounts are usually very small, but one unemployed family man who had moved to Ajegunle after being expelled from Ghana was sent £25 every month.

Nigerians were most likely and Ghanaians least likely to make some gift to their visitors; except in Tema; men and women were about equal in this. The gift tends to take the form of a small sum of money (sometimes only enough to cover transportation) and/or drinks, food, or clothing. The drinks are usually consumed on the spot, but the cloth or clothing is taken home and, like the money, may be for someone other than the visitor. Thus, a sibling who comes to town may collect school fees for himself or money or clothing for his parents. The larger sums which tend to characterize these exchanges in the Gambian and Nigerian suburban towns may be explained by the fact that visitors are somewhat less frequent and from farther away than those coming to the Ghanaian or, especially, the Nigerian provincial towns. However, the earlier date of the Ghanaian surveys and the depressed economy at that time mean that £5 was a relatively larger gift there than elsewhere.

TABLE 5.7
Gifts from and to Visiting Kin, by Town and Sex (Percentages)

	Ashaiman		Tema		Banjul		Serekunda		Aba		Abeokuta		Ajegunle		Kakuri	
	M	F	M	F	M	F	M	F	M	F	M	F	M	F	M	F
Gifts from kin																
Nothing	22	17	25	28	31	11	60	41	31	32	17	8	24	9	27	25
Food[a]	74	75	75	72	48	67	35	18	66	53	57	49	71	87	64	67
Other	4	13	0	4	21	22	5	41	3	15	26	43	5	4	9	8
Total[b]	100	105	100	104	100	100	100	100	100	100	100	100	100	100	100	100
Gifts to kin																
Nothing	19	25	25	48	15	6	19	29	11	7	19	10	7	4	5	12
Under £5	63	58	57	29	23	6	33	29	60	42	36	45	37	46	32	33
£5 or more	13	2	15	2	54	39	44	6	20	15	26	16	48	33	54	42
Amount unknown	2	2	4	0	0	0	2	0	1	5	5	5	1	0	0	0
Goods	13	15	13	21	38	72	33	59	65	54	41	53	78	83	71	75
Total[b]	110	102	113	100	130	123	131	123	157	123	127	129	171	166	162	162
N	120	53	71	58	48	18	63	17	119	41	86	38	67	24	91	24

[a]Includes food sent from home to Ghanaian urban residents.

[b]Totals may be over 100 percent because of multiple gifts.

Frequent, casual visitors may get only beer or palm wine on some visits and a contribution on special occasions, whereas the parent or sibling who comes only every year or two expects, or at least hopes, for something substantial. One man whose mother-in-law had been helping with the new baby said he was expected to provide her with new clothes for her return to the village. Generally, these expectations are fulfilled without resentment to the extent that the urban resident can manage. Men go into debt to satisfy what they consider reasonable demands of close kin, whether made in person or through a message from home. This is partly a question of "face." Most men want a reputation for success and generosity to precede their return to the village.

Substantial contributions are more often sent or brought home than given to visitors. About three-quarters of the Nigerian male migrants, two-thirds of those interviewed in The Gambia, and half of those in the Ghanaian towns reported sending money home, at least in emergencies. More money is sent than brought, except perhaps by frequent visitors, and women both send and bring less money than men (see Table 5.8).

Women are less likely to send money, and send smaller amounts, because many have no income at all and most earn only small amounts through petty trading. A woman who sends a pound to her mother three or four times a year may be making as large a contribution, in proportion to her resources, as a man who sends £5 with the same frequency. However, women are not solely dependent on their own earnings. Ghanaian housewives were almost as likely to send money home as women with an income. This suggests that some husbands make it possible for their wives to send small contributions home, especially in emergencies. Nevertheless, parents are aware that most of the support for their old age will come from their sons; this increases their desire to educate sons—if necessary, at the expense of daughters. But women who get good jobs undertake considerable responsibility for helping kin. Dinan (1977, p. 171) reports on the substantial gifts of professional women in Accra to a wide range of kin.

Although only a minority reported sending money every month, the "amount sent" section of Table 5.8 is divided so that pounds per month can be calculated. Of those who sent anything in the past year, the majority of Ghanaians and Nigerian women sent the equivalent of £2 or less per month; only men in The Gambia averaged more than £4 per month. These differences are partly due to inflation. Ten pounds was a much larger sum, relative to local wage rates in the Ghana of 1968 than in the Nigeria of 1972 or, especially, the Gambia of 1976. But even small amounts can prove a significant factor in national income transfer. Caldwell (1967, pp. 142–43) estimates that about £5 million per year was sent from Accra. In a large sample of rural households throughout Ghana, one-third claimed to receive money from kin living in towns. Nearly 70 percent of Yoruba households surveyed in a Nigerian study received help

	Ashaiman		Tema		Banjul		Serekunda		Aba		Abeokuta		Ajegunle		Kakuri	
	M	F	M	F	M	F	M	F	M	F	M	F	M	F	M	F
Sent Money Home[b]																
Never	43	80	67	82	37	66	34	79	23	53	13	15	29	57	24	43
Emergency only	3	5	1	3	28	7	29	17	41	36	23	43	39	25	49	39
Regularly[c]	54	15	32	15	29	27	35	0	29	9	52	39	25	18	21	7
Investment[d]	..	..	..	..	6	0	2	4	7	2	12	3	7	0	6	11
Total	100	100	100	100	100	100	100	100	100	100	100	100	100	100	100	100
N	175	64	146	106	68	15	86	23	140	45	60	33	154	40	148	28
Amount Sent																
£1–12	49	92	37	85	4	0	8	17	33	43	13	37	14	32	25	45
£13–24	24	0	32	15	3	11	8	28	22	21	23	23	20	14	24	12
£25–48	20	0	24	0	9	14	31	17	12	11	24	19	30	14	33	31
£49+	7	8	7	0	84	75	53	38	33	25	40	21	36	40	18	12
Total	100	100	100	100	100	100	100	100	100	100	100	100	100	100	100	100
N	123	26	56	20	90	28	95	18	114	28	82	43	111	28	110	16
Brings Home																
Nothing	16	11	23	30	14	0	0	33	8	11	5	3	2	21	7	16
£1–5	47	46	39	27	8	5	14	27	51	38	28	24	7	14	20	9
£6–10	17	18	22	11	2	16	15	20	12	15	14	30	16	21	12	22
£11–20	12	7	7	6	10	16	33	0	6	4	28	21	22	17	20	22
£21+	7	0	4	0	39	26	14	0	2	0	19	6	50	17	36	3
DK how much	1	0	1	0	4	0	2	0	2	2	0	0	1	5	1	0
Goods	16	29	14	31	62	63	56	33	82	83	53	85	80	64	68	72
Total	100	100	100	100	100	100	100	100	100	100	100	100	100	100	100	100
N	234	111	110	105	139	126	134	113	163	153	147	169	178	159	164	144
N		83	153	113	51	19	52	15	144	47	58	33	137	42	123	32

[a] Amounts are given at the widely accepted rather than the official exchange rates (i.e., £1 = NC 2, D 4, and £N 1); these were fairly close at the time of the studies.

[b] Migrants in employment only. Those in town less than a year who have not yet sent have been omitted. Ghanaians were not asked about investments.

[c] Includes giving money monthly to parents in town.

[d] Many of these also sent regularly.

179

from children; almost all of those which did not either had no adult children or were rich enough not to need such assistance (Caldwell 1976, p. 233).

There appears to have been more money going home in the relatively affluent early 1960s than at the time of my Ghanaian study; Caldwell's rural households which got remittances received an average of £50 per year, much more than my Tema or Ashaiman respondents claimed to send. However, the small amounts sent in Ghana compared to The Gambia suggest that remittances probably fluctuate with the urban economy; it must also be remembered that emergencies, which count most at home, were not included in the Tema/Ashaiman figures. When times are good, money flows home.[8] Unfortunately, severe inflation and job insecurity can cut these flows just at the time when more money is needed at home. Nevertheless, the desire to send remains. Migrants may send smaller amounts, but may continue to send at regular intervals unless they are unemployed. Those at home can thus depend on something coming without their specific request, even though it is only two to four times a year.

The data do not allow the computation of a total yearly contribution for each respondent because only the more regular or recent contributions were reported. Money brought home probably varies with the visitor's current finances and his family's pressing needs. More is given when school fees fall due, there is a funeral or memorial service to celebrate, or someone is ill; it is these emergencies which also bring money from migrants who are not regular senders.

In any case, it was felt that sums mentioned on these questions should be taken as rough approximations of the amount of income transferred from urban to rural areas. Kaufert (1976, p. 164) found that there was about 25 percent difference in the frequency of visits and sending money reported by a matched sample of migrants and their rural kin. Because of the moral connotations of such behavior, migrants tend to overestimate and their kin to underestimate both the frequency and the value of transfers. Records would have to be kept over a long period to accurately measure the total aid given. Most of the evidence suggests that requests are frequent and are answered if possible, though not necessarily to the family's satisfaction.

Money sent or brought home is only a partial measure of the process of income transfer from urban migrants to their extended families, and it may be misleading in situations where transfers actually take place in town. Byerlee (1976, p. 61) found that in Sierra Leone money sent home was relatively unimportant compared to support given to kin in town. About 17 percent of migrants' income was spent on scholars and the unemployed who were living in town (often with the migrants), compared to about 5 percent sent home. Food received from home was worth about half of the remittances sent, though some of this helped feed indigent kin in town.

Pfeffermann (1968, p. 223) suggests that in Dakar workers have some choice in whether to send money home or support kin in town, but either way the system results in considerable equalization of incomes between rural and urban residents. Elkan (1976) reports a similar situation for many Nairobi migrants, and Table 4.3 shows the high proportion of urban householders in these samples who are providing accommodation for kin, both children still in school and adults. While some of these adults are self-supporting, many are a drain on household resources. Thus, even the worker who never sends or brings money home may be making a considerable contribution to his extended family.

The figures for regular remittances in Table 5.8 include people who are living as dependents (usually in their parents' or brothers' households) and pay something every month as their share of expenses. They rarely send anything to their hometown, since their major responsibility is within the household, but the monthly contribution is more in the nature of a remittance than of payment for room and board. They are helping parents or kin with whom they happen to live. This is another illustration of the difficulty of separating support given to kin at home and in town.

Patterns of generosity are clearer in sending money home than in gifts to visitors, though there is some evidence that people who have close ties with kin through visits (in town and at home) and are generous to visitors are also more likely to send money home than others whose contacts of all types are rare. (The frequency of contact rienforces the value of generosity.) Those who send regularly and fairly often usually send more money than those who send only rarely. There are a few cases of people who come up with £100 or even £1,000 once a year, but most people never accumulate such sums; kin who can be sure of a monthly or quarterly remittance of a few pounds are likely to receive more overall than those who must depend on a grand gesture every year or two. This is especially important to women, and mothers are the most frequent recipients of remittances.

The most important factor is ability to pay. If clerical workers and professionals send more than all types of manual workers (as they consistently do), and if middle-aged men send more than young newcomers, it is because they can afford to. Price (1975, p. 62) and Byerlee (1976, p. 57) both report that remittances increase with urban incomes, and this is confirmed in the present study. Rather than cutting themselves off from their kin, civil servants moving up the hierarchy tend to take on more responsibility for family and hometown affairs, even though they can be sure of a pension on retirement. University students, as the aspirant elite, feel a strong obligation to help their families, who have helped them achieve educational success (Caldwell 1965, p. 192; Price 1975, p. 62), and Oppong's study of the elite in Accra (1974, pp. 55, 63) shows how well this debt is paid off.[9]

Although in some towns men in commercial occupations send home as much money as clerical workers and professionals, on the whole the wage-employed are more generous than the self-employed. Not only do the former tend to have somewhat larger incomes, but wages are more dependable than income from self-employment. The man or woman who knows how much money will come in each month can more easily promise to send a certain amount at regular intervals than one whose income is highly variable and uncertain. At the same time, since salary scales are widely published, relatives of the wage-employed know how much they are earning and can make demands accordingly, whereas it is easier for the self-employed to conceal the size of their income.

There are few notable differences in the frequency or amount sent between migrants of varying origin and urban experience, and these are probably due to differences in income. Migrants who grew up in a town feel the same obligation to kin at home as men originating in a village, and men who migrate several times are no more likely to lose contact with home than those who go directly to a city and stay there. Although the proportion of the population growing up in cities is increasing, the continued importance of mutual aid within families seems assured. The largest group of people who send nothing home are nonmigrants, but these are helping kin in town. Nevertheless, some nonmigrants are still sending money "home," so the responsibility is maintained into the second generation.

Conclusion

The study of forms of marriage and relationships with kin illustrates the maintenance of customary values and structures in a time of otherwise rapid change. A strong continuity of family norms is demonstrated in every section of this chapter. The forms may change somewhat (outside wives instead of polygyny, paying school fees rather providing skill training, a narrowing of extended family ties, support for kin in town rather than sending money to the village), but the principle remains.

While data on the incidence of polygyny and interethnic marriage in the past are inadequate, it appears that the former is still highly valued and the latter remains an unpopular choice. Polygyny will probably decline only when women refuse to participate—a long-term result of increased education. Interethnic marriage may have been more common among migrants twenty years ago than it is today; newcomers can now find someone of their own group to marry and improved transportation makes it relatively easy to court a girl at home if this is preferred.

The direct relationship between age and polygyny makes any calculation of polygyny rates which does not control for age highly misleading. Few men under 35 are polygynous and (contrary to the stereotype repeated in many novels) women under 25 are less likely than older women to be involved in polygynous marriages. The other important factor is religion, with notable differences between Christians and followers of either Islam or traditional religions. Various aspects of social change appear to have relatively little effect on the social value of polygyny; education, non-manual occupations, and the experience of living in a large urban center may make polygyny possible for more men rather than putting them under pressure to remain monogamous.

Interethnic marriage levels are affected by the characteristics of individual ethnic groups, but also by the environment in which prospective partners meet. Propinquity and choice make it more likely that migrants will marry across ethnic lines than nonmigrants. Cities with a high level of ethnic tolerance and mixing (as in The Gambia) have higher rates of intermarriage than those where political competition tends to foster ethnic factionalism (as in Nigeria). The generally low levels of exogamous marriage suggest that ethnicity continues to be an important part of family as well as individual identity among urban residents and, as such, inhibits the formation of permanent relationships across ethnic lines. Less intense forms of social interaction will be discussed in later chapters.

Marriage tends to change the nature of an individual's social life. More time is spent on family and household responsibilities, so less is left for friends. Personal networks open to include affinal as well as cognatic kin, though there may be relatively little interaction with the former unless they live nearby. Married people whose spouses live elsewhere appear to have somewhat less full social lives than the unmarried or those with coresident spouses; this group needs more study to sort out the factors involved.

Whereas the stereotype of African migrants in the past held that children were left at home, most now grow up with their parents in town. The urban child population is further increased by schoolchildren sent to live with siblings and uncles, though this appears to be rarer than in the past because the expanding educational system has made it unnecessary for most children to leave home to attend school; many small towns and large villages now have secondary schools. Servants have been almost as widespread in some towns as in Victorian England, but expanding education and alternative opportunities are increasing the cost of household labor beyond what ordinary families can pay. It seems likely that within ten to twenty years only "waifs and strays" and young people being trained for certain occupations (apprentice craftsmen and traders) will be providing domestic labor in any but the most affluent households.

The question on a £100 windfall shows the differences between husbands and wives in contributions to domestic finances and the aspirations of people at different income levels. Women's contributions to the costs of food and clothing and their readiness to send money home if they have any to spare is especially evident in the data. Both men and women at all income levels consider it possible to save money for future needs, though far more would use it for immediate investment. Given the low rates of interest in these countries (and negative interest in the savings societies which many people prefer to banks), investment in housing or businesses is probably more likely to lead to the desired goal.

The data on visits and gift exchange consistently support the hypothesis that kinship bonds are highly valued by urban residents of all social levels. Those who have more usually give more; though they may occasionally complain about the demands made on them, most place a high value on family solidarity. Most adults have kin in town, and those who live nearby are seldom seen less than once a week. Women tend to see somewhat less of their kin than men due to their lower mobility, but age, education, occupation, and place of origin seem to have relatively little influence on the frequency of visits. Within certain socially acceptable limits, urban residents can choose how much time they want to spend with kin, especially those who live in other parts of town. Close ties are developed with some relatives because of personal attraction or perceived advantage, whereas others can be avoided or at least "greeted" only rarely. Most visits appear to be for socioemotional rather than instrumental reasons.

Visits from home are more often instrumental, in that visiting kin often expect gifts of money or in kind from their urban relatives; they may come especially to explain their needs. However, the desire to maintain social ties through face-to-face interaction is also very important. From the urban resident's point of view, a visit is sometimes most unwelcome because demands are made on living space and financial resources which cannot easily be filled. People who are relatively well-off are especially subject to the unannounced arrival of kin needing medical care, school fees, a job, and so on, who plan to stay for an indefinite period; the poor are often subject to the same appeals, and find themselves in debt by the time the visitor returns home. Complaints that people at home do not understand the constraints of urban living are to a certain extent based on fact, but the even partial satisfaction of most visitors' demands shows that family and hometown status are considered to be worth the sacrifices involved.

There is considerable pressure on migrants to come home at least once a year, especially for the community festival. This provides an opportunity to meet fellow migrants as well as those who have remained at home, and hometown ties are strongly reinforced in the convivial atmosphere. Migrants to nearby towns may get home more often, depending on their financial status and the demands made on them by their families. Women generally feel less need to visit home than men, as their ties to their kin are to some extent attenuated by marriage and few can expect to play important roles as lineage or community decision makers.

Kinship ties are reinforced by the exchange of gifts, which make it difficult to quantify the so-called exploitation of rural by urban areas. The man who never sends money home or gives anything to visitors is less likely to be forgiven than the man who never visits his hometown. But the necessity to provide something to help, in emergencies if not regularly, is taken so seriously that few who are not truly indigent would maintain a stand against all aid. The range of people helped may be narrowing (a higher proportion is given to parents and siblings and less to distant kin), but the lack of data from the past makes comparison hazardous; we should beware of assuming the increasing importance of the nuclear family. Extended kinship continues to be an important factor in urban social relations. The next two chapters will examine two other foci of social inter-action, informal and formal relations with people who are usually not kin.

6 □ FRIENDS

Sunday Akpan was a 26-year-old store assistant, not yet married. An Efik from Cross River State, he had worked in Benin and Onitsha before being transferred by the Electricity Corporation to Abeokuta in 1963. He left his linesman's job for better pay as a steward; when his employer left the country, he found his present job. Several of his cotenants were young migrants like himself, and the two who were interviewed named Sunday and each other among their close friends. The others mainly chatted and occasionally shared meals. Sunday, as an active Jehovah's Witness, involved them in Bible study. Sunday's own list of close friends did not include the cotenants he was trying to convert. Instead, he listed three couples (a very unusual occurrence) and another man whom he saw three times a week at the Kingdom Hall, plus one coworker. Two of the couples were Egba; the other three Witnesses were Efik. He had met all of them through the sect. The third friend listed was a Catholic coworker, who came from Sunday's hometown; this man knew his other Efik friends, and Sunday had met him at work rather than at home. Thus, his sources of friends were religion, ethnicity, and work, whereas his cotenants found their friends where they lived. In both cases, all or almost all the close friends listed knew each other well. Sunday's best friend was both an Efik and a Witness; he was older and better placed than Sunday and could be looked to for help if he needed money or had other problems.

Sunday hadn't been home for six years and no longer belonged to an ethnic association, but he had been visited recently by a brother and sent money home regularly. He planned to go home when he had saved enough to start trading. Meanwhile, he had a very active social life in Abeokuta. Much of his nonworking time was spent on Bible study or spreading the faith, but his outgoing nature made this a social occasion. He knew everyone in the house and six of his neighbors well, talked with them frequently, visited their rooms, and occasionally shared meals with them. He sometimes gave a party for his friends, including cotenants, on weekends.

One of sociologists' major concerns has been communal relationships—strong attachments among members of a group based on multiple shared roles; mutual social, economic, and moral support and shared residence over a considerable period of time. The argument as to whether communities are lost, saved, or liberated by modern society has engaged many writers over the past thirty years (see Wellman 1979). Is modern society, with its mobility, impersonality, and great increase in scale inimical to the development of communal attachments? Do people become isolated, anomic, and alienated, or do they find satisfying personal relationships which are less tied to a small locality than was necessary in the past?

Fischer et al. (1977, pp. 6–13) is a strong proponent of the view that communal-type relations may benefit from but are not dependent on coresidence, especially now that modern technology makes frequent communication over considerable distance possible, and that such relations are in fact maintained by a majority of urban residents. Modern urban society should be seen as offering more choice than in the past, within a framework of structured constraints. It is the disadvantaged members of the society (the poor, the old) who become socially isolated, regardless of their geographical mobility or continued residence in the "community" of their youth, because they have much less choice in the formation and continuance of friendships than the rest of society.

This hypothesis is supported by data from a number of American studies and, with some modification and elaboration, by Wellman's Canadian data (1979). However, as Fischer points out (1977, p. 186), these studies may be quite inadequate tests because contemporary American society may lack "true communities" in the conventional sense to which comparison could be made. Even small towns have been profoundly changed by recent developments in American society as a whole.

A comparative study of West African towns provides a useful framework for testing this hypothesis. First, although the social life of African towns has also been deeply penetrated by new values and norms, a high proportion of their residents have a clearer idea of community, in the sense of a corporate group providing its members with primary relations, moral support, mutual aid, and so on, than do most Americans. The villages they come from are closer to that ideal, or at least to the reality of small-scale communal living which is known in the developed world mainly through novels and history books.

Second, observers of cities in developing countries have often commented on their "urban village" characteristics, though they have seldom presented systematic data to support their impressions. Some West African towns have been far less marked by "modernity" than others; they have grown slowly and maintained both a core of lifetime residents and the values of mutual support based on long-established and frequent social interaction and attachment to place. These can be compared to newer towns, where most residents have only short-term ties with those around them. Finally, technology is as yet only modestly developed in these towns, so distance is a greater constraint than in urban America. Few people have cars or telephones and the mail tends to be slow and sometimes unreliable. Therefore, it is far easier to contact people living or working nearby than to maintain close relationships with distant friends. If distant ties are maintained, they must be seen as considerably more rewarding than local ties.

This chapter examines the nature of informal social interaction, especially the friendship networks of urban residents with people to whom they have no ties of blood or marriage. What sort of people are socially isolated? To what extent are intimate social relations localized? Do people establish social networks mainly with others who live nearby, who are socially and economically their equals, or on some other basis? Do locals have different patterns of social relations from migrants? How do choice and constraint affect friendship patterns?

Individuals need contacts at varying levels of society in order to get what they need, and social relations built up in one sphere may later prove useful in a very different context. If people have only limited time for social interaction (as a result of the constraints of earning a living and maintaining a family), the choices of contacts they make on arrival and at other points of occupational and residential change may have a considerable effect on their later success, in whatever way this is measured.

The belief that people are more isolated and social life is less satisfying in large cities than in small towns, which is as widely held in Africa (for example, by university students) as in America, is not supported by observation in most West African towns on weekends. Towns of all sizes and types usually provide considerable scope for social interaction between people of widely differing background and social status, should they choose to make such contacts.

However, it is well to remember at the outset that a high proportion of residents of these towns would be classed as poor, using international or local criteria. Friendship and associational networks and even contacts with kin may be limited because an individual has no money for drinks, new clothing, transportation, or mutual aid. This could result in social isolation or a tendency to form ethnic or occupational ghettos, with small, homogeneous groups of people interacting mainly with each other and having only necessary economic contacts with other residents. (See Mayer 1961 for a classic African example.)

The most important factors interfering with this are the high value placed on kinship ties, discussed in chapter 5, and the shortage of housing, which makes it necessary for a newcomer to find a room wherever he can, and the consequent heterogeneity of neighborhoods and even houses (see chapter 4). Employees (nursegirl, driver) live with well-off families and apprentices often live with their masters; this means that more informal interaction occurs than if they lived elsewhere. Thus, a top civil servant or businessman may have in his household a nurse, a clerk, a photographer, a trader, several students, and/or a steward. Insofar as these have wide social networks within the town, the elite have many indirect sources of knowledge about public opinion and many ordinary people in the society have indirect if not direct social contact, at least on a patron/client basis, with these "big men" (see Luckham 1971, pp. 112–13; Yusuf 1975, p. 180).

Potential for interaction is not enough; it is important to measure how much people actually mix. To what extent are migrants to town dependent on their kin or other migrants from home for their social life, as opposed to mixing with "strangers" in the urban environment? To what extent do they choose friends who are much like themselves, thus reinforcing boundaries? Does multiform interaction vary with sex, age, education, occupation, or intention to remain indefinitely in town? It was expected that considerable evidence of heterogeneous friendship networks would be found, especially among males of moderate socioeconomic status who intend to remain in town indefinitely (though, given West African norms, not permanently). This wide range of contacts is fostered by a low level of class consciousness and by the importance of patron/client and extended kinship relationships, which were discussed in the last chapter.

Appendix A shows the questions which were asked of the various samples. Experience showed that only very detailed questions would provide adequate data on membership in associations and specific types of social interaction. Long periods of participant observation would have been useful in providing a wider range of information, but it was not possible to do this in so many towns. The aim here is to quantify the relationships of a large number of people on a comparative basis; small-scale observation too often presents an unrepresentative picture. So far, depth has been much better served in African urban studies than breadth, and this is an attempt to restore the balance.

Sociability

One of the goals of the original studies in Tema and Ashaiman was to develop a scale which would differentiate the more social from the less social members of the population so that the background and circumstances of these types of people could be examined. Sociability can be used to recreate networks reminiscent of home, and/or to build up support for leadership roles. In many of these societies, leaders ("big men") are expected to have large numbers of contacts at all social levels, through whom they obtain information and exercise influence. There is little objection to wealth, even if it is gained through corruption, if at least some of it is shared widely—the holder does not cut himself off but has a wide circle of kin and clients (Lloyd 1975, p. 199). Among ordinary people as well, social isolates are suspect.

Work on the Ghanaian data led to dropping some questions and adding others in subsequent studies, so the data are not precisely comparable. However, the addition of more towns provides an opportunity to examine additional structural factors in sociability. Some towns "feel" more friendly than others; it is useful to see whether the data reflect this and to examine the causes of these varying levels of sociability.

Housing

Certain types of housing seem to foster social interaction, whereas other types may inhibit it. The size and density of houses, the orientation of rooms, and the availability of amenities within the compound are all relevant. In small houses, a resident owner will take the new tenant around and introduce him or her to the other tenants, and the tenants may formally greet the owner each morning. Disputes between cotenants may be easier to handle in small than in large houses because social control can more easily be maintained. However, some tenants see this control as a constraint. Large houses have greater turnover of tenants only in Abeokuta (where small houses are kept mainly for the family); in Kakuri, Aba, and the Gambian towns there were more recent arrivals in the small houses, and in Ajegunle and Ashaiman size appears to have little effect on turnover.

Pellow and Schildkrout, both reporting on relatively large houses, provide conflicting evidence. Pellow (1977, pp. 187–89) found only limited interaction among women cotenants in central Accra, unless they were kin or of the same ethnicity. However, Schildkrout (1978, pp. 105–12) reports that frequent interaction in the heterogeneous Kumasi *zongo* leads to the adoption of new cultural patterns, including language, food, and behavior. People who are contenants over a long period sometimes take on fictive kinship roles. This may be due to the northerners being strangers in Kumasi to a greater extent than southerners are in Accra, or to the greater availability of kin in Accra.

Second, the orientation of rooms affects the frequency of interaction between cotenants. Where each room has its own entry to the road, cotenants come and go without meeting each other, though those who sit outside their doors in the evening to watch passersby often talk among themselves and with visiting friends. Shopkeepers, craftsmen running small businesses, and prostitutes prefer outside rooms because they provide easy access for customers.

The two major alternatives feature a single entry giving access to individual rooms, either by way of a long hallway (common in Ajegunle) or an interior or fenced-in courtyard (Ashaiman, the Gambian towns). This courtyard provides communal space for the women to cook, braid each other's hair, look after children, wash clothes, and so on, and for the men to sit in their free time; it also encourages interaction between cotenants (see Aribiah 1976, pp. 43–44). Space is needed in Kakuri for the activities of secluded women and in Banjul for Koranic instruction. Houses with rooms facing a hallway may have a courtyard at the rear, but this tends to be small in relation to the number of tenants and is mainly used for the latrine and washing space rather than for informal socializing. People living in multistoried buildings (which are becoming the norm for new urban housing in Nigeria) generally have less contact with cotenants than those living in single-story buildings.

It is interesting that housing in Tema, the only planned community among the towns studied, seems to have been designed to discourage interaction. The first three "communities" to be built included many multistoried buildings with minimal space for contact at ground level. Other areas have rows of houses, each opening on the street with its own small, hedged garden. A third form, in Kortu-gon (Community 1), has eight two-room "houses" attached around a single core, each opening on the back of the next so that neighbors have to walk around in order to meet. These methods of ignoring or avoiding neighbors may be suitable to a society such as England, where family privacy is an important value. They are quite contrary to African values of sociability. The differences between Tema and Ashaiman in the number of neighbors respondents know well and in conversations with cotenants and neighbors show that Ashaiman neighborhoods are more social, especially for women.

The opportunity for informal interaction in the neighborhood is further increased in Ashaiman because most houses lack their own water supply and sanitation. Waiting at the public standpipe is a common way to get to know one's neighbors. Though standpipes are often a source of quarrels over queue jumping, they do provide a chance to meet neighbors regularly. Waiting for water takes less time in Banjul than in Ashaiman because the supply is more dependable, but many people still find time to gossip at the standpipe. Where compounds have their own water supply, cotenants interact when collecting water there and neighbors may come to buy water.

The high density of most houses might well increase conflict, leading to more friendly social relations with neighbors than with cotenants. More Ghanaian and Nigerian respondents reported no regular conversations with neighbors than with cotenants, but there was usually a somewhat higher proportion reporting frequent conversations with five or more neighbors than with a similar number of cotenants (see Table 6.1). The number of cotenants is not an important factor in this; there was no difference between the frequency of contacts with cotenants and with neighbors in either Ajegunle or Abeokuta, though Ajegunle houses average five households and Abeokuta houses three. While housing density does appear to depress social relations in Ajegunle, it affects both co-tenants and neighbors. Very few people in any of the towns listed a cotenant or former cotenant as a friend, in spite of the fact that nearly a third had shared a meal with a cotenant during the previous week. Frequent interaction with cotenants is probably more through necessity than choice, and a move to another house usually ends the relationship.

Informal Contacts

Research on social networks in East and Central Africa has produced several interesting reports (Mitchell 1969; Parkin 1969; Stren 1972; Jacobson 1973; Ross 1975; Weinrich 1976), but little quantitative data and nothing based on more than one town. Thus, it has not been possible to take the nature of the urban environment or the relevance of different social structures into account. For example, Parkin found that women's contacts on a Kampala housing estate were mainly with cotenants and neighbors, while men usually had wider social networks and only limited contacts on the estate. This was certainly influenced by the fact that very few women were in the labor force and that most of the men worked in another part of town.

Informal contacts between urban residents can be examined in two ways: the relative attraction of various types of interaction, such as gossiping with workmates or sharing meals with cotenants, and differences in overall levels of sociability between people in varying positions in the society. Inevitably, there is a certain amount of overlap between these two, since people vary in the type and amount of informal recreation they prefer. Fischer's choice/constraint hypothesis (1977) proposes that, aside from personality, certain people will be more sociable than others because their position in society allows them more opportunities and resources with which to expand their networks. Opportunities are likely to be affected by age, sex, migration experience, occupation, and income, and the maintenance of contacts by the balance between perceived rewards and costs. It is easier to maintain contacts with neighbors than with people living farther away, but if the latter have provided social and/or material support over the years and are thought of as intimate friends, considerable effort may be made to see them at least occasionally.

Many theorists would argue that size of place and the level of communal attachment are also important. There is thought to be less choice of contacts and more pressure for friendly interaction in a small town or a neighborhood with a strong sense of community than in a large town with a transient and unattached population. However, Fischer argues that long residence may promote knowledge of neighbors but not necessarily frequent or intimate interaction with them. Given the choice, people may prefer close friendship with people who live at a distance and may remain merely acquaintances to their neighbors.

Applying this hypothesis to the West African context, the towns studied provide a wide range of communal environments, from the hometown atmosphere of Abeokuta and, to a lesser extent, Banjul, to the new town impersonality of Ajegunle and Tema. If communal relations are dependent on long residence and neighborhood attachment, there should be considerable differences between towns. If, on the other hand, they are fairly independent of place but rely on opportunities within structured constraints, there should be more differences between respondents of differing position in the society than between people of the same relative position living in different towns. Given the size of the samples, the possibilities cannot all be adequately tested, but the trend of the findings should broaden our understanding of the factors involved.

Women were expected to have narrower networks than men, because as housewives they have limited financial resources and geographical mobility and as working women they have only limited time for sociability. Differences between the young, middle-aged, and old are likely to be hidden by other variables; the young tend to be hampered by being new arrivals in town, but they need to spend less time in the household and have relatively few family responsibilities, so they have more time available for an active social life. Short-distance migrants, who are least strangers in the town, should have more contacts than long-distance migrants, even though the latter often choose a town where they know someone.

If urban experience has a damping effect on sociability, as the decline of community hypothesis suggests, people of rural background should be more sociable than those who grew up in town. On the other hand, insofar as adjustment to urban conditions improves with time and the opportunities it provides to get to know people, long-term residents and those who grew up in a town should be more sociable than recent arrivals who miss the easy familiarity of the village. People who have made several moves should find it easier to make new friends than recent direct migrants, but more mobile people may not bother to form strong local ties. Since people with many friends probably find interaction rewarding, the more social individuals are expected to have more favorable attitudes toward their neighborhoods or town than those with only limited contacts.

The stratification variables (education, occupation, and income) affect the resources available. With the possible exception of trading, wage employment should provide more opportunities to meet people than self-employment, though workers in a large-scale enterprise, like residents of large cities, may find the atmosphere too impersonal to foster friendship among coworkers. Employees in higher-level positions, which usually require considerable education and provide higher income, generally have more resources than ordinary workers; these can be used to develop and maintain networks. The assembly-line operative, on the other hand, may have a large number of coworkers from which to choose but have little time to socialize with them. Yusuf's study of a trader's network (1975) suggests that having many contacts helps to promote a business, but Imoagene (1976, chapter 5) found that businessmen and civil servants had comparable social networks, both narrower than ex-politicians.

Kin can be seen as an alternative to friends. Those who choose to have extensive contacts with kin and people from home will have less time for socializing with people met in town. In much the same way, coworkers may be an alternative to neighbors; those who spend considerable time with people met at work may have little interest in the area in which they live. To the extent that these are alternatives, people who know a majority of their neighbors and interact frequently with them should think more favorably of their neighborhoods than those who choose to spend their free time elsewhere.

Tables 6.1 and 6.2 show two approaches to testing these hypotheses; the first compares the towns on specific interaction variables and the second focuses on individual differences to determine which factors increase sociability. As expected, people in Banjul and Abeokuta are most likely to know large numbers of their neighbors well; residents of small towns (for whom alternative contacts would be some distance away) come second. People in Ajegunle (a large, rapidly growing, mobile population) have the least contact with their neighbors, or with people in most other categories. Both men and women in Ajegunle are more likely than residents of other towns to say that they know none of their neighbors well and few men have much to do with their cotenants; the houses are large and many spend considerable time each day getting to and from work.

Although Banjul houses have relatively few households and the prevailing style (a walled compound or courtyard shared by all residents) should foster cotenant interaction, comparatively few of those interviewed in Banjul reported contacts with cotenants, coworkers, or acquaintances living in other parts of town. Only in neighboring were they as social as Serekunda residents and more social than residents of most other towns. Moreover, although the locally born do know more of their neighbors well, migrants who have been in town at least five years often report more frequent contacts with more people. Given the small size and easy accessibility of all parts of Banjul and the size and heterogeneity of friendship groups (see below), there is no apparent explanation for their low level of sociability outside the neighborhood.

A wide social network may be less important in provincial than in more heterogeneous towns because of the high accessibility of the extended family in the former. In Abeokuta in particular the extended family (either sharing the house or living in the neighborhood or in a nearby village) can

TABLE 6.1
Informal Social Contacts, by Town and Sex (percentages)[a]

| | Ghana | | | | Gambia | | | | Nigeria | | | | | | | |
| | Ashaiman | | Tema | | Banjul | | Serekunda | | Aba | | Abeokuta | | Ajegunle | | Kakuri | |
	M	F	M	F	M	F	M	F	M	F	M	F	M	F	M	F
Number of neighbors R knows well																
0–1	11	20	6	6	7	8	3	4	9	18	11	3	17	27	4	16
2–9	4	33	50	56	23	24	31	36	49	57	33	38	54	40	45	39
10–25[b]	39	37	25	19	34	44	45	35	31	18	25	34	27	29	29	27
26+					36	24	21	25	11	7	31	25	2	4	22	18
Total	100	100	100	100	100	100	100	100	100	100	100	100	100	100	100	100
Talks regularly with[c]																
Cotenants: none	8	0	11	16	34	26	14	12	10	10	11	12	12	4	8	5
5+	44	67	...	...	22	29	25	38	36	20	33	19	19	28	26	30
N	72	24	119	77	142	42	124	34	143	51	92	48	163	53	156	43
Neighbors: none	19	12	22	33	13	10	11	18	28	45	17	19	21	30	15	27
5+	32	44	...	...	49	42	53	49	21	9	34	23	22	16	33	31
Coworkers: none	5	10	20	33	23	42	12	17	6	10	11	7	8	9	7	19
5+	49	20	...	...	42	32	46	17	42	50	39	18	42	53	57	38
N	59	10	196	116	140	31	134	30	133	42	123	44	144	32	136	16
Others: none	15	16	37	30	43	56	32	31	16	29	46	59	22	43	26	42
5+	42	40	...	...	35	29	22	24	36	22	27	17	45	23	42	44
Visits rooms																
Never	8	19	15	18	7	14	7	4	1	2	10	12	5	7	3	7
Cotenants, neighbors	86	78	79	76	90	84	89	87	92	93	79	75	87	84	94	89
Coworkers, others	59	45	171	65	76	49	78	64	94	73	76	51	90	68	80	73
Total[d]	153	142	165	159	173	147	174	155	187	168	165	138	182	159	177	169

196

Shares a meal[e]

Never	50	57	40	55	31	16	17	31	9	22	18	25	13	27	15	31
Cotenants	32	37	22	18	14	18	26	24	45	29	37	34	26	32	52	47
Neighbors	18	8	20	17	16	6	21	28	29	26	35	25	25	18	43	18
Kinsmen	22	15	49	28	33	57	64	59	62	38	50	43	55	38	48	33
Coworkers	{			}	38	14	39	12	65	42	61	40	53	27	53	13
Others					18	12	20	26	52	29	24	22	50	20	50	31
Total[d]	122	115	131	118	150	123	187	180	262	186	225	189	222	162	261	173
Had a party	36	4	…	…	63	76	57	72	53	51	64	60	47	36	34	36
Mean sociability score[f]	8.6	6.6	9.0	7.6	10.7	9.6	10.6	9.8	12.5	10.2	12.2	10.0	11.2	9.0	12.1	9.9
Maximum N	318[g]	142[g]	298	152	152	51	152	53	152	55	137	65	171	56	161	45

[a] Although bases for percentages differ slightly because of don't knows, only the maximum has been given at the base of the table in the interests of readability. Where the bases differ considerably, in talking with cotenants and coworkers, they are given in the table.

[b] The top category for Ghanaians (9+) is shown here as 10+.

[c] Ashaiman data are from the 1970 study. Tema data on talking use a more general question, which shows only the proportion who rarely or never talk with such people.

[d] Totals are over 100 percent because of multiple answers.

[e] In the last week, shared a meal with someone outside the household.

[f] Maximum score is 19. For Ashaiman 1970, means are 11.3 for men and 9.4 for women, with maximum score. 17.

[g] For data on talks and party, Ns are 73 males and 25 females.

provide a full social life. This might make it difficult for strangers to settle down in the town, but most migrants are able to find friends among the local population; few isolate themselves physically or socially. The provincial milieu seems to be more important than migration status or the availability of kin. Aba and Abeokuta, the former with large numbers of recent migrants and the latter with relatively few, have the highest sociability scores of the towns studied, for both men and women.[1]

The differences between these towns are that Aba residents appear to be more selective within their neighborhoods (as befits more recent arrivals) but more inclusive outside it; they are choosing their friends over a wider area. As in America, community does not require propinquity. Communalism continues to be very important in Aba, and friendships outside the neighborhood reflect the dispersion of housing of members of communal networks. With length of residence controlled, both men and women in Aba know and associate with fewer neighbors than respondents in other towns, and women with fewer than five years in Aba also reported fewer contacts with cotenants than women elsewhere. Nevertheless, they obviously find congenial companions elsewhere in town.

The utility of using a variety of measures is demonstrated in the greater importance of certain activities in one town than in another. Giving parties is most common in the Gambian and Nigerian provincial towns and least common in Ashaiman, which also had relatively low levels of visiting rooms outside the neighborhood and of sharing meals. Gambians also shared meals less often than Nigerians. Residents of Aba and Ajegunle were more likely than people living in other towns to visit the rooms of coworkers and other friends.

Visiting people in their rooms was included as a measure of intimacy, since normally only close friends or important people would be invited into one's room. However, it also measures space for entertaining visitors; where the area around the house is crowded or not amenable to visiting because there is no shade or protection from rain, visiting is necessarily transferred into the room, however crowded it may be. Thus, the abundant rain in Aba and crowded external conditions in Ajegunle probably increase the proportion of visits which take place indoors. Ashaiman is in one of the driest areas in coastal West Africa and there is plenty of exterior space in which to visit, so there is no need to enter the host's room. Tema residents may be no more likely to visit outside their neighborhoods than those in Ashaiman, but the division of land around the houses into minute "gardens" discourages its use for entertaining and promotes the privatization of visiting.

The typical West African meal requires considerable time in preparation. Hence, it is often more convenient to buy ready-cooked food or share with someone rather than prepare one's own meal.[2] Men often eat with coworkers during their breaks and men living alone may arrange to eat with members of other households, either regularly or occasionally. Women may share meals when their husbands are out. Sharing food is an important symbol of hospitality, so kin often eat together as part of weekend visits and other guests are encouraged to share the family meal. Thus, a majority of those interviewed, except in Ashaiman, had shared at least one meal during the previous week, most often with kin and (among the men) with coworkers.

Contrary to expectation, women did not share meals with cotenants more than men, and cotenants were preferred to neighbors only in Ashaiman and among women in Ajegunle and Kakuri. The single, widowed, or divorced are, on the whole, not more likely to share meals than married men and women living with their spouses. Thus, sharing is best seen as a form of sociability rather than convenience. This is confirmed by its consistently high positive correlation with other forms of sociability such as conversations and visiting rooms.

Parties are less closely correlated with the other measures of sociability than meals. They appear to occur mainly as part of rites of passage (the celebration of marriages and the outdooring, circumcision, or christening of children) though birthday parties were also mentioned in The Gambia. Thus, they may take place at home rather than in town and middle-aged or older people are more likely to report having a party than young, single people.

A large party affirms the status of the host, especially if important people attend. People of higher socioeconomic status can better afford parties than the poor, but the latter may invite large numbers of people to a ceremonial party in hopes that the gifts they bring will more than offset the cost of drinks, music, and other expenses. Records are often kept so that the host can return an equal gift should the guest invite him to a similar party. Thus, parties are reciprocal mutual aid institutions which make it possible to celebrate rites of passage in a suitable manner. Except among the young and well-educated, less formal events are probably not classed as parties.

A Sociability Scale

These aspects of social life have been brought together in a sociability scale. It includes many of the same variables as the index of social orientation used in chapter 2 (frequency of talking and eating with nonfamily members, visits to friends' rooms, and membership in associations), but omits contacts with kin in town and at home and substitutes the number of friends listed, the number of neighbors known well, and whether the respondent has given a party.[3]

The scale is useful for examining the effects of various individual and structural characteristics on sociability. Making towns and countries into dummy variables showed that town explains 12 percent of the variability in sociability scores of both men and women or, alternatively, country explains 8 percent of male and 9 percent of female variance. Most of the individual variables explain much less; particular characteristics seldom add more than two points to an individual's score.

The towns chosen in each country provide different social environments, from the new town industrial bureaucracy of Ghana, where the 1968 sample had the lowest mean scores, through the stable small towns of The Gambia, to the Nigerian provincial towns where sociability levels were highest. The low Ghana 1968 scores were partly due to the use of somewhat different items, but the 1970 scores, which were based on items much closer to the Nigerian and Gambian scales, produce much the same means as Ajegunle, the least social of Nigerian towns.

Gambian men's relatively low scores disprove the hypothesis of the efficacy of small size and long residence in facilitating communal relations. The hypothesis receives some support in the low sociability of Ajegunle, but the minimal difference between the mean scores for Kakuri and Abeokuta shows that many other factors must be taken into account. As expected, mean scores for women are lower than those for men in all eight towns, though in The Gambia these differences are not significant. Nevertheless, there are very few men or women without informal contacts; less than 1 percent of the Gambian respondents, 2 percent in Nigeria, and 5 percent in Ghana had scores below three.

On the whole, sociability as measured by the scale is only moderately and inconsistently related to individual characteristics and attitudes (see Table 6.2). The most important characteristics appear to be income and origin (size and distance combined), which each explain between 5 and 12 percent of the variance in male and female scores. Other useful variables for women are length of residence, age at arrival, employment sector, occupation, and education. Most characteristics of respondents are significantly correlated with sociability scores in less than half of the measured cases; for several (notably age, rural/urban origin, going home, liking for the neighborhood, and ethnic heterogeneity of best friends) the direction of the relationship varies from one town to another. This suggests considerable interaction between variables and over time as well as the influence of different urban environments. There is no obvious explanation as to why the relations are more often significant for women in Serekunda and Ajegunle and for men in Banjul and Tema; similar types of towns and the opposite sex in the same town often produce different results. This is yet another warning of the danger of limiting research to a single place.

In spite of this variance, certain hypotheses are clearly supported. The most stable relationships are distance from place of origin and length of residence. Mitchell (1973) found that short-distance migrants to Zambian

TABLE 6.2

Correlations between Sociability Score and Individual Characteristics, by Town and Sex[a]

Column groups: **Ghana 1968** (Ashaiman, Tema) · **Ashaiman 1970** · **Gambia** (Banjul, Serekunda) · **Nigeria** (Aba, Abeokuta, Ajegunle, Kakuri)

	Ashaiman M	Ashaiman F	Tema M	Tema F	Ashaiman 1970 M	Ashaiman 1970 F	Banjul M	Banjul F	Serekunda M	Serekunda F	Aba M	Aba F	Abeokuta M	Abeokuta F	Ajegunle M	Ajegunle F	Kakuri M	Kakuri F
Origin	-.12	-.19	-.30	-.37			-.30		-.13	-.34	-.21			-.22	-.12	-.43	-.15	
Length of residence	.25	.17	.20	.19			.33		.20	.40	.15		.17	.35	.15	.36		.13
Number of moves							-.14			-.26		.24		-.21		-.24		
Rural/urban	-.18	-.14					.21			.25							.18	
Income[b]	⋯	⋯	⋯	⋯	⋯	⋯	.21		.19	.33	.15	.23			.24	.43	.23	.26
Employment sector		.23		.31	.29		.23	.23		.35					.33	.57	.23	.35
Occupation			.19							.24	.16	.29				.45		
Education			.37		.20	.48	.20			.37		.24	.16					
Age at arrival							-.30			-.39		-.28	-.14	-.29			.17	-.33
Age						-.39		-.38										
Marital career	.11		.14								.14	.25						
Visits with kin			-.13	.44	-.51						-.23	-.55	-.30	-.47	-.20	-.34	-.35	-.42
Visits home[c]	.18		.29				.24		.27		.42		.27				.35	
Going home[c]				-.15					.35		-.17					.38		-.28
Friends																		
Easy to make[d]					.38			.25			.14		.21	.39				
Mixed ethnicity	.49	.47	.40	.29			.31	.25		.38	-.22		.22	-.24				
Network density[d]					.42		.27	.34		.35	.24		.16	.37				

[a]Only correlations significant beyond the .05 level are shown.
[b]No data available for Ghana.
[c]Migrants only.
[d]No data for Ghana 1968.

towns are more active socially than those from farther away. He attributes this to the need for long-distance migrants to be absent from town if they are to maintain their (more important) rural ties. West African migrants from a long distance tend to handle this problem by attenuating their links with home, but in all three countries they have significantly lower sociability scores than other migrants. Short-distance migrants are more socially active in Tema and Ashaiman than the indigenes, but in The Gambia and Nigeria only a long distance makes a notable difference.

This suggests that the important factor may be cultural difference rather than distance. Migrants from another country or, in Nigeria, from well outside the cultural area of the majority of residents of a town, find it harder to make wide-ranging contacts and thus develop smaller and more selective networks. It is less a question of withdrawing to keep up contacts with home (they seldom go home and do not stay away long), than of being more of a stranger than other migrants.

Length of residence also has the effect predicted. Migrants who have been in town up to ten years are less active socially than long-established residents, and those with less than five years in town tend to have the lowest scores. Age at arrival may be a factor in this; those who arrive after age 25 are significantly less social. They probably make less effort to build up an urban network because men expect to return home relatively soon and older women migrants are often satisfied to confine their social life to the household. Moving more than once appears to affect the sociability of women more than of men, usually by lowering the range of their contacts. It probably takes women somewhat longer than men to build up networks of friends, and those whose husbands are subject to transfer may make less effort to do so.

Of the stratification variables, income differentiates most clearly and education is a better predictor of sociability than occupation. Those with the least resources (no income, no education, no employment) have a lower level of sociability than the rest, but those with the most resources are not necessarily more social than people in the middle of the range. Only the poorest seem to be disadvantaged by a lack of economic resources. There is usually little or no increase in the proportion with high sociability scores beyond the £200–299 category and the proportion drops somewhat for men in Banjul and the Nigerian provincial towns with incomes over £750.

Female education correlations tend to be insignificant and inconsistent, but the few Gambian and Nigerian women who had gone beyond a middle level of education were significantly more social than the majority. Resources appear to be of more importance to the sociability of women than of men because they help women to get out of the house and thereby broaden their contacts, especially if they have enough education to become wage employed.

Men in wage employment are slightly more social than the self-employed, which suggests that the opportunity for contacts on the job is more important than the self-employed's availability to visitors. Occupation is, on the whole, the least reliable measure of resource differentials. This is partly because of the broad and necessarily heterogeneous categories used, but also because other factors unconnected with occupation are more important. The preemployed and unskilled laborers have, on average, the lowest sociability scores, but indigenes in this position often lead active social lives.

Occupational differentials tend to disappear when education is added to the regression equation, but men in skilled work are still significantly more social than the unskilled. Men in commerce tend to have about average mean scores. Rather than develop wide networks to improve their business, they seem to prefer to limit friendships in the interests of husbanding their capital. Women traders are more sociable than housewives in Ghana and Nigeria but not in The Gambia.

Age and religion have relatively little effect which is independent of other variables. The differences between Muslims and Christians are largely due to Muslims having less education and (in Ghana) being long-distance migrants. The effect of education for men in Ghana disappears when religion is added to the regression equation, indicating that religion (and place of origin related to it) is more important than education in the formation and maintenance of contacts in these towns.

Several studies in America have shown that adults with children tend to make more friends in their neighborhoods than those without children; parents meet through their children (see Fischer 1977, chapter 5). The criteria used here divide respondents into single, divorced or separated without children in the household, either a spouse or children in the household, or both spouse and children present. This appears to have only a limited effect on overall sociability in West Africa, and to be more important for men than for women. All the correlations are negative in The Gambia (indicating that those with children are less social), and none was over .06.

Only in Aba does marital state significantly affect the social interaction levels of both men and women, though men and women in other Nigerian towns had more contacts with neighbors and (men only) with cotenants if they were living with both spouse and children. What probably happens is that family responsibilities do increase neighborhood contacts because they keep parents closer to their rooms; people living on their own have a wider choice of contacts and thus have less to do with their neighbors.

The correlation of visits with kin with sociability is consistently negative, showing convincingly that this is an alternative to socializing with nonkin. The people who see their kin daily, either because they live nearby, through choice, or because of family pressures, tend to have little time for neighbors, coworkers, or other friends, whereas those who see kin less than once a week usually spend their spare time with friends and neighbors.

Visiting home, on the other hand, appears to be quite compatible with a wide urban network, since this is often done during holiday periods when many urban residents are visiting their homes. In two-thirds of the male samples, those who visited home often were more sociable in town than those who seldom went. As the frequency of visits is closely related to distance, this supports the findings of Mayer (1964, pp. 32–33) in South Africa and Mitchell (1973) in Zambia that migrants from nearby can make the most of both worlds, maintaining contacts at home while enjoying the income and amenities of urban life. This makes for greater security and wider social networks. The insignificant relationship between women's visits home and sociability is because, as noted in chapter 5, they have less control over the frequency of visits than men do.

In The Gambia and Abeokuta those who intend to stay in town permanently are usually more sociable, but they tend to have lower scores than intended returnees in Kakuri, Aba, and among the Tema women. This appears to be a difference between towns with low and high proportions of migrants. In the former, those intending permanent residence are the majority, and tend to be well established in their relationships with the indigenes and each other. In the latter, most residents consider themselves strangers in town and they tend to have more choice of people with similar background and attitudes than the few who intend to settle in town.

People who find it easy to make friends do not necessarily have wider contacts than those who find it difficult, and there is no consistent relationship between liking the neighborhood (comparing it favorably to other parts of town) and overall sociability. Both of these findings suggest the importance of constraints. People who enjoy making friends have few because of limited resources (in time as well as finances), and residence in a particular neighborhood is often due to a lack of alternatives rather than because it is socially satisfying. Women who seldom sit and talk with neighbors nevertheless often think well of their locality, but Nigerian men with the most neighborhood contacts are the most positive about their areas. Whether having friends nearby makes it seem a more pleasant neighborhood or whether liking the area makes it easier to make friends there is difficult to say.

The more social respondents in Ghana and The Gambia tend to have friends of different ethnic groups, but in Nigeria friendship networks of the more social tend to be ethnically homogeneous. This supports the impression of greater interethnic tension in Nigeria, to be discussed in chapter 8. Nigerians with ethnically mixed networks of close friends tend to be locals (Kakuri) or long-distance migrants (Ajegunle); in both cases they are members of minority groups who are under some constraint to choose "strangers" as friends.

The density of friendship groups (the likelihood that all members know one another) increases with sociability, indicating that more social individuals are better able to bring their friends together or, because they see them more often, friends are more likely to meet. This probably increases the rewards of friendship, since the company of several friends can be enjoyed at once. Less social individuals may prefer to see friends one at a time, or merely visit with each one so rarely that their friends do not meet.

These data may be summarized by saying that the most social individuals tend to be males living in the Nigerian provincial towns or Kakuri, who know many of their neighbors and visit regularly with other people around town, in their rooms as well as on the street. They tend to have lived in the town for some time, to be locally born or short-distance migrants and to have a moderate level of income and education. They see relatively little of their kin and usually have friends of other ethnic groups. In other words, they have had time to settle down and make friends and have the resources to expend on an active social life, which they choose to spend with coworkers and neighbors rather than with kin. This does not mean that they have no contacts with kin, but rather that kin are only part of much wider networks.

Friendship Networks

Some indication of the nature of individuals' extended networks was given in the last section. This section will focus on a much smaller group characterized as friends. In Epstein's term (1961, p. 57) this is the effective social network, the people with whom respondents interact more regularly, who care about them and who are most available to give them advice and (perhaps) economic support.

Because "friend" can sometimes mean the sort of person who leads a young man into trouble or repeats secrets told in confidence (see Pellow 1977, pp. 195–98), respondents were asked about the people they move with/see often. They were encouraged to provide details on five people; a few listed even more, but most stopped after two or three. They were not asked about the degree of intimacy of the link, but most appear to have understood the question as referring to what Nigerians call "tight friends," people to whom they felt particularly close. A few people who said they had no friends obviously had many acquaintances; on the other hand, a few young people listed several companions of the moment as well as one or two long-established relationships. Most of the friends were living in the same town and were seen at least once a week, though a few people listed friends they saw as rarely as once a year.

Jackson, Fischer, and Jones (in Fischer 1977, p. 46) differentiate four characteristics of networks (density, homogeneity, dominant source, and dispersion of sources) and five characteristics of the links (intimacy, frequency, duration, role multiplexity, and source). Because of space limitations, the discussion here will be focused on the networks as a whole, though mention will be made of variations in link characteristics.

The density or mesh of the network (the extent to which all members know each other well—ideally, are close friends) was mentioned above. A dense network provides more support for individual members, but may be used to cut the group off from the rest of society, at least in their free time. It can exert more pressure on members to conform to group norms, which may be used to maintain allegiance to traditional values or to speed the adoption of new values.

Homogeneity may be measured in terms of age, education, status, ethnicity, or other characteristics of network members. To the extent that friendship networks are homogeneous (all members have the same characteristics and fill the same roles in society), boundaries develop which may interfere with societal integration. People hesitate to interact across well-established boundaries, and intergroup conflict may be difficult to resolve because the competing parties have little in common and seldom contact one another socially (Blau 1975, p. 229).

Members of a network may be drawn from a single source (hometown, church, work) or from many sources. If all or most members met in a particular context, the group is likely to be more homogeneous than if they met at different times and in various contexts, though this homogeneity may be limited to certain characteristics. For example, friends met at work are likely to be similar in education and status but some will be different in ethnicity; friends met in childhood will probably be similar in age and ethnicity but different in status. Networks drawing from several sources should also be less dense, since members are likely to have less in common.

Intimacy refers to the closeness of the tie, whether they are "tight friends" or merely acquaintances. Links may also be characterized by the frequency of contacts, the length of time since they were established, and the context in which the two individuals met. Frequency will be dealt with here in terms of the activity level of the group as a whole, the regularity with which the respondent sees everyone he or she has listed. This tells us something about their use of what are seen as close friendship ties.

If friends are all seen often, they are likely to know each other and collectively provide a focus for network social activities. Members of the network who are seldom seen are unlikely to be known to the others; they often live some distance away. They probably provide less support than friends seen frequently, but may be useful as an alternative source of information and help in a crisis. They may be more intimate than nearby friends; the friendship survives in spite of distance because the tie is strong (Fischer 1977, p. 173).

Some friends share many roles (as when they are kin, coworkers, and members of the same association), whereas others share only the role of friend. To the extent that the link is long-established and based on several roles, it can be intimate without frequent contact. On the other hand, a friendship of short duration without much intimacy or role multiplexity may soon wither if frequent contact becomes impossible, perhaps because one member moves away; costs become greater than rewards. This is especially important in urban situations, where moves are common.

Density and Activity Level

Table 6.3 shows relatively little difference between men and women or between towns in the mean number of friends listed, with the exception of men in Ashaiman; the effective network averages about three people. Between half and three-quarters of the friendship groups listed consisted of people who all knew one another well. Here again, the differences between men and women are small, but (except in Ajegunle) women appear to have somewhat less dense friendship groups than men. It is easier for men to meet geographically dispersed friends and they are more likely to have friends at work, so new friends can be introduced into a group activity and, through regular meeting, get to know other members of the network. Since their free time is less predictable than men's, women are more likely to see friends one or two at a time; therefore, density takes longer to develop.

The densest networks are usually those with an exclusively hometown, childhood, or school source, closely followed by those entirely drawn from coworkers. Networks based on other urban sources (church, association membership, met at parties) are less likely to be dense and, as expected, those with several sources have the loosest mesh. Nevertheless, except among women in Aba and Kakuri, at least a third of mixed-source networks were fully dense.

Since density levels are considerably higher for all sources than in Detroit (see Fischer 1977, p. 56), African urbanites appear to be more likely than Americans to introduce friends to one another. They tend to have more localized networks, and may feel more comfortable if all their friends at least know each other. Where one member of the network is not known to the others, he or she is usually (1) from another source, often from home, (2) living in another town (village friends are almost never listed), (3) of a different status from the respondent and other network members, or (4) a prospective marital partner, though in many cases these are integrated into the network.

TABLE 6.3

Size and Density of Friendship Networks, by Town and Sex

| | Ashaiman 1970 | | Gambia | | | | Nigeria | | | | | | | |
| | | | Banjul | | Serekunda | | Aba | | Abeokuta | | Ajegunle | | Kakuri | |
	M	F	M	F	M	F	M	F	M	F	M	F	M	F
Mean number of friends	4.5	2.5	2.8	2.8	2.4	2.3	2.7	2.6	3.4	2.6	3.0	2.2	3.4	3.5
Percent of fully dense networks														
Total sample	62	54	70	65	64	52	53	45	76	77	55	75	57	59
By source:														
Home, school	100	100	87	100	89	100	77	75	96	100	100	77	82	82
Work	100	67	71	100	90	NA	82	75	90	83	77	80	73	100
Other urban	62	67	88	82	45	60	50	50	68	75	53	85	52	73
Mixed	52	33	53	47	43	60	41	27	63	44	33	62	45	27
Percent seen at least weekly														
Fully dense	80	43	93	96	96	100	85	83	95	91	87	94	88	87
Less dense	54	50	81	79	95	88	59	82	85	80	64	82	81	69
Maximum N[a]	63	13	126	40	131	35	119	40	112	44	144	44	137	39

[a]Density measures include only those with two or more friends.

Men and women tend to see their friends with about equal frequency, but there is considerable difference between towns in how often friends are seen. There is more daily visiting in the Gambian towns than in Ashaiman and Kakuri, though these towns are comparable in size and respondents in the latter two are no more likely to report that friends live some distance away. Some Ghanaians were doing shift work, but this was not a factor in Kakuri. Gambian friends may be more likely to meet at the local mosque, or may give greater preference to spending their free time with the same people.

The three largest towns show the least visiting on a daily basis; about a fifth of Aba respondents saw at least some of their friends less than once a week. As expected, the relationship between density and frequency of visits is positive, but considerably stronger for men than for women. Men have more control over their activity levels, because time is less of a constraint for them. All members of dense networks are usually seen more often than those in loose networks, because the distant and infrequently seen friends tend to be unknown to the others.

The relationship of density to sociability and the characteristics of respondents are seldom significant and usually inconsistent from one town to another. Thus, the density of an effective network appears to be independent of the range of the individual's extended network and of age, education, occupation, income, place of origin, and length of residence in town. This is partly due to the high proportion of dense networks; people of all types appear to prefer them. The lowest density for both men and women tends to be between the ages of 25 and 34, which suggests that new friends are being made during the period of early marriage and parenthood.

As predicted, density and homogeneity are positively correlated; dense networks are usually more homogeneous in their membership than loose networks. This is partly because people are more likely to introduce friends who are seen to have much in common than friends of different background. In addition, the more diverse sources and greater geographical spread of many loose networks make it more difficult for members to meet.

Homogeneity and Source

Table 6.4 shows the variables used in measuring the homogeneity of the friendship group. Selectivity is clearly related to both cultural expectations and opportunities. Most of the friends mentioned are of the same sex and marital status as the respondent. Ethnicity is a more salient criterion for potential friends in Nigeria than in The Gambia, but about half of the respondents in the highly heterogeneous Ajegunle and Kakuri had at least one close friend belonging to a different ethnic group.

TABLE 6.4

Heterogeneity of Friendship Networks, by Town and Sex (Percentages)

| | Ashaiman | | Gambia | | | | Nigeria | | | | | | | |
| | | | Banjul | | Serekunda | | Aba | | Abeokuta | | Ajegunle | | Kakuri | |
	M	F	M	F	M	F	M	F	M	F	M	F	M	F
Percentage whose reported friends are all														
Same sex	92	87	89	82	94	93	74	64	78	78	80	62	82	76
Single/all married	35	43	54	50	71	69	90	78	83	83	90	76	89	78
Same ethnic group[a]	49	52	39	46	36	42	42	31	50	52	45	65	47	43
Same religion	39	59	82	84	85	87	31	35	17	18	32	29	22	16
Aged within 5 years	30	32	46	42	55	49	31	31	44	53	38	35	42	49
Same level occupation[b]	28	43	30	42	32	47	23	41	30	55	28	25	27	40
Same education	32	48	49	42	46	53	16	16	27	55	21	27	34	51
Same hometown	17	17	44	56	38	42	18	9	39	45	20	24	24	27
N	75	23	142	50	140	45	161	45	172	55	138	64	152	55
Mean score[c]	5.1	4.4	5.1	4.9	4.9	4.8	4.2	3.7	4.0	3.1	5.6	5.1	5.4	4.6

[a] For Aba and Abeokuta, same subgroup.

[b] Six categories were used: farm/unskilled, semiskilled, skilled, commerce, clerical/uniformed services, administration/professional.

[c] Possible range is 0–12; a higher score indicates greater heterogeneity.

Subethnicity becomes important in provincial towns such as Aba and Abeokuta, and relatively few respondents crossed this boundary. Similarly, 90 percent of the residents of the Gambian towns are Muslim, so friendships with Christians are limited by opportunity as well as by differences in social status and culture between Muslims and Christians.

Age is somewhat more important in Serekunda than elsewhere; some Gambians still consider that true friends are those who went through the initiation school together. Though closely related to social status, occupation and education are not very important criteria of friendship; a high proportion with the same education usually means that few people in that town attended school. Many people report friends they have made at work, but they usually have other friends in different occupations as well. The elderly Nigerian prophet who listed a university vice-chancellor and two lawyers (friends since childhood), the chief superintendent who listed his car mechanic, the teacher who included her seamstress and a trader she met in the hospital, and the Gambian electrician who listed two government ministers were less unusual in West Africa than they would be in the United States.

Harries-Jones (in Mitchell 1969, pp. 298–99) compares the use of "home-boy" ties in Zambia and South Africa. The nature of urbanization and the attitude of political authorities affect these relationships, but use also varies with the migrants' economic and social position and need in a particular situation. As a basis for close friendship, a common hometown is relatively unimportant in West Africa; the majority have friends met in town, though a substantial number have come from the same district, region, or state. Between a fifth and a quarter of respondents mentioned only friends they had met at home or in school, but these are mostly nonmigrants rather than long-distance migrants forming a small, closed community.

It was expected that social networks would be most homogeneous in the provincial towns, moderate in the suburbs (which, except for Ajegunle, are small in size), and most heterogeneous in central cities, where the potential for multiform contacts is greatest. Table 6.4 shows the lowest mean scores in the provincial towns, but only relatively minor differences between the other towns. Ajegunle men have the most heterogeneous friendship groups, followed by Kakuri men. Both towns are highly mixed ethnically and respondents there tend to report few friends from home. Ajegunle men are especially likely to have friends of different education and Kakuri men, of different religion—reflecting the relatively high level of Christian/Muslim mixing in Kakuri.

In both Abeokuta and Banjul, people born in the town are more homogeneous in their friendship choices than migrants, which suggests that the political conflicts which have arisen in many towns between a large local population and migrants are probably aggravated by a lack of close personal ties across this boundary. Lloyd's report on Warri (1974) and Baker's study of Lagos indigenes (1974) support this. Migrants make new friends because they need to; it is easy for the indigenes to associate mainly with old friends.

Differences in mean scores on the heterogeneity scale are often small, but women's networks are consistently somewhat more homogeneous than men's except in sex and marital status. This is partly due to the greater homogeneity of female respondents. As a high proportion of women are illiterate or have only primary education and most are either housewives or petty traders, women are more likely than men to have friends with the same education and occupation as themselves. They also tend to have a somewhat narrower linguistic competence, which should increase the probability that friends will be of the same ethnicity.

An interesting exception is heterosexual friendships. Some men object to their wives trading because of the opportunities this provides for meeting other men. In all but Abeokuta, women were at least slightly more likely than men to report friends of the opposite sex. This may be the result of somewhat different definitions of friendship, but the implications of cross-sex friendships must be taken into account. These are usually re- ported by young, unmarried respondents with a wide circle of friends or by high-status individuals listing their spouse, but in Abeokuta the high level of polygyny apparently made it acceptable for both married men and women to form close heterosexual attachments outside the marital bond. These are sometimes of long standing without marital change on either side.

On the basis of at least five out of seven correlations in the same direction, at least two of which are significant beyond the .05 level, heterogeneity of friendship for men increases with education, level of occupation, employment sector (wage- more than self-employment), and income, and is inversely related to the length of time spent in town. For women, it increases with education and decreases among long-term residents. Correlations with size of place or origin are small, but tend to be negative for men. Rural and long-distance migrants are not segregating themselves more than men of urban origin. Exceptions to the above trends are often the Gambian towns, indicating that a different pattern may be operating there.

As a result of his study of social networks in Mbale, Uganda, Jacobson (1973) suggests that friendships are formed at least partly in anticipation of the future. Members of the elite who are subject to transfer from one town to another have networks which are "wholly contained among the elite" (1973, p. 129) because these are the people they expect to meet again in other towns; their networks are ethnically heterogeneous because other characteristics, such as equality of education and income, are more important at this level. Nonelite people, on the other hand, usually have ethnically homogeneous friendship networks, composed largely of people from home, because they expect to retire to their homes and hometown affairs continue to be of great importance to them.

Jacobson (1973, p. 131) suggests that West African elite members probably maintain wider ties than those in East Africa because they tend to settle for life in one town (such as Ibadan) which has many people from home (of all social levels) rather than move about, and because they want access to land at home, which must be obtained through communal ties. On the whole, the West African situation is much more complex than this. Land purchase is more open and widespread than Jacobson assumed, and access to land is a relatively unimportant reason for maintaining contacts with home.

There may be a significant difference in the frequency of close friendships between elite and nonelite residents of East and West African towns, but the chief problem with this comparison is that it refers to people in different situations. The mobile elite of Mbale should be compared to mobile administrators in small West African towns, not to the stable elite of Ibadan or Lagos. The most comparable respondents are the four in Abeokuta and six in Aba who were living in the Government Residential Areas. The men held senior administrative or professional positions (doctor, accountant, chief superintendent) and the women were teachers or health professionals. It is striking that all four in Abeokuta said it is hard to get to know people and had correspondingly small networks, whereas those in Aba said it is easy to get to know people and had average or relatively high levels of sociability. Obviously, high-level transients find it difficult to move into Abeokuta social life, whereas the greater mobility of Aba residents makes this less of a problem.

All of these elite respondents except one woman (who said she had no friends) had friends of other ethnic subgroups. The majority of their friends were connected with their work, but a car mechanic (seen weekly), a trader (from the same village), and some private sector and self-employed elites were included. Some friends were known from school or had been met in other towns when both were working there. The Abeokuta respondents usually knew several of their elite neighbors, but none of them ate or talked with neighbors.

In Aba, on the other hand, the neighbors reported as known were also visited. In neither town is there much eating out, but friends are seen for a chat and (among the men) for a drink about two to four times per week. Women are busier, and chat with friends mainly at work. Thus, the picture is not too different from that presented by Jacobson. These mobile elites make friends mainly with people like themselves.

Comparison of these with people of similar occupations and income living elsewhere suggests that Government Residential Areas provide an atypical environment which inhibits social interaction. A high proportion of the administrators and professionals living in other areas in these towns were teachers or nurses, but there were also lawyers, managers, and religious leaders. Most knew more of their neighbors and interacted with more of them than the GRA residents. Almost all had interethnic friendships.

An examination of the data for all the Nigerian and Gambian towns shows that high-income administrators and professionals are only rarely more likely to have interethnic friendships than people of lower-level occupations and income, in spite of the fact that they probably have the greatest opportunity to meet people of different ethnic background at work. Thus, it should not be concluded that the elites as a whole are more universal in their interaction patterns or are cutting themselves off from the rest of the society; one must take into consideration the nature of the housing in which the elite being studied live. Insofar as the housing is isolated, its residents may also be; if they live in mixed areas, they will probably have much the same levels of sociability as other sectors of the population. The development of housing estates for people with high incomes (which in increasing in all three countries) will probably lead to greater isolation than at present.

As expected, the most homogenous friendship groups are those where all the members met at home or in school and the least homogeneous tend to have several sources. Coworker groups are only moderately homogeneous, as they tend to differ in age and/or ethnicity. They sometimes include occupations at different levels, as in the case of the machine operative with a friend who was a supervisor (both members of a pentecostal church) and the skilled mechanic whose friend was a clerk at the same factory. Two-thirds of the networks from "other urban" and mixed sources are over the mean heterogeneity score for their town and sex, compared to only a third of those who all met at home and school and three-fifths of those who met exclusively at work. Groups drawn from urban sources are also most likely to be educationally and ethnically heterogenous. Thus, migrants who make friends in town (the majority) usually broaden their sources of information and support by so doing.

Conclusion

It should now be possible to answer some of the questions posed at the beginning of the chapter. Relatively few people in West African cities of any size are socially isolated, but these tend to have the least choice, to be most constrained by age (especially older women), poverty, and lack of education or employment. These disabilities limit their mobility within the town and their ability to reciprocate hospitality.

However, it is important to emphasize that (1) the contrary is not true. Those with the most resources in terms of income and education are, on the whole, fairly average in their sociability. Most neither isolate themselves nor set a pattern of widespread hospitality, perhaps because both of these life-styles would involve greater costs than a middle road, the first in loss of status for unsocial behavior and the second in time and demands for assistance. (2) A narrow social network may not indicate isolation but merely a preference for one or two old friends or, more often, for the companionship of the other members of the household. Kin are a viable alternative to friends for many urban residents. (3) Very few of the correlations are significant for both men and women or for a majority of towns, so that structural variables and personal characteristics explain only a relatively small part of the variance in sociability. The urban environment explains as much as any single individual variable.

Time is an important factor in establishing and maintaining relationships. It often takes several years in a locality to get to know a large number of neighbors, but neighborhoods have more meaning in towns which are growing slowly than in those with much recent change. Men participate in a wider range of social activities than women because of their greater access to resources in time as well as money. Women with good jobs often have little time for socializing because they have domestic duties as well, whereas men earning less often have considerable free time.

The available evidence does not demonstrate conclusively that the size or density of housing affects residents' social interaction, though the size of a town may inhibit contacts between residents who live at some distance from each other. Small houses and small towns often seem more social, but the data suggest that individuals make social opportunities in varying ways so that observation of contacts in a particular situation may be misleading. For example, young people may have little to do with the neighbors because they find friends elsewhere in town; older people with children to look after are more likely to find friends among their neighbors. Few people have close friends among their cotenants, regardless of the size or type of house they live in.

Most West Africans appear to favor closure in their effective networks; the majority of their good friends all know each other well and segregated friendships involving frequent interaction are rare. Network density appears to be unrelated to sociability and individual characteristics; the occurrence of a dispersed network may be due to chance, and the maintenance of segregated ties may be the result of events in the individual's earlier career. Because the intensity of the links was not measured, it is impossible to say whether loose ties are more or less important to respondents than dense ones.

Although social segregation is on some measures somewhat more common at the top- and bottom-status levels than for the majority in these societies, there is little evidence that coterminous boundaries are leading to exclusive subgroups which resist incorporation into the urban society or cut themselves off from the rest of the population. Insofar as some long-distance migrants encapsulated themselves in the past, the increasing education of today's migrants and their greater commitment to urban living makes it likely that such groups are declining in importance. At the other extreme, the elites may be gradually moving in the direction of segregation, but so far few of them are willing or able to isolate themselves from frequent social contacts with nonelite people.

7☐ASSOCIATIONS[1]

> Dupe Okunlola is a trained teacher of 29 who came to
> Ajegunle from Western State to join her husband when he
> got a clerical job in Apapa. Her three friends come from
> different Yoruba towns, all are teachers, and all know one
> another well although they do not teach in the same
> school and one lives in another part of Lagos. Membership
> of the Nigerian Union of Teachers is a result of her job, but
> she feels that, if necessary, teachers should strike to make
> their needs known to the government. She is also active in
> several other associations: the Baptist Women's Society in
> Ajegunle, the social circle of people from her village
> (which meets in Lagos), a netball team associated with her
> school, and a savings society. She has a joint bank account
> with her husband, but the savings society is useful for
> accumulating capital for her private business. With super-
> vising her household (including a five-year-old son), pre-
> paring lessons, attending meetings, seeing her friends
> regularly, and trading, she has a very busy life.

Voluntary associations have received much more attention in the literature than informal recreation, largely because of the role they are supposed to play in the socialization of new migrants to the cities (see Banton
1956; Little 1957; Parkin 1966). However, in recent years this function
has been questioned (Kerri 1976). There has been increasing evidence
that association membership is fairly selective and varies with individual
background, personality, and status; with local customs of affiliation; and
with urban social structure and the process of migration experienced by
members of various groups.

Individuals of identical background may participate in different types
of associations when living in different types of towns, and the same individual may prefer different types of associations, or no association at all, at
different times in his or her career, either because of changed personal
needs or of changed external conditions. For example, membership in
political parties was a popular form of participation prior to and just after
independence (Wallerstein 1964; Mackintosh 1966, p. 349), but they
existed only in The Gambia at the time the studies were made and most

Gambians limited their party activism to the period just prior to an election.

Early studies of associations, especially in the 1950s, drew their data largely from officers, and probably overstated their importance and the size and level of activity of their membership. As the research generally covered only a short period of time, the authors failed to note the ephemeral, or at least irregular, nature of many voluntary associations. The small ones (the majority) tend to be highly dependent on the enthusiastic leadership of a few and fade away quickly when one or two individuals take up other interests; they only come into effective existence again if a new leader appears. Thus, a town improvement association (probably the most widespread type today) may be very active for a year or two, lapse into quiescence for a few years, then be resurrected by the old leader or a new one; this circular pattern is likely to be more typical than continuous activity.

Voluntary associations are groups of people who join together freely to further their mutual goals. They differ from informal groups of people in having (1) a hierarchical leadership, (2) specified goals, (3) formal or informal norms as to members' behavior, and (4) a distinct identity, symbolized by a name (Edwards and Booth 1973, p. 3). The prominence of these characteristics, and the continuity of the associations' existence, probably increase with size, but the value of associations to their members in African towns may be inversely proportional to their size. Small associations are more limited in the resources of their members and more ephemeral, but they probably provide better social support, on the particularistic basis their members expect, than the more bureaucratized large associations. However, the most effective size depends on the goal to be achieved. A savings society requires mutual trust, and thus all members should know one another well; if a tribal union is to influence the government to favor a particular part of the country, it must demonstrate its backing by a large number of voters.

Ghanaian respondents were asked about membership of ethnic or other mutual aid associations and of church or savings societies. Respondents in other towns were questioned more systematically on past and present membership of a wider variety of associations. The discussion of the factors involved in association membership of any kind will be followed by an examination of participation in specific types of associations: primary (ethnic, hometown, and family), religious, occupational, savings, and recreational. As frequency of attendance was not included in the Nigerian interviews and leadership data are available only for The Gambia, less can be said on these topics than on the characteristics of people who claim to be members. Nevertheless, these data provide a more comprehensive picture of association membership than has previously been available.

Membership

The level of membership varies considerably with the size, hetero-geneity, and political and social structure of the town as well as with the age, socioeconomic and migration status, ethnicity, and religion of individuals. Table 7.1 shows that membership is most common in Aba, more widespread in Nigeria than in The Gambia, and least common in the Ghanian towns. Cultural propensity to form associations is a factor in this,[1] but some towns also provide a more favorable environment for associations than others.

Small towns, where it should be easier to know one's neighbors and make friends, could be expected to have a lower level of participation in formal associations than larger, less personal cities. This hypothesis is supported in the differences in the proportion of members between Ashaiman and Tema, between Kakuri and the other Nigerian towns, and between males in Banjul and Serekunda. Chapter 6 showed how informal social contacts are fostered in Ashaiman (as contrasted with Tema) by the residents' ability to choose their own rooms and by the necessity of using public standpipes. Although membership is at about the same level in Ajegunle and Abeokuta, members appear to be less assiduous in attending meetings unless they occur in Ajegunle itself because of transportation difficulties in the Lagos area.

Migrants might be expected to be more active in primary associations in heterogeneous towns where their position is less secure than where they feel at home. This seems to explain the relatively low participation in such associations in Abeokuta, where the indigenes are unquestionably dominant and migrants accommodate themselves to this situation. In Aba, which is ethnically homogeneous but where the indigenes are not dominant and where subethnic competition is important, there is strong pressure to belong and many men join more than one primary association.[2] In The Gambia, ethnic competition is muted and there is little interest in such associations. Thus, the important factor in the strength of primary associations seems to be competition for local or national political resources which emphasizes ethnic or subethnic boundaries or migrant versus host interests. Other types of associations tend to flourish where primaries are common, but in Abeokuta and the Gambian towns other types are more important: church and work groups in the former and recreation and savings societies in the latter.

Pressure to belong to an association and the rewards of membership are such that men and women who join an association tend to belong to more than one. Three-fifths of the Nigerian and Gambian members of primary, church, and occupational associations, and nearly as many members of savings societies, belong to at least one other association. The proportion declines to half of the members of recreation associations. Multiple

TABLE 7.1
Current Membership in Associations, by Town and Sex (Percentages)

Type of Association	Ghana Ashaiman M	Ashaiman F	Tema[c] M	Tema[c] F	Gambia Banjul M	Banjul F	Serekunda M	Serekunda F	Nigeria Aba M	Aba F	Abeokuta M	Abeokuta F	Ajegunle M	Ajegunle F	Kakuri M	Kakuri F
None	90	93	68	65	39	43	52	40	10	11	13	28	16	29	24	44
Primary[a]	8	2	21	19	15	24	13	21	73	45	32	14	42	40	40	20
Ethnic	(16)	(1)	(17)	(15)	(10)	(20)	(9)	(9)	(24)	(16)	(9)	(6)	(9)	(5)	(27)	(16)
Hometown	(2)	(1)	(4)	(1)	(5)	(4)	(2)	(6)	(31)	(20)	(10)	(5)	(16)	(16)	(6)	(2)
Family	(0)	(0)	(0)	(0)	(0)	(0)	(2)	(6)	(30)	(13)	(13)	(5)	(24)	(20)	(10)	(2)
Religious	4	4	9	16	7	14	6	17	40	67	42	41	30	42	40	33
Occupational	...	...	3	1	14	2	18	4	47	27	57	36	33	29	23	13
Savings	0	0	0	d	15	17	17	30	16	5	15	26	20	14	15	22
Recreational	...	...	10	2	27	10	17	11	34	9	28	17	19	4	26	4
Total[b]	102	100	111	103	124	114	124	123	220	164	183	162	160	158	168	136
N	316	144	372	325	152	51	152	53	152	55	137	65	171	56	161	45
Belong to 2 or more	1	1	7	3	19	12	20	24	73	51	56	38	47	39	45	27

[a]Only one membership is counted in the totals. Subgroup figures are shown in parentheses.

[b]Totals exceed 100 percent because of multiple memberships. Doubles within the same category (i.e., two religious societies) have not been counted. Gambian totals include other associations (i.e., political) which are not shown separately.

[c]Figures for Tema are from the Tema Activities Survey. Nonmembership among respondents in the Tema/Ashaiman Network Survey was 68 percent for males and 67 percent for females.

[d]Less than 0.5 percent.

memberships are as common in these as in other types in Nigeria, but only a quarter of Gambians in recreations societies belonged to any others.

This pattern of activity makes it useful to compare associationally active and inactive individuals (in terms of multiple membership and nonmembership) Ghanaian respondents are not included in this discussion because very few reported membership in associations. Tema and Ashaiman were too new to have developed the dense associational life of older towns in Ghana (see Acquah 1958, pp. 105, 146–47) and elsewhere. The following profiles of four particularly active individuals demonstrate some of the factors that appear to be important, but also reveal how ordinary such people often are in terms of social background. Although they spend considerable time on formal association activities, they also find time for frequent contacts with kin and friends:

1. Urban primary teachers may not be the community leaders they used to be, but many are more active in formal associations than men in other occupations. Alagy is a Gambian-trained teacher of 32 who grew up in Banjul and now lives in Serekunda with his wife and three children. He has lived in several other places during his teaching career, and moved into a house owned by a cousin because there was no room in Banjul. He often sees numerous kin and friends in Serekunda and Banjul. The friends include a teacher, a clerk, a fitter, a goldsmith, and a factory worker, some known since childhood and others recent acquaintances. He is an officer in four associations (church and ethnic groups, the Boy Scouts, and a youth committee) and member of three others (the teachers' union, a savings society, and a dancing group). He attends meetings of three of these at least once a week, the ethnic group once a month, and the union and youth committee only once a year.

2. Benedict is a 30-year-old soldier who completed primary school in Nigeria's Middle Belt and has lived in Kaduna or Kakuri during most of the past fourteen years. He left the textile mills in 1969 to join the army, where he does technical work. He sees his kin and friends at least weekly. Three friends are in the same workshop and a factory operative and clerk work nearby; only one of these is the same ethnicity as himself. He belongs to an ethnic cultural association, a Bible study group, an army dining hall group, a drinking club, a savings group, and the YMCA. There is no information on how often he attends meetings, but he appears to spend most evenings with friends.

3. Cecilia is a 47-year-old woman who moved to Aba with her husband in 1939. He spends half of every month at home, and so must be either self-employed or retired; she stays in Aba and supports herself by sewing bags. Although she had only three years of primary education, her two sons both attended universities overseas. She has only one sister in Aba, whom she sees daily. Her three friends are all traders, and are visited at least once a week; two of them are from her hometown. She belongs to her

hometown women's association, but most of her social life appears to be focused on the Catholic Church; she listed six church associations to which she belongs. This proliferation of church activities, and their special importance for women, were documented for Accra by Acquah (1958, pp. 146–47); they appear to characterize Lagos and provincial towns as well.

4. Mama Aduke demonstrates a pattern of activity characteristic of many women traders (see Lewis 1976). She is a 54-year-old mother of four children, two of whom have not yet left home although they are in wage employment. She had no education and moved to Lagos from Abeokuta in 1934 to trade; she still earns a modest income selling in the market. She sees her brother and sister two or three times a week and two of her three friends daily. All are Muslim traders and two also come from Abeokuta. Though her days are full of "business" (from 9:00 A.M. to 10:00 P.M.), she is able to fit in activities related to trading, family, and mosque. She belongs to the Market Women's Association, the Muslim Women's Union, a savings society, and her family association, and has participated in sending delegates (probably from the market women) to see local council officials.

These four individuals illustrate the importance of age and long residence in town in multiple memberships. Only Mama Aduke is outside the boundaries generally accepted as middle-aged. Young people, usually newly arrived in town, are seldom as actively involved in associations as those who have found stable employment, settled down, and married. As their commitment to the town and responsibilities increase, the potential of voluntary associations as a source of support becomes more important.[3] Men and women in their forties and fifties may find satisfying leadership roles in voluntary associations which compensate for their relative lack of success in other fields, but this often means that young people find associations less rewarding because there are few leadership roles for them. (Even societies with "young" in their titles often have members in their forties.) As few married women with young children have time for associations, they tend to leave such activity to older women. However, traders have more need of associations than housewives and therefore are more likely to participate regardless of age and home responsibilities.

Multiple memberships were most common among men between 35 and 49 in three of the Nigerian towns; in Kakuri the men under 25, who constitute a much higher proportion of the population, were as likely as older men to be multiple members. The young men were most likely to be multiple members in Banjul, though men in their fifties were not far behind. In this case, many young men are indigenes, with better-developed local interests than young men in either Serekunda or Ajegunle.

However, the effect of social structure on participation appears to be more important for older men than for younger ones. There was no difference between suburban and provincial Nigerian towns in the proportion of men under 25 belonging to no associations or to two or more, but men over 50 were more likely to be muliple members if they lived in the provincial towns or in Banjul as opposed to Serekunda. Age gives more status in such towns and older men are expected to move into responsible positions. There are few men over 50 in Kakuri or Ajegunle, and as their working life nears its end their interests are expected to shift from town to home, leaving urban leadership roles to the next cohort. Even in provincial towns, membership drops off after age 60.

Membership in associations in industrial nations tends to be highly correlated with socioeconomic status (education, occupation, and income; see Cutler 1973, p. 135). The reasons for this (especially greater economic resources and ability to communicate) seem likely to apply in African towns, but it appears that the relationship is less close in West Africa, both in societies where the level of membership is very high and in those where it is moderate. The low-income, relatively uneducated majority of the population provides the bulk of membership and even of association leadership in these cities, partly because most associations are so small. There are few elite clubs outside the capitals and the mutual aid form of most associations (whether they draw members from the same ethnic group, hometown, church, occupation, or friendship group) attracts the ordinary members of society, who want this type of affiliation.

However, additional resources do tend to lead to wider participation in associational life. Correlations between the number of memberships and all three indices of status are significant for the Nigerian towns taken together, but only income is significantly related to the number of memberships in all four towns taken separately. In The Gambia, none of the correlations, except for income for men in Banjul, are statistically significant. Socioeconomic status appears to be a more important factor in membership for provincial residents than for people living in the suburbs. This may be because there is more scope for high-status residents to exercise leadership in a provincial town; in a suburb, the important decisions tend to be taken elsewhere and there is probably a wider range of alternative uses of time.[4] The correlation between income and number of memberships is higher for men in the provincial towns (.33) than in the Nigerian suburbs (.19) and the correlations with education and occupation are also significant for men in the provincial towns (.29 and .27) but not in the suburbs.

Income is also the most important factor in multiple memberships among women, but the correlations are lower than for men. The female samples are smaller, women belong to fewer associations than men, and their incomes are lower. The most important differences are due to labor force participation; housewives are most likely to be nonmembers and the wage employed to be multiple members. While women in wage employment tend to be better educated and have higher incomes than self-employed women, their relatively greater mobility and shorter hours of work, allied to income, are probably more important in fostering associational activity than their education. Women who stay at home lack resources and are often caring for young children, whereas women traders often spend very long hours on their trading. It appears that women primary teachers—like male teachers—have the most memberships, though the level of activity may be higher for other women.

These relationships are often curvilinear rather than linear. Whereas the poorest residents, who tend to be unskilled and illiterate, may lack the resources to participate in an association (or in more than one) because they cannot afford the dues, clothing, or even the time for meetings, many of the most advantaged members of these societies prefer to spend their free time in informal socializing with friends or family rather than engaging in associational activities (Lloyd 1967, p. 148; Jacobson 1973, p. 67). The field is therefore left open for the moderately successful—the primary teachers and more prosperous manual workers, men without university degrees or advanced diplomas. The more politically oriented members of the elite are sometimes leaders or patrons of large numbers of associations, but they are probably the exception rather than the rule.

Other background variables can be treated briefly. Another indicator of the mass appeal of these associations is the finding that growing up in a town or village and the extent of migration experience appears to make very little difference in the number of memberships, though this is usually inversely related to the distance of migration. Short-distance migrants tend to be somewhat more active in joining associations than long-distance migrants, for the same reasons that they are more active in other types of social activities. However, this difference is not statistically significant, so the lower level of sociability of long-distance migrants demonstrated in the last chapter applies less strongly to participation in associations.

Length of stay appears to be more important for women in the suburbs and in Banjul than for provincial women or for men. It may take longer to work into the associational life of Ajegunle and Kakuri than Abeokuta or Aba because women in the former come from farther away and are less often in the labor force. Men born in Aba or Ajegunle are more likely than migrants to these towns to belong to three or more associations, but the locally born in Kakuri and Abeokuta are more likely to be nonmembers than multiple members; this may be due to their relatively low socioeconomic status.

Both men and women who have lived in town less than three years are likely to be nonmembers; new migrants get help from kin rather than from associations. The exception to this pattern is Serekunda, where membership tends to decrease with length of residence for men; there is no difference among the women. Nearly half of recent migrants to Serekunda are between 25 and 34, and these are the most common multiple members in this town; half have already put down roots in the sense that they intend to stay in town permanently. Thus, they are in many ways different from new arrivals in the Nigerian towns or even in Banjul.

Rather surprisingly, ethnicity proved to be a relatively unimportant indicator of membership, which suggests that local structural factors and alternatives are more important for associational activity than cultural predilection. Insofar as it is relevant at all, ethnicity should be germane mainly for primary association membership, except that those who join one association are likely to join another. Both the Yoruba and the Igbo have the reputation of being joiners,[5] but the data suggest that they are no more active than many other Nigerians. The Igbo had high levels in Aba but low levels in Kakuri, where they were recent arrivals and not very secure. In Ajegunle, they were about average, as were the Yoruba. The Hausa consistently showed little interest; for them, religion is probably as important as ethnicity (see below). In The Gambia, there is considerable variance between men and women and between towns as to which ethnic group is the most active, so ethnicity is obviously not the causal factor.

This suggests that the level of associational activity is situational and personal rather than cultural. Although the experience of immigrants to America, especially to the large cities such as New York, suggests that newcomers to a heterogeneous, impersonal environment find support and satisfaction in associations, in West Africa kin provide much of this help and pressures to join associations are stronger in homogeneous societies with dense networks of personal ties; newcomers have less need for associations.

This is partly a problem of method. We do not know what proportion of immigrants to American cities between the 1880s and 1920s belonged to voluntary associations, just as we have no comparable data for African cities in the 1950s. The potential alternative of political activity is likewise untested, as Nigeria was under military rule at the time most recent studies were made. Henderson (1966, p. 384) found that interest in primary associations in Onitsha declined considerably when migrants found other ways to influence the local political system. A survey of membership in 1982, after Nigeria has returned to civilian rule and local councils are fully operational, could turn up quite different figures from these of 1972.

The participation of members of various religious groups is related, through education, to income, but religion *per se* also has some influence. Muslims are consistently somewhat more likely than Christians to be nonmembers, partly because religious adherence is not fostered through associational activity as it so often is for Christians. Muslims do not need associations to study the Koran as Christians seem to need Bible study groups, and Muslims have no equivalent of the singing band. Rather, they tend to group themselves informally under a mallam or headman for prayer and study and for other group activities which they find useful (Cohen 1969; Schildkrout in Cohen 1974, pp. 211–12). So far, few have gone to secondary school, so they do not belong to old boys' or old girls' societies.

Participation levels vary considerably between Catholics, members of Protestant mission churches, and those belonging to various separatist sects, so it seems unlikely that religious belief is an important factor for them. Members of the separatist sects usually belong to at least one religious association, but their concentration on religion tends to inhibit other types of affiliation, as is the case for some Muslims.

The place of associations in social life should not be overemphasized; most participants spend little time attending meetings and only leaders are active between meetings. Primary associations occasionally meet once a week, but once or twice a month is more common and some meet much less often. Savings societies tend to hold meetings weekly or monthly; some religious societies meet more than once a week. Recreational associations vary according to type. Sports and drinking groups may meet every week or even more often and dancing groups meet weekly or after payday, but associations of old boys or old girls gather only once a year.

Many of the members attend irregularly; sometimes only a few of the officers show up. Less than one in ten of the Ghanaians who reported attending meetings went as often as once a week and nearly three-fifths reported that they attended no more than once a month. Gambians spent somewhat more time attending meetings. Nearly two-fifths said they went, on average, to at least one meeting a week, but about the same proportion went only once a month or less.

Frequency of attendance appears to be related to the number of memberships and convenience of meetings. There was little difference between Banjul and Serekunda in the frequency of attendance among men; though Banjul men are more likely to belong to an association, equal proportions in both towns belong to two or more, and these are more likely than members of one association to go to at least one meeting a week. However, women in Banjul are slightly more likely than those in Sere-kunda to attend at least one meeting a week even though they average somewhat fewer memberships. This may be because Banjul women travel shorter distances to meetings than those in Serekunda. Unfortunately, there are no data from Nigeria to test these relationships.

Functions

In addition to overall levels of participation, there are also important differences in the characteristics of various types of associations which lead people of varying background to select one or another. Nigerian women are less likely than men to participate in primary associations because these are mainly male-dominated. This is not the case for Gambian women, who are less active in associations than the Nigerians and probably less concerned with female autonomy. The Nigerian women are likely to focus their activity on church or work associations, as a high proportion are in the labor force.

Except in the Nigerian provincial towns, young people are more likely than older, married residents to belong to a society centered around recreation. As the average age of members increases, the nature of recreation associations changes from Scouts and dancing to drinking, and the participation rate of females drops sharply. Savings societies are more popular among older people, who find banks too formal and bureaucratic, than among the better-educated young people; this is particularly true for women.

Associations oriented around primary ties, religion, occupation, savings, and recreation attract members in roughly that order. As many of these provide much the same rewards (welfare services, an opportunity to gain status through leadership, personalized social contacts), they are to a certain extent alternatives. But the manifest goals of each type (supporting customary ties, promoting religious adherence, seeking economic prosperity, accumulating capital, having a good time) influence individuals to join and to maintain their membership.

Primary Associations

Although associations based on primary ties (ethnicity, kinship, and a common place of origin) have had the most attention in studies of affiliation in African towns, it is important to note that they seldom attract a higher proportion of the population than any other type of association. There may be many of them, and they may be of considerable importance in some towns and to at least some of their members in all towns, but the majority of urban residents (except for men in Aba) are not even nominal members. Ethnic associations were more prominent forces in national politics in the preindependence and immediate postindependence period than they are today; governments of several countries have seen their potential for disrupting national unity and have banned them. Those that remain tend to belong to subgroups or minorities, or at least to keep a low profile.

Hometown associations are seen as less disruptive because of their much smaller size and therefore political potential, and they may be viewed positively because they finance local development projects which would otherwise require government funds. Family or lineage associations take in even smaller groups, and are mainly supportive of kinship ties.

Primary associations have typically been seen (i.e., by Little 1957, 1965) as important in socializing new migrants to the towns, helping them find jobs and housing, and providing mutual aid and welfare services which in European societies would be provided by the government. However, their welfare services have become less important as the associational provision in towns has broadened and as a rising standard of living has brought increased security to many potential members. There are now many other associations, such as church and savings societies, which provide similar assistance to their members with less emphasis on the maintenance of village values and authority structure—aspects of primary associations which are not very popular with young, educated migrants.

Most people who join primary associations these days become members only after spending three to five years in town; only in The Gambia is the membership of recent arrivals relatively high. This suggests that they may still be socializing the relatively less educated new migrants in The Gambia but that this function is performed by other agencies (notably kin) in the other two countries.

Their more common use today (in addition to contributing to hometown development and mutual aid) is as a means of increasing status and exerting political influence. The men who are most likely to participate in (and lead) primary associations are over 35 and of moderate educational and occupational attainment. Men who are beginning to think of resettling at home and have relatively little to show for their time in town may seek leadership roles in the local branches of the hometown or ethnic associations, where they can influence hometown politics and demonstrate their ability to act as community elders.

Southall (in Lloyd 1966, p. 352) found that membership in primary associations in East Africa is related to a group's numbers, residential distribution, and traditional hierarchical structure, and to the potential members' socioeconomic standing, attitude toward urban life, and distance from home. While some of these factors are operative in West Africa, most appear to be relatively unimportant there. As mentioned in chapter 4, ethnic groups are usually residentially mixed in West African towns, but dispersion only affected membership in Ajegunle. The size of the Lagos metropolitan area and its transportation problems make attendance at meetings in other parts of town difficult; scattered housing is not a problem in smaller towns. Group size may pose problems at the hometown level, but associations are often small and if people want a primary association they can usually find enough people of common origin at some level to form one. On the other hand, numbers can be a disadvantage; there are very many Egba migrants in Lagos, but few belong to the Egba Association. It is easy for families to assume that their support is not needed.

Nor is there clear evidence that peoples from traditionally hierarchical, centralized ethnic groups or from acephalous societies are more likely to form voluntary associations in town. The Yoruba and the Hausa both had important kingdoms before the advent of colonial rule; yet the Yoruba are far more active in both primary and other types of associations than are the Hausa, regardless of whether they are short- or long-distance migrants. The Igbo and the Frafra both lacked centralized, hierarchical authority and migrated about the same distance to Lagos and the Accra/ Tema area respectively; but the former are very active in forming primary associations while the latter prefer informal groupings under prominent personalities and are seldom successful in forming associations (Hart 1971, pp. 28–29). Three-fifths of the members of primary associations in the Ghanaian samples are Ewe, relatively short-distance migrants whose national position as a minority group with more education than local resources may be responsible for their interest in organizing migrants to help those left at home. This description could also apply to the Igbo in Aba.

Socioeconomic status does make a difference in membership, but it is the reverse of the "normal" pattern. Well-educated Ghanaians tend to look down on such associations as suitable only for illiterates, and in both The Gambia and Nigeria men in manual and commercial occupations are more likely to be members than are professionals. Education and occupation make less difference in female membership, but women traders are slightly more likely to belong than other women in all four Nigerian towns. Primary associations tend to attract the self-employed more than the wage employed, partly because of socioeconomic background, but also because associational contacts can bring in business and because leadership in these associations can be another form of entrepreneurship.

Finally, it was expected that members of primary associations would be more oriented toward home and kin than nonmembers, but this does not appear to be the case. Men and women who plan to stay in town permanently are no less likely to belong than those who intend to retire eventually to their homes. Nigerian men who say they will go home when they are rich enough are the most likely to belong, reinforcing the impression that the possibilities of political patronage attract some members to primary associations. In Nigeria, membership increases with the frequency of visits home and is higher among those who send money home than among those who do not, but these differences are not found in The Gambia or Ghana, where membership is much less common. The one exception to this is that Ghanaian women who send money home more than once a year are more likely to belong to associations than other women. Since most of them send only very small sums, their membership may be an expression of their ties with home to a greater extent than it is for male members.

General satisfaction with life in town is not a very good measure either; Nigerian men who belong to primary associations are, on the whole, more satisfied with urban life than are nonmembers, but there is no difference among the women or among those interviewed in The Gambia. It seems likely that the background factors already discussed are more important than the closeness of kinship or hometown ties in predicting membership. Some urban residents get the support they need from primary associations, while others prefer other types of contacts.

Religious Societies

A majority of West African urban residents attend religious services in mosques or churches regularly, though membership of religious associations is considerably less common. Nevertheless, these associations are often at least as important as primary associations in the lives of women; they are somewhat less important for men, but still draw a higher proportion of male participants than would be found in most West European countries. Both religious attendance and associational activity were lower in Ashaiman than elsewhere because few churches had been built there. Tema and Kakuri were somewhat better provided for, and the other towns had many churches and mosques.

In addition to specifically religious activities, such as Bible study and hymn singing, many of these groups provide the opportunity for small-group interaction and mutual aid which are attractive aspects of primary associations. Indeed, many are very similar to primary associations in that all of their members are drawn from the same ethnic group. Some mission churches have sought conversion in only one area; those with wider establishment may divide into separate ethnic congregations in towns (so that hymns and sermons in one language will reach all participants) or provide a range of ethnically based societies to solve the language problem at that level. For example, a Catholic church in Tema has a service and associational meeting for the Ewe one night, the Frafra another night, and so on through the week. Lagos parishes often have several ethnically based societies, which attract mainly older people. They help to organize a large parish for the Harvest Festival, but interest in them has declined in recent years. Young people, who can communicate in English, prefer groups that better serve their interests and that they can run.

Steady (1976, p. 225) suggests that church associations in Freetown are basically conservative institutions, especially in preserving male dominance in the society. She argues that they exist to provide church support and an opportunity for women to exercise leadership without challenging the male clergy, and to uphold the double standard of morality for men and women. She ignores religious societies for men, but presumably they fill mainly church support and leadership functions. Fund raising is certainly important for churches, which could not survive on Sunday collections. In addition to the money collected, fetes, bazaars, and raffles provide social activity, a chance for those who participate to broaden their contacts and, for the many officers, status enhancement.

Unlike primary associations, which are usually for men and women of all ages, religious societies tend to segregate men and women, young people, and the middle-aged. This gives women a better chance to assume leadership roles and may explain why so many women are active in these societies. Although women prophetesses are active in several separatist churches, the mission churches have maintained an all-male clergy, and women's supportive role in associations is the only religious leadership role open to them. Women's societies probably place more emphasis on upholding a monogamous moral code than do those for men, but the latter often include attempts on the part of the clergy to promote monogamy among men. However, while these associations may help to reinforce the commitment of members to the church's moral norms, they have little effect in changing the values of the society at large.

Occupational Associations

Membership in associations based on occupation appears to be more important for the self-employed than for wage employees. Trade unions are seldom mentioned, either by Ghanaian factory workers (for whom they were at the time obligatory) or by Nigerian or Gambian employes, who can choose whether to belong. Those who do mention trade union membership are more likely to be teachers, nurses, or clerks than manual workers. This is in line with membership figures; the National Union of Teachers has several times as many members as the country's next largest union, even though many teachers do not belong to it (Waterman 1976, p. 164; Sami 1978).

Waterman, who included Kakuri factory workers in his samples, suggests that trade unions have had relatively little impact on Nigerian society because of the basic conservatism of the workers, especially in the north as opposed to Lagos. At all levels, they continue to believe in individualism, the possibility of progress through hard work, and the rights of the successful to enjoy the fruits of their labors. This makes it very difficult for them to work together for a common goal; occupational associations are therefore often looked on as entrepreneurial opportunities (by their leaders) or as sources of mutual aid and welfare (by their members). Insofar as they have been less successful than primary or religious societies in providing mutual aid, unions have not attracted much interest from potential members except during wage negotiations.

Craft guilds attract a higher proportion of potential members than most trade unions in Nigeria, but they appear to be relatively unimportant elsewhere. They have a long history in Yoruba provincial towns (Lloyd 1953), and flourish best where most craftsmen are self-employed and it is possible for most men in a particular craft to know each other. Guild membership was mentioned by 37 percent of skilled men in Abeokuta, compared to only 13 percent in other towns. Two other Yoruba provincial towns (Oyo and Ede) have much higher levels of guild membership, 96 and 56 percent respectively; Ede has 88 percent membership in those crafts which have guilds and in both towns there is considerable pressure on craftsmen to conform to guild norms (O.Y. Oyeneye, personal communication). At the other extreme, only one man in Tema (a mason) mentioned belonging to a craft association and all the Gambian skilled workers who belonged to occupational associations were trade union members in wage employment.

The potential for frequent interaction is important if a guild is to retain authority over its members. Yoruba craftsmen in Abeokuta find guilds more useful than those in Lagos because anyone can set up a business in Lagos and follow his own inclinations as to the prices charged for goods and apprenticeship training; collective action becomes difficult to maintain. In this competitive, individualistic situation, guilds appear to be more feasible in trades which are well established (the guild pattern was set before increasing urban scale caused problems), with relatively long apprenticeships (strengthening the socialization process), and a fairly high level of income which can be improved through group action.

A study of self-employed craftsmen in Lagos found that almost all of the goldsmiths belonged to guilds (there were several in different parts of town), compared to over half the fitters and none of the radio or watch repairmen or shoemakers. There were guilds of printers, electricians, and painters, but few belonged. As most men in these trades are wage employed, trade union activity is probably more important for them, leaving the few self-employed to think of themselves as businessmen or contractors rather than as craftsmen.

Goldsmithing has a long history; apprenticeships usually last at least four years and include rituals which increase the identity of workers with their craft. Goldsmiths also need group action to deal with government regulations on the acquisition and use of gold. Fitters have a similarly long apprenticeship, usually work with other fitters, and tend to have relatively high incomes, at least in Lagos. These characteristics promote group action and make it rewarding, even in a highly individualistic environment. Shoemakers and watch repairmen, on the other hand, have short apprenticeships, usually work alone and, as a consequence of low income, tend to be less committed to their trades than other craftsmen. These factors discourage guild formation and membership.

Whereas trade unions and craft guilds are mainly male institutions, both men and women traders form associations to further their interests. Women's trading associations have attracted more interest because of the prominence of women traders in this area. Lewis (1976) found that competitive individualism and ethnic heterogeneity made it very difficult for women market traders in Abidjan to form viable associations, though they often belonged to other types of societies. The Dioula have a long tradition of associations, often of the rotating credit variety. Dioula traders usually belong to several of these outside the marketplace. Members of these *moni* are all of the same ethnicity and religion, and can further their individual goals on the basis of equality of contributions and benefits by all members of the associations. Southern women have fewer associations, but these are also usually ethnically homogeneous. Their most common purpose is insurance; a member faced with sickness, a funeral, a marriage, or other crisis can draw benefits without regard to taking turns, so that some members get more than they pay in and others less. Thus, their expectations are somewhat different from those of Dioula women.

A traders' cooperative association, whether its goal is buying merchandise cheaply or negotiating with the local council for better market conditions, demands considerable effort on the part of some for collective goals; those who contribute little may benefit as much as those who contribute a great deal. But the market situation favors competition, not cooperation. Some have more resources and/or ability than others, and their goal is to improve on this rather than share with others; members' inexperience in interethnic cooperation outside the marketplace is an added handicap. Thus, though the need is evident and many attempts have been made, traders' associations have not been successful in Abidjan.

They have had a larger measure of success of Ghana and Nigeria, perhaps because of more able leadership or the rewards in status and political influence available to the women who have led them. The National Council of Ghana Women, the national mouthpiece of women traders, was an integral wing of the party during Nkrumah's rule and was consulted on government decisions. Nigerian traders' associations have been mainly concerned with local rather than national affairs and have had less political impact than the importance of their votes would warrant (Bretton 1966, p. 61; Baker 1974, pp. 241–43). However, while they lack the concern for wider political issues and ability to cooperate economically which outsiders see as their legitimate goals, they are usually successful in terms of their members' goals. They provide an institutionalized means of settling conflicts between traders and putting pressure on local government for specific market concerns, a source of aid in emergencies and, in their rotating credit form, a way of systematically accumulating capital. Their leaders operate with the traditional style of personalized authority and patronage which the largely illiterate market women understand. In Accra, organized market women have been able to maintain monopolies over certain products and thus increase their income.

These associations are largely limited to market traders; the majority, who trade outside the market, operate on a small scale and are seldom organized. Because they have more capital invested and work in more centralized locations, male traders are somewhat more likely to belong to trading associations than women. But only a minority are members; 36 percent of the Nigerian male traders and 28 percent of the women belonged to traders' associations, compared to a fifth of the Gambian male traders and none of the Gambian women.

Savings Societies

As the Eureka Savings Services of Aba advertisement put it, "Money is a defense." Educated people, with relatively high incomes, can use banks, but many people at all levels like the regularity, ease of access, and credit facilities of savings societies. About a sixth of respondents in The Gambia and Nigeria reported belonging to rotating credit associations. These are known in The Gambia as *osusu,* in Ghana as *susu,* and in Nigeria (where the word seems to have originated) as *esusu* or (in the north) as *adashi.* Because they demand trust that all members will continue to pay their share until the cycle is complete, these societies tend to be formed by small groups of friends, who may be coworkers, neighbors, or even kin. Urban residents with no longstanding contacts may prefer to contribute to collecting agencies which pay out regularly, deducting a small commission for the collector. These appear to be more common among market women in Aba than elsewhere. Lewis (1976) reported similar arrangements among Abidjan market women and Hill (1972, p. 203) found that *adashi* formed by Hausa village women take this form because the norms of seclusion make it impossible for them to meet. Where the members do not know each other and never meet, the "group" becomes a business operation rather than a voluntary association.

Almost everyone appreciates the possibility of drawing a lump sum of considerable size. Traders find these associations useful for accumulating capital to increase the size of their businesses; other people use them to facilitate savings for major expenses such as school fees or consumer goods (furniture, a sewing machine) or, for the wealthy, a trip to Mecca or the materials to start building a house. They are also helpful as sources of loans, either for business or for emergencies. Bank or government loans are available only to the rich, leaving the poor at the mercy of the extremely high interest rates demanded by money lenders (25 percent per month in advance is not uncommon). Thus, a savings society which grants loans to its members at half the local rate performs an important service. Some societies also loan money to outsiders at higher rates. This is more speculative, but the shared income makes it a highly profitable use of pooled funds.

Savings societies tend to be more popular with women than with men, but this is not the case in Aba or Ajegunle. Women in these towns may have found it more difficult than women elsewhere to form the close ties needed for such associations, either because so many were new arrivals (Aba) or because of heterogeneity and competition (Ajegunle, where men also have relatively low levels of membership). People with little or no education find this a useful way to accumulate capital with only a small weekly or monthly commitment. Relatively few professionals belong, but people in other occupations are about equally likely to participate.

This confirms the impression that there is a widespread need for savings and credit facilities in these societies. Many people with low as well as high incomes are able to save regularly, even though the amount saved may be small. Recent rapid inflation, especially in Ghana, has made saving impossible for some and difficult for many, but savings societies among coworkers are still popular. Because of the advantages of collecting money early in the cycle (in effect, a free loan) and the need for a lump sum at more frequent intervals than a large group of thirty to fifty individuals can provide, men and women who can afford it may belong to several groups.

Partly in response to expansion of education and rising standards of living, the use of banks is spreading among both men and women of relatively low incomes, who would not have considered a bank account ten years ago, but now use one as an alternative or in addition to a savings society. The banks have found it difficult to cope with illiterates and until recently have not been interested in the small sums which most people have to offer, but they are beginning to learn that these can amount to considerable sums if many people save with them.

Differential use was clearer for women than for men. No woman with four or more years of secondary-school in Nigeria or senior secondary schooling in The Gambia belonged to a savings society and no illiterate woman had a bank account. Men show similar preferences, but some men without formal schooling had bank accounts and some well-educated men also found savings societies useful. Nigerian and Gambian clerical workers were as likely to have accounts as professionals, and women with incomes of between £300 and £499 were as likely as women with higher incomes to use banks. The expansion of banking will probably affect savings societies insofar as interest on an account increases the return on money saved, but interest rates have remained low and until bank loans are easily available to small savers, the societies will continue to be popular.

The greatest problem with these associations is the betrayal of confidence on the part of leaders or members. Hart (1972, p. 29) reports that Frafra savings societies in Accra inevitably break up amid charges of

TABLE 7.2
Participation in Football Pools, by
Town and Sex (Percentages)[a]

Town	Males	Females
Banjul	38(152)	8(51)
Serekunda	48(152)	19(52)
Ajegunle	25(170)	4(55)
Abeokuta	35(133)	5(65)
Aba	32(151)	7(55)

[a]Numbers in parentheses are bases for percentages.

misuse of funds. The need for security and help from fellow migrants (in lieu of absent kin) leads to repeated attempts at collective savings in spite of the realization that trouble is likely. As low-income, long-distance migrants from a highly egalitarian and acephalous society, the Frafra probably experience greater difficulty in group formation than members of most other ethnic groups.

Another method of accumulating capital (at least in theory) is participation in football pools (see Table 7.2).[6] These appear to be a growth industry in many towns, and regular betting may to a certain extent be replacing regular saving, in hopes of a higher payoff. Respondents were not asked about this in Ghana or in Kakuri, as there was little sign of pools activity in these towns at the time. In contrast, there were few streets in Ajegunle which did not have an office of Rocky Pools, Face to Face Pools, or other agents. The federal government owns Niger Pools, the largest in the country, and several state governments also compete for income by running lotteries (aimed at attracting migrants to other states as well as local people). The main season for pools is from August to April; they are run on Australian football results during the British off-season, but these games generate less interest among punters.

Some agents collect from door to door, but most people go to a kiosk or office to place their bets. These offices are often a focus of considerable social activity on Fridays and Saturdays, as people discuss the possibilities and wait for the results. Regulars get to know one another and sometimes become friends, sharing the celebration when anyone wins.

The pools attract more men than women, as the former have more disposable income with which to bet. People of all ages and social levels play, from illiterates to university students and from the unemployed young to the retired elderly. Men and women traders in The Gambia are particularly drawn to them, though their chances of increasing their capital are better with savings societies.

Recreation Associations

All of the above types, with the possible exception of savings groups, provide recreational opportunities. The concern here is with groups whose main focus is on recreation: sports clubs; drinking, dancing, and debating societies; associations of former students of prestigious secondary schools; and international organizations such as the Boy Scouts and Girl Guides, the YMCA, and the Red Cross. About as many people belong to associations based on recreation as to savings societies, but the former are more selective of the younger, better educated sector of the society.

This is partly a question of the type of recreation sought and the nature of the urban environment. Participation in sports teams (especially football) is popular among young factory workers in Tema/Ashaiman and Kakuri and, to a lesser extent, among young clerical workers elsewhere. The high proportion of young people who leave school in these three towns makes it easy to get a team together; unmarried men have plenty of time to practice, and alternative entertainment (drinking, cinema) tends to be more expensive. There are fan clubs for major football teams such as Accra Hearts of Oak, but sports are more often participant in these towns than in developed countries. Eight Tema industries sponsor teams.

Older, married men, especially in the provincial towns, tend to prefer drinking as a form of social activity, whether this is done individually or as part of an organized group. Drinking is most common on weekends following payday. The large number of small bars tends to localize participation, so the same group of men patronize a particular bar regardless of whether or not they form a drinking club. Allegiance to one bar is fostered by the limiting of credit to regular customers, a necessary precaution if the owner hopes to stay in business (Hart 1973, pp. 79–81). Data on the frequency of drinking were collected only in Ghana: 58 and 43 percent of the men in Tema and Ashaiman respectively (but only 3 percent of the women) reported drinking as a regular social activity. Of the men who did drink, a quarter in Tema and half in Ashaiman did so during the week as well as on weekends and about a fifth drank in groups of more than five people. While these may not be formalized into voluntary associations, they probably provide more regular companionship than formal groups (see Pons 1969, pp. 152–60).

Traditional dancing is often done under the aegis of primary associations, one of whose goals is to maintain customary values. Other groups feature a variety of dances as a way of attracting young people; many of these serve some mutual aid functions as well as providing recreation

(Banton 1957, pp. 162–83; Meillassoux 1968, pp. 130–42). The socialization of newcomers to the towns, which Banton found to be an important
function of the Freetown Ambas Geda, is much less important today than
it was twenty years ago, and with the growth of community centers
attached to churches or built by municipalities (as in Tema) there are
probably fewer associations specifically for dancing than in the past. Most
towns have one or more night clubs which provide better music and more
convenient amenities for dancing than small associations can; they are
patronized by young and middle-aged people of moderate and high
income.

Membership in recreation associations is higher among men and
women who have attended secondary school than among residents with
little or no education. Certain groups, such as Scouts and "old boy"
societies are limited to those who have been to secondary school, and the
better-educated tend to have more money for recreation. Cohen (1971)
reports on the importance of Masonic membership among the Creole elite
of Freetown. Frequent banquets and meetings provide occasions for
talking over political and economic events; the cooperation thus engendered gives the Creoles much more political power than would otherwise
be possible for such a small group. The Masons appear to be more important in Sierra Leone and Liberia than in Ghana or Nigeria, but indigenous
secret societies became of sufficient importance in Nigeria for the military
government to forbid civil servants to belong. Some of these are now
ethnically mixed, at least in Lagos; prospective members' social and
economic position is considered more important than their ethnicity.

Men participate more than women in recreation associations; the latter
have less free time and usually drop participation in sports and Guides
when they leave school, whereas some men continue to be active. Insofar
as recreation associations are an expression of local interests, including
political interests, they should attract local men. This appears to be the
case in The Gambia, where locally born men are more likely to belong
than migrants. However, in Nigeria such interests are probably articulated
in other ways, including kinship and patronage networks; none of the
locally born belonged in Kakuri and in other towns they had about the
same levels of membership as migrants. Newcomers to Kakuri and
Abeokuta tend to join within a year or two of arrival, but migrants to the
other towns take somewhat longer.

The most important factor in membership is probably personality.
Rather than serving as sources of contact and socialization for strangers,
these associations help the more gregarious residents to widen already
extensive friendship networks. Men who belong are more likely than
nonmembers to have large numbers of friends (though they do not
necessarily see them more often; friends are seldom met through association membership). They maintain the same level of contacts with kin at

home and in town as other people of similar background. Recreation associations are not drawing them into new, exclusive networks, but merely providing additional outlets for their interests.

Conclusion

Voluntary associations are only one alternative in urban social inter-action. Their importance has probably been overrated in the literature because previous researchers have focused on the associations, inter-viewing leaders and active members rather than surveying the general population. However, formal associations are more important in some periods (as in the buildup to independence) than in others, so their position in the 1970s is relevant to the needs of urban residents and the constraints of local social structures at that period.

Individuals have different needs at various points in their careers, and this affects the types of association they join. The young have the time and energy for sports and dancing; facilities for such activities are increasingly provided by commercial organizations rather than voluntary associations. Other types of associations are more attractive to the more settled seg-ments of the population, who can use interest groups to pressure those in authority—the local council, the church, or the hometown—and to en-hance their own status in the society.

Since associations are formed by people of all social levels (even the unemployed, though theirs do not usually last very long), membership is a widespread phenomenon, especially in Nigeria. The poorest often find it difficult to participate, but many people of very modest circumstances are active members and even leaders. Many wealthy people participate less than those of lower income because they have other ways of gaining status and exercising influence. The indigenous nature of associational activity is shown by its equal popularity among people of rural and urban back-ground and of varying migration experience. While some forms of associ-ation are recent developments, they are largely a local response to local needs. This is quite different from the situation in Zimbabwe, where forms of recreation are mostly imported from the white community via the black elites (see Weinrich 1976, chapter 10).

The forms of associations and their popularity in a particular town depend on its history and demographic structure, the nature of its labor force, the cultural ethos which encourages or discourages interest in group formation, government policy, and the nature of competition for resources. New towns have few associations because it takes time for leaders to develop them. A town with a high proportion of young, un-married migrants shows a different organizational patttern than one whose population is mainly of long-settled families. The educational experiences of teachers and clerks help them to found certain types of societies which are of less interest to semiskilled and unskilled manual workers who have not gone beyond primary school. The latter, and the self-employed, tend to have less secure incomes than the former and thus favor associations which emphasize mutual aid and welfare.

Members of certain ethnic groups may find it easier and more rewarding than others to form associations (for instance, the Igbo and Yoruba as compared with the Hausa and Akan), but the extent to which they do so depends partly on the local stimulus of the town in which they are living. Ethnic homogeneity seems to make it easier to join together (in primary and other types of groups), or at least to exert pressure on individuals who might otherwise fail to join. There are times when it is good politics to emphasize ethnic or subethnic group membership through an active association, and other times when a "low profile" is more politic, or may even be required by the government. Ethnic and occupational groups which are actively competing for local resources are most likely to be successful if they can demonstrate their ability to recruit a large number of members into an efficiently run association which can be mobilized for demonstrations and/or lobbying as needed. The importance of kinship ties and patron/client relations in these countries means that a group of even moderate size will probably have some close links to the elites and that these links will be used at least as much as more formal methods for attaining individual and group goals.

8 □ PROBLEMS

Mamadu Kuti is a 42-year-old Mandingo son of a farmer/
fisherman who moved to Banjul from North Bank Division
because he found farming at home unprofitable. He has
been a self-employed fisherman ever since, and now considers Banjul his home. His three closest friends are all
from his hometown; they go out fishing together. He
belongs to no voluntary associations. Mamadu supports
two wives (both housewives) and two children on about
£150 per year; they have two rooms and both children are
in primary school. When he needs money, he borrows
from a friend. If he wanted a job, he would ask an acquaintance he has known for eight years who is a government official. If there were trouble at work he would go to
a policeman he has known for eighteen years; this is his
right. However, if there were a dispute within the family
or trouble with the police he would take the matter to his
elder brother; he has done this on one occasion with a
police problem. The brother also lives in Banjul, and they
visit three times a week. As Mamadu's only kinsman in
Banjul, he fills the roles of elder and supporter in town.

Mamadu believes that "inequality has been handed
down from God" and must be accepted; there should be
more difference between the top and bottom incomes in
The Gambia than there is now. Nevertheless, he com-
plains about the high cost of living and says that farmers
should make much more money than they do now. High
government officials and executives, on the other hand,
are being paid too much; clerks, teachers, and manual
workers are paid about the right amount. In rewarding
work, size of the family being supported and efficiency
should be the most important factors; experience and
loyalty are not very important. If he got a £100 windfall, he
would buy a good fishing net.

This chapter will examine the way people handle certain problems which
arise in towns—some which are easily observed, such as poverty, unemployment, and trouble with the police, and others which commentators
on urban life in developing countries have felt to be important, such as
political efficacy and relations between members of different ethnic and
economic groups. Some of these topics have been discussed at length

elsewhere (Peil 1975b, 1976b); a brief summary of the findings is included here because it helps to round out the picture of urban life.

Whereas the previous three chapters have discussed relations of kinship and friendship and alliances in associations, the concern here is interaction at a somewhat less personal level, the extent to which ordinary citizens are able to penetrate the government bureaucracy when in need and their categoric relations with fellow citizens to whom they have no personal ties. Even though particularistic contacts are preferred, there are bound to be situations in which an urban resident must operate outside his or her personal networks. Modernization theorists have argued that urban experience and especially employment in a large universalistic organization such as a factory will make it much easier for individuals to handle these situations (see, for example, Inkeles 1969). These data provide an opportunity to see whether the nature of the urban environment has any effect which is independent of the characteristics of individuals, and to explore the ways in which both locals and migrants see themselves as part of a wider society.

Getting Help

Most people need help from time to time. They run short of food or chairs because visitors arrive unexpectedly, or they face an emergency demand for more cash than they have at hand, someone in the family falls ill, or they need something from the government bureaucracy and lack the appropriate contacts. Generally speaking, the lower a person is in socioeconomic status, the more likely he or she is to need help and the more likely he or she is to have difficulty getting that help. Since primary-group relations are important for many types of help, especially in emergencies, recent migrants with small networks are likely to have more trouble getting help than long-established residents who know the rules of the game and have developed exchange relationships with a number of urban patrons.

Litwak and Szelenyi (1969) suggest that technological development has changed the functions of primary groups so that groups structured around different bases (kinship, neighborhood, and friendship) perform different functions for urban residents than in the past. Kin continue to carry the responsibility for long-term support in major crises, but neighbors are more available for short-term aid; friends are often a preferable reference group to either kin or neighbors because they tend to have a similar or hoped-for position in society. While the technology available to most West African residents is considerably below that of the Americans and Hungarians on which these hypotheses were developed, many of them are sufficiently separated from most of their kin to make it necessary, or at least convenient, to get assistance from other people from time to time.

Ghanaians were asked about borrowing from neighbors, how many of their neighbors and cotenants they talked to about their mutual problems or asked for advice or help, and whether they ever discussed their problems with kin, coworkers, or fellow migrants from home. They were also asked whether they had ever gone to the Tema Development Corporation, the police, or the school to complain, and whether they got the help they sought. Nigerians and Gambians were asked what they would do if faced with certain specific problems: if they needed money or a job, had trouble at work or with the police, or had a dispute with a spouse or kinsman. In each of these cases, they were asked whom they would consult, where this person lived, how long they had known him or her, the reason for the choice, and whether they had ever done so. They were also asked whether people like themselves could make their needs known to the government,[1] how they could do this, and whether they had ever tried it.

It was expected that residents of industrialized towns would be more aware of the availability of professional advice and more willing to use it than residents of more "traditional" towns such as Abeokuta, though the size of the town would affect the opportunity for consultation; Aba is large enough to have lawyers and welfare services, whereas residents of Kakuri and Ashaiman would have to go to the neighboring cities for such help. In addition, individuals with secondary or higher education and nonmanual employment should have the experience to make them fairly confident in their use of official agencies, whereas housewives and people with no education and laboring jobs would probably feel safer seeking help from family or friends regardless of their ability to provide it.

Table 8.1 shows, as expected, that women seek help from their husbands and kin to a far greater extent than do men. Very few husbands expect any help from their wives, but when they do it is usually when money is needed. Specialist help is sought mainly when outsiders are involved (trouble at work and with the police), but even then only a minority would go beyond their extended networks. "Other individuals" includes friends, people from home, cotenants, neighbors, coworkers, and landlords—anyone contacted in a personal rather than an official capacity. While lawyers and employers were the most commonly named specialists, religious and trade union or guild leaders, policemen, a chief, the labor office, public services commission, and bank were also mentioned.

Men in Abeokuta and Banjul were most likely to seek specialist help; the relative stability of population and multiple ties of many residents make it likely that some extended link could be established between individuals needing help and specialists in these towns. Aba women are at the

TABLE 8.1
Assistance Sought, by Problem, Town, and Sex (Percentages)[a]

| | | Gambia | | | | Nigeria | | | | | | | |
| | | Banjul | | Serekunda | | Aba | | Abeokuta | | Ajegunle | | Kakuri | |
Problem	Help Sought From	M	F	M	F	M	F	M	F	M	F	M	F
Dispute with kin, spouse:	Spouse	1	16	0	21	0	30	3	23	1	39	0	16
	Kin	78	72	74	70	74	65	57	50	78	39	59	72
	Other individuals	5	6	14	6	22	5	40	25	21	22	37	12
	Official, specialist	16	6	12	3	4	0	0	2	0	0	4	0
	Total	100	100	100	100	100	100	100	100	100	100	100	100
	N	121	38	120	38	111	40	94	52	137	44	118	32
Money:	Spouse	4	51	3	36	0	68	3	33	0	53	1	26
	Kin	61	39	56	46	63	26	22	19	64	30	34	36
	Other individuals	21	8	24	14	27	6	64	43	30	17	61	36
	Official, specialist	14	2	17	4	10	0	11	5	6	0	4	2
	Total	100	100	100	100	100	100	100	100	100	100	100	100
	N	124	46	129	47	125	51	132	64	155	53	142	42
Need job:	Spouse	1	30	1	36	0	70	0	28	0	45	0	52
	Kin	55	52	58	39	51	30	19	17	47	22	40	29
	Other individuals	14	8	24	14	30	0	74	51	29	14	39	19
	Official, specialist	30	9	17	11	16	0	6	4	22	13	17	0
	Total	100	100	100	100	100	100	100	100	100	100	100	100
	N	97	23	78	28	69	33	104	57	125	40	105	21

TABLE 8.1 (continued)
Assistance Sought, by Problem, Town, and Sex (Percentages)[a]

| | | Gambia | | | | Nigeria | | | | | | | |
| | | Banjul | | Serekunda | | Aba | | Abeokuta | | Ajegunle | | Kakuri | |
Problem	Help Sought From	M	F	M	F	M	F	M	F	M	F	M	F
Trouble	Spouse	1	29	0	49	0	59	2	30	1	34	2	21
at work:	Kin	38	36	29	30	40	23	9	20	29	9	20	15
	Other individuals	8	6	11	4	30	7	64	38	22	27	31	48
	Official, specialist	53	29	60	17	30	11	25	12	48	30	47	16
	Total	100	100	100	100	100	100	100	100	100	100	100	100
	N	115	31	103	23	118	44	123	61	156	33	125	19
Trouble	Spouse	2	37	1	35	1	71	0	50	1	58	0	49
with	Kin	52	30	52	45	57	25	24	31	64	32	38	26
police:	Other individuals	10	14	18	8	21	2	60	15	23	8	41	17
	Official, specialist	36	19	29	12	21	2	16	4	12	2	21	8
	Total	100	100	100	100	100	100	100	100	100	100	100	100
	N	120	43	114	40	128	47	99	55	150	47	112	40
	Contacted government	37	10	18	13	24	16	27	8	6	4	10	4
	N	152	51	152	53	152	55	137	65	171	56	161	45
Mean problem score[b]		3.4	1.4	2.9	1.2	2.6	0.7	4.0	2.2	2.8	1.4	3.2	1.3

[a]Those who said they would solve the problem themselves or that it would not arise have been omitted.

[b]Minimum 0 (all help sought from family, kin); maximum 12.

other extreme; only a third of them admitted the possibility of consulting anyone outside their kinship network; for any problem but disputes with their husbands, a majority would expect husbands to provide whatever help they need. Dependency on husbands is considerably lower in other towns, though about a third of the women would usually go to their husbands for help. They are seen as "in charge" of their wives, as having a duty to help them. Older women also expect help from their children.

Whereas it might be expected that the most useful friends would be those who are better placed than the individual seeking help, respondents who said they would use their friendship networks tended to refer to people who were of the same age and socioeconomic status as themselves and had been known a relatively long time. Banjul residents and women in Ajegunle most often referred to somone of higher status or wealth. Gambians were more likely than Nigerians to mention someone not on their friendship list, selecting an acquaintance who would best fit the particular problem. This tended to be someone known since childhood who was now highly successful; one woman said she would go to the President if she needed a job. This type of contact is more likely in the small-scale Banjul society than in Nigeria. These are the "weak ties" which Liu and Duff (1972) and Granovetter (1973) show are particularly useful for the diffusion of information and influence and which help to bind various segments of a community together. The strength and diversity of these ties in Banjul is probably an important factor in its relatively stable political situation.

Friends of about the same age and socioeconomic status can be solicited for help more often and on a more reciprocal basis than wealthy and successful patrons. Several men named friends who provided cash when they needed it and to whom they supplied cash in emergencies. These exchanges generate security without the burden of clientship. Length of acquaintance is less important for information on job opportunities than for other needs; all contacts are mobilized for this. Money may also be borrowed from someone who is a new friend or neighbor if this person is seen to be favorably inclined and able to help. For family disputes, however, long-term friendship is more important, as the arbitrator must know the parties well or have considerable authority in the community if he is to stand in for absent kin.

Disputes within the conjugal or extended family are usually solved by kin who are immediately available rather than by kin living at home, even though the latter may be more closely related and thus more appropriate for conflict resolution. Only in Aba would more than 4 percent of respondents take a dispute home for settlement, and this is because so many Aba residents come from nearby villages and go home frequently. For the rest, propinquity is more important; a kinsman living nearby would be consulted and at least a fifth would seek help from nonkin. In Nigeria, these are almost always friends, but in The Gambia the imam (or, for Christians, the pastor) acts as a counselor for family disputes and some-times for other problems. This happens in Ghana too; Lowy (1977, p. 26) reports that disputes between spouses are the most common type brought to religious leaders in Koforidua, a provincial town.

Landlords are also used for "household cases." Nearly three-fifths of the landlords surveyed in Koforidua had settled tenant disputes, about a third of which concerned family matters. Landlords were seldom sug-gested as arbitrators in The Gambia or Nigeria, but observation and informal discussions of their role indicate that their position as elders and as relatively wealthy members of the community reinforces their authority as owners. Landlords who are resident in their houses not only keep the peace but are also consulted about other problems that their tenants have.

The proportion who would consult kin at home for other problems is about the same as for family disputes. Aba respondents (especially the women) are about twice as likely as those in other towns to say that they would seek help for any problems at home. This confirms their closer hometown ties, which were reported in chapters 5 and 7. Residents of other towns tend to see people at home as uninformed about urban prob-lems and thus unable to help, in addition to being physically unavailable. This is particularly true in The Gambia, where residents are more likely than in Nigeria to cut their ties with home.

Five percent of the Nigerian men but only two Gambians would try to get money from home. The major source of cash is kin living in town, except in Abeokuta and Kakuri, where both men and women would ask their friends. About a third of respondents in these towns said they had no kin living there, so friends are a necessary substitute. Friends or patrons are also used where they are seen as more affluent than kin; part of the price of friendship is a willingness to help out in emergencies. Banks were mentioned more often in The Gambia than in Nigeria; they were thought of mainly for holding savings rather than for providing loans. Only one person thought of a savings society as a source of cash in an emergency.

As in most countries, low-income people look to kin, neighbors, and friends as sources of information about jobs. Men in Banjul are most likely to register for employment; men elsewhere said they would try factory gates or "the man who owns the job." Patrons, brokers, or "long legs" are seen as particularly important in getting the job once a vacancy has been located. This question is irrelevant to a majority of the women, since most expect to be self-employed when they enter the labor force. Neverthe-less, their answers demonstrate the relatively narrow networks they would mobilize should they seek wage employment. This is likely to lower their chances of finding such jobs.

A major characteristic of modernization is held to be the separation of work from home, so that the particularistic family relationships should not intrude on the universalistic relationships of the former. However, the data show that large numbers of West Africans still handle trouble connected with their employment through the use of personal networks. Between one- and three-fifths of the women would expect their husbands to take care of it, which seems inordinately high given the reputed economic autonomy of these women. Significantly, the proportion is highest for Aba women, who are shown on other measures to be the most dependent. Igbo women in Ajegunle were more willing than those in Aba to seek specialist help; the local environment may encourage autonomy, or they may be driven to it by the lack of appropriate kin.

Between half and two-thirds of the men in wage employment in all six towns would take work disputes to officials, especially their employers but also trade union officials and other people in authority such as policemen. The proportion is lowest, as predicted, in Abeokuta, but the differences between towns are not significant and Kakuri, with its large textile factories, is second lowest. Nigerian men in semiskilled work[2] or the uniformed services were more likely than other workers to use officials to handle work disputes; they may be more subject to large-scale bureaucracy than the average laborer, clerk, or professional. Nevertheless, the relatively high proportion in all occupations who would use personal mediators indicates that customary norms still affect the application of authority in the workplace.

The police pose a potentially more threatening problem, especially for the poor. Work disputes seldom lead to loss of employment, but an accusation of wrongdoing by the police could lead to considerable expense if not to loss of liberty. Refusal to answer the question on trouble with the police was relatively high; people sometimes resented the implication that they might break a law, even inadvertently. The majority of these who did reply, except in Abeokuta and Kakuri, said they would get help from kin (or husbands); between an eighth (Abeokuta) and a third (Banjul) of the men would seek official help, usually from a lawyer, but (more often for Nigerians) also by going to the man in charge of the local police station. One gets the impression that police officers are seen as more reliable than ordinary policemen, but perhaps they are also easier to arrange things with.

The use of brokers in this case showed that a large number of people have at least an indirect connection with the police. Either they or one of their friends have a kinsman or friend on the force. Another use of friends in this sort of emergency is the provision of transportation; one young man said his friend would provide a motorcycle for the trip to the station. This service could also be useful to get the police should they be needed for neighborhood trouble and for medical emergencies.

From the standpoint of Litwak and Szelenyi's hypothesis, the striking finding in these data is the little use made of contenants or neighbors, with the exception of the landlord, and the comparatively wide use made of friends. Given the level of technological development, the continuing preference for help from kin is to be expected, and the evidence consistently shows that friends are often a substitute for absent kin. Relationships with contenants and neighbors are apparently too tenuous for the problems posed; a better indicator of the availability of their help is the exchange question asked only in Ghana.

About two-thirds of the men and women in Ashaiman occasionally borrow provisions, dishes, and other household items from contenants, compared to a third of the men and a quarter of the women in Tema. Contenants are more often parties to these exchanges than neighbors, and the relationships within houses must therefore be seen as stronger (as well as more convenient) than those between residents of neighboring houses. Part of the difference between the two towns is due to the lower incidence of contenants in Tema, but the ability of Ashaiman residents to choose their houses (and, implicitly, their contenants) and the presence of resident landlords probably improve relations as well. This question shows the use of local acquaintances for small-scale, short-term help, but on the whole there appears to be little formation of primary groups on a neighborhood basis, perhaps because most people can still have face-to-face contacts with kin and see their residence in the neighborhood as temporary.

Although a majority of people think it is possible to make their needs known to government officials, either by direct contact, letters to the newspapers, or through associations or intermediaries (see Peil 1976b, pp. 143–53), only a minority have actually done so. The proportion is, as expected, highest in Banjul and the Nigerian provincial towns, where government is physically as well as psychologically closer to the people than in the suburbs. The relatively high level of active women in Aba is surprising in the light of their demonstrated dependence on their husbands; perhaps the activist stance inherited from the Aba women's riots of 1929 makes it easier for them to react to the government than to take independent action in other fields. The comparatively low rate for women (otherwise quite able to act independently) is also surprising. Yoruba custom provides a political role for women, including chieftaincy. The women in Abeokuta are as likely to be locally born as the men, and should therefore have as many long-term contacts in local government; nevertheless, they are less than a third as likely to have attempted to exert influence.

The score at the bottom of Table 8.1 summarizes the use made of kin, personal contacts, and officials in handling problems. In each case, handling the problem oneself or seeking help from kin or spouse is worth no points, use of an unrelated individual one point, and asking for help from a specialist two points (including contacts made with government regardless of how this was done). Men in Banjul rely most on specialists and men in Abeokuta and Kakuri rely least on kin. Men and women in Aba are most dependent on kin, but the negligible difference between the mean scores for men in Aba and Ajegunle indicates much more reliance on kin in the capital than would be expected given the metropolitan nature of the environment and the relatively infrequent visits to kin by Ajegunle residents. What appears to be happening is that the highly competitive atmosphere in Lagos and the relative unavailability of specialists in Ajegunle lead men to seek the comparative security of kin when they need help.

As the questions asked Ghanaians were more general than those used in Nigeria and The Gambia, they provide much less information. Nevertheless, the results are worth summarizing. None of the Ashaiman 1970 respondents would take a serious problem to a specialist. About half would seek help from kin, a quarter from friends, and the rest from fellow migrants from home, cotenants, or coworkers. About four-fifths of the men and three-quarters of the women interviewed in Ghana in 1968 discussed their problems with others at least occasionally; people in Ashaiman were more than four times as likely as Tema residents to do this often. This may be partly because they had more problems to discuss; the environment in Ashaiman (quality of housing, amenities) makes community problems more salient than in the higher-quality Tema environment. Personal problems also tend to be greater in Ashaiman, as the people there have less stable employment and lower average incomes than Tema residents.

Both men and women in Ashaiman discuss problems with more cotenants and neighbors than do Tema residents; contenants are more often involved in such discussions in Ashaiman and neighbors in Tema. Although people in Tema are somewhat less likely to have kin in town, they discuss problems with them more often than Ashaiman residents do; the latter make about the same use of migrants from home as of kin, whereas these are seldom party to problem discussions in Tema. About a fifth of the men and women in both towns reported conversations about their problems with coworkers; few mentioned other friends, but this may be due to the structure of the question. Only ten percent of the men in Ashaiman and women in both towns said they had made a complaint to the TDC or the police; this was up to 29 percent for men in Tema, who had more to complain to the TDC about. Women and Ashaiman residents were somewhat less likely to be satisfied with the help they received than Tema men, who are probably better placed to make effective complaints.

The most important personal characteristics which distinguish those who get all their help from kin from those who are able to mobilize other contacts and specialist resources are income and type of employment. Housewives and the unemployed are the least likely to look beyond kinship networks, whereas men and women in wage employment and especially professionals and administrators earning more than £750 per year are more likely than those with lower incomes and manual work to seek professional help. This is partly because in a corrupt society such help often costs money, but also because the experience of wage employment and access to an above-average income increase the efficacy of those who seek such help; they have a better idea of what to ask for and how to go about it. Education and occupational level are relatively unimportant and count more for women than for men; the well-educated woman in a nonmanual job can potentially use specialists more efficiently than her illiterate sister, though she is more likely to do so in Aba and the Gambian towns than elsewhere.

Although both old and young tend to prefer mobilizing personal contacts rather than involving themselves with unknown and untested specialists, older men are more likely than young newcomers to have acquaintances in the bureaucracy whom they can consult. Long-term male residents of Tema and Banjul and locally born men in Serekunda had higher scores than more recent arrivals.

The frequency of visits to kin and an individual's level of sociability make little difference when a crisis arises. In The Gambia, Ajegunle, and Abeokuta, women who usually see their kin less than once a week are more likely to seek them out for help than women who visit more often, whereas Ghanaian men who see kin daily are more likely to ask their help than those with less contact. The least social Ghanaians and women in the Nigerian industrial towns are more likely than others to rely exclusively on kin, but the same is not true for respondents elsewhere.

Given that it is usually kin in town rather than at home who are asked for help, it was expected that visits home and intention to return there might have no effect on asking for help in town. However, it appears that Nigerians who visit home less than once a year are more likely than those who go more often to think of kin in town as their main source of help. They do not visit these kin more often, but may feel closer because of their lack of contact with home.

Strangers and Hosts

Relations between the local people and migrants have given rise to difficulties in several West African towns, notably in Nigeria and in Abidjan. Differences tend to be expressed in ethnic terms, but this is often flexible and situational. The hierarchy of acceptability is affected by perceived cultural distance, education, religion, and the level of competition for political, economic, and social resources. With independence, nationality has become an increasingly important boundary; several West African countries have expelled aliens because they were perceived as having as undue share of the economy (Peil 1971). This is more important in the towns than in the rural areas; alien farm laborers are more controllable than urban entrepreneurs (see Bonacich 1973, p. 592).

Most ethnic groups have provisions for the assimilation of outsiders, but they vary considerably in the conditions under which this is possible. In the precolonial period, it was probably most common for slaves; more recently, it has involved migrating farmers (usually from a short distance) and the children of interethnic marriages who choose to emphasize the local side of their inheritance. In the urban situation, both individual migrants and groups vary in their willingness to accommodate to local customs and their interest in assimilation. The majority who do not come to town permanently are usually content to remain strangers, providing this does not interfere too much with their ability to find work and live in reasonable security.

Levine (1979) has expanded Simmel's concept of stranger into a typology which defines the relative position of the outsider in terms of his interest in the local society and the host's response. Migrants who are short-term visitors may be seen as guests or intruders; those who stay longer may be termed newcomers or marginal men, more or less permanent in the community but not of it. Because both nationality and community membership are usually seen by Africans in terms of ethnicity, full integration in one generation is virtually impossible and even second-generation residents who have not intermarried may still be seen as sojourners; to the extent that strong ties with home are maintained, this is probably justified. Schildkrout (1978) shows that second-generation Mossi in Kumasi are usually assimilated into the *zongo* culture. As this is dominated by Hausa-influenced Muslim values, the Mossi are effectively prevented from integrating into Ghanaian society, which they have been socialized to reject. This weakens their security in Kumasi and encourages them to maintain ties with the Mossi community.

Competition

On the basis of his work in Indonesia, Bruner (in Cohen 1974, p. 269) proposes the hypothesis that interethnic relations will be much more relaxed in a town where the local people are in a majority and retain control over the local power structure than in a town with no majority or dominant culture. In the former, migrants will tend to adapt local norms, whereas the latter will be characterized by competition and tense relationships which keep people apart because it is difficult to predict behavior if there is no local norm to which all can refer. This seems to apply quite well in West Africa, but other factors such as the resources of the migrants, the alternative opportunities of the indigenes, the number and size of competing groups, and their relative national support must also be taken into consideration.

The response to the influx of migrants may be favorable at first; increasing numbers are good for trade. But if the migrants are better educated than the locals, they begin to take over the best jobs and to be influential in policy making. Their demand for housing may also be seen initially as beneficial, but when they begin to buy land, pushing up prices and taking over a commodity which is basic to community identity, and when as landowners and a numerical majority, they start to take over local politics, the hosts are likely to feel that guests have become intruders.

Two towns where this has happened, Warri and Lagos, have been studied by Lloyd (1974) and Baker (1974). In both cases, communal nationalism emphasized the status of traditional leaders, but the mass of the people seem to have had much less to gain in Warri than in Lagos. Partly for this reason, the latter case developed into a truly populist movement, embracing Lagosians of all social levels who resented being relegated to the status of unimportant slum dwellers in a city belonging to the nation. After about twenty years of agitation, the Lagosians won autonomy in a state of their own which, given the attachment of most migrants to other parts of the Federation, they could largely control. This, in turn, has meant that a "stranger town" like Ajegunle, which houses low-income sojourners, gets little attention from state authorities.

Other hosts are less concerned about protecting their position because their most enterprising men migrate. The indigenes of Abeokuta, for example, have been relatively uninterested in the local civil service, preferring trade or crafts if they stay at home, or the greater opportunities of the Lagos or Ibadan bureaucracy if they have the appropriate education. The migrant status of most civil servants has been maintained even though Abeokuta is now a state capital.

The Ngwa of Aba were outnumbered in their hometown after the war, but recovered their position somewhat when Owerri was made the state capital. By the late 1970s, the Ngwa were able to play a strong role in local politics. Competition in these provincial towns is more on an economic than a cultural basis, since almost everyone has the same basic culture.

Kaduna is at the other extreme in having no indigenes, but there are so many ethnic groups represented in Kakuri that conflict over potential dominance, except perhaps between the Hausa and Yoruba because of their national links, is muted. However, another important factor in the Kakuri situation is that struggle for relative advantage has tended to be for control over state policy; the town is one of the prizes to the victor.

A large proportion of the migrants are content to be strangers, though they are probably more likely to put down roots than rural-urban migrants of thirty years ago because their education and the rising standard of living make town life more satisfying. People in Lagos like to feel that they are near the seat of power, even though they can have no meaningful part in it.

A sense of disadvantage occurs mainly over the provision of amenities, when migrants are aware (as in Ajegunle) that other parts of town are better served than their own. This was expressed by a man in Ashaiman who said, in response to a question on the effect the expulsion of aliens was likely to have on Ashaiman, that perhaps the government would now develop the town because it would no longer be seen as only a residence of aliens. However, the provision of services is usually best in residential areas reserved for the governmental elite, and may be nearly as bad in the more indigenous center as in the largely migrant outskirts. The Ghana government was spending its money to make Tema a showplace new town, and had little left for Ashaiman regardless of who lived there.

The relations between the host community and the strangers also depend on the former's sense of security. Large numbers of migrants can be accommodated by a secure host community, whereas a community which feels itself under threat may see even a few strangers as intruders. The insecurity may be due to a struggle for power ("we must make the decisions or we will be exploited"), for economic resources ("our young men need jobs; too many migrants are going into trade"), or to social considerations ("our language and the quality of life in our town must be maintained"). To some extent, self-confident egocentrism can make for good community relations, especially if the strangers do not make too many demands.

The uncertainties of independence have tended to worsen relations both between aliens and citizens and between majority and minority ethnic groups within the country. Aliens can have no part in national unity because their allegiance—regardless of where they were born—is elsewhere. Internally, the competition for political and economic resources has made ethnic identity a greater source of conflict than in the past, when Africans could unite against the colonial overlords. To a certain extent, the acceptance of dependency theory and the denunciations of expatriate capitalism are an attempt by national leaders to revive this sense of national unity.

The level of economic competition and prosperity and the work sought also affect the welcome which newcomers get. The hosts prefer that they fill unwanted jobs at the bottom rather than compete for more attractive opportunities, though better-educated migrants expect better jobs than uneducated locals. Opposition tends to be greatest to middleman minorities (Bonacich 1973), to strangers who monopolize certain commercial opportunities and can be seen as exploiting the local population through their control over the price of daily necessities. But the authorities may also find it convenient to develop a negative stereotype against those living at the margins of subsistence by emphasizing their crime rates and unemployment.[3] Van Velsen (1975, p. 307) found that residents of squatter settlements in Lusaka are resented and looked down on by both trade unionists and politicians in spite of their substantial contributions to urban development. He suggests that an unfavorable stereotype is a useful way of legitimating one's antagonism to a competitor. This helps to explain rising levels of opposition to strangers in times of stress.

It is interesting that the government itself has little to say about competition for high-level jobs, though this may involve more specifically ethnic competition than lower-level employment. Harris (1978, pp. 303–306) found considerable agreement among top Nigerian politicians, businessmen, and professionals in the mid-1960s that the public service took political and ethnic affiliation into consideration in appointments, promotions, and general dealings with the public. About half of the top public servants interviewed agreed that this was the case. Discrimination can be legitimated if the strangers are aliens (as in campaigns for laws against small alien businesses), but is more difficult to assert against fellow citizens. However, discrimination against aliens almost inevitably serves as a warning to citizens who are also strangers to develop personal relations with the locals and not flaunt their success if they want to avoid local opposition. In deciding who is eligible for jobs, regional or state boundaries may be as important as national ones and discrimination (real or imagined) in one area soon spreads to others.

Aliens

Because of the salience of these issues, questions were asked about relations with aliens in Ashaiman in 1970 and relations with members of other ethnic groups in Nigeria. Before the expulsions of 1969–1970, about a fifth of the Ashaiman population was alien; most respondents had known aliens as cotenants, coworkers, or neighbors. Most considered them to be compatible cotenants and hardworking coworkers. Respondents who had had unfavorable experiences were usually reluctant to generalize to all aliens and it was evident that once personal relationships develop ethnicity and nationality become relatively unimportant to Ghanaians. "Alien" appears to be a category of government manufacture rather than a natural development; any "we-they" boundary is normally at a lower level than nationality.

The two areas where aliens had a bad reputation were as traders and criminals. As happens in most parts of the world, alien traders are often seen as grasping, cliquish, and unfriendly. This applies especially to Nigerian traders, who have tended to maintain greater separation from the Ghanaian population than northern immigrant laborers and whose lack of kinship ties (outside the trading community) is useful in building up their businesses (see Eades 1979).

Ashaiman had a bad reputation as a home of thieves and smugglers and the government's campaign to identify crime with aliens was well received there. Unexpectedly, respondents who claimed to have known aliens well were more likely than others to say that there would be less crime in Ashaiman now that most of the aliens had gone. The drop in crime between 1968 and 1970 seemed to confirm this, but it was partly due to a new head of the police post and a drive against thieves that encouraged some to move elsewhere. However, some aliens (like Ghanaians in similar economic circumstances) did engage in illegal activities.

Nationals

Competitors for national resources in Nigeria are usually citizens, though the economic prosperity of recent years has brought in increasing numbers of aliens from less fortunate neighboring countries. Unlike The Gambia, where ethnic groups are scattered and thus not identifiable with a particular area, ethnic groups in Nigeria are geographically based, so demands of a particular region, state, or locality can be identified as the demands of a particular ethnic group. This inevitably increases interethnic hostility. As in Ghana, this competition does not preclude satisfying interpersonal relations between members of various groups; previous chapters have shown that housing and friendship are often ethnically mixed, though marriage is only rarely so. However, because individuals are acquainted with members of only a few of Nigeria's approximately six hundred ethnic groups and because the struggle for political and economic resources has so often been phrased in ethnic terms, stereotyping has been more widespread there than in many smaller-scale nations.

Nigerians were asked a standard social distance question for twelve ethnic groups: would they marry or allow a child to marry one of these people, share a house with them but not marry, work but not live with them, or prefer to have nothing to do with them? Answers were scored from one to four, from negligible to great social distance. The groups selected included northerners and southerners, and majority and minority peoples: Edo, Efik, Fulani, Hausa, Ibibio, Igbo, Kalibari, Kanuri, Nupe, Tiv, Yoruba, and Zugu. The last were included because they are relatively unknown; how do people respond when they have no stereotype except stranger?

Ratings vary with sex, education, migration experience, exposure to a particular group, and relative position in the town's ethnic hierarchy. The most consistent difference is by sex. Women's ratings show greater social distance than men's for all groups, though the differences are not significant for Ibibio and Yoruba. If each individual's ratings are aggregated, the mean scores for women are also somewhat higher than for men; in this case the difference is significant only in Aba, where men have a mean score of twenty and women's scores compare with those of men in other towns (twenty-seven to twenty-eight). To some extent, this is due to differential exposure; women probably have fewer opportunities than men to know strangers well, though only in Ajegunle are they less likely to have interethnic friendships. As the largest differences are all for northern peoples, there may be more north-south distance among women than among men.

Respondents with secondary or university education and/or administrative or professional occupations generally showed a lower level of prejudice than those with less education. Thus, the opportunity to socialize with members of other groups at school and the ability to communicate with them in a neutral language (English) appear to pay off in more universalistic relationships. The few who reported Muslim schooling were the most tolerant of all, presumably because of their acceptance of Islamic teaching, which minimizes ethnicity among Muslims. However, this was much less evident for Muslims as a whole. It does not appear that primary education, which is all that most Nigerians get, has any effect in lowering prejudice.

Length of residence in town and migration experience have different effects in different types of towns. In industrial towns, by their nature ethnically heterogeneous, recent arrivals and men from rural areas are less interested in associating with strangers than men and women who have spent more time in town and men of wider urban experience. Newcomers probably feel more secure with people from home and are more determined to marry endogamously than those who have had more time to get to know members of other groups as individuals.

However, the experience of living in more than one town tends to increase the ethnocentrism of women. This may be related to competition among women traders or to housewives having greater difficulty than their husbands in coping with strangers, though why this should be a greater problem for women of urban than of rural background is not clear. In the provincial towns, it is the nonmigrants who show the highest levels of ethnocentrism, probably because they find it satisfying to maintain their own superiority and feel threatened by strangers. This could be a case of more sheltered people finding it easiest to maintain stereotypes.

Differential exposure, regionalism, and relative political, economic, and social power in the town seem to cause the greater social distance shown toward minority than majority peoples. Most people living in heterogeneous towns have met quite a few Yoruba and Igbo (and, in the north, Hausa) and have been able to form opinions about them, whereas they may never have knowingly met anyone belonging to any of the minority groups mentioned. Respondents in all towns show the greatest social distance toward the Zugu and the least toward the Yoruba (who are "at home" in both northern and southern states). In addition, the group with highest local status (Yoruba in Ajegunle, Hausa in Kakuri) received the most favorable ratings; marriage into this group may well be perceived as a step up. Schildkrout (1978) shows this for the Kumasi Hausa.

Members of both southern and northern minorities look more favorably on peoples from their own area than on those from other parts of the country, regardless of whether they are living in the north or south. Both religion and culture play a part here. Fellow northerners are more likely to be Muslim and fellow southerners to be Christian, but there are also cultural continuities among many Middle Belt minority groups and among the peoples of the Niger Delta which facilitate intermarriage.

Last, there is the question of whether ethnically mixed housing tends to increase or decrease prejudice. This seems to depend partly on the type of town. In the ethnically mixed industrial towns, both men and women in monoethnic houses showed the highest levels of ethnic distance. Provincial residents in houses limited to single subgroups also had relatively high levels (presumably because so many of these are local family houses), but residents of the relatively few ethnically mixed houses showed the greatest prejudice against strangers. Thus, encapsulation probably increases ethnocentricity among residents of hetereogeneous towns (where differences are widely accepted) whereas the strain of coping with differences may be more readily noticed in environments where homogeneity is expected.

Inequality

Because of the increasing interest in social class formation and because so little sociological research has been done in The Gambia, a series of questions was asked on the socioeconomic backgrounds of respondents, their ideas of occupational prestige and remuneration, and the level of inequality which should exist in Gambian society. Although these data refer only to The Gambia, some comparisons can be made with studies carried out elsewhere.

Social Mobility

The rating of an individual's inherited socioeconomic status (SES) is based on father's occupation while that individual was growing up and the education obtained by both parents. Those classed as low in Table 8.2 had fathers in farming or manual work, with a few years of primary education or none at all. Those in the high category had fathers in business or nonmanual employment, with at least secondary education, and mothers with at least primary education. While there are very few cases of downward mobility, there is abundant evidence of upward mobility among both men and women. Thus, while over three-quarters of those who did not go beyond primary school came from low-SES backgrounds, the same is true for over two-fifths of the men and nearly a third of the women who got as far as senior secondary school, in a country where this is still a rare achievement. Half of the men and a third of the women in clerical and professional occupations had also greatly surpassed their parents' positions.

From the opposite point of view, it is clear that well-educated parents have largely passed on their educational advantages to their children,

TABLE 8.2

Inherited Socioeconomic Status, by Sex, Education, Occupation,
and Income, The Gambia (Percentages)

	Males					Females				
Respondent's	Low	Medium	High	Total	N	Low	Medium	High	Total	N
Education										
None	98	2	0	100	40	86	14	0	100	28
Muslim	89	11	0	100	90	84	16	0	100	32
Primary	76	21	3	100	38	64	18	18	100	11
Junior secondary	57	39	4	100	54	25	58	17	100	12
More	44	30	26	100	82	24	29	47	100	21
Occupation										
Unskilled/ semiskilled	91	9	0	100	70 }	57	43	0	100	14
Skilled	70	25	5	100	61 }					
Commerce	88	6	6	100	55	71	21	7	100	28
Clerical	52	35	13	100	63 }	32	24	44	100	25
Administrative, professional	47	35	18	100	55 }					
None						81	16	3	100	37
Income										
Low[a]	81	18	1	100	93	78	17	4	100	23
Medium	71	22	7	100	148	72	22	6	100	32
High[b]	54	27	19	100	52	16	37	47	100	19

[a]Males: under D1200 (£300); females: under D400 (£100). Those with no income excluded.

[b]Males: D3000+ (£750); females: D2000+ (£500).

though they have been less solicitous toward their daughters than toward their sons. About three-fourths of the children of high-SES parents have found clerical, administrative, or professional occupations. While this is high, it is also clear that not all the advantaged children maintain their position. The main benefits demonstrated in these data are the ability of medium-SES children (whose parents had some education) to move into secondary schooling and nonmanual jobs, and the large share of female nonmanual posts held by high-SES daughters. This is partly because so many low-SES daughters follow custom and remain out of the labor force or go into trade, but relatively few middle-SES daughters did not yet have enough education to qualify for such jobs. Skilled work proved attractive to both sons and daughters of middle-SES parents; these jobs often satisfy the aspirations of junior secondary leavers and provide opportunities for stable and reasonably well-paid employment.

Inherited SES is also an advantage for income, but again more for women than for men. Over half of the men in the top quartile of income had low-SES parents. With discrimination in education and more limited occupational opportunities, it is much more difficult for women than for men to overcome initial disadvantages and achieve high individual income, but a woman's social status may also be raised by her husband's position, a situation most likely to be useful to moderately well-educated middle-SES daughters.

Occupational Prestige

Measures of occupational prestige in many developed and developing countries produce generally similar results, with professional and administrative occupations at the top and unskilled manual occupations at the bottom (Hodge 1966; Treiman 1977). Since most African prestige studies have used student respondents, one purpose of including an occupational prestige question in the Gambian questionnaire was to see how close the ratings of students and the general population were. (The same scale was administered to 138 secondary students in two Banjul schools.) The second purpose was to examine the relative placement of certain occupations in a small-scale, highly Islamized, and relatively nonindustrialized town. Respondents were asked to rate thirty-two occupations as very high, high, not high or low, low, or very low in the "prestige and respect" given them by Gambians and to give the reasons for their ranking of one high and one low occupation.

There was general agreement on the relative position of most occupations between the adult and student samples, between men and women, and between the two towns, which supports the hypothesis of a widely accepted ranking of occupations. However, differences from rankings in Ghana and Nigeria show the influence of local culture on this hierarchy. For example, imam was ranked second by adults and fourth by students in The Gambia, whereas religious leader (priest or imam) was only tenth in Ghana (Peil 1972a, p. 118). Gamble (1966, pp. 105–06), who found imam was rated very high in Sierra Leone, explains that Muslims usually rate both imam and priest higher than Christians because of the prestige they give to anyone who teaches people to pray. Christians place more emphasis on (Western) education and income, and thus give less prestige to religious leaders.

Farmers and blacksmiths both got less prestige than in Ghana although, as will be seen below, there is considerable sympathy for the economic position of farmers. Blacksmith (twenty-eighth) is considerably lower than other skilled trades because of the low position of blacksmiths in the Senegambian caste system. Although some urban dwellers farm on the outskirts of town, many residents who stay in Banjul and Serekunda during the farming season have made a definite choice not to farm, so their ranking of farmer (twenty-sixth) reflects its low prestige in their eyes. It was rated somewhat higher in Serekunda, where ties to the rural areas are stronger, than in the more cosmopolitan Banjul. Commercial occupations, especially storekeeping and petty trading, get more respect in Banjul, where they are better represented and more successfully practiced.

Service is the most important criterion of high prestige and income of low prestige. Thus, the big businessman (sixth) is given considerable respect but not ranked as high as a doctor, imam, or judge. Education and the ability to exercise authority and leadership are more important factors in positive than in negative prestige; occupations lose respect when they are morally ambiguous, physically hard, unimportant to the community, or require subservience. Thus, the independence of skilled craftsmen wins them more respect than they would merit on income alone.

Economic Inequality

Respondents were also asked whether they thought incomes in The Gambia should become more equal, should continue to have about the same range or should have a greater spread between top and bottom, and why they thought so. About three-fourths of the Banjul respondents and two-thirds of those in Serekunda thought that incomes should become more equal. The main reason given was the cost of living; as several people put it, "We use the same market." This common use of markets by people at all economic levels was also used to symbolize common need by secondary students in Ghana and Nigeria to whom the same question was put, so it should be seen as an important aspect of striving for equality in all of these countries.

Most of the rest opted for the *status quo,* commenting on the country's development needs, noting that The Gambia had chosen capitalism and this is the way things are in a capitalistic society, or otherwise accepting present circumstances. Only one woman and 9 percent of the men (but considerably higher proportions of secondary students in all three countries) felt that differentials should be greater. These and some of the people who preferred the *status quo* felt that more qualified people, in responsible jobs, should have a higher income and/or that the elites would only be satisfied if they were well rewarded for their efforts.

The attempt to distinguish certain categories of people who feel strongly about inequality was largely unsuccessful; there is no obvious source of potential revolutionaries. The only significant differences are that men who have spent less than five years in town (and women who have recently arrived in Serekunda) are more likely to want greater equality and the locally born men to favor a greater spread of income. Income and occupational differentials are in the direction Marxists would predict (administrators, professionals, and those with above-average income are somewhat more likely to favor the *status quo*) but the poor/illiterate/disadvantaged are apparently more interested in leaving open the chance to rise, or at least are reasonably satisfied with things as they are, than they are in demanding radical change in economic differentials.

To get more specific information on attitudes toward various sectors of the society, respondents were asked two more questions. In response to "If some people earn more than others, on what should this difference be based?" they had to rank experience, family size, education, and other qualifications (efficiency/good work, loyalty/good conduct, and seniority). Then they were asked to assess the justice of the income of high government officials; administrators and executives; primary teachers; clerical, skilled, and unskilled workers; and farmers: "Should they earn more, about the same, or less than they do now?"

There was considerable overall agreement between men and women and between respondents in the two towns in the answers given to these questions. This supports the findings of Jasso and Rossi (1977) that there tends to be fairly general agreement within a society on the level of remuneration for jobs having varying characteristics. Jasso and Rossi found that the agreed levels varied little with the demographic characteristics of respondents and concluded that equally distributed income would not be considered just; structured variance would be more acceptable, even to those disadvantaged by such an arrangement. This does not negate the tendency to desire greater equality, but suggests that most people neither want nor expect that differentials will disappear.

The overall agreement in The Gambia hides some interesting differences in the way people of varying background answered these questions. These differences are often not statistically significant, and thus do not contradict the hypothesis. But where they show up in a number of tables, they suggest that certain sectors of the population are more satisfied with the *status quo,* or more concerned about modifying their position, than others.

Table 8.3 shows that women placed less emphasis on education and more on family size as criteria for fair income distribution than men. Women usually have less education than their husbands and face discrimination in jobs because of this lack. They also face the problem of family size more acutely than men because it is they who must feed the family, regardless of its size. Differences between Banjul and Serekunda tended to be smaller than those between men and women, and to a certain extent reflect the background of residents in the two towns. Banjul people are somewhat better educated, so they feel safer using education as the key to a good income, while middle-aged houseowners in Serekunda favor efficiency and loyalty.

An examination of first and last choices shows a few easily explainable

TABLE 8.3

Mean Ranking of Bases for Differentiated Income, by Town and Sex

		Education	Efficiency	Experi-ence	Loyalty	Family Size	Seniority
Males:	Banjul	1.61	2.68	3.05	3.86	4.45	4.50
	Serekunda	2.60	2.30	2.90	3.56	4.64	4.72
Females:	Banjul	2.04	2.69	3.06	3.57	3.47	3.71
	Serekunda	2.21	2.32	2.81	3.40	4.17	4.60
Total		2.07	2.65	2.97	3.68	4.14	4.50

differences, though we would expect much older men to opt for experience or seniority and the well-educated women to emphasize education to a greater extent than they do. Nevertheless, a certain amount of self-interest is evident in preferences for structural changes in the system, hardly a surprising finding. In spite of this, the low demand for payment by family size shows that the system of family allowances, an important component of wages in Senegal, is not very attractive to Gambians. Likewise, the use of annual increments would seem to be less acceptable than the more difficult-to-measure reward of the worker's experience and ability to do a good job. Increasing demands on the educational system can be foreseen in the widespread acceptance that certification should mean higher salaries.

About three-fifths of those answering the question on the justice of incomes favored regressive changes, much more income for farmers, and less or about the same income for high government officials; only 5 percent favored a wider range. Although certain predictable differences do show up, the data are more remarkable for the lack of differentiation shown by this question than for any evidence it provides of demands for greater equality. Illiterate men, those in unskilled occupations, and women traders were more likely than others to want a general leveling of incomes, but there was no difference between people of varying income levels and no evidence of the advantaged wanting to increase their differentials. Income, education, length of residence in town, and age apparently make little difference in one's overall view of the justice of present incomes, though occasionally people take a more subjective view of their own income position.

There appears to be general agreement throughout this urban population that farmers deserve much more income than they get. Only one man thought they should get less and three-quarters of the respondents said they should get much more. This need not be at the expense of higher consumer prices, as Gambian farmers mostly produce groundnuts for export. Those most removed from farming (long-term urban residents, professional men) were most likely to feel that farm incomes should stay about the same, but only a small minority of people in these categories said so.

Of the other occupations listed, skilled workers and primary teachers got the most sympathy (the latter, especially from women). Unskilled and clerical workers were thought to be paid about what they deserve; as the unskilled had recently had a large wage increase, this is not as unfeeling as it seems. The average respondent thought that both high and middle-level government officials were making as much as or somewhat more than they should, though about a fifth said they should be paid more. On the whole, men with junior secondary education and clerical jobs tended to be most generous, advocating that people both above and below them in the occupational hierarchy should earn more. Men in administrative, professional, and skilled jobs were more parsimonious; administrators and professionals tended to feel that skilled workers and farmers were sufficiently well paid and the skilled wanted the income of those above them, including primary teachers but not necessarily clerks, to be cut down.

Nonmanual workers and the semiskilled were more likely than other men to say that administrators and executives should get more, while skilled and semiskilled workers tended to support no further increases for the unskilled. These are the clearest indicators of class interest in the data, but not all the differences are statistically significant and they are not supported by comparable variance by education or income. Neither men nor women with low income were strongly dissatisfied with their position, and women's occupational position had little relevance to their opinions on relative wages. Even among the men, the unskilled tended to give answers very close to those of professionals.

From the comments of various respondents as well as the answers given, it becomes clear that pressure for greater equality is largely based on the assumption that it should be achieved by raising the income of the poor rather than by lowering that of the rich. In other words, what people want is a high standard of living for everyone rather than a revolutionary overthrow of those at the top. High income is seen as a good thing; more people should have it (see Waterman 1976).

Lloyd (1975, p. 203) points out that class consciousness can be seen in terms of perceived inequality, collective action to further group interests, or attempts to revolutionize social structure. There is no question that the first type is found widely in African cities. Collective action occurs sporadically, in demonstrations and elections where these are allowed and in general strikes. Whereas the rich are often seen to be making the most of their opportunities (in a situation where wealth usually means power), this is likely to be due to individual rather than to collective action. Various members of the elites (and their followers, who are often far from elite) are often in direct competition for greater access to national resources. The poor are usually more concerned that the avenues of individual mobility remain open than that the structure of the society be changed to give them (as a group) a better deal.

Sandbrook and Arn (1977, pp. 55–58) found that the majority of residents of Ashaiman and Nima (a low-income area in Accra) were either acquiescent or populist in political orientation; 23 percent of the household heads interviewed in Ashaiman compared to only 1 percent in Nima expressed a class orientation. The authors argue that employment in large-scale enterprises, shift work, and relative isolation contribute to the formation of class consciousness in Ashaiman. As these factors are present in relatively few African towns (except mining towns), it is unlikely that urban residents will provide the vanguard to revolution in the near future.

There may be considerable dissatifaction with urban life and with the arrogant behavior of the powerful, but the majority (even in Ashaiman) feel that they are better-off than they would be at home. As informal-sector workers value their independence and accept urban conditions to a greater extent than factory operatives, a decline in their relative position seems unlikely to push them to collective action. The presence of even a few successful entrepreneurs in the neighborhood (which is more common in Nima than in Ashaiman) reassures the poor that they may yet find urban life the road to opportunity.

Conclusion

The three sections of this chapter deal with quite different topics: getting help, ethnic relations, and class perceptions. Yet these are three ways of measuring the nature of competition in a society. To what extent are people in varying positions able to mobilize the formal bureaucracy or their personal contacts to get what they need and to what extent do individuals erect boundaries between their own and other sectors of their society? The unemployed squatter may be as much an economic stranger as the new migrant is an ethnic stranger, and societies vary considerably in the part they allow such people to play. The material discussed here and in earlier chapters suggests that the most marginal people in West African cities are those who fail to develop wide personal networks, and that ethnicity is more important than economics as a basis for division. On the whole, ethnic and family solidarity remain strong obstacles to class formation.

Problems are solved mainly with the help of long-term personal contacts, even though an individual goes to someone whose official position would make him a universalistic giver of this type of aid. Kin living in town are the chief source of help for serious difficulties, even by people who do not otherwise have much to do with their kin. Friends take second place, but they provide considerable support for individuals who do not happen to have kin in town.

Authority figures in the local community have an important role in resolving conflicts which get beyond family control, especially for first-generation migrants who prefer that customary norms be applied. The use of specialists such as trade union leaders and government officials is probably increasing, but given the prevalence of particularist norms this may be a last resort because other means have failed—applicants will probably try to develop a personal relationship as the surest way of getting what they want. The expectation of the efficacy of a personal approach makes it almost impossible to eliminate corruption and nepotism from these societies.

So much attention has been given to interethnic tensions in Nigeria and Ghana's expulsion of aliens that Europeans might be forgiven for believing that peaceful relations across ethnic boundaries are impossible in these countries. This is far from the case, as data on housing and friendships have shown. Nevertheless, the strains which arise between groups competing for limited economic, political, and social resources cannot be ignored. These are as important at the town as at the national level because hosts and strangers, majority and minority peoples must compete for jobs, housing, amenities, and so on. The level of identity used varies from one situation to another, but ethnicity is likely to continue as a vital part of most Africans' self-image, because it symbolizes roots and community in a changing environment. Higher levels of education, wider acquaintance with members of other groups, and increasing equalization of opportunities seem the most likely ways of lowering the boundaries between groups.

It would be difficult to be unaware of inequality in West African towns. The important questions, therefore, are the level of demand for greater equality and the extent to which resentment against inequality is leading to a class-conscious proletariat or an elite determined to maintain its benefits and cut itself off from the rest of the society. The Gambia may be a poor place to ask these questions, as its small size provides a high level of contact between rich and poor. Islam also contributes to the satisfaction with the *status quo* in that economic differences can be seen as the "will of Allah."

However, the ability of people to get help from kin and friends who have been more successful than themselves also hinders the development of class consciousness, and this is as characteristic of Ghana and Nigeria as of The Gambia. So long as those at the top share their rewards and upward mobility through personal effort remains possible, the less successful continue to accept the system because they can overcome their disadvantages to some extent by building up patron/client relations. So far, though the desire for greater equality is widespread, this is usually seen in terms of raising the poor rather than pulling down the rich; most people remain optimistic that the system as it is can bring them at least some of the success they seek.

9□CONCLUSION

This book has examined the nature of life in West African towns, to test the myths and assumptions which have grown up about African urbanization and answer the question, "What does living in town involve?" Only a limited number of topics and certain aspects of the data could be dealt with, but it should now be possible to generalize about the various types of towns and the effect of varying patterns of social structure and social interaction on urban life, West African style. This provides a basis for speculation on future developments.

Urban Typology

A basic task in this project has been to examine the differences between towns, to see what categories are most useful, and to provide a clearer idea of the limits of valid generalization. It is tempting to conclude that one should never generalize, even with data from several towns, because so many untested variables affect the results that one is necessarily dealing with biased evidence. Nevertheless, some systematic relationships are clearly present. Figures 9.1 and 9.2 show that some clustering does occur; this provides a basis for categorization of towns.[1]

New, Industrial, and Provincial

Ghanaian data are not available for Figure 9.2, but the isolation of these towns in Figure 9.1 suggests that this does not seriously affect the clustering. The small size of the Ashaiman 1970 sample (especially for females) and the necessity of adjusting scale scores for missing data makes its position suspect. A line can be drawn from Abeokuta to Tema/Ashaiman in Figure 9.1 and from Abeokuta to Ajegunle in Figure 9.2 which corresponds roughly to an increasing level of industrialization/complexity of the labor force and exposure to influences of national development. At one extreme is a fairly typical Yoruba provincial town, where traditional influences remain strong. At the other is a new industrial town, highly subject to national planning decisions, or (in Figure 9.2) a metropolitan population whose quality of life is strongly affected by such decisions. The

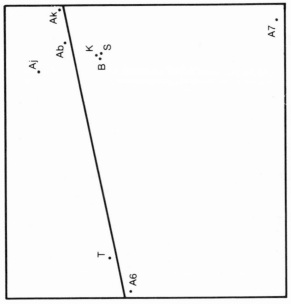

Males. Two dimensional solution,
Guttman-Lingoes Coefficient of Alienation .001.

Females. Two dimensional solution,
Guttman-Lingoes Coefficient of Alienation .006.

(A6 = Ashaiman 1968; A7 = Ashaiman 1970; Ab = Aba; Aj = Ajegunle
Ak = Abeokuta; B = Banjul; K = Kakuri; S = Serekunda; T = Tema)

Figure 9.1 Smallest Space Analysis of Similarities in Mean Scores for Premigration,
Subjective Adaptation and Sociability Scales, Males and Females, Euclidian Metric

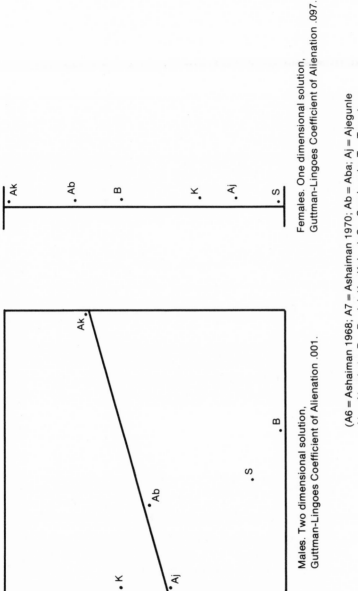

Males. Two dimensional solution,
Guttman-Lingoes Coefficient of Alienation .001.

Females. One dimensional solution,
Guttman-Lingoes Coefficient of Alienation .097.

(A6 = Ashaiman 1968; A7 = Ashaiman 1970; Ab = Aba; Aj = Ajegunle
Ak = Abeokuta; B = Banjul; K = Kakuri; S = Serekunda; T = Tema)

Figure 9.2 Smallest Space Analysis of Similarities in Mean Scores for Seven Scales, Males and Females, Euclidian Metric

Gambian towns remain somewhat apart, but lie midway on this continuum except for Serekunda in 9.2b.

It is evident that Tema and Ashaiman 1968 have more in common with each other than with any other town. Thus, the case that a new town, with a highly industrialized labor force, provides a quite different milieu from older and more conventional towns is sustained. City and suburb have different socioeconomic composition, different size, and widely differing provision of amenities, but the pressures of bureaucratized, large-scale wage employment and/or the lack of roots give residents of both towns a common orientation. "New town," or possibly "industrial town," is a more useful description in this case than city or suburb.

The "new" may be a better distinction than "industrial," given that Kakuri is clearly not in the same cluster. As Tema and Ashaiman grow, diversify, and age, it seems likely that they will become more like other Ghanaian and Nigerian towns instead of serving as a model of modernity for others to follow. On the other hand, the continuance of a high pro-portion of large-scale industrial employment (and, in Tema, public hous-ing) may help them maintain their differences from more conventional towns.

To return to Figures 9.1 and 9.2, the similarities between Banjul and Serekunda and their differences from other towns which have been noted so often throughout this book are evident in both figures. Gambian women are closely related to Nigerian women in 9.1a (especially to Kakuri, where Muslim influence is important), but the men remain segregated. The Gambian cluster is notable in 9.2a, but disappears in 9.2b. The influence of culture is important here, as it affects many aspects of social structure and interaction in the Gambian towns.

Kakuri and Ajegunle are somewhat closer together than either is to Aba in Figure 9.2, but Aba and Kakuri are closer and Ajegunle more isolated in Figure 9.1. This suggests that the wider range of scales used in Figure 9.2 brings out more clearly the provincial characteristics of Aba. Labor force characteristics (relatively industrialized males and housebound females) have a greater influence in the Economic, Political, and Problem Scales used in Figure 9.2 than in the three scales in Figure 9.1.

Aba is clearly less provincial than Abeokuta, as has been shown in many examples, but relationships there are influenced by the ethnic homo-geneity, preponderance of short-distance migrants, and strength of ties to the area which give Aba more in common with Abeokuta than with the other two Nigerian towns. A study made in 1980 would probably show them to be considerably closer together than they were in 1972 because of recent development in Abeokuta.

Ajegunle males are pulled toward the Ghanaian towns (see Figure 9.1a). Many are drawn by the same opportunities that draw migrants to the Tema area, though in the case of Ajegunle, Lagos provides a much wider range of jobs and Ajegunle is usually seen mainly in terms of housing. Both have relatively well-educated male labor forces, very rapid growth, little commitment to permanent residence, and little control over local development.

The conclusion to this exercise seems to be that the clearest type is the new town; established industrial towns and provincial towns are more influenced by local culture than new towns. They do have distinctive patterns of social relations, but the extent of these differences depends on cultural, historical, economic, and political factors. Political insecurity (as in Aba) or a decline or rise in economic activity (as in Kakuri in the late 1960s and Abeokuta in the late 1970s) has a strong influence on the number, qualifications, and interests of newcomers, and the attitudes of the stable population. Therefore, social relations in a town may change notably over a relatively short period.

Three examples of the effect of political change can be given. Ajegunle residents reported that there was no point joining together to improve the community, as had sometimes been done during the period of civilian rule. Anyone who tried to organize such activity could get into trouble with the military government, and it was therefore best just to mind your own business. The prevailing atmosphere in Ajegunle was "each for himself; this is nobody's town." The Ashaiman Development Committee, an active force for interaction between religious and communal groups in 1970, also withered when the military took over.

In Sekondi, Jeffries (1978, pp. 182–83) found that most of the voluntary associations reported as so prevalent by Busia (1950, chapter 6) had ceased to exist by the early 1970s. Problems of administration and trust in large associations made small, informal groups of people from the same village and of the same economic position a more viable source of mutual aid. Jeffries shows considerable continuity in Sekondi as a "working class town" over several decades, but also demonstrates the effect of political changes at the national level on the residents' perception of their societal position and their social relations with other residents.

Cities and Suburbs

The distinction between cities and suburbs is most meaningful in terms of political dependence; residents of suburbs are often cut off from decision makers who can have a strong influence on the quality of their lives. Beyond this, life in the suburb is affected by the level of its economic independence. Are residents employed locally, as in Kakuri, or mainly in other areas, as in Ajegunle? Coworkers are more likely to be neighbors in the former case.

Social contacts with the central city also depend on distance and the availability of transportation. In all the cases studied, transportation seems to be improving; this will tend to widen the horizons of suburban residents and lower their sense of being a separate community. As town and suburb grow toward each other, the distinctive nature of the suburb becomes harder to maintain. This is already the case with Ajegunle, though the administration seems determined to preserve what has for years been an artificial boundary.

The similarities between the suburbs studied and their central cities, and the differences between the suburbs themselves are instructive. Although the standard of living in Ashaiman is much lower than in Tema, residents in the two towns show many similarities in background and attitudes. The same is true of Serekunda and Banjul, though here the differences are more in the use of space than in standard of living. Kakuri's position in Figure 9.1 shows that the influence of its provincial town (Kaduna) is more relevant than its similarities to Ashaiman in size, industrialized work force, or recency of development. In a sense, Kakuri should be more industrialized in atmosphere than Ashaiman, since the factories are on the site, whereas Ashaiman workers must commute to Tema factories.

However, the central city type exerts a strong influence on the suburb. Differences in the level of urbanization between Tema and Ashaiman are mitigated by the common work experiences of large numbers of men, whereas workers in the Kakuri factories who live in Kaduna are only a small part of its basically administrative and commercial labor force. The Kakuri workers are therefore living in a more provincial environment and Ashaiman workers in a more industrial one.

Ajegunle partakes of the metropolitan nature of its central city; this is what differentiates it from the other three suburbs, though less from Serekunda than from the other two. Its residents must cope with the complexity and heterogeneity of Lagos, and use it as their reference for success or failure. Their aspirations are increased by what they see around them in the city and by their being, on the whole, better educated than residents of Ashaiman or Kakuri. Nevertheless, when migrant characteristics and satisfaction are less important and labor force characteristics and political/bureaucratic position are more important (Figure 9.2), Ajegunle's nearest neighbor is Kakuri. It is clear that all of these towns are truly suburbs, dependent on their central cities for their existence and growth, though they are officially listed as independent towns.

A valid question at this point is the extent to which the findings about the different types of towns are useful for predicting the nature of social relations in towns not studied. It seems to me that it is now fairly clear what characteristics to look for. While the configuration of cultural, historical, and locational factors will affect what happens in towns which otherwise fit into the same type, it seems reasonable to expect, for instance, that San Pedro (a new industrial town in Ivory Coast) will have much in common with Tema. Relationships observed in Benin City,

Enugu, or Owerri should be familiar to one who knows Aba, though their position as state capitals will give them a more politicized and bureaucratized environment than Aba. Ogbomosho, Oshogbo, and Oyo, in turn, seem to have much in common with Abeokuta, though this may decline as Abeokuta's status as a state capital leads to more rapid development.

The examination of the way towns differ should make one alert to the difficulty of making precise comparisons, but the overall picture provides some confidence that generalizations are possible so long as one keeps the implications of cultural and structural differences in mind. Southern Nigerian provincial towns probably have more in common with southern Ghanaian provincial towns than they do with northern Nigerian ones, but this may change if Nigeria becomes more culturally integrated.

Urban Development

The data provide information on three interrelated aspects of urban development. First, African governments often express concern over the rapid growth of towns and proclaim the importance of rural development as a panacea which will keep the rural population at home. Some of the assumptions behind this approach must be challenged with the reality of migration of the 1970s, which has a large component of educated or trained workers moving to places where they can earn a much larger income working at jobs which are not needed in villages. Second, the findings on housing have policy implications which planners and politicians should keep in mind. Third, urban size is less important to social relations and the satisfaction of residents than the composition and differentiation of the labor force and the level of conflict over resources.

The history of a town, its location, and its structure affect the number and qualifications of the migrants it attracts and thus its rate of growth. Governments can produce relatively large towns within ten years by making a village (or an open space) the site of new industry or administration, since large numbers of prospective migrants are looking for employment opportunities and will travel long distances if necessary. However, willingness of either the government or the indigenes to provide infrastructure, especially housing, is an important constraint because few West Africans will invest in a town before they have spent many years there. Two industrial developments in Ghana, at Juapong and Komenda, have produced little urban growth because the infrastructure was not developed; factory workers have had to find housing in nearby villages.

Migrants and Indigenes

The costs of growth are more easily borne if projects are located in towns, so that the basic infrastructure is already available and the established population can contribute to its development. The most obvious recent cases are the new Nigerian state capitals, only one of which had less than twenty-five thousand people in 1963. The effects on the indigenous population of a massive increase in migration and thus in the scale and complexity of social structure have been indicated in some of the discussion of the differences between the provincial towns and the suburbs and between indigenes and migrants in various towns. The first reaction tends to be "business as usual; this doesn't concern us," though it soon becomes clear that it does concern everyone.

The more entrepreneurial residents (and many of these towns are based on trade) soon decide to make the most of new opportunities, to use their access to land to build houses for rent, and to develop businesses by providing the goods and services the newcomers need. Social interaction with the new arrivals will depend on the extent to which indigenes take them into their houses and neighborhoods,[2] whether they work together or form a dual labor market (self- and wage-employed) and the level of competition for local resources. So far, mixing has been more common than isolation, but in some towns competition has led to conflict, which has been exacerbated by lack of social contact.

A potential source of conflict is the higher level of qualifications of migrants than of indigenes, so that the former tend to get the best jobs. It is often assumed that migrants flooding into the towns are relatively unqualified (school leavers with no training at best) and thus are unable to compete with the locally born. However, the data show that the spread of development produces better qualified migrants. With the exception of Banjul, indigenes were not better educated than migrants and were more likely to find employment in trading or other informal sector activities, while the high-level formal sector jobs went to migrants. In Banjul, as in other towns, relatively well-qualified indigenes often experience long periods of unemployment because they are unwilling to accept jobs which migrants (with lower aspirations) will take.

The drive for self-improvement which motivates migrants makes them more interested than many indigenes in using educational and training facilities in the towns, but they are also more concerned than nonmigrants with the relative advantages of various towns and will take their training (wherever received) to the best job they can find. In the case of Banjul, slow development elsewhere in the country means that the capital has an overwhelming advantage in both education and wage employment; indigenes are, on the whole, better qualified for and more likely to hold good jobs than newcomers. However, some of the Banjul indigenes are the well-qualified migrants who arrive (on transfer) in smaller Gambian towns, just as the qualified indigenes of Abeokuta migrate to other towns during their careers while those with less chance of prospering stay at home.

The towns may be better equipped with schools than the rural areas, but many young people born in town see little of them. Aside from the cost of school fees and incidental expenses, factors such as overcrowding and shifts in urban schools, the prominence of commerce as an alternative route to success which does not require education, the lack of control of urban parents over their children because of the long hours they spend working, and the lack of success in examinations which makes schooling seem a waste of time all lower the enthusiasm of urban parents for their children's education. This is especially true of urban manual workers. Cooksey (1978) found that very few manual workers' children were successful in the Yaoundé primary school examinations; the children of small farmers who had been sent to Yaoundé to complete their primary schooling did much better. Thus, the incentive for the poor to keep their children in school may be slight.

There are several implications of this. First, since urban host peoples remain relatively traditional in their outlook, they tend to see strangers as intruders and may become increasingly restive at the power which one man one vote gives in their town. The insistence of Imo State in 1977 that people vote in their hometown rather than in the place in which they were living was partly to maintain migrants' support for their place of origin, but was also due to pressure by urban indigenes to keep local power in their own hands.

Second, the assertion that rural-urban migration can be stemmed by rural development must be modified by the realization that no amount of rural development will produce the jobs which the better-qualified migrants can find in town. Rural development which increases educational participation can only encourage more migration. The larger farms engendered by development will take space from small farms and need less labor; this will also push many from the land.

Third, insofar as migrants holding middle- and high-level positions are encouraged to see themselves as belonging to their home villages rather than to the town, they will fail to contribute their share to urban development. Yet these are the people who should be working for responsibility and probity in local government and for improvements in urban standards of living (for all, not just for themselves), and who could contribute leadership, capital, and expertise to the towns if they found it worthwhile to do so. Their contributions at home are welcome and are rewarded by considerable prestige there, but urban development needs much more attention from elite and subelite residents than it gets at present. The indigenes are often unable to mobilize sufficient resources to fill the gap.

Heterogeneity

The more complex the labor force and the wider the catchment area for migrants, the more diverse the resulting urban population. This diversity is increased by improvements in national and international transportation systems and the centralization of government which encourages the transfer of employees to all parts of the country. For example, whereas mining towns have in the past tended to draw labor from certain areas according to their location on transportation routes[3] and the accidents of early recruitment, long-distance transportation today is well enough organized that opportunities are more important than distance. There was no notable ethnic specialization of Ghanaian mining towns in 1960.

The amount of social interaction between groups in the resulting heterogeneous population depends partly on differential occupational recruitment but also, to a large extent, on mixing in housing. Government housing projects are an important factor in lowering the amount of mixing and thus seem likely to promote the development of class consciousness. People of different economic levels usually have little opportunity to know each other at work, but if they live in the same neighborhood they are likely to have some social contacts, however rare and tenuous these may be. For example, a relationship may be initially based on the occasional purchase of cigarettes or vegetables from a streetside trader or meeting at the local pools agency or bar.

The low level of recreational interaction between people of differing income levels in Sekondi (Jeffries 1978, p. 181) seems to be clearly related to the fact that they live in different parts of town, often on estates built for specific groups of employees. The heterogeneous housing in Banjul, Ajegunle, and the provincial towns is all privately owned rental property. Thus, an increase in the provision of public housing seems likely to result in more homogeneous neighborhoods (both for those who get these houses and for those who don't because they are not eligible) and greater social differentiation along economic lines.

The nature of the labor force is more important than size in its effect on the complexity of social structure. There are many West African towns which have achieved considerable size (well over one hundred thousand) with relatively low social and economic differentiation—where in the past over 70 percent of the population were farmers for at least part of the year and where there was relatively little difference in standard of living between rulers and ruled.

Social and economic differentiation have increased in all towns in the postindependence period. The limited opportunities in provincial towns restrict this process, but politics and government encourage it even there. Those who obtain the most education and/or have the highest aspirations usually leave the smaller towns and the least successful find it easiest to get the social and economic support they need at home. Thus, it is in towns like Lagos (and, to a lesser extent, Ajegunle) where the gap between rich and poor is most visible. Where a high proportion of a town's labor force is in small-scale crafts or trading or in middle or lower-level civil service jobs, migrants and indigenes tend to be culturally and socially more homo-geneous and the society more integrated than in central cities where the full range of opportunities is available.

With a few exceptions of towns which are bypassed by development, time seems likely to bring growth in size and complexity. The ethnic numbers game means that towns in all parts of a country will claim their share of development money. The government or industrial jobs which this money finances will draw long- as well as short-distance migrants, depending partly on how open wage and entrepreneurial opportunities are. This could do more to foster national integration than any amount of government propaganda or rural development to minimize migration. It is therefore important to monitor developments in urban social structure and social interaction so that the cities of the 1990s will be more satisfying places to live and work than those of the 1970s.

APPENDIX A☐THE INTERVIEW SCHEDULES

Tema/Ashaiman, 1968 (The diagram and some of the precoding have been omitted.)

I. (Unemployed and 1968 arrivals only)
    1. Why did you decide to move here instead of going someplace else?
    2. Why did you decide to come just at that time?
    3. Did you know anyone who was already here? 0..no 1..yes: Who?
    4. A. Did you just sleep out at first, or did you share with someone?
       0..out 1..shared: Who?   For how long? _____ months
       B. Did you stay with . . . until you moved to this house or have you also lived somewhere else?
       C. How did you find this room?
    5. How long did it take you to find a job? _____ months
    6. (1968 arrivals only)
       A. Would you say that people in this house are quite friendly, or that they are hard to get to know?
       B. How long did it take you to get to know people living in this house? 0..1 day 1..2–3 days 2..4–7 days 3..8–14 days
       4..15–30 days 5..longer
       C. How does someone who moves into a house get to know the other tenants?
    7. (1968 only) When you moved to . . . , did you go and make yourself known to the tribal headman?
    8. (1968 married males)
       A. Does your wife live here in . . .?
       B. (If no) Would you like your wife to come to live with you here?
          i. (If no) Why?
          ii. (If yes) When do you think she will come? _____ months

II. (Everyone) Do you have any relatives in Tema or Ashaiman? (Include wife's kin, children)

Relationship to R		

Where lives		
How often visits		

III. We are studying how people get along with their neighbors and how much they visit with friends and cotenants. By neighbors we mean the people living in the houses near this one. (Draw this and neighboring houses.)

    1. About how many of the people in the houses around this one would you recognize by sight if you saw them in a large crowd? 0..few, none 1..half or more

    2. A. How many people living in nearby houses do you know fairly well? _____

       B. Which houses do they live in? (Mark 2 on diagram)

    3. Do you and your cotenants or neighbors ever entertain one another to drinks?

       A. This house: 0..never 1..sometimes 2..often

       B. Neighbors: 0..never 1..sometimes 2..often (Mark 3 on diagram)

       C. What about people you work with who live elsewhere in Tema or Ashaiman—do you ever go for drinks with them or invite them here? 0..never 1..sometimes 2..often

       D. (If ever drinks) When do you usually drink with your friends? 0..just after payday 1..Saturday nights 2..Sunday 3..1–2 evenings after work 4..nearly every night 5..other

       E. How many of you usually get together and relax in this way? _____

    4. Do you ever eat together with your cotenants or neighbors?

       A. This house: 0..never 1..sometimes 2..often Times in the last week: _____

       B. Neighbors: 0..never 1..sometimes 2..often Times in the last week: _____

       C. What about workmates or other friends or kin—do you ever eat with them? 0..never 1..sometimes 2..often Times in the last week: _____

    5. A. Do you ever go to the cinema? How often? _____ times per _____

       B. Do you usually go with someone or meet someone there? Who?

    6. A. What about dances and concert parties—do you ever go to them? _____ times per _____

B. Do you usually go with someone or meet someone there? Who?

7. How many of your cotenants or neighbors' homes have you ever been in?

A. This house: _____   C. Workmates: _____

B. Neighbors: _____ (7 on diagram)   D. Other friends: _____

8. If you were having a party—say an outdooring—who would you invite?

A. Kin in Tema/Ashaiman (Who?)

B. Kin living elsewhere (Who?)

C. Number of cotenants: _____

D. Number of neighbors: _____

E. Number of workmates: _____

F. Number of other friends: _____

9. A. About how often do you sit and talk with friends about problems? 0..never 1..sometimes 2..often

How many of your neighbors or cotenants have you ever talked to about their problems when they were worried (troubled) or have you asked for advice or help?

B. This house: _____

C. Neighbors: _____ (Mark 9 on diagram)

D. Do you ever talk to your kinsmen or workmates or other friends about their problems or your own: 0..never 1..kin _____ 2..work 3..other: _____

E. Have you ever gone to the TDC or the police or school to complain about something? 0..no 1..yes: What about? Did they help you?

10. How many names of people in nearby houses do you know? _____

11. About how many of the people in these houses do you greet when you meet them by chance on the street? _____

12. Do you and your neighbors exchange or borrow things from one another such as dishes, provisions, clothes, etc.?

A. Cotenants: _____

B. Neighbors: _____

13. How often do you sit and talk with cotenants or neighbors?

A. Cotenants: 0..never, rare 1..sometimes 2..often

B. Neighbors: 0..never, rare 1..sometimes 2..often

What about workmates or friends who live farther away—how often do you sit and talk or play games with them?

C. Workmates: 0..never 1..sometimes 2..often

D. Friends: 0..never 1..sometimes 2..often

14. With how many of these people do you sit and talk fairly frequently?

A. This house: _____   C. Workmates: _____
B. Neighbors: _____   D. Friends: _____

15. (Point to diagram of houses in the neighborhood)
    A. These neighbors whom you know well and do things with—are
       any of them related to you or your wife? (Mark K)
    B. Are any of them from your hometown? (Mark HT)
    C. Are there any that are not . . . (R's tribe?) Other tribes: _____

16. These other friends and workmates whom you see fairly frequently:
    A. Are they kin of yours or your wife's?
    B. Do they come from your hometown? (If yes) How many? _____
    C. Are they all . . . (R's tribe)? (List others)

17. A. Do you belong to a susu or a tribal assocation or any other
       mutual aid association? (If yes) How often do you attend meet-
       ings? _____ times per _____
    B. Do you ever attend church services? How often? _____ times
       per _____
    C. Do you belong to any church societies such as a study group or
       fellowship or singing band? 0..no 1..yes: _____

18. Do you have a radio? (If yes) Do your cotenants often come to
    listen to it?

19. A. What do you like most about living in . . .?
    B. What do you dislike about living in . . .?
    C. Do you think it is better for older people to live in town with
       their children or should they go back home when they retire?
       Why?

20. (Those over 49)
    A. (If working) Do you think you will stay in . . . after you retire?
       Why?
    B. How long do you think you will stay here? (If DK) What would
       make you decide to leave?
    C. Where will you go then—to your hometown or someplace else?
       Why?

21. A. How many brothers and sisters do you have, same father, same
       mother?

	1	2	3	4	5
B. Br or Si?					
C. Education					
D. Occupation					
E. Where living?					

22. A. During the last year, how many times have relatives from out-
       side . . . come to visit you? _____

B. Who was it?

C. Where did they come from?

D. Did they bring you any gifts? What?

E. Did you give them any money or other things? What (or) How much?

(If living with parents, go to 23G)

23. A. Has anyone at home sent you food or other gifts during the last year? What?

    B. About how often do you send money home? _____ times per year

    C. Who do you send it to?

    D. How much do you send each time? NC _____

    E. Have you sent any money recently for emergencies, school fees, etc.? NC _____

    F. In the last year, how much have you sent home? NC _____

    G. (Lives with parents) Do you give any money to your parents when you get paid? (If yes) How much each month? NC _____

24. A. What place do you consider your hometown?

(If Tema or Ashaiman, go to 25)

    B. When was the last time you visited your hometown? 19____ Month: _____

    C. How long did you stay?

    D. How often have you visited since you first went away? _____ times per year(s)

    E. How long do you usually stay?

    F. Do you usually take gifts or money along? How much/What do you take?

25. A. What place outside . . . (hometown and here) do you visit most often?

    B. How often do you go there?

    C. When do you visit?

Ashaiman 1970, Nigeria and The Gambia[1]

1. A. Why did you move to . . .?

    B. In comparison to other parts of . . ., do you think this is a good place to live or not such a good place? Why?

2. A. Is it easy or hard to get to know people here?

    B. Which do you think gets to know more people, a man (woman) who lives alone or one who is living with his wife (husband)?

3. Have you always lived in this house since you came to . . .? (If no) Why did you move?

1. A, N, or G after the question indicates that it was asked only in Ashaiman, Nigeria, or The Gambia. Long questions asked in only one country are given at the end. Some of the precoding has been omitted. Interviewers circled the number before the answer given.

4. In addition to the people living with you now, was there anyone else who spent a night with you in the last two weeks? (*G:* also "in January") Relationship to Head _____ Sex _____ Age _____ Employment _____ From _____

5. Have you any relatives in town, not living with you in this house?

	1	2	3	4	5
Relationship to R					
Distance					
How often sees					
Activities					

6. A. What year did you marry? 0..never 1–19 _____ 2–19 _____ 3–19 _____ 4–19 _____

   B. Has your wife (wives) always lived in the same town/village with you, or have you sometimes left her behind when you moved to a new place? Wives now: _____ Lived apart for _____ months in 19_____. Divorces 19_____. Widowed in 19_____

7. How many children do you have (from all sources? _____

Age				
Sex				
Where living				
Schooling				

8. Do you think parents should send all their children to school if they can, or should they send only the boys, only the bright ones, or is it best not to send any children to school? (*N, G*)

9. We would like to know about the work you have done and the places you have lived since you left school/grew up. (Start at age 15 or school leaving.)

	1	2	3	4	5
A. What was your next job?					
B. How long were you unemployed?					
C. When did you start work?	/19 ____	/19 ____	/19 ____	/19 ____	/19 ____
D. Age at start					
E. Where were you living?					
F. How long was your training?					
G. How long did the job last?					
H. Why left (N, G)					

10. How many people living in nearby houses do you greet when you meet them by chance on the street? _____

11. About how many people in nearby houses do you know fairly well? _____

12. Do you ever eat together with your relatives, cotenants, neighbors, or other people you know well?
    A. This yard: 0..never 1..sometimes 2..often Times in the last week _____
    B. Neighbors: 0..never 2..sometimes 3...often Times in the last week _____
    C. Kinsmen: 0..never 2..sometimes 3..often Times in the last week _____
    D. Workmates: 0..never 2..sometimes 3..often Times in the last week _____ During the lunch break at work or at other times?
    E. Townsmen or others: 0..never 1..sometimes 2..often Times in the last week _____

13. How many people do you sit and talk with fairly frequently?
    A. This yard: _____
    B. Neighbors: _____
    C. Relatives: _____
    D. Workmates: _____ At work or other?
    E. Townsmen and others you know well: _____

14. How many of your cotenants' or neighbors' rooms have you ever been in?
    A. This yard: _____   C. Workmates: _____
    B. Neighbors: _____   D. Other: _____
15. Have you ever had a party? (If no) If you had one, whom would you invite? (If yes) What was the occasion? _____ Whom did you invite?
    A. This yard: _____   C. Kin: _____ in town and _____ elsewhere
    B. Neighbors: _____   D. Workmates: _____
    E. Townsmen/others: _____
16. Could you tell me something about the people you move with/see often?

	1	2	3	4	5
First name					
Sex					
Age					
Education					
Where grew up					
Year moved here					
Married?					
Ethnicity					
Occupation					
Employer					
Religion					
Where/how first met					

	1	2	3	4	5
How often sees					
Activities					

17. How many of these friends know each other?
    0 = does not know
    1 = knows, but not well
    2 = knows well

	2	3	4	5
1				
2				
3				
4				

18. If you had a serious problem—say you needed money quickly, whom would you go to for advice or help?

	Relationship to R	Where lives?	How long known?	Why this person?	Ever done this?
A. Need money					
B. Need job					
C. Trouble at work					
D. Dispute with wife or kin					
E. Trouble with police					

19. Do you think that people like yourself can make their needs known to the government? (G, N: "local government")
    (If yes) How can they do this? Have you ever . . .?
    (20 to 25 are G,N only)

20. Have you ever belonged to any associations?

	Title	Officer (G)	Attends meetings	Past only
A. Ethnic/family/clan/ homeplace				
B. Church: (brotherhood, women's)				

20. Have you ever belonged to any associations?

	Title	Officer (G)	Attends meetings	Past only
C. Work: (union, guild, cooperative)				
D. Recreation (sport, dance, drink)				
E. Savings				
F. Other (veterans, old boys, Scouts, debating)				
G. Do you ever bet on the pools?				

21. See below.
22. A. During the last year, has anyone in your family come to visit you here in . . .? Parents _____ Wife _____ Children _____ Brothers _____ Sisters _____ Other kin _____
    B. Where did they come from?
    C. Did they bring you any gifts? What?
    D. Did you give them money or any other things? Cash _____ Gifts _____

23 and 24. See Tema/Ashaiman 1968 schedule, 23 and 24.

25. A. Would you say your income (if self-employed, profit) for the last year was (precodes in local equivalents) 0..under £100, 1..between £100 and £200, 2..£200–£300, 3..£300–£500, 4..£500–£700, or more than £750? _____
    B. If someone gave you £100, how would you spend it?
    C. Do you own a house or plan to build one either at home or here in . . . (G)

26. Lastly, we would like to know how you spent your time on four days, over a weekend and during the week, just the ordinary things you did and people you met.
    First day _____

Time	Place	Activity	Contacts

Questions Asked in Only One County

(N only:)
21. Here are four houses. I am going to name various people who live in Nigeria and I would like you to tell me in which house you would put them. In the first house are people you would feel free to marry or allow your children to marry. In the second house are those you would not want to marry but would live within the same house. In the third

house are those you would not want to live near, but would not mind working with (if you had a choice). In the fourth house are those you would not want to have anything to do with.

DRAW HOUSES See MS 331 for space

1. marry   2. cotenant   3. work   4. none

A. Edo   D. Hausa ___   G. Kalabari ___   J. Tiv ___
B. Efik ___   E. Ibibio ___   H. Kanuri ___   K. Yoruba ___
C. Fulani ___   F. Igbo ___   I. Nupe ___   L. Zugu ___

(G only:)
6. A. What was your father's main occupation while you were growing up?
   B. If your father went to school, what education did he have?
   C. If your mother went to school, what education did she have?
21. A. Some jobs give the men who do them high prestige and respect; others are considered much less important or even without prestige. For each of these jobs, say how you think it rates among Gambians.

Occupation	Very high	High	Not High or Low	Low	Very low	Don't know
Policeman	5	4	3	2	1	9

(Occupations listed:) building laborer, headmaster, senior clerk, judge, carpenter, typist, education officer, blacksmith, traditional healer, imam or priest, community welfare officer, medical doctor, storekeeper, newspaper reporter, chop-bar keeper, district commissioner, secondary teacher, diplomat, electrician, steward, motor car fitter, big businessman, factory worker, petty trader, football player, musician, farmer, lorry driver, shop assistant, messenger, and nurse.
   B. Pick one occupation that you have rated high or very high. What is it about this job that makes it high? Why do people respect men who have this job?

C. Pick one occupation that you have rated low or very low. Why does this work have a low standing?

D. Which of these statements do you most agree with?

   1. People's incomes in Gambia should become more equal than they are now.

   2. People's incomes in Gambia should stay about as they are now.

   3. There should be more difference between top and bottom incomes than there is now.

E. Why do you say this?

F. If some people earn more than others, on what should this difference be based? Put these in the order of importance from first to sixth (1 = most important).

   ____Experience

   ____Size of the family they must support

   ____Education and qualifications

   ____Ability to do good work (efficiency)

   ____Loyalty and good conduct

   ____Length of time on the job (seniority)

G. Generally, how just do you think the income of the following groups of people is? Do you think they should earn more, about the same, or less than they do now?

	Much more	More	About the same	Less	Much less
High government officials	5	4	3	2	1

(As above for:) Administrators and executives, primary teachers, clerical workers, skilled workers, unskilled workers, and farmers

(A only:)

20. A. Have you ever known any Togolese or Nigerians or other aliens well? (If yes) How did you get to know them? Do you think they were (are) typical of . . .? Why?

B. Have you ever lived in the same house as any aliens? (If yes) Where were they from? Did you find them easy to get on with, compared to Ghanaians? Why?

C. Have you ever worked with any aliens? (If yes) Where were they from? Did you find them any different from Ghanaians?

D. Do you think it has made any difference to Ghana that many aliens have left?

E. Do you think it has made any difference in Ashaiman that many aliens have left?

APPENDIX B□BACKGROUND VARIABLES

Coding categories have been devised which are based on local conditions but vary as little as possible from one town or country to another. The most notable sources of divergence are at the middle of the educational system and in ethnic divisions. Problems of data collection and the relative scarcity of representatives of certain categories have also affected the way age, size, and location of place of origin, date of arrival, occupation, religion, and relationship to the head of the household have been coded. As the first studies were made in Ghana, coding of later studies has had to be similar to make comparison possible. Occupational coding is discussed on pages 80–82.

Age was reported in single years, but because of the propensity to round off and inaccuracies due to the lack of records of birth date, it was considered more reliable to group ages in ten-year categories. The Ghana census considers 15 as the beginning of adulthood, so this age was adopted for the study. Although retirement from government service was set at 60 in Ghana and 55 in Nigeria, the age of 50 was used as the beginning of old age because men of this age are taking over the role of elders in their communities and beginning to think of returning home (if they have not done so before) and because at about 50 women either retire from trading or begin to lessen their participation.

In the Ghanaian educational system, secondary school may be entered after Primary 6 or Middle Form 2, 3, or 4. Most Secondary 1 pupils have had eight or nine years of schooling and most school leavers who migrate to towns have had ten years of primary and middle school. Technical and commercial education is available to middle-school leavers; they may also enter training college with the goal of becoming teachers, but training college places are increasingly being reserved for those who have completed at least five years of secondary school and passed "O" level examinations. Most students entering the university have completed an additional two years of secondary schooling (sixth form) and passed "A" level examinations.

The Nigerian system is fairly similar hierarchically, but there is no middle school as such. Primary schooling dropped from seven or eight years to six at various dates in different parts of the country, mostly in the 1950s. In the late 1950s, a three-year secondary modern program was introduced (following a new British pattern) for those who could not get into a secondary grammar school. This was most popular in the then Western Region and made no impact in the north, which is educationally far behind the south. Grammar schools and most training colleges are entered directly after Primary 6, though training colleges are gradually upgrading their entry. The same five years to "O" level and two further years to "A" level are followed, except that a higher proportion of students in Nigeria than in Ghana enter universities for a preliminary year instead of doing a two-year sixth form course.

The middle levels of the Ghanaian and Nigerian systems have been equated by considering Nigerians who completed more than six years of primary school or attended secondary schools of any type for less than four years as in the same category as Ghanaians with middle schooling. Since very few Ghanaians reported dropping out of secondary school before Form 4 and until the mid-1960s it was common to complete Middle Form 4 before starting secondary school, a Ghanaian with secondary schooling and a Nigerian with four or more years in secondary school appear to be equivalent. Relatively few respondents had any form of commercial or technical schooling or attended universities; these are put in the same category as the ex-secondary students (more than middle).

Junior secondary schooling in The Gambia approximates secondary modern schooling in Nigeria and was coded accordingly. Senior secondary school is similar to secondary grammar schools in Ghana and Nigeria. Given the small numbers involved and their potential role in the society, they were coded as more than middle schooling, as was training college.

The large number of ethnicities represented, especially in Ajegunle and Kakuri, means that some grouping was necessary; this was usually based on categories which were used locally, and resulted in a combination of identities which can best be described as geo-ethnic. (Wolpe 1969, p. 486). Where an ethnic group was well represented, they could be treated separately; where there were few, they were joined to others from the same general area because that is usually how local people refer to them. For example, Efik, Ibibio, and Kalabari living in the north were often called easterners. Some suffered the same fate as Igbo in the 1966 riots because northerners did not distinguish between them. Migrants from Upper Volta, Mali, and Niger tend to speak Hausa as a *lingua franca* and are often identified as generic if not ethnic Hausa by southern Ghanaians. Thus, it seems reasonable to put them in the same category for purposes of analysis of their relative position in the community.

The Ghana census sets five thousand as the minimum population for a town and refers to towns of ten thousand or more as large towns. All those places designated as cities in the 1960 census had populations of over forty thousand. Because many places of less than ten thousand in Ghana are large agricultural villages with few central place functions, ten thousand was used as the urban base rather than five thousand, and the same base was used in Nigeria. There is no official urban/rural line in Nigeria, but there are many towns of over ten thousand and there is no adequate information on the size of towns of less than twenty thousand. Places of over forty thousand were coded as cities. The sizes given in the 1960 and 1963 censuses in Ghana and Nigeria respectively were used. Many of the places referred to were much smaller when the respondents were growing up, but this was only taken into consideration in exceptional cases such as Tema, where the urban boundary had been very recently passed. In The Gambia, places of 2,500 or more were counted as urban. These are all locally considered to be towns.

A few studies have carefully measured the distance migrants have come. Since many of the migrants in these studies grew up in villages which are not on any available map, this was not possible. Rather, the Region (in Ghana), State (in Nigeria), or Division (in The Gambia) have been used. This provides an adequate indicator of distance and also of cultural differences between place of origin and place of residence. As it was not possible to get accurate reports on the month of arrival, migrants have been divided into those who arrived in the year of the survey (usually within the last six to eight months, but in Kakuri within the last three to four months) and those who have lived in the town for one to two years, three to five years, six to ten years, or more than ten years.

A difficulty arose in Aba because residents fled during the war; since most were very vague on exactly how long they had been away, it seemed more reasonable to count from the time of first arrival. The few migrants who had spent more than one period in the other towns were treated in the same way, because it was quite possible that at least some had continuing contacts with the town while they were away.

The importance of religious affiliation varies from one town to another, but generally it is useful as an additional indicator of socioeconomic background. Protestant churches have been united for comparative purposes, since different churches are prominent in each town. Catholics and Muslims were usually present in sufficient numbers to form separate categories, though no Muslims were found in Aba and all Christians in The Gambia were put in one category. Members of apostolic and pentecostal sects were oversampled for interviewing so that there would be enough to say something about how their way of life differs from that of Muslims and members of longer-established Christian churches, but there are still too few to make any reliable statements about individual groups. The "other" category (which includes Jehovah's Witnesses and the Salvation Army) and the "traditional" category represent even smaller numbers.

Interviewers were instructed to list the head of the household first on census forms. In case of difficulty, the head was defined as the person with major responsibility for the household, implying (1) authority over the others and (2) payment of rent for the room. Where a child pays the rent because a parent has retired, a father is usually considered head because he retains authority. A mother may be head of a household including her daughter and grandchildren, but usually a son is head of the household if his father is not present. Where brothers share a room, the eldest is usually the head, but if a younger brother has been in town longer and originally took the room, he may be considered head, especially if he is married while the elder brother is still single. Other household members were categorized by their relationship to the head or their function: wife, child, sibling of head or wife, other kin, employees (apprentices and maids), and other nonkin. Kinship took precedence over function, so that a maid who was the wife's sister would be categorized as sibling.

APPENDIX C☐THE SCALES

The variables included in these scales are not necessarily highly correlated with each other, but are varying ways in which the characteristic being measured can be expressed. This was essential because social patterns differ so much by town and sex. The scales are additive in that various combinations produce the same score, though some variables have been given greater weight than others. Factor analysis was not used to examine the configurations of variables because in this I am an atheist. However, extensive work on the data has provided considerable information on the relationships beween variables.

The variables used differ somewhat between countries because equivalent data are not always available. In order to produce the same maximum score, substitutions have been made where possible. House ownership was added to the Gambian subjective scale even though there are no data on this for other towns because it is the best predictor of satisfaction. Where maximum scores are not the same, they have been equalized statistically.

Some variables which on theoretical grounds might belong in the scale (such as the location of spouse and children as part of social or subjective adjustment to the town) have been dropped because analysis of their roles showed them to be irrelevant.

The scales of social factors in adaptation in chapter 2 and of sociability in chapter 6 are basically similar; their differences in composition and weight reflect differences in the purpose which each serves. People who have adjusted socially to living in town should not need to rely only on kin; they should have made friends and acquaintances in town whom they see fairly often and can consult on problems. Associations provide an occasion to meet people and some economic and psychological support. Visiting home frequently makes it easier to stay in town than living so far away that home visits are almost impossible. The sociability scale, on the other hand, is not concerned with adjustment *per se*. It thus omits the kinship variables and emphasizes friendship, allotting three points each to talking, eating, and visiting friends in their rooms; it also includes the number of friends and giving a party.

Differential weighting is also illustrated in the heterogeneity scale. Differences in origin, ethnicity, and occupation better express diversity in a friendship network than having friends who are of another marital status or who have spent more or less time in the city. In this case, weighting is based on the degree of diversity; the respondent whose friends are mostly in a different category gets more points than the one whose friends are mostly like himself. The discussion of heterogeneity is based on those with two or more friends because the concern is with networks rather than dyads. It is recognized that those with many friends are likely to have more heterogeneous networks than those with only two, but it seems reasonable that this "hidden credit" should be given to the large networks.

Chapter 2: Adaptation (Migrants only)

Premigration (11)[1]

Education: none = 0; primary, Muslim = 1; middle, secondary modern, junior secondary = 2; secondary, other post-middle = 3; university = 4
Rural/urban: rural = 0, mixed = 1, urban = 2
Type of migration: direct = 0, indirect = 1
Ethnic distance: far = 0, near = 1, local group = 2
Age at arrival: 15–24 = 0, 25+ = 1, by age 15 = 2

Social (18)

Kin seen: daily = 0, 1–6/week = 1, less often = 2
Guttman scale of talk, eat, and rooms:
  Talk with cotenants, neighbors, kinsmen, coworkers, others: 1–2 = 1, 3–4 = 2, 5+ = 3 for each category, sum scores. If total is 8 or more, add 1 point.
  Eat with others outside household: breakpoint at 1–3 categories, depending on country
  Rooms visited: 2 or more = 1 point
Friends of another ethnic group: some = 1, most = 2
Consult friends on problems: 5 problems, maximum score 3
Visits home: under 1/year = 0, 1–3/year = 1, more often = 2
Membership in associations: Up to 5 types, maximum score 3
Know: 0–1 = 1, 2–9 = 2, 10–25 = 2, 26+ = 3 (Ghana: 2–4 = 1, 5–9 = 2, 10+ = 3)
  Ghana 1968: If church attendance 1/week, add 1 to association score
  Ghana 1970: No home visit or assocation data; consult friend = 1 (11)

Political (6, Nigeria and The Gambia only)

---

1.   Numbers in parentheses are maximum scores.

Local government activity: never tried = 0, has tried = 2
Influencing government possible: no = 0, yes = 1
Contacting officials: 5 problems as above, maximum score 3

Economic (14 for males, 11 for females)

Occupation: Males: farmer or unskilled = 1, semiskilled = 2, skilled =
3, commerce = 4, clerical or uniformed services
= 5, administrative or professional = 6
Females: commerce = 1, manual = 2, nonmanual = 3
Unemployment (males only): 13+ months = 0, 1–12 months = 1, never
over 1 month = 2
Time on the job: none yet = 0, under 12 months = 1, longer = 2
Income: none = 0, £750+ = 4, middle points depend on national distri-
bution for each sex
Ghana: occupation only (6 or 3)

Subjective (Gambia—8, Nigeria and Ghana 1968–6, Ashaiman 1970–4)
Easy to know people: hard = 0, unsure = 1, easy = 2
Satisfied with neighborhood: no = 0, ambivalent = 1, yes = 2
Plans to go home: soon = 0, eventually = 1, never = 2
House ownership (Gambia only): at home = 0, no plans = 1, here = 2
Ghana 1970: no data on going home

Chapter 6: Friendship

Sociability (19)

Know and membership in associations: as above
Talk: scored as above, 1–5 = 1, 6–8 = 2, 9+ = 3
Eat: scored as above, 3–4 categories = 3
Rooms visited: 3+ categories = 3
Party: has given = 1 (Ghana: invited few = 1, invited many = 2)
Number of friends listed: 1–2 = 1, 3–4 = 2, 5+ = 3
Ghana 1968: no data on friends, drink with others: seldom = 0,
middle = 1, often/many = 2
Ghana 1970: no data on associations (17)

Heterogeneity (12, no Ghana 1968)

Friend's age: range greater than 5 years = 1
Friend's sex and education: either different = 1, both different = 2
Friend's origin: some different state, area = 1; most different state,
area = 2

Friend's arrival: greater than 2-year range = 1
Friend's marriage: any different from R = 1
Friend's ethnicity: most same as R = 1; most different from R = 2
Friend's occupation: same type and level as R = 0, same type (manual/
    nonmanual/commerce) = 1; greater difference = 2
Friend's religion: different from R = 1
(those with no friends omitted)

Chapter 8:

Problems (12, Nigeria and The Gambia only)

5 cases for consultation: for each kin = 0, individuals = 1, officials = 2
Local government activity: see political above

NOTES

Chapter 1

1. Ten have been or are being built.

2. In 1971 there were sixty-two primary and forty-seven middle schools with 22,908 pupils and one secondary school with 622 students in the Tema Metropolitan Area. Most of these were in Tema proper (Ministry of Education statistics).

3. Plans for a bus service were announced in 1979.

4. Alayabiagba is the only part of town east of Boundary Road; an army camp and navy barracks are in this area.

5. The rest live in Kaduna. See Hinchliffe (1973) for details of the age, education, origin, and income of the textile workers.

Chapter 2

1. As respondents are anonymous, common names have been used for these sketches, which are based on real people.

2. Brydon (1977) suggests that education is increasing the propensity of Ghanaian girls to migrate for work as their brothers do rather than to wait at home until they are married.

3. See Appendix C for details. There are no income or political data for Ghana and ownership of housing was added to the subjective scale in The Gambia.

4. Gove *et al.* (1979, p. 78) comment that the explained variance for multiple regression based on individual data is likely to be far smaller than when aggregate data are used. Since "the size of the relationship is determined largely by the nature of the data," it is better to compare the effect of various sets of independent variables than to trust some general rule as to what a strong relationship is.

5. A good example is a Voltaic who had spent forty-two years in Ghana, serving in both the army and the police; he had made only one visit to Upper Volta, and no longer had contacts there. He owned his house and served as elder for the Voltaics in Ashaiman.

6. See Hutton (1973) for comparable data on Uganda.

7. Or, under a will or new legislation, as individuals.

8. See comparative data presented by Caldwell (1969, p. 188) and Nelson (1976).

9. One had completed his education in London, but spent the whole of his working life in Abeokuta.

Chapter 3

1. S. Benson (personal communication) found that Hausa women in Kano are freer to work outside the house after menopause than when they are younger; therefore, many take up low-paid wage employment in their fifties.

2. See Dinan (1977) for a discussion of the position of professional single women in Accra.

3. Nearly half the population of Abeokuta is Muslim, but Yoruba values have proven stronger than Islamic ones in allowing women freedom to trade.

4. Clignet (1976, p. 53) found that local people and short-distance migrants have no advantage in Yaounde, but in larger and more industrialized Douala the indigenes are better represented in the civil service and in self-employment than in private industry. Thus, they have better access to culturally preferred entrepreneurship and local political institutions and leave less preferred (though not necessarily less rewarding) jobs to strangers. This gives Douala some characteristics of Banjul and some of Abeokuta.

Chapter 4

1. See Schildkrout (1970, 1978) for a report on the changing position of the Hausa community in Kumasi and the development of *zongo* housing.

2. Adepoju (1977, p. 9) divides Abeokuta into indigenous, mixed, and migrant zones. While the proportions of migrants do vary between these zones (34, 53 and 64 percent respectively of adults in my sample living in these areas were born outside Abeokuta), local people are not as isolated from outsiders as Adepoju suggests and the difference between the mixed and migrant zones is not statistically significant. Clustering is increased by the convenience of living in family houses, but even in these, extra rooms are sometimes rented to strangers. The same pattern is evident in central Lagos (Marris 1961). This mixing was missed by Adepoju because his sample included only one household per house; the strangers were usually tenants, not landlords, and so were less likely to be chosen.

3. Lobo (1976, p. 124) reports that in Peru migrants often value the sociability of urban crowding instead of finding it burdensome.

4. Overcrowding is probably more typical of industrial than of provincial towns. Adepoju (1975, p. 50) found densities of about two per room in Ife and Oshogbo in southwestern Nigeria; only 17 percent of households in these towns had three or more people per room, though migrants were somewhat more likely to be crowded than nonmigrants.

5. Hinderink and Sterkenburg (1975, p. 291) found high-density areas in all parts of Cape Coast, but densities under 1.5 per room were all on the periphery.

6. Morgan and Immerwahr (n.d., pp. 25, 28) found that 21 percent of the 3,550 households they studied in metropolitan Lagos contained a single individual. The forty-nine upper-class households averaged 8.49 people, compared to 4.64 for the sample as a whole. These households averaged twice as many kin as the total sample, nine times as many nonkin (mainly domestic servants), and nearly twice as many children. The absence of single-person households and high proportion of wives present suggest that the households in this subsample are on average older than those in the sample as a whole. There is probably less difference in household size for families at the same stage in family life. B. Cooksey (personal communication) found that the households of 2,700 Primary 6 pupils in Yaounde, Cameroun varied only from an average of eight to ten with fathers in different occupational categories.

7. The Ghanaian Statutory Planning Areas regulations and the Nigerian Land Use Decree of 1978 are attempts to bring greater order and government control to the land acquisition process. It is too soon to assess their impact.

8. Schildkrout (1973, p. 56) reports that successful women traders in Kumasi plan to use their profits to build houses for their children.

Chapter 5

1.   See Oppong 1970 for a discussion of the effect of a wife's economic contribution on marital decision making.

2.   The Hausa and Fulani are often considered separate groups, but combined political authority, mixed residence, and intermarriage over the last 150 years have produced considerable cultural convergence, so that some individuals see themselves as belonging to both groups. Therefore, treating them as parts of a single entity seems a better expression of reality.

3.   Okediji (1975) describes the networks of rural patrons and urban middlewomen which supply domestic servants to elite households in Lagos. Arrangements in other towns appear to be less structured than in Lagos.

4.   Weisner (1976) and Ross and Weisner (1977) demonstrate the importance of rural-urban contacts in Kenya. They suggest that migrants and their kin must be seen as part of a single social field. Unfortunately, they have very little data on women's contacts with their kin, though they consider these of "crucial importance" (1977, p. 371). Ferraro (1973) found that Kikuyu living in one area of Nairobi spent as much time in interaction with kin in town (in both economic and recreational roles) as Kikuyu in a relatively isolated rural area. He sees this as a result of economic insecurity in both areas. Differences between males and females were small; new arrivals in town had somewhat less contact with kin than "old timers."

5.   Young and Willmott (1957) and Gans (1962) have shown the continuing importance of kinship among low-income residents of British and American cities.

6.   Yoruba are very precise in calculating shades of seniority and ensuring that all visiting is "up" rather than "down" (inferiors visit superiors). The questions asked about how often kin and friends were seen, without specifying who visited whom.

7.   Many of the comments in this section draw on Kaufert (1976). She analyzes the effects of these visits on villagers.

8.   The Hausa appear to be an exception to this pattern. Hill (1977, p. 146) reports that 57 percent of the migrants from the Kano Close Settled Zone village she studied had "vanished" and only those who went no farther than Kano were likely to keep in contact or eventually return. This is partly because migrants sell their land rights before leaving. Further study is needed, but the connection between maintaining contact and eventual return confirms the belief of southern village leaders.

9.   Odimuko and Riddell (1979, pp. 59–60) found that 57 percent of households in eight Igbo villages received cash remittances and 71 percent gifts in cash or kind during the year previous to their 1976–1977 study. In comparison, Caldwell (1969, p. 152) reported that 36 percent of the Ghanaian rural households he studied in 1962 received money from urban migrants; 63 percent of the migrants interviewed in town said they sent money home. About a fifth of the Igbo households received cash and/or noncash remittances worth ₦20 (about £15); nearly a fifth got ₦100 or more. The Igbo remittances benefited from inflation and relative economic prosperity. Much of this extra income was spent on secondary schooling, which will provide the next cohort of migrants.

10.   Ross and Weisner (1977, p. 367) found that both visits home and money sent by Nairobi migrants were significantly correlated with income and education. Rempel and Lobdell (1978) summarized the data on remittances in various countries. They concluded that these are more important in Africa than elsewhere and that they are used mainly for improving the rural standard of living and education rather than for agricultural development. The amount sent increases with income, but those with a moderate income tend to send a higher proportion of it than the wealthy. There is a widespread concern to repay

parents for the cost of education, and older migrants may no longer send money home because their parents are dead.

Chapter 6

1. Liu and Duff (1972, p. 366) use Philippine data to show that information crosses class lines most readily in mixed neighborhoods. Contacts between neighbors across class lines need not be frequent to achieve "remarkably wide circulation."

2. Their edge over Kakuri is slight.

3. Another alternative is to reheat a stew again and again until it is finished, which causes a considerable decline in its nutritional value.

4. See Appendix C for details. Talk, rooms, and eat form a Guttman scale for both men and women in all eight towns. The mean item-to-scale correlations (omitting the item concerned) are .42 for talk, .38 for rooms, .32 for eat, .29 for number of friends, .25 for number of neighbors known well, .20 for giving a party, and .07 for membership in associations. The last would be .20 without The Gambia. While combining various forms of sociability causes problems because different processes may be involved in each and these forms may vary in their attraction for people of different social positions, the project proved to be analytically useful. It should be remembered that the scale score tells us more about the range of a person's sociability than about its depth.

Chapter 7

1. Some of the issues raised in this chapter have been more fully discussed in Barnes and Peil (1977).

2. In a study of seven nations, N. Nie found that Nigerians were second only to Americans in the proportion belonging to associations; Nigerians of low "Social Economic Advantage" had a higher level of membership than similar respondents in any of the nations studied (personal communication).

3. Callaway (1972, p. 408) reports that there were over four hundred village and clan associations in Aba in 1966. These had an important role in local politics.

4. Dutto (1975, pp. 147–48) found that young, single people were less likely than those who were over 30 and married to participate in associations in the small Kenyan town he studied. Marriage is necessary to signify full maturity and to take one's place in the community, and older people are expected to take part in community activities, which have increased considerably since independence.

5. Imoagene (1976, chapter 6) found a very high level of participation among the Yoruba ex-politicians, civil servants, and elite businessmen he interviewed (mostly in Ibadan). Only 1 percent belonged to no associations and 32 percent belonged to five or more. Politicians, upwardly mobile men, those over 35, and migrants with more than twenty years in town had the most memberships. Older men were much more involved as leaders than young men, but men with the highest-status occupations attended meetings less often than lower-level clerical workers. Unfortunately, he did not distinguish between those currently living in Ibadan and other respondents; he also had too few manual workers in his samples for a valid comparison and treated church attendance equally with membership in church associations. Members of the elites in Ibadan have far more recreational, philanthropic, and professional associations than are available in smaller towns.

6. Inkeles (1969) found higher participation among the Yoruba than among respondents in five other countries. Smock (1971), among others, reports on the high level of Igbo membership in ethnic and hometown associations before the 1966 coup.

7. The Nigerian military government banned pools in the 1979 budget.

Chapter 8

1. The Nigerian question specified local government.

2. Except in Abeokuta, where semiskilled workers are usually self-employed.

3. Figures, if provided, may have little basis in reality (see Peil 1971, pp. 218–19).

Chapter 9

1. The differences on a number of scales between the mean score for a particular town and all the other towns for which data are available were squared and summed to provide an index of dissimilarity. These were inverted, producing a similarity matrix for use with the Smallest Space Analysis and Hierarchical Linkage programs. Results of the former are shown, as they moved more meaningful. The Social Adjustment Scale was not included because the Sociability Scale better represents these characteristics.

2. Rather than isolating them in newly developed parts of town, as is planned for Owerri, for instance. See Galantay (1978).

3. See Mitchell (1954) for a southern African example.

BIBLIOGRAPHY

Abloh, F. A. *Growth of Towns in Ghana.* Kumasi: Department of Housing and Planning Research, University of Science and Technology, 1967. Mimeographed.

Acquah, I. *Accra Survey.* London: University of London Press, 1958.

Adepoju, A. "Living Conditions of Migrants in Medium-Sized Towns, Nigeria, 1971," *Ghana Journal of Sociology* 9 (1975):42–53.

Adepoju, A., ed. *Internal Migration of Nigeria.* Ile-Ife: Department of Demography and Social Statistics, University of Ife, 1976. Mimeographed.

Adepoju, A. *Policy Implications of Migration into Medium-Sized Towns: The Case of Abeokuta, Nigeria.* Ile-Ife: University of Ife, 1977. Mimeographed.

Ajaegbu, H. I. *Urban and Rural Development in Nigeria.* London: Heinemann, 1976.

Ajisafe, A. K. *History of Abeokuta.* Lagos: Kash and Klare Bookshop, 1948.

Akinnusi, A. "Migration and Occupational Mobility: The Small-Scale Industrialists in Western State of Nigeria in Perspective," Paper presented at the seminar on Population Problems and Policy in Nigeria, University of Ife, 1971. Mimeographed.

Amachree, I. T. D. "Reference Group and Worker Satisfaction: Studies among some Nigerian Factory Workers," *Nigerian Journal of Economic and Social Studies* 10 (1968):229–38.

Amartefifio, G. W. et al. *Tema Manhean: A Study of Resettlement.* Accra: Universities Press, 1966.

Anon. "The Challenge of Rapid Urbanization to Nigerian Local Government." Paper presented at the Fourth National Conference on Local Government, University of Ife, 1971. Mimeographed.

Aribiah, O. "The Politics of Rehousing," *Lagos Notes and Records* 5 (1974):5–13.

———. "Community Creation in a Rehousing Estate," *Urban African Notes* Series B 1, No. 2 (1976): 39–54.

Aronson, D. R. "Cultural Stability and Social Change among the Modern Ijebu Yoruba." Ph.D. thesis, University of Chicago, 1970.

———. "Ijebu Yoruba Urban-Rural Relationships and Class Formation," *Canadian Journal of African Studies* 5 (1971):263–79.

———. . "Capitalism and Culture in Ibadan Urban Development," *Urban Anthropology* 7 (1978a):253–69.

————. *The City Is Our Farm.* Cambridge, Mass.: Schenkman Publishing Co., 1978b.

Aryee, A. F. "Christianity and Polygamy in Ghana: The Role of the Church as an Instrument of Social Change," *Ghana Journal of Sociology* 3 (1967):98–105.

Baker, P. *Urbanization and Political Change: The Politics of Lagos 1917–1967.* Berkeley: University of California Press, 1974.

Bannerman, J. Y. *The Cry for Justice in Tema.* Tema: Tema Industrial Mission, 1973.

Banton, M. "Adaptation and Integration in the Social System of Temne Immigrants in Freetown," *Africa* 26 (1956):354–67.

————. *West African City.* London: Oxford University Press for the International African Institute, 1957.

Barnes, S. "Becoming a Lagosian," Ph.D. thesis, University of Wisconsin, 1974.

————. "Political Transition in Urban Africa," *Annals, American Academy of Political and Social Science*, No. 432 (1977), pp. 26–41.

Barnes, S. and M. Peil "Voluntary Association Membership in Five West African Cities," *Urban Anthropology* 6 (1977):83–106.

Bascom, W. "Urbanization as a Traditional African Pattern," *Sociological Review* 7 (1959):29–43.

Betts, R. F. "The Problem of the Medina in the Urban Planning of Dakar, Senegal," *African Urban Notes* 4 (3) (1969):5–15.

Blau, P. M. "Parameters of Social Structure." In *Approaches to the Study of Social Structure*, edited by P. M. Blau. New York: Free Press, 1975.

Bonacich, E. "A Theory of Middleman Minorities," *American Sociological Review* 38 (1973):583–94.

Bretton, H. L. "Political Influence in Southern Nigeria." In *Africa: The Primacy of Politics*, edited by H. J. Spiro. New York: Random House, 1966.

Bryant, J. "The Petty Commodity Sector in Urban Growth." London: n.p., 1976. Mimeographed.

Bryant, K. J. *Kaduna—Capital of Northern Nigeria.* Zaria: Gaskiya Corporation, n.d.

Brydon, L. "Factors Affecting the Migration of Women in Ghana, with Particular Reference to Avatime Women." Report MR4604 to the Social Science Research Council, London, 1977.

Busia, K. A. *Report on a Social Survey of Sekondi-Takoradi.* London: Crown Agents for the Colonies, 1950.

Byerlee, D. et al. *Rural-Urban Migration in Sierra Leone: Determinants and Policy Implications.* African Rural Economy Paper No. 13. East Lansing: Department of Agricultural Economics, Michigan State University, 1976.

Caldwell, J. C. "Extended Family Obligations and Education: A Study of an Aspect of Demographic Transition amongst Ghanaian University Students," *Population Studies* 19 (1965):183–99.

———. "Migration and Urbanization." In *A Study of Contemporary Ghana,* edited by W. Birmingham *et al.,* Vol. 2. London: George Allen and Unwin, 1967.

———. "Determinants of Rural-Urban Migration in Ghana," *Population Studies* 22 (1968):361–77.

———. *African Rural-Urban Migration: The Movement to Ghana's Towns.* Canberra: Australian National University Press, 1969.

———. "Fertility and the Household Economy in Nigeria," *Journal of Comparative Family Studies* 7 (1976):193–253.

Callaway, B. "Local Politics in Ho and Aba," *Canadian Journal of African Studies* 4 (1970):121–44.

———. "Transitional Local Politics: Tradition in Local Government Elections in Aba, Nigeria and Keta, Ghana," *African Studies Review* 15 (1972):403–12.

Clignet, R. and J. Sween "Social Change and Type of Marriage," *American Journal of Sociology* 75 (1969):123–45.

Cohen, A. *Custom and Politics in Urban Africa.* London: Routledge and Kegan Paul, 1969.

———. "The Politics of Ritual Secrecy," *Man* 6 (1971):427–48.

Cohen, A., ed. *Urban Ethnicity.* London: Tavistock, 1974.

Cohen, M. A. *Urban Policy and Political Conflict in Africa: A Study of the Ivory Coast.* Chicago: University of Chicago Press, 1974.

Cooksey, B. "Education and Social Class in Cameroun," Ph.D. thesis, Birmingham University, U.K., 1978.

Cutler, S. J. "Voluntary Association Membership and the Theory of Mass Society." In *Bonds of Pluralism,* edited by E. O. Laumann. New York: Wiley, 1973.

Dahlberg, F. M. "The Provincial Town," *Urban Anthropology* 3 (1974): 171–83.

Dinan, C. "Socialization in an Accra Suburb: the Zongo and its Distinct Subculture." In *Legon Family Research Papers,* No. 3: *Changing Family Studies,* edited by C. Oppong. Ghana: University of Ghana Institute of African Studies, 1975.

———. "Pragmatists or Feminists? The Professional Single Women in Accra," *Cahiers d'Etudes Africaines* 65 (1977):155–76.

Doudu, C. *The Gab Boys.* London: Andre Deutsch, 1967.

Duncan, O. D. "A Socioeconomic Index for All Occupations." In *Occupations and Social Status,* edited by A. J. Reiss, Jr. New York: Free Press, 1961.

Dutto, C. A. *Nyeri Townsmen Kenya.* Nairobi: East African Literature Bureau, 1975.

Eades, J. "Kinship and Entrepreneurship among Yoruba in Northern Ghana." In *Strangers in Africa,* edited by W. A. Shack and E. P. Skinner. Berkeley: University of California Press, 1979.

Edwards, N. J. and A. Booth (eds.) *Social Participation in Urban Society.* Cambridge, Mass.: Schenkman Publishing Co., 1973.

Ejiogu, C. N. "African Migrants in Lagos Suburbs." Ph.D. thesis, Australian National University, n.d.

Elkan, W. "Is a Proletariat Emerging in Nairobi?" *Economic Development and Cultural Change* 24 (1976):695–706.

Epstein, A. L. "The Network of Urban Social Organization," *Rhodes-Livingstone Institute Journal,* No. 29 (1961), pp. 29–61.

Fapohunda, O. J. *The Informal Sector in Lagos: An Inquiry into Urban Poverty and Employment.* Report to the I.L.O., Lagos, 1978. Mimeographed.

Ferraro, G. P. "Tradition or Transition?: Rural and Urban Kinsmen in East Africa," *Urban Anthropology* 2 (1973):214–31.

Fischer, C. S. *et al. Networks and Places: Social Relations in the Urban Setting.* New York: Free Press, 1977.

Fraenkel, M. *Tribe and Class in Monrovia.* London: Oxford University Press for the International African Institute, 1964.

Free, L. A. *The Attitudes, Hopes and Fears of Nigerians.* Princeton, N.J.: Institute of International Social Research, 1964.

Gailey, H. A. *A History of The Gambia.* London: Routledge and Kegan Paul, 1964.

———. *The Road to Aba.* London: University of London Press, 1971.

Galantay, E. Y. "The Planning of Owerri," *Town Planning Review* 49 (1978):371–86.

Gambia. *The Gambia: Ten Years of Nationhood.* Banjul, n.p., 1975.

Gamble, D. P. "Occupational Prestige in an Urban Community (Lunsar) in Sierra Leone," *Sierra Leone Studies,* New Series No. 19 (1966), pp. 98–108.

Gans, H. J. *The Urban Villagers.* New York: Free Press, 1962.

Garlick, P. C. *African Traders and Economic Development in Ghana.* Oxford: Clarendon Press, 1971.

Ghana. *1960 Population Census of Ghana,* Vol. 2: *Statistics of Localities and Enumeration Areas.* Accra: Central Bureau of Statistics, 1962.

———. *1960 Population Census of Ghana,* Vol. 4: *Economic Characteristics.* Accra: Central Bureau of Statistics, 1964.

———. 1970 Population Census of Ghana, Vol. 2: *Statistics of Localities and Enumeration Areas.* Accra: Central Bureau of Statistics, 1972.

Ghana Development Secretariat. *Tema: Ghana's New Town and Harbour.* Accra: Ministry of Information, 1961.

Goldlust, J. and A. H. Richmond "A Multivariate Model of Immigrant Adaptation," *International Migration Review* 8 (1974):193–225.

Goldstein, S. *et al.* "Migration and Urban Growth in Thailand: An Exploration of Inter-Relations among Origin, Recency and Frequency of Moves." In *Internal Migration: The New World and the Third World,* edited by A. H. Richmond and D. Kubat. Beverly Hills, Calif.: Sage, 1976.

Goode, W. *World Revolution and Family Patterns.* New York: Free Press, 1963.

Goody, E. "The Fostering of Children in Ghana," *Ghana Journal of Sociology* 2 (1966):26–33.

———. "Kinship Fostering in Gonja." In *Socialization,* edited by P. Mayer. London: Tavistock, 1970.

Gove, W. R. *et al.* "Overcrowding in the Home: An Empirical Investigation of its Possible Consequences," *American Sociological Review* 44 (1979):59–80.

Granovetter, M. S. "The Strength of Weak Ties," *American Journal of Sociology* 78 (1973):1360–80.

Grillo, J. *African Railwayman.* London: Cambridge University Press, 1973.

Gugler, J. *Urban Growth in Subsaharan Africa.* Nkanga Editions No. 6. Kampala: Makerere Institute of Social Research, 1970.

Gugler, J. and W. G. Flanagan *Urbanization and Social Change in West Africa.* London: Cambridge University Press, 1978.

Guttman, L. "A General Nonmetric Technique for Finding the Smallest Coordinate Space for a Configuration of Points," *Psychometrika* 33 (1968):469–506.

Haeringer, P. "San-Pedro 1969: la Premiere Vague d'Immigrants" and "San-Pedro 1973: Quatre Années d'Evolution," *Cahiers OSTROM, Serie Sciences Humaines* 10 (1973):245–87.

Hake, A. *African Metropolis: Nairobi's Self-Help City.* London: Chatto and Windus for Sussex University Press, 1977.

Harrell-Bond, B. E. *Modern Marriage in Sierra Leone.* Paris: Mouton, 1975.

Harris, R. L. "The Role of Higher Public Servants in Nigeria: As Perceived by the Western-Educated Elite." In *Studies in Nigerian Administration,* 2nd ed., edited by D. J. Murray and L. Adamolekun. London: Hutchinson, 1978.

Hart, K. "Migration and Tribal Identity among the Frafras of Ghana," *Journal of Asian and African Studies* 6 (1971):21–36.

———. "Informal Income Opportunities and Urban Employment in Ghana," *Journal of Modern African Studies* 11 (1973):61–89.

Henderson, R. N. "Generalized Cultures and Evolutionary Adaptability: A Comparison of Urban Efik and Ibo in Nigeria," *Ethnology* 5 (1966): 265–91.

Hill, P. "Landlords and Brokers: A West African Traditional System," *Cahiers d'Etudes Africaines* 6 (1966): 349–66.

———. "Hidden Trade in Hausaland," *Man* 4 (1969):392–409.

———. *Rural Hausa*. London: Cambridge University Press, 1972.

———. *Population, Prosperity and Poverty: Rural Kano 1900 and 1970*. London: Cambridge University Press, 1977.

Hinchliffe, K. "The Kaduna Textile Workers: Characteristics of an African Labour Force," *Savanna* 2 (1973):27–37.

———. "Labour Aristocracy—A Northern Nigerian Case Study," *Journal of Modern African Studies* 12 (1974):57–67.

Hinderink, J. and J. Sterkenburg *Anatomy of an African Town: A Socio-Economic Study of Cape Coast, Ghana*. Utrecht: Geographical Institute, State University of Utrecht, 1975.

Hodge, R. W. *et al.* "A Comparative Study of Occupational Prestige." In *Class, Status, and Power*, edited by R. Bendix and S. M. Lipsett. New York: Free Press, 1966.

Hull, R. W. *African Cities and Towns before the European Conquest*. New York: Norton, 1976.

Hutton, C. *Reluctant Farmers? A Study of Unemployment and Planned Rural Development in Uganda*. Nairobi: East African Publishing House, 1973.

Imoagene, O. *Social Mobility in Emergent Society*. Canberra: Australian National University Press, 1976.

Inkeles, A. "Making Men Modern: On the Causes and Consequences of Individual Change in Six Developing Countries," *American Journal of Sociology* 75 (1969):208–25.

Jacobson, D. *Itinerant Townsmen: Friendship and Social Order in Urban Uganda*. Menlo Park, Calif.: Cummings Publishing Co., 1973.

Jasso, G. and P. H. Rossi "Distributive Justice and Earned Income," *American Sociological Review* 42 (1977):639–51.

Jeffries, R. *Class, Power and Ideology in Ghana: The Railwaymen of Sekondi*. London; Cambridge University Press, 1978.

Johnson, M. "Technology, Competition, and African Crafts." In *The Imperial Impact: Studies in the Economic History of Africa and India*, edited by C. Dewey and A. G. Hopkins. London: University of London Press, 1978.

Jules-Rosette, B. "Alternative Urban Adaptations: Zambian Cottage Industries as Sources of Social and Economic Innovation," *Human Organization* 38 (1979):225–38.

Kaufert, P. A. L. "Migration and Communication: A Study of Migrant-Villager Relationships in a Rural Ghanaian Community." Ph.D. thesis, Birmingham University, U.K., 1976.

Kennedy, P. "Patterns of Indigenous Enterprise in Ghana." Ph.D. thesis, Birmingham University, U.K., 1974.

———. "African Businessmen and Foreign Capital: Collaboration or Conflict?" *African Affairs* 76 (1977):177–94.

Kerri, J. N. "Studying Voluntary Associations as Adaptive Mechanisms: A

Review of Anthropological Perspectives," *Current Anthropology* 17 (1976):23–47.

King, K. *The African Artisan.* London: Heinemann, 1977.

Lewis, B. C. "The Limitations of Group Action among Entrepreneurs: The Market Women of Abidjan, Ivory Coast." In *Women in Africa: Studies in Social and Economic Change,* edited by N. J. Hafkin and E. G. Bay. Palo Alto, Calif.: Stanford University Press, 1976.

Levine, D. N. "Simmel at a Distance." In *Strangers in African Societies,* edited by W. A. Shack and E. P. Skinner. Berkeley: University of California Press, 1979.

Little, K. "The Role of Voluntary Associations in West African Urbanization," *American Anthropologist* 59 (1957):579–96.

———. *West African Urbanization.* London: Cambridge University Press, 1965.

Litwak, E. and I. Szelenyi "Primary Group Structures and their Functions: Kin, Neighbors and Friends," *American Sociological Review* 34 (1969):465–81.

Liu, W. T. and R. W. Duff "The Strength of Weak Ties," *Public Opinion Quarterly* 36 (1972):361–66.

Lloyd, B. B. "Education and Family Life in the Development of Class Identification among the Yoruba." In *The New Elites of Tropical Africa,* edited by P. C. Lloyd. London: Oxford University Press for the International African Institute, 1966.

Lloyd, P. C. "Craft Organization in Yoruba Towns," *Africa* 23 (1953):30–44.

———. "The Yoruba Town Today," *Sociological Review* 7 (1959):45–63.

———. "Ethnicity and the Structure of Inequality in a Nigerian Town in the mid-1950s." In *Urban Ethnicity,* edited by A. Cohen. London: Tavistock, 1974.

———. "Perceptions of Class and Social Inequality among the Yoruba of Western Nigeria." In *Migration and Development: Implications for Ethnic Identity and Political Conflict,* edited by H. I. Safa and B. M. duToit. Paris: Mouton, 1975.

Lloyd, P. C., ed. *The New Elites of Tropical Africa.* London: Oxford University Press for the International African Institute, 1966.

Lloyd, P. C. *et al.,* eds. *The City of Ibadan.* London: Cambridge University Press, 1967.

Lobo, S. B. "Urban Adaptation among Peruvian Migrants," *Rice University Studies* 62 (3) (1976):113–30.

Lowy, M. "Establishing Paternity and Demanding Child Support in a Ghanaian Town." In *Law and the Family in Africa,* edited by S. Roberts. Paris: Mouton, 1977.

Luckham, R. *The Nigerian Military.* London: Cambridge University Press, 1971.

Lux, A. "The Networks of Visits between Rural Wage-Earners and their Kinsfolk in Western Congo," *Africa* 41 (1971):109–28.

Mackintosh, J. P., ed. *Nigerian Government and Politics.* London: George Allen and Unwin, 1966.

Marris, P. *Family and Social Change in an African City.* London: Routledge and Kegan Paul, 1961.

Mauss, M. *The Gift,* trans. by I. Cunnison. London: Cohen and West, 1925.

Mayer, P. *Townsmen or Tribesmen.* Cape Town: Oxford University Press, 1961.

———. "Labour Migrancy and the Social Network." In *Problems of Transition: Proceedings of the Social Sciences Research Conference,* edited by J. F. Holleman *et al.* Pietermaritzburg: University of Natal Press, 1964.

Meillassoux, C. "The Social Structure of Modern Bamako," *Africa* 35 (1965):125–41.

———. *Urbanization of an African Community.* Seattle: University of Washington Press, 1968.

Mitchell, J. C. "The distribution of African Labour by Area of Origin on the Coppermines of Northern Rhodesia," *Human Problems of British Central Africa* 14 (1954):30–36.

———. "Theoretical Orientations in African Urban Studies." In *The Social Anthropology of Complex Societies,* edited by M. Banton. London: Tavistock, 1966.

———. *Social Networks in Urban Situations.* Manchester, U.K.: Manchester University Press, 1969.

———. "Distance, Transportation and Urban Involvement in Zambia." in *Urban Anthropology,* edited by A. Southall. London: Oxford University Press, 1973.

———. "Perceptions of Ethnicity and Ethnic Behaviour: An Empirical Exploration." In *Urban Ethnicity,* edited by A. Cohen. London: Tavistock, 1974.

Morgan, R. W. and G. E. Immerwahr "Family Structure in Lagos, Nigeria." Lagos: n.d. Mimeographed.

Morgan, R. W. and V. Kannisto "A Population Dynamics Survey in Lagos, Nigeria," *Social Science and Medicine* 7 (1973):1–30.

Nelson, J. M. "Sojourners Versus New Urbanites: Causes and Consequences of Temporary Versus Permanent Cityward Migration in Developing Countries," *Economic Development and Cultural Change* 24 (1976):721–57.

Odimuko, C. L. and J. B. Riddell "Remittances in South-Eastern Nigeria," *Area* 11 (1979):58–62.

Ohadike, P. O. "A Demographic Note on Marriage, Family and Family Growth in Lagos, Nigeria." In *The Population of Tropical Africa,* edited by J. C. Caldwell and C. Okonjo. London: Longmans, 1968.

Okediji, O. O. "On Voluntary Associations as Adaptive Mechanisms in West African Urbanization: Another Perspective," *African Urban Notes,* Series B, No. 2 (1975), pp. 51–73.

Oppong, C. "Conjugal Power and Resources: An Urban African Example," *Journal of Marriage and the Family* 34 (1970):676–80.

———. *Marriage among a Matrilineal Elite: A Family Study of Ghanaian Senior Civil Servants.* London: Cambridge University Press, 1974.

Osborne, O. H. "Census Reliability in Anthropological Field Work." In *Survey Research in Africa,* edited by W. M. O'Barr et al. Evanston, Ill.: Northwestern University Press, 1973.

Oyeneye, O. Y. "The Apprenticeship System in Southwestern Nigeria: A Case of Human Resource Development." Ph.D. thesis, Birmingham University, 1979.

Paden, J. "Communal Competition, Conflict and Violence in Kano." In *Nigeria: Modernization and the Politics of Communalism,* edited by R. Melson and H. Wolpe. East Lansing: Michigan State University Press, 1971.

Parkin, D. "Urban Voluntary Associations as Institutions of Adaptation," *Man,* New Series, 1 (1966):90–95.

———. *Neighbours and Nationals in an African City Ward.* London: Routledge and Kegan Paul, 1969.

Peace, A. "Industrial Protest in Nigeria." In *Sociology and Development,* edited by E. deKadt and G. Williams. London: Tavistock, 1974.

———. *Choice, Class and Conflict: A Study of Southern Nigerian Factory Workers.* Brighton, Sussex: Harvester Press, 1979.

Peil, M. "Reactions to Estate Housing: A Survey of Tema," *Ghana Journal of Sociology* 4 (1968):1–18.

———. "Unemployment in Tema: The Plight of the Skilled Worker," *Canadian Journal of African Studies* 3 (1969):409–19.

———. *The Ghanaian Factory Worker.* London: Cambridge University Press, 1972a.

———. "Male Unemployment in Lagos," *Manpower and Unemployment Research in Africa* 5 (2) (1972b):18–24.

———. "The Expulsion of West African Aliens," *Journal of Modern African Studies* 9 (1971):205–29.

———. "Female Roles in West African Towns." In *Changing Social Structure in Ghana,* edited by J. Goody. London: International African Institute, 1975a.

———. "Interethnic Contacts in Nigerian Cities," *Africa* 45 (1975b): 107–22.

———. "African Squatter Settlements: A Comparative Study," *Urban Studies* 13 (1976a): 155–66.

————. *Nigerian Politics: The People's View.* London: Cassell, 1976b.

————. "Unemployment in Banjul: The Farming/Tourist Trade-off," *Manpower and Unemployment Research* 10 (1) (1977):25–29.

————. "West African Urban Craftsmen," *Journal of Developing Areas* 14 (1979):2–22.

Peil, M. and D. Lucas, *Survey Research Methods for West Africa.* Lagos: Human Resources Research Unit, University of Lagos, 1972.

Pellow, D. *Women in Accra: Options for Autonomy.* Algonac, Mich.: Reference Publications, 1977.

Pfeffermann, G. *Industrial Labor in the Republic of Senegal.* New York: Praeger, 1968.

Plotnicov, L. "Going Home Again—Nigerians: The Dream Is Unfulfilled," *Transaction* 3 (1965):18–22.

————. *Strangers to the City.* Pittsburgh, Penn.: Pittsburgh University Press, 1967.

Pons, V. *Stanleyville.* London: Oxford University Press for the International African Institute, 1969.

Potakey, A. "Tema Flats Survey," *Tedeco* (Tema) 2 (1975):2–7.

Price, R. M. *Society and Bureaucracy in Contemporary Ghana.* Berkeley: University of California Press, 1975.

Rempel, H. and R. A. Lobdell "The Role of Urban-to-Rural Remittances in Rural Development," *Journal of Development Studies* 14 (1978): 324–41.

Richmond, A. H. and R. P. Verma "The Economic Adaptation of Immigrants: A New Theoretical Perspective," *International Migration Review* 12 (1978):3–38.

Riddell, J. B. and M. E. Harvey "The Urban System in the Migration Process: An Evaluation of Stepwise Migration in Sierra Leone," *Economic Geography* 48 (1972): 270-83.

Robertson, C. "Ga Women and Socioeconomic Change in Accra, Ghana," In *Women in Africa,* edited by N.J. Hafkin and E. G. Bay. Palo Alto, Calif.: Stanford University Press, 1976.

Ross, M. H. *Grass Roots in an African City: Political Behavior in Nairobi.* Cambridge, Mass.: MIT Press, 1975.

Ross, M. H. and T. S. Weisner "The Rural-Urban Network in Kenya: Some General Implications," *American Ethnologist* 4 (1977): 359–75.

Sada, P. O. "The Rural-Urban Fringe of Lagos: Population and Land-Use," *Nigerian Journal of Economic and Social Studies* 12 (1970):225–41.

Salamone, F. A. "Becoming Hausa: Ethnic Identity Change and its Implications for the Study of Ethnic Pluralism and Stratification," *Africa* 45 (1975): 410–24.

Sami, E. "The Social Status of Primary School Teachers: A Case Study of the Rivers State of Nigeria," Ph.D. thesis, Birmingham University, U.K., 1978.

Sandbrook, R. and J. Arn *The Labouring Poor and Urban Class Formation: The Case of Greater Accra.* Montreal: Centre of Developing-Area Studies, McGill University, 1977.

Schildkrout, E. "Strangers and Local Government in Kumasi," *Journal of Modern African Studies* 8 (1970):251–69.

———. "The Fostering of Children in Urban Ghana," *Urban Anthropology* 2 (1973):48–73.

———. *People of the Zongo.* London: Cambridge University Press, 1978.

Skinner, E. P. *African Urban Life: The Transformation of Ouagadougou.* Princeton, N.J.: Princeton University Press, 1974.

Smock, A. C. *Ibo Politics.* Cambridge, Mass.: Harvard University Press, 1971.

Steady, F. C. "Protestant Women's Associations in Freetown, Sierra Leone." In *Women in Africa,* edited by N. J. Hafkin and E. G. Bay. Palo Alto, Calif.: Stanford University Press, 1976.

Stouffer, S. A. "Intervening Opportunities: A Theory Relating Mobility and Distance," *American Sociological Review* 5 (1940):845–67.

Stren, R. "A Survey of Lower Income Areas in Mombasa." In *Urban Challenge in East Africa,* edited by J. Hutton. Nairobi: East African Publishing House, 1972.

Tema Development Corporation "Tema Industrial Survey," *Tedeco* (Tema) 2 (1977):5–13.

Treiman, D. J. *Occupational Prestige in Comparative Perspective.* New York: Academic Press, 1977.

Turner, J. C. "Housing as a Verb." In *Freedom to Build,* edited by F. C. Turner and R. Fichter. New York: Macmillan, 1972.

Udo, R. K. *The Geographical Regions of Nigeria.* London: Heinemann, 1970.

Van Velsen, J. "Urban Squatters: Problem and Solution." In *Town and Country in Central and Eastern Africa,* edited by D. Parkin. London: International African Institute, 1975.

Wallerstein, I. *The Road to Independence.* Paris: Mouton, 1964.

Waterman, P. "Conservatism amongst Nigerian Workers." In *Nigeria: Economy and Society,* edited by G. Williams. London: Rex Collings, 1976.

Weinrich, A. K. H. *Mucheke: Race, Status and Politics in a Rhodesian Community.* Paris: UNESCO, 1976.

Weisner, T. S. "The Structure of Sociability: Urban Migration and Urban-Rural Ties in Kenya," *Urban Anthropology* 5 (1976):199–233.

Wellman, B. "The Community Question," *American Journal of Sociology* 84 (1979):1201–31.

Wolpe, H. "Port Harcourt: Ibo Politics in Microcosm," *Journal of Modern Studies* 7 (1969): 469–93.

Young, M. and P. Willmott *Family and Kinship in East London.* London: Routledge and Kegan Paul, 1957.

Yusuf, A. B. "Capital Formation and Management among the Muslim Hausa Traders of Kano, Nigeria," *Africa* 45 (1975):167–82.

INDEX

Aba, Nigeria, 15, 16, 17, 22–23, 126, 157, 173, 247, 249, 253; demographic data, 31–40

Abeokuta, Nigeria, 15, 16, 17, 18, 22, 23–25, 71–72, 253, 300; demographic data, 31–40

Abloh, F. A., 123, 305

Accra, Ghana, 9, 10; housing estates in, 8

Acquah, I., 221, 222, 305

Adaptation, urban, 53–63, 77–78

Ademola II, Alake, 24

Adepoju, A., 24, 300, 305

Age: labor force participation and, 89; migration and, 43, 47–50, 77; polygyny and, 182–183; urban adaptation and, 55–56, 69, 140–142, 144–146, 175, 291; associations and, 222–223

Aid, emergency, 6–7, 242–251

Ajaegbu, H. I., 22, 305

Ajegunle, Nigeria, 15, 16, 17, 25–27, 250; demographic data, 31–40

Ajisafe, A. K., 24, 305

Akan, 40, 118, 128, 149, 150, 240

Akinnusi, A., 24, 108, 305

Akorley-Djor, Ghana, 19

Aku, 118, 150

Aliens, relations with, 118, 254–256
    See also Ethnicity

Amachree, I. T. D., 175, 305

Amartefifio, G. W., 18, 305

Americo-Liberians, 10

Apapa, Nigeria, 25

Aribiah, O., 10, 192, 305

Army, 102

Arn, J., 7, 108, 265, 315

Aronson, D. R., 73, 85, 100, 131, 163, 305, 306

Aryee, A. F., 147, 306

Ashaiman, Ghana, 15, 16, 20–21, 62, 167, 250, 254–255, 265; demographic data, 31–40

Assistance, getting 6–7, 242–251

Assimilation, 251–252

Associations, 6, 13, 217–240, 302; functions of, 226–239; membership in, 219–226; occupational, 231–234; primary, 227–230; recreation, 237–239; religious, 230–231; savings societies, 234–237

Baker, P., 53, 212, 233, 253, 306

Banjul, Gambia, 9, 10, 16, 17, 18, 29–30, 31; demographic data, 31–40

Banks, 235, 247

Bannerman, J. Y., 20, 306

Banton, M., 10, 217, 238, 306

Barnes, S., 65, 66, 70, 130, 131, 148, 302, 306

Bascom, W., 11, 306

Benson, S., 299

Betts, R. F., 9, 306

Blau, P. M., 206, 306

Bonacich, E., 251, 254, 306

Booth, A., 218, 308

Bretton, H. L., 233, 306

British colonial rule, West African towns and, 8

Bruner, E. M., 252

Bryant, J., 108, 306

Bryant, K. J., 28, 306

Brydon, L., 299, 306

Burial, 66, 73, 78

Busia, K. A., 3, 8, 271, 306

Byerlee, D., 51, 180, 181, 306

Caldwell, J. C., 10, 50, 64, 65, 93, 178, 180, 182, 299, 301, 307

Callaway, B., 23, 302, 307

Central cities, 13, 271–272

Children: attitude toward, 155–156, 183; migration and, 49, 156, 174

Christianity, 5, 17, 23; polygyny and, 143, 147, 183

Class consciousness, 6, 116
    See also Elites, Inequality

Clignet, R., 142, 143, 147, 148, 300, 307

Lagos, Nigeria, 9, 10, 11, 17, 26–27; water problem, 23
Laissez faire attitude, 8, 10
Landlords: *see* Housing
Landowners, 130–134
Leaders, 70, 190, 218, 222–223, 231, 233, 260, 275; traditional, 12, 14, 23–25, 29
Levine, D. N., 252, 311
Lewis, B. C., 222, 233, 234, 311
Little, K., 217, 228, 311
Litwak, E., 163, 242, 248, 311
Liu, W. T., 246, 302, 311
Lloyd, B. B., 116, 124, 163, 164, 228, 311
Lloyd, P. C., 11, 130, 190, 212, 224, 232, 253, 264, 311
Lobo, S. B., 300, 311
Lobdell, R. A., 301, 314
Lowy, M., 47, 311
Lucas, D., 80, 81, 314
Luckham, R., 190, 311
Lugard, Sir Frederick, 27
Lukhero, M. B., 163
Lunsar, Sierra Leone, 14
Lux, A., 175, 312

Mackintosh, J. P., 217, 312
Makera, Nigeria, 28
Mande, 118
Mandinka, 40
Marriage, 90–91, 128, 140–155, 173, 302; effect on social life, 55, 151–155, 183; interethnic, 149–151, 182, 183.
    See also Polygyny
Marris, P., 115, 124, 300, 312
Mauss, M., 176, 312
Mayer, P., 189, 204, 312
Meillassoux, C., 81, 238, 312
Migration, 4, 41–78, 93–98, 182, 202, 224, 256, 274–275, 293; age and, 43, 47–50, 77; career, 42–53; children and, 49, 156; contacts and, 51–53; direct, 42, 44; education and, 50–51, 77; indirect, 44, 49, 50; labor force participation and, 93–99; multiple, 42, 43, 45; occupation and, 46–47; retirement and, 72–78; return home, 50, 63–78; step, 42; urban adaptation and, 53–63, 77–78; women and, 47, 52, 77
Mitchell, J. C., 82, 116, 193, 200, 202, 204, 211, 303, 312
Monrovia, 10
Morgan, R. W., 122, 300, 312
Mossi, 252

Nationalism, 57
"Native quarters," 9
Nelson, J. M., 299, 312
Ngwa, 40, 133, 253
Nie, N., 302
Nigeria, 22–29
Nupe, 256

Occupational associations, 231–234
Occupational mobility, 4, 100–103
Occupational prestige, 260–261
Occupations, 37–39, 46–47, 148, 248, 263–264, 79–83; migration and, 46–47; associations, 231–234; categories, 280–283; mobility, 100–103, 259–260; prestige, 81, 260–261
Odimuko, C. L., 201, 312
Ohadike, P. O., 142, 312
Okediji, O. O., 301, 313
Oppong, C., 93, 158, 163, 182, 301, 313
Osborne, O. H., 11, 128, 165, 313
Ouagadougou, 9, 10
Owerri, Nigeria, 22, 40
Oyeneye, O. Y., 106, 232, 313

Paden, J., 114, 121, 313
Parkin, D., 163, 176, 193, 217, 313
Patronage, 247–249
Peace, A., 38, 57, 313
Peil, M., 19, 20, 38, 39, 42, 53, 64, 69, 81, 82, 90, 101, 105, 107, 121, 126, 242, 249, 251, 260, 302, 303, 313, 314
Pellow, D., 191, 205, 314
Pfeffermann, G., 163, 181, 314
Plotnicov, L., 63, 114, 314
Police, 245, 248
Polygyny, 5, 37, 140, 142–149, 182–183; age and, 182–183; education and, 142–143; religion and, 143, 147, 153; urbanization and, 147–148
Pons, V., 42, 110, 237, 314
Pools, 236
Population statistics, 31–40
Port Harcourt, Nigeria, 14, 22
Potakey, A., 126, 314
Price, R. M., 181, 182, 314
Problems, handling of, 241–266
Prostitutes, 90, 92

Recreation associations, 237–239
Religion, 39–40, 225, 230–231, 293; polygyny and, 143, 147, 183
    See also Islam

Religious associations, 230–231
Rempel, H., 301, 314
Retirement, 72–78; women and, 78
Richmond, A. H., 53, 58, 77, 96, 308
Riddell, J. B., 42, 301, 312, 314
Robertson, C., 132, 314
Ross, M. H., 163, 193, 301, 314
Rossi, P. H., 262, 310

Sada, P. O., 25, 314
Salamone, F. A., 149, 314
Sami, E., 231, 314
Samples, 15–18
Sandbrook, R., 7, 108, 265, 315
San Pedro, Ivory Coast, 14, 272
Sapele, Nigeria, 14
Sarahuli, 85, 118
Savings, 162–163; societies, 234–237
Scales, 295–298
Schildkrout, E., 8, 115, 130, 155, 191, 226, 252, 257, 300, 315
Secret societies, 238
Segregation, housing, 114–115
Sekondi/Takoradi, 3, 8, 14
Self-employment, 14, 23, 38, 42, 71, 77, 79, 80, 82, 85, 89, 94, 99, 107, 109, 229.
    See also Commerce, Craftsmen
Serekunda, Gambia, 16, 17, 18, 30–31; demographic data, 31–40
Servants, 5, 128, 155, 156–158
Sex ratios, 140
Skinner, E. P., 9, 10, 315
Smock, A., 303, 315
Sociability, 110, 151–155, 172, 190–205; housing and, 191–193
Sociability scale, 199–205
Social interaction, 5, 137–277
Social life, 5, 17; effect of marriage on, 55, 151–155, 183
Social mobility, 258–260
Social structure, 1–136
Socioeconomic status (SES), 223, 229, 258–260
    See also Elites, Income
Southall, A., 228
Steady, F. C., 230, 315
Sterkenburg, J., 80, 300, 310
Stouffer, S. A., 96, 315
Strangers, relations between hosts and, 7, 251–258, 274–275.
    See also Aliens
Stren, R., 193, 315

Suburbs, 13, 14–15, 17, 271–273
Sween, J., 142, 143, 147, 148, 307
Szelenyi, I., 163, 242, 248, 311

Takoradi, 11
Tema, Ghana, 11, 15, 16, 18–21, 167, 192; demographic data, 31–40
Tema Development Corporation (TDC), 18–21, 121, 243, 250, 315
Towns: ancient, 7; colonialism and, 8–10; industrial, 13, 14, 267, 270, 271; new, 37, 267, 270–271; provincial, 13–14, 17, 267, 271; sample, 15–18; satellite, 14; social interaction in, 5, 137–277; social structure of, 1–136; stable, 37; types of, 13–15, 62–63, 91–92, 195, 211, 223, 258, 267–273
Trade Unions, 231
Treiman, D. J., 80, 260, 315
Turner, J. C., 126, 315

Udo, R. K., 22, 315
Umahia, Nigeria, 22
Unemployment, 38–39, 64, 83
Urban adaptation, 53–63, 77–78
Urban development, 273–277
Urban typology, 267–273
Urbanization, 7–15; colonialism and, 8–10; indigenous response to, 10–13; literature on, 3; polygyny and, 147–148; types of towns, 13–15
Urhobo, 149

Van Velsen, J., 254, 315
Variables, background, 291–294
Verma, R. P., 96, 314
Visiting, 165–176, 198, 203, 251

Wallerstein, I., 217, 315
Waterman, P., 231, 264, 315
Weinrich, A. K. H., 163, 176, 193, 239, 315
Weisner, T. S., 301, 314, 315
Wellman, B., 188, 315
Willmott, P., 301, 316
Windfall, uses of a, 159–163, 183–184
Wollof, 29, 40, 150
Wolpe, H., 292, 315
Women: 37–39, 47, 52, 67, 76, 89–94, 98–99, 148, 157, 161, 164, 178, 194, 212, 224, 231, 235, 243, 248–249, 256–257, 262, 299; labor force participation and, 90–93; retirement and, 78
Work, *see* Labor force; Occupations